BOOKS BY THOMAS MERTON

The Seven Storey Mountain

The Sign of Jonas

New Seeds of Contemplation

Conjectures of a Guilty Bystander

Zen and the Birds of Appetite

The Collected Poems of Thomas Merton

The Literary Essays of Thomas Merton

Mystics and Zen Masters

The Hidden Ground of Love (Letters I)

The Road to Joy (Letters II)

The School of Charity (Letters III)

The Courage for Truth (Letters IV)

Witness to Freedom (Letters V)

Love and Living

The Monastic Journey

The Asian Journal

Run to the Mountain (Journals I)

Entering the Silence (Journals II)

A Search for Solitude

THE JOURNALS OF THOMAS MERTON / Volume 3: 1952–1960 / Patrick Hart, O.C.S.O., General Editor

Thomas Merton

A Search for Solitude

Pursuing the Monk's True Life

EDITED BY LAWRENCE S. CUNNINGHAM

HarperSanFrancisco
An Imprint of HarperCollins*Publishers*

Grateful acknowledgment is made to New Directions Publishing Corp. for permission to reprint lines from "Hugh Selwyn Mauberley" by Ezra Pound, from *Personae*. Copyright © 1926 by Ezra Pound. Reprinted by permission of New Directions Publishing Corp.

HarperCollins Web Site: http://www.harpercollins.com
HarperCollins®, 📖®, and HarperSanFrancisco™ are trademarks of HarperCollins Publishers, Inc.

Book design by David Bullen

FIRST EDITION

Library of Congress Cataloging-in-Publication Data
Merton, Thomas, 1915–1968.
    A search for solitude : pursuing the monk's true life / Thomas
Merton ; edited by Lawrence S. Cunningham. — 1st ed.
    (The journals of Thomas Merton ; v. 3)
    ISBN 0–06–065478–3 (cloth)
    ISBN 0–06–065479–1 (pbk.)
    1. Merton, Thomas, 1915–1968—Diaries.   2. Trappists—United
States—Diaries.   3. Catholic Church—United States—Clergy—
Diaries.   4. Monastic and religious life.   5. Solitude—Religious
aspects—Catholic Church.   I. Cunningham, Lawrence.   II. Title.
III. Series : Merton, Thomas, 1915–1968.   Journals of Thomas
Merton ; v. 3.
BX4705.M3515A3   1996
    271'.12502—dc20   95-46821
[B]

96 97 98 99 00 RRDH 10 9 8 7 6 5 4 3 2 1

What it all comes down to is that I shall certainly have solitude but only by miracle and not at all by my own contriving. Where? Here or there makes no difference. Somewhere, nowhere, beyond all "where." Solitude outside geography or in it. No matter.

December 17, 1959

Contents

Acknowledgments

A few words of recognition and thanks are in order. First, I am grateful to the Thomas Merton Literary Trust, and especially Anne McCormick, for their confidence in appointing me as one of the journal editors. Next, I would like to recognize Brother Patrick Hart, O.C.S.O., of the Abbey of Our Lady of Gethsemani both for his support and his friendship over the years. Doctor Robert E. Daggy, director of the Thomas Merton Study Center at Bellarmine College, was always helpful in guiding me through the byways of Mertoniana. My graduate assistants, Therese Johnson, Michael Novak, and Michael Sherwin, O.P., did a lot of work for me while this project was underway. The indefatigable labor of Monsignor William H. Shannon was of invaluable assistance as I correlated my text and the letters of Merton published under his general editorship. John Loudon of Harper San Francisco and the editorial staff there were thoroughly professional in overseeing the metamorphosis of manuscript to book. My Notre Dame colleagues (James Vanderkam, Joseph Blenkinsopp, Thomas O'Meara, O.P., Albert Wimmer, Bernard Doering, and Daniel Sheerin) helped clarify some vexatious issues. Anne Fearing, my administrative assistant, kept me on an even keel in our department, and Dorothy Anderson ran more than one diskette of this manuscript with good humor. The three women in my life – my wife, Cecilia, and our daughters, Sarah Mary and Julia Clare, always made home a welcome port after a day at the computer.

This volume is dedicated to the Cistercian Community of Our Lady of Gethsemani and its abbot, Father Timothy Kelly. If one wishes to experience monastic hospitality deeply, that is the place to go.

Introduction

A monk is a man who is separated from all and who is in harmony with all. *Evagrius of Pontus*

A monk should be like the seraphim and cherubim: all eye. *Abba Macarius*

This third volume of Thomas Merton's private journals covers, sporadically, the period between July 1952 and 1960. When he wrote his 1952 entries, Merton had already been at the Abbey of Gethsemani for over a decade. He made his final vows as a Cistercian monk in 1947 and was ordained a priest on Ascension Thursday in 1949. The publication of *The Seven Storey Mountain* (1948) had already made him a household name in the Catholic world.

Merton kept rather brief journals in the last months of 1952 and in 1953, with a hiatus in 1954–1955. It was in this period that Merton gave up his position as master of scholastics, training the young monks in preparation for final vows (he was appointed to that post in 1951) to become, in 1955, master of novices. In 1956 he again began keeping his journal on a regular basis. The journal entries from 1956 through 1960 must be read against his role as novice master, as he saw to the formation of the many young men who were coming to Gethsemani to try their hand at the monastic life. Since he was in such a crucial position, it is no surprise that his thought constantly focused on who and what a monk was. It was André Louf, I think, who once wisely said that a monk is a person who every day asks, "What is a monk?" It was a question that was very much on the mind of Merton in this period.

These journals were written in those brief moments in his crowded schedule or on those days in which he had a bit of freedom to go for a few hours either to the little woodshed that he called his "hermitage" and named in honor of St. Anne, or into the woods that were part of the abbey property. What the journals mention only in passing is that he kept the full monastic horarium, taught, did his share of manual labor, kept up an enormous correspondence, and continued to write for publication. Not counting pamphlets, essays, and reviews, Merton published ten books between 1952 and 1960.

Merton wrote on legal-sized ledgers, dating his entries either with a calendar notation alone, or with a mention of the feastday of the liturgical calendar. Like all good monks, he was frugal. Every line was filled and, not infrequently, he wrote on the wide white top of the page. His daily entries were often separated with a series of crosses. He rarely crossed out words, and only in a very few places was his rather tight handwriting illegible; erasures and illegible words are noted in the text in brackets.

He rarely wrote in parallel columns (mostly when doing literary "experiments"), but when he did I have tried to reproduce the columns as he wrote them. He often used abbreviations (for example, John of the Cross became John of the †; Frater [Brother] was usually Fr., and so on) and these are retained in the text.

It is very difficult to specify the contents of this journal. Sometimes he was speaking to himself in reaction to his reading, or musing about possible strategies for a project. In other places he commented on what he was researching or what he did on a particular day. Some of his most beautiful lines are impressions of what he saw, people he met, or snatches of conversation. Finally, there were arguments with himself, pleas to God, or unverbalized comments to others.

In order to let Merton speak in his own voice, I have only added notes where it was necessary to clarify matters under discussion or to add the final titles of Merton's own works, which often had other working titles while in the process of being written. No attempt was made to identify every book or article he mentioned in passing, even though I have tracked down most of them. Rather than clutter the text with footnotes, translations are put in brackets immediately after the original citation; they are my rather free translations except in those few cases where Merton himself did the translation as preparation for a published work. I resisted correcting Merton's sometimes hasty annotations or miscopying from a book or article; in places where he says something is on a particular page, it might, in fact, spread over to an adjacent page.

A glossary of commonly used monastic terminology is appended to this work to aid those readers who might not be familiar with the more arcane usages of religious and monastic nomenclature.

Assiduous readers of the published works of Merton will benefit from these private journals in a quite particular fashion: They will see in raw form his own reflections and observations and be able to compare them with their finished form in some of his published work. A not insignificant portion of *Conjectures of a Guilty Bystander* (1966) makes a first appearance in these pages, while the seeds of such works as his essays on Boris Pasternak as well as his translations from the Spanish are portrayed in an unfinished fashion. Other published works, such as his translation of the desert solitaries entitled *The Wisdom of the Desert* (1960) and his *Thoughts in Solitude* (1958), appear on these pages as embryonic projects struggling to mature. Some will note that his duty on the night fire watch (which is so movingly described at the end of *Sign of Jonas*) is the subject of more than one entry in his journal.

Beyond all these matters of interest to the serious student of Merton there is something more elemental reflected in these jottings: the voice of the man and the monk. I have lived with these journals for well over two years, and hope you will indulge me in a few reflections about what struck me as they were being transcribed from his page to my computer.

First, there are the wonderful passages where Merton lets his poetic eye capture the natural environment in which he lived. Everything from the patois of the monastery's neighbors to the "knobs" (hills) and woods within which they live get set down with a sympathetic and uncondescending accuracy. He had a feel for the sky and the flight of birds (recall that contemplation first meant to look for portents in a portion of the sky); for the trees planted or culled on the monastery grounds; for the emergence of spring flowers; for the brush fires that would erupt in the knobs around the monastery; and for the avian and animal life of the woods that he loved so much.

That same discerning eye could be turned to the monastic community itself. He had the fiction writer's sharp eye and ear for the beauties as well as the idiosyncrasies of his brethren; for the rhythms and tediums of regular observance; for the strengths of the monastery and for its weaknesses. If he could be judgmental at times, it was only in the journal that he could be so; after all, vagrant conversations were hardly the norm in the Gethsemani of that day. So much of the journal is a form of talking to himself. Indeed, one is led to think that some of these entries would not be here at all if sustained conversation with another person were the rule rather than the exception in a Trappist monastery.

However vexed Merton could be with his monastic life, it is quite clear that he took it with utmost seriousness, both in terms of what he demanded of himself and what he expected of those under him (as well as those over him). It is important to note that when he pursued his readings in everything from literature to Marxist philosophy, he did so with this imperative question in mind: How can a contemplative monk in the twentieth century not be concerned with these issues?

In fact, it was his preoccupation with the question of what it meant to be a monk in his own time that gives this journal its most lasting value, both because it does honor to monasticism in its own right, and because it is instructive for all who value the contemplative life.

Merton, in fact, had a rather original angle on what we might call "ecumenism" as it derives from, and finds nurturance in, the contemplative life. During 1956 and 1957, he was reading widely in the writings of Russian Orthodox theologians and thinkers. Through those readings he came to the conclusion that he could, at a deep and interior level, join within himself East and West by a sympathetic openness to the best that the East could offer. He set out that program for himself on April 28, 1957, when he wrote: "If I can unite *in myself*, in my own spiritual life, the thought of the East and West of the Greek and Latin Fathers, I will create in myself a reunion of the divided church and from that unity in myself can come the exterior and visible unity of the Church." (Merton's emphasis; these lines would reappear in *Conjectures*.)

His eager embrace of the writings of Boris Pasternak, after all, derived from his sense that beneath the prose of *Doctor Zhivago* he could detect a strain of sophianic christology, Christ as the Wisdom of God, which he had discovered more explicitly in the writings of Berdyaev and Bulgakov in the same period. His eager desire to correspond with Pasternak was a kind of enfleshment of this interior desire to be in communion with those who were by temperament and work fellow seekers.

That desire to combine in his heart Eastern and Western Christianity (through a contemplative synthesis) also motivated his passionate concern for the world of Latin America. Spurred by his friendship with Ernesto Cardenal (then his novice), Merton read Latin American writers, corresponded with them, translated their poetry, commissioned their art, and eagerly welcomed them as novices at Gethsemani. He mentions in passing that he was taking lessons in Portuguese to add to his linguistic repertoire of French, Italian, and Spanish. Frequently, he writes in his journals of his desire to bridge the gap between North and South America; to become a builder of a view of a single America in which human solidarity and love would replace the tensions between the two Americas. Further, let it be noted, he wanted to do this from his perspective as a monk. In a very real sense, Merton was a liberation theologian *avant la parole.*

These were not the only projects of reconciliation that preoccupied him. We see him wondering how, as a contemplative person, he might cross over to the world of Zen and existentialism and the serious Marxism of his day. Careful readers of this journal will note that these were not mere fancies of a promiscuously restless mind (although his mind *was* restless). These interests were grounded in his intuition that at the base of reality was the transcendental presence of God's Wisdom (*Sophia*) present in the world from the beginning and, to quote from a source he loved and referred to constantly, beside God "rejoicing before Him always, rejoicing in his inhabited world" (Proverbs 8:30–31).

The figure of Sophia/Wisdom is at the heart of his discussions with his artist friend Victor Hammer, whose own attempts to depict the figure of Sophia would inspire Merton to write his wonderful liturgical poem, "Hagia Sophia." It was the Sophia that he found in the Orthodox theologians, in the art of his friend, and in subtle but detectable ways, in the great intellectual debates of his time. It is, in short, in Sophia that one finds the thread that holds these journals together.

In the late 1950s, Merton records a kind of vocational crisis. He is unhappy in the monastery, finding it too successful and too busy (its success and busyness, ironically, caused in part by his own books' and articles' celebration of its life and virtues). His old desire for a more retired life with its attendant temptation to look to the more eremitical Carthusians and Camaldolese comes back with a vengeance. The chance visit of a Benedictine prior who offers him a new life in a Cuernavaca (Mexico) monastery unleashes a frenetic year of correspondence, plans, poring over maps for suitable monastic sites in Latin America, canonical strategies to leave Gethsemani for other places – either in the rural areas of the West, or more likely in Central or Latin America.

This restlessness not only brought forth moments of faintly hilarious enthusiasms (as he dreamed of far-away islands and idyllic monastic settlements), but painful and sometimes uncharitable private criticisms of his superiors in general and his abbot in particular. Transcribing those entries could be an irritating business – one wants to give him an avuncular scolding when criticism veers off into moments of self-pity. Notwithstanding those moments of irritation, one does appreciate what he himself noted in an entry dated May 21, 1960: that in the journal he "could speak freely," and what he wrote for others was, in contrast to these journals, "more controlled, more responsible, more objective and therefore better . . ."

It was while working on those entries that I stumbled on some pages in the *Institutes* of the old fourth-century monastic writer John Cassian. Describing the temptation to *accedia*, Cassian (borrowing rather freely from Evagrius of Pontus's *Praktikos*) sets out the symptoms of monastic *accedia* (boredom; listlessness) with almost clinical exactitude. The monk begins to feel a "horror of the place where he is" and "disgust with his cell." The same monk begins to "complain that he is making no progress" and is "devoid of all spiritual progress." Finally, he "sings the praises of monasteries located in other places" and concludes that "he cannot get any better as long as he stays in his present place" (*Institutes* X.2).

Ironically, I first read those words while sitting one evening on the porch of Merton's hermitage in Kentucky as the sun slowly went down on a lazy June evening. I wrote Cassian's words in my journal with the notation: "an exact description of TM in 1959." One must agree that these ancient monastic writers were shrewd students of human psychology and exact observers of human frailty. They seem to intuit that it was not the harshness of the monastic life but its regularity, its sameness, its boundedness, that could enervate a person. In that sameness one could fancy other places, other settings, other people who would add vigor and freshness to the routines of the ordinary monastic round. As Peter Levi once put it in his study of monks (*The Frontiers of Paradise*, 1987): "If a monk realized that his vocation as a young monk was to become an old monk, I think he would be terrified."

The end of the story, of course, is that Merton's superiors did not permit an exclaustration, official permission to leave Gethsemani; Merton got that word directly from the Vatican. It is striking, given the passionate character of his earlier entries in his journal, that Merton received this news with a calm sense of acceptance. It is then that he notes, briefly, that he will devote himself to the search for "solitude outside geography."

My story ends in early 1960, when arrangements had already been made for Merton to have a combination hermitage and retreat center, Mount Olivet, on the monastery property for the many visitors who came for ecumenical discussions. He could spend time there, and eventually he moved there permanently as a hermit. One does not get Dom James's side of the story, but given those arrangements it is clear that Merton's superiors had the shrewd sense to give him enough latitude within the community to fulfill his heart's desire for a life of contemplation and solitude.

PART I

Master of Students

July 1952–March 1953

I am trying to get myself adjusted to the fact that, twenty four hours ago, I had just left Columbus, Ohio, in an American Airlines plane, although forty eight hours ago, I was here at Gethsemani, working quietly enough, just as I am doing now. Once again – the problem of always arriving where I already am – the problem that confronts me in my dreams – beats me here. (I am slowly getting rid of the violence of that one day's journey.)

How did I happen to get away from Gethsemani, gather myself together in the middle of Ohio, then take a running jump at the place and land back here in the evening after every one else had gone to bed? This is extraordinary behaviour for a Trappist.

Was it last week Reverend Father told me I was to drive up and meet him in Columbus to see some property near Newark, Ohio, that was being offered us for a foundation?

I said Mass yesterday morning at 2:15 in the back sacristy. Bro. Clement and Bro. Wendeline served me. We drove off together about sunrise. They are bringing back some hay from Ohio, where there has been plenty of rain. Everything is burnt up in Kentucky this year – corn, hay, beans, everything except the tree seedlings we planted in the forest this Spring.

About a half hour on the other side of Louisville, I suddenly realized this was a marvelous journey. We were going along the Ohio River and I saw that it was wide and serene and blue and I saw the wooded hills sweeping down to the broad water, and soon we came to a great curve in the river and passed a river boat coming down with great paddles kicking up the water at her stern. It had already been a happy journey from the beginning (I said the votive Mass for Travellers), but now it became a brilliant one. We crossed the bridge at Cincinnati where the state trooper tried to arrest me for taking a snapshot in 1941, when I first came to Gethsemani on retreat. We sailed up the side of a big hill, a couple of hundred feet above the river, with the city unrolling behind us. There are corners where you come upon churches and monasteries springing up on the hilltops, and over your shoulder you see the weird domed towers of Covington, and you are no longer sure whether you are on the Ohio River or the Danube. Finally, somewhere on the way out of Norwood, we stopped at an intensely dull little soda fountain to get a sandwich and it all seemed inexpressibly beautiful. The man who ran the soda fountain was called Shorty and someone reproved him harshly for his high prices, but we were to discover that his prices were much less high than elsewhere, for now everywhere prices are high.

Out in the plains of Ohio, with red clover in the fields and corn growing high, we raced along the empty highway under the blue sky full of clouds, and I sang the praises of flat country, which I love, and Brother Clement talked of the offspring of bulls.

It seemed, at the moment, that I must be going to make a foundation in Ohio. Why else would Reverend Father get me to go all the way up there unless he intended me to be Superior of the foundation? Afterwards this turned out to be by no means certain.

At Washington court house, the county fair was just about to open and I realized that I loved the small towns of Ohio. We skirted around the outsides of Columbus, but I saw the city in the distance and was filled with the mysterious awe that still comes over me when I think of the nineteen twenties. That tower, and the other less tall buildings, all haunt the memory of those innocent days when Pop[1] was making money for Grosset & Dunlap and Father played the piano in the movie [house] in France and one of the books that made money for Grosset and Dunlap was a reprint of Sinclair Lewis' *Babbit*.

The awe grew on me when I realized that, in heading for Newark, we were also headed for Zanesville, where Pop came from and my mother was born. I was inexpressibly moved by the thought that perhaps I would start a monastery in this land which is mine without my ever having lived in it.

Of course, we did not get as far as Zanesville, and now that I am home again and have woken up in Kentucky, I am sobered by our own solitude, and the poor land, and the cedars, and the hills I have looked at and lived in for eleven years . . .

July 26, 1952
We arrived in Newark, Ohio, and found the house of our benefactor on 7th street. When I was trying to find the house, a painter, working a few blocks up the street, said the house had not been occupied for years. But

---

[1] Samuel Jenkins, Merton's maternal grandfather.

we found it occupied by a quiet, dignified little old man with the same kind of stiff collar that Pop used to wear, and an immense collection of Indian arrowheads in his cellar. Here we met Reverend Father and Fr. Francis de Sales who had flown in from Chicago where they had been looking up equipment for a new monastery infirmary.

We had dinner and went out to the farm at Hebron.

Driving through Granville on the way to Newark I had hoped the farm would be as beautiful as those around this little college town. It was not and yet it is a beautiful farm. The corn was taller than our Kentucky corn. There was woodland with great old maples and walnut trees, and I was fascinated by a corner of the land where there was a wooded hollow and a spring and an old tumbledowned house and barn, and a few Guernsey cows swishing about in the bushes and the deep grass.

Everybody else wanted to build a monastery on an open hillside looking out over the wide valley, but in my distractions at prayer my mind returns to this hollow . . .

Whether or not we accept this gift depends on whether we can buy some more land around the 600 acres offered us, for protection and greater solitude. It is crowded country, and there are many factories in the valley. You have only to go over the shoulder of the hill to see them spread out before you.

At Port Columbus, where we went to take the plane, there was a former lay-brother postulant from Gethsemani who got in a conversation with Bro. Clement and Reverend Father.

As we rose off the ground I was saying Hail Marys, and when we leveled off – not too high to miss anything below – I recited Matins and Lauds of Our Lady's Office, living in the sky between two worlds. Below us, Ohio was very neat and flat. The brown hayfields looked like thread-bare rugs and the cornfields looked like thick rugs, and the roads went off for miles and miles in straight lines, and all the farms were neat and white and prim. All this was half veiled by a purple haze which came up to our own level, so that we seemed to be skimming the surface of a clean, thin sea. Off in the distance, on a level with our eyes, a few clean clouds floated in this sea like icebergs or strange wandering islands and I settled back to enjoy the solitude of the sky.

The flight became more beautiful after Cincinnati, where we were held up for an hour, and where the airport seemed to be infected with some moral corruption that had been brought in by plane from New York. (But in the distance the city itself was beautiful and grand, enshrined in hills and gleaming in the late sun. I only saw it when we got off the ground again.)

We flew South West over the big river, with our propellers ringing a halo of ice around the sinking sun. I challenged the country below to tell us something about my destiny. These were fiercer fields, all on hills. The slanting rays of the sun picked out the contours of the land, with waves and waves of hills flying away from the river, skirted with curly woods or half-shaved like the backs of poodles, farms sitting in the crooks of valleys or under the elbows of wooded elevations, and dirt roads twisting to them through the fields. Thus I knew that I was in my state again, which is Kentucky.

When I got home, I thought I was not tired, but it has taken me two days to get out of the trauma of this journey.

When we were coming into Dayton, Reverend Father told me he had no intention of making me superior of the foundation, if there was a foundation. So I threw away all the plans I had been drawing up since the morning and felt as if I was making a sacrifice. But now, back at Gethsemani, and especially at the altar, as I get quiet once more and seem to find myself comparatively sane, I beg God, in fervent terror, to keep Reverend Father from changing his mind.

August 12, 1952. Feast of St. Clare

Yesterday morning before Prime I went out to the wagon shed to practice our[2] sermon for the Assumption – in fact, to finish writing it. They have a new electric fence all around the place because the horses are there, and when I was just beginning to get into the sermon, the brother came through with all the horses, to take them out to work. Some of them shied away from me and our sermon.

After that, a brother novice came to feed the turkeys. I had seen no turkeys in the turkey pen. I thought they were in the house. But as soon as the brother appeared, there was a turbulent stirring of foliage and a great noise of wings in the orchard, and the huge young turkeys flew out of every apple tree and sailed down gracelessly into the yard below the turkey pen. One of them hit the electric fence on his way down and flopped sideways in the dirt. I walked away from this distraction to the place where the old

---

[2] The plural "our" was often used in monastic life instead of "my" to indicate lack of personal possessions. Merton did not employ this monastic usage with consistency.

horsebarn was, and sat on a slab pile and preached on the Assumption to the hills and the woods and to the weeds in the future park. It starts out at present, "Why do we venerate the relics of the saints?" and goes on all about the resurrection of the body and the power of the Holy Spirit and our Lady bringing back the captives of Sion.

My Lord, I am supposed to have only your heart to love with, to see and carry out only your intentions, in my work for the souls You have given me. And yet, what is the mystery behind this? "Whatsoever you shall bind on earth is bound in heaven" [Matthew 16:19]. You have made our intentions your own, provided they are sincere intentions, provided we desire them to be, as far as we know, Your own. The priest does not have to make infallible decisions: but if he honestly tries to make good decisions, You will preserve him from error. It is here, in my own human and defectible heart, that union with You is found – for You descend to me to make my heart Your heaven, even in the midst of business and of banal decisions.

The life of Christ in the soul of the priest depends in large measure on the priest's attitude toward the "needy and the poor" – the materially poor, if he deals with them, or, at heart, the spiritually underprivileged in the community where *all* are supposed to be materially poor together.

Deut. XV:7–10.

God manifests His greatness most of all in pardoning: *qui omnipotentiam tuam parcendo maxime manifestam* [whose power is most manifest in forgiving] – collect of the last Sunday or the one before (9th. or 10th. after Pentecost). The priest is a man of sacrifice and a man of pardon, and just as Christ speaks in the words of consecration, so too He speaks in the words of absolution. But He must also be seen everywhere in the mercy, the compassion, and the long-suffering of the hearts of His priests.

August 13, 1952. Day of Recollection
Direction.[3] Spiritual direction does not consist merely in giving advice. The man who has only an advisor does not really have a director in the fullest sense. Since the spiritual life does not consist in having and thinking, but in being and doing, a director who only gives ideas has not begun to *form* the one he directs. He forms him by counsels and "precepts" (qualify for theologians), by exercising him, by testing him, by giving him, when necessary, penances. The penitent is not formed by listening, but by

[3] These notes are part of the reflections used by Merton before he published the pamphlet *Spiritual Direction and Meditation* in 1960.

complying, if possible, in his whole being, thought, desire, and action, with the precepts of the director.

But in order for this to be fruitful, the Director must be, as St. Benedict says, a "loving Father," humble and discreet, aware of his own limitations, docile and respectful before the Holy Ghost.

A good director must have almost as much respect and veneration for the ones he directs as the penitent should have for his director.

Spiritual direction cannot be really fruitful, ordinarily, unless there is a real spiritual affinity between the director and his penitent. Not necessary that there be a *natural* affinity or community of tastes on the human level, but the penitent must have complete confidence in the director, and the director must have enough confidence in and respect for the penitent to correct him firmly, lovingly, and without fear or passion, if the need should arise.

The director should be willing to sacrifice himself and his time for everyone who needs him, but particularly for anyone who shows by his attitude that he *relies* on him.

The quasi-contract between director and his subject is formally complete as soon as the subject makes up his mind, after serious thought and prayer (not necessarily after a long *time*), that he really can and does rely on this particular director . . . sense that here is one who can discover God's ways in their particular soul. But to merit direction, he must live up to this grace and actually rely on the director – which is proved by obedience – by what he does.

The director, on his side, must be ready with untiring patience to listen and to observe and to advise and to guide the soul, realizing his own deficiencies.

If a director has a real supernatural love and respect for the souls he directs, he will be hardly tempted to impose upon that soul a pet system of his own devising. Such a temptation and such ill-considered guidance is the sin of natural and unmortified spirit in one who directs for direction's sake, who does not love those he directs, but guides them for his own satisfaction, seeking only to make copies of himself, to multiply and then contemplate himself in them.

August 15, 1952. Feast of the Assumption

It was when Adam desired to be as a god that mankind became capable of bargaining with God. Not because we are able, by ourselves, to deal with

Him as equals, but by His mercy He makes us promises and, if we receive and keep them, we can be said to live up to our share in an alliance.

The Old Testament is the record of men getting further and further away from God, so that the alliance between man and God becomes less and less mystical and more and more juridical. The further you are from God, the more your dealings with Him take on the air of a formality.

To Noah, who had not yet descended as far as the law courts, God gave the rainbow as the sign of His alliance with men. This means that some men, with some of the simplicity of Noah, will always be capable of seeing nature and created things for what they are, signs and pledges of our union with God.

But creatures are signs of the alliance only in so far as we use them chastely. As soon as we possess them, they become the objects of haggling and litigation, and we must drive a bargain.

Now the rising sun comes over the bank of lowly slate-colored clouds out there, and I can no longer look straight into the East, beyond the woods where the crows are breaking silence.

The three scarecrows in the vineyard begin to be crucified in fire: at least one of them. The others hang against the mist that is more northward and less red. The door of the hayloft in the cowbarn yawns into the rising sun, the grass is full of crickets, and black birds whistle softly under the water tower.

Last evening – in the joy of being cleansed by bitterness – I renounced the thing I had been praying for under the pressure of temptation: a separate scholasticate in the mountains of Colorado (where someone has offered us a splendid house). I had already proposed it to the General[4] but the proposal will probably never get anywhere.

First bell for Prime . . . Are they going to build a tower, then, for the new bells?

August 18, 1952

Correcting proofs of _The Sign of Jonas._[5] Writing a journal and publishing it are two different things. The Georgia censor has already attacked the scruple which prompted me to say too many things I did not mean, but which I felt I had to say because they were things I did not like about myself. You have to distinguish what is ugly in you and what is _willed_ by you and what is

[4] The Abbot General of the Cistercians, Dom Gabriel Sortais.
[5] _The Sign of Jonas_ was published by Harcourt, Brace & Company in 1953.

ugly – or silly – and *not* willed. The latter is never really interesting, because it is usually quite unreal – and therefore not a matter for a journal – gives a false picture.

Bouyer's book *Bible et évangile* is brilliant but makes me nervous. Marmion never made anybody nervous but he does not always keep me awake. Where is the happy medium? What book was St. Benedict reading as he sat so calmly at the monastery gate and did not even look up to see the Goth approach, driving the tied peasant?

Recollection cannot be really achieved without interior self-humiliation. If there is no fear of God to open up the depths of the soul and admit Him from within, you might as well keep your eyes open to recognize some trace of him in His visible creation.

August 23, 1952

On the Feast of St. Bernard, in the evening, Msgr. Larraona, the secretary of the Sacred Congregation of Religious, came to Gethsemani. He stayed overnight and spoke twice to the community in Italian. The second time I had to do the interpreting. He spoke for about an hour in the morning Chapter, went through all the gifts of the Holy Ghost, and said some wonderful things. But I especially liked the way in which he said them. Italian is a wonderful language to preach in.

One of the points that struck me in his sermon was the truth that, under the influence of the gifts, not only the theological, but the infused moral virtues, become immediate avenues of contact with God. The main theme of his talk was the unity of all virtues of the active and contemplative lives in charity, under the influence of the gifts of the Holy Ghost.

More important for me – I had two conferences with him in Spanish. I like his Italian but liked better his Spanish, his native language. The Italian was melodious – and I think, perfect – and full of unction and devotion. The Spanish – in which we talked canon law – was sober, wise, full of counsel, and good sense. He gave me a full history of the canon about manifestation of conscience 518.3.[6] But that was not chiefly what I wanted to talk about; it was the scholasticate. I had been thinking for some time

[6] In the old canon law, canon 518 dealt with confessors for religious houses. Paragraph 3 discussed the freedom of a religious to seek out a confessor.

that the scholastics ought to be in a house of their own (?), or, anyway, in a house where more perfect conditions for prayer and study and the contemplative life could be found than here where there is necessarily so much activity and noise. The big difficulty is that a separate scholasticate is entirely foreign to the spirit of our order. I recognize the difficulty. The monks are supposed to develop in the bosom of *one* monastic community. We are not like Mendicants[7] with their provinces. It would not do to have them graduate from a scholasticate and "go to work" to serve the needs of this or that monastery, as if their life were primarily a kind of ministry. It would be a false and harmful mental attitude. Nevertheless, for a priest in our order now, his vocation amounts in large part to just that.

But anyway, Msgr. Larraona was not only in favor of my ideas, but said the congregation was bringing out an Instruction on this very point. Even in monastic orders there are to be special houses of study in which the right conditions are maintained, in which the students do not hold important offices in the community, where the best professors and spiritual directors can be concentrated, where they can really live the Rule and live the contemplative life as perfectly as possible. He said he was going to talk to Dom Gabriel about it.

He told me very authoritatively that the Holy See desired as much as possible to be done to ensure the right formation of priests in religious orders. In order not to infringe on the rights of the autonomous abbey by the constitution of a scholasticate that would be a separate house of no definite class, the scholastics would gather in certain abbeys of the Order and make their studies there. However, in America, all kinds of solutions could offer themselves for our own particular problems.

He told me, also authoritatively, that it was most desirable for me to go on writing. I gather that this seems to be the general opinion in Rome.

What most struck me about the whole visit was the grace and peace it brought with it – the realization that Christ was speaking, that the Church was making known God's thoughts and His will to us – the sense that the Church definitely has Gethsemani in her mind and in her heart and has things to say to us. The awareness of being in the *center* of the life we live by, the life of Christ and His Church. It had a deep effect on my prayer, indeed, a tremendous effect – freedom, light, "lightness," union. And the sense of renewal that always comes with special grace.

---

[7] The "begging" friars: Franciscans, Dominicans, Carmelites, and Augustinians.

August 28, 1952. Feast of St. Augustine

The other day – Feast of St. Louis[8] – the scholastics had enormous candle-sticks on the altar and enormous wine cruets with lids on them, used for pontifical masses in the days of Dom Edmond.[9] I could hardly handle them.

That night I was on the fire watch. The new moon had already gone down. There was a light in the ladies guest home over on the hill by Nally's. But everything else was dark and quiet. Sitting on the tower, I looked up into the enormous darkness of the clear sky full of stars and stars seemed to come falling down upon the world like snow. They fall and fall and never arrive!

Finished the proofs of *Bread in the Wilderness*[10] Tuesday, concluding in my heart that *The Sign of Jonas* is a better book and that it is perhaps useless for me to write anything more like *Bread*. It seemed to me an im-pertinence and waste of time to write a book about St. Bernard, as I am supposed to do.

– But don't you love St. Bernard?

– Of course I do. I love him well enough not to write a book about him. Since it is obedience, however, I take it to be somehow necessary for me to find out a new way to write about St. Bernard. What need is there for me to do all over again what has been done by Gilson and Leclercq and by our own Father Pacificus from Tilburg in Rome, these recent days!

If obedience thinks it desirable for me to write about St. Bernard, obedi-ence must also make it *possible* for me to do so! Where will I get the time to write anything? Frs. Bertrand and Eudes came over to the scholasticate from the novitiate this morning. That brings us up to 28 – and this is only the beginning.

Fr. Stephen made me enthusiastic signs about his eight year old niece who is visiting him. He reads to her out of the bible, especially about King Nebuchadnezzer who was changed into the likeness of an ox and ate grass.

So now I must get busy and prepare a conference on the typical sense of scripture.

[8] This feast day, August 25, held special importance for Merton, whose religious name was Louis.

[9] Dom Edmond Obrecht was abbot of Gethsemani from 1898 to 1935.

[10] Published by New Directions in 1953.

———

When I ended the night watch the other night and went down to the place where we change back from sneakers into our own shoes, I found a note from Fr. Tarcisius in an envelope in one shoe, a feast-day note and prayer he wrote for me to Our Lady of Solitude.

September 1, 1952. St. Giles

While great Apostles went into the city to bring men back to God, Antony went into the desert to bring material creation back to God by being holy in the midst of it and driving out the devil from the nature he had usurped as his possession. Material creation sanctified by our *hope* – i.e. by our poverty. See Romans 8.

The ascetes[11] taught their disciples not only by words but especially by actions. The novices watched the ascete work and pray and tried to do as he did. Fasted as he fasted, slept when he slept, got up to pray when he got up to pray. Hence, the ascete had to be content to be watched, without self-consciousness. To be watched by someone he had repeatedly scolded and corrected. The charity of Christ forming a son for the Father by the actions of a son and a father working together at simple things in silence.

Father John of the Cross and his parents and sisters sitting on ancient solid chairs under the sweet gum trees out in the front avenue, partly protected from the view of passerbys by a line of parked cars. I went out to them twice, which is inordinate I suppose. His little brother Robert chased a lizard on the enclosure wall. Afterwards, I was astonished at the patience and indifference with which his sisters submitted to having a lizard placed on their bare arms, on their hands. Only his mother seemed to mind a little. She was apologetic after she had shaken the thing off her wrist, as if she had given in to some kind of weakness. Ann did not want to enter the Louisville Carmel because the new building did not seem like a convent, did not seem to have Christ in it. She is going to try Cleveland. I liked the attitude they all had towards her. She is the one who is entering the convent. When it was dark, in church, while we sang the *Salve* a firefly came flashing over our heads. "We thought it was something coming to Ann – an apparition or something," they said. "The light was this big," said

---

[11] The early Desert Fathers and Mothers.

Gretchen, making the size of an apple. Gretchen is the youngest of the sisters and she ate a lot of apples. And Carol is the eldest, who says she wants to be a saint in the world.

The last one who came to communion on Sunday morning, when I said Mass for them in the secular church, was Hanekamp, the hermit, and after that, it was impossible for me to be the least bit distracted by any of Fr. John of the †'s visitors at all, or by anything that was said.

September 3, 1952

I am now almost completely convinced that I am only really a monk when I am alone in the old toolshed Reverend Father gave me. (It is back in the woods beyond the horse pasture where Bro. Aelred hauled it with the trax-cavator the day before Trinity Sunday.) True, I have the will of a monk in the community. But I have the *prayer* of a monk in the silence of the woods and the toolshed. To begin with: the place is simple, and really poor with the bare poverty I need worse than any other medicine and which I never seem to get. And silent. And inactive – materially. Therefore the Spirit is busy here. What is easier than to discuss mutually with You, O God, the three crows that flew by in the sun with light flashing on their rubber wings? Or the sunlight coming quietly through the cracks in the boards? Or the crickets in the grass? You are sanctified in them when, beyond the blue hills, my mind is lost in Your intentions for us all who live with hope under the servitude of corruption!

The prayer for solitude is answered when my will is moved by Your Spirit to reach out and find You in solitude. I receive what I want as soon as I want it, when it is You who moves me to want it. The lack of interior solitude is simply the *inability* to desire solitude with an efficacious desire. That desire cannot be perfectly acquired without a certain degree of exterior solitude. You know how much is necessary for each one who is called to union with You.

You have called me into this silence to be grateful for what silence I have, and to use it by desiring more.

Prayer should not only draw God down to us: it should lift us up to Him. It should not only rest in His reflection (which the soul, still resting in the house of the body, finds within itself). It should rise out of the body and seek to leave this life in order to rest in Him. This is true solitude, unimaginably different from any other solitude of body or of soul. But it is hard to find, under the pressure of desires that make us heavy and anchor us to earth when we are immersed in the active life of a community.

Heaven and earth are full of Thy glory. Full of Thy mercy. And I who am nothing have been placed here in silence to behold it and to praise Thee!

September 13, 1952

I have been making decisions.

The chief of these is that I must really lead a solitary life. It is not enough to try to be a solitary in community. Too much ambivalence. Wednesday – a conference with Fr. Bellarmine. He is the first person who has ever told me point blank that I belonged in a Charterhouse and *not* at Gethsemani.

As soon as he said it, I saw that he was completely right and everything inside me affirmed it by peace and happiness. I cannot doubt him, as far as my vocation to solitude is concerned. Whether it is to be the Carthusians, Camaldolese or somewhere else remains to be seen.

Wrote to Dom Humphrey at Sky Farm, to Dom Porion in Rome and to the Prior of Camaldoli Thursday afternoon. First letter was to Camaldoli and I didn't feel so great about it. Writing to Dom Humphrey – everything sure and serene. Praying a lot. I feel that my desire for solitude is now the one thing that most unites me to God. Prayer in hope – swimming in the Holy Ghost and at the same time utterly pure. The hope alone is wonderful. It is a solitude of its own!

Complete new attitude. I have been fooling myself about my "compassion" for the scholastics – my interest in them is uselessly human, and the job itself, even when most supernatural, is something less than I need and therefore – practically speaking – an obstacle – an occupation that complicates my mind too much for the simplicity of God.

I do not see how I can possibly write the books I am now supposed to write. At the moment I think I would rather lie down and die than attempt the book everyone thinks I should write about St. Bernard: as if someone who just made a vow of virginity was told to get married[12]

One of the best things that has ever happened to me is this decision. Fruit of one of the worst trials of my life – 4 days last weekend – real tribulation – ground between millstones. At that same time Ann Wasserman

---

[12] He would, in fact, finally write the book: *The Last of the Fathers*, published by Harcourt, Brace & Company in 1954.

(Fr. John †'s sister) was in Cleveland to see about entering Carmel there. Yesterday a letter arrived from her that the Cleveland Carmel was "just right" – spoke of the big trees looking over the wall and speaking to her of God who was there!

September 15, 1952

Out here in the woods I can think of nothing except God and it is not so much that I think of Him either. I am as aware of Him as of the sun and the clouds and the blue sky and the thin cedar trees. When I first came out here, I was sleepy (because we are in the Winter season and no longer have meridienne) but I read a few lines from the Desert Fathers and then, after that, my whole being was full of serenity and vigilance.

Who am I writing this for, anyway! It is a waste of time! Enough to say that as long as I am out here I cannot think of Camaldoli either; no question of being here and dreaming of somewhere else. Engulfed in the simple and lucid actuality which is the afternoon: I mean God's afternoon, this sacramental moment of time when the shadows will get longer and longer, and one small bird sings quietly in the cedars, and one car goes by in the remote distance and the oak leaves move in the wind.

High up in the late Summer sky I watch the silent flight of a vulture, and the day goes by in prayer. This solitude confirms my call to solitude. The more I am in it, the more I love it. One day it will possess me entirely and no man will ever see me again.

September 17, 1952. Ember Wednesday

The woods all smell of malt because the South wind blows, bringing us news of the distillery a mile away. Clouds in the sky. It will rain and tomorrow will suddenly be cold and the year's end will be upon us. Already the leaves seem to be changing color – and they are, not because it is fall. They were dried up by the dry summer.

This morning I did not say Ember day Mass but the mass of St. Francis because it is the feast of his stigmatization.

September 19, 1952. Ember Friday

At the end of the lesson from Osee the Holy Spirit says "The ways of the Lord are right – straight *(rectae)* and the just shall walk in them, but the transgressors shall fall in them" [Hosea 14:9]. This cannot be properly understood unless we know, from the Gospel, what are the ways of the Lord. They are simple and plain. The ways St. John Baptist came to make straight are ways of penance. Penance is love which is simple enough and enlightened enough to seek *mercy* and because it seeks mercy, it has already been forgiven. Hence today's gospel of Mary Magdalen in the house of Simon the Leper. "Many sins are forgiven her because she has loved much" (Lk. 7:47). The first are those who have received mercy and who know that the ways of the Lord are simple because they are the ways of love. Simon and the Pharisees who do not understand love cannot receive the teachings of Jesus about forgiveness. On the contrary, they are scandalized when He forgives Mary's sins. It does not even occur to them that they themselves need forgiveness, and since they do not feel any need of mercy, the question of forgiveness and love is a purely abstract one, a canonical question, a matter of jurisdiction. So the truth remains that Jesus is the Way, the Truth, and the Life. In Him the Father has forgiven us and no man comes to the Father but by Him. Penance without the love of Christ is, therefore, wasted. It is useless. All penance is perfected *in gratia* [in grace].

September 25, 1952

Still no reply to those letters.

I was talking with Dr. Law[13] today and he agreed that I ought to go somewhere else. Said he thought of it for a long time. Rather than go to the Carthusians, he thought I should start something new – a "really contemplative order." I explained to him the Camaldolese set up and he said that sounded fine. Offered to help in any way he could. Said it was useless to try to introduce something new into the Trappists. And I agree. All that the Trappists need to be is what they are meant to be, namely, Trappists. And that means fully admitting that the Trappists are not a purely contemplative order.

Trials lately. Their function seems to be to *force* me into solitude and to make me realize at the same time that I exist for no other reason than for God's will to be fulfilled in me. Not to desire the slightest thing for myself – not to use any of my faculties merely for my own satisfaction – to take only those satisfactions which accompany the giving of glory to God, so that in all things He is glorified and lives in me. To see His will in its purity,

---

[13] Philip Law of Chicago was a psychiatrist friend of Merton.

not clouded by human respect or prejudice or wishful thinking. To live by faith and beyond that to be nothing.

September 26, 1952

Yesterday, extra work, cutting corn in the middle bottom. Bright sun, hot work, dust in the throat and sweat in the eyes. It was good. That side of Trappist life is very good. All of it is good, but the cornfield side is good for *me*. It would be the aspect of life I would miss most if I became a Carthusian or a Camaldolese. Hence, perhaps the real solution is to be a hermit in America, on your own, and *work* for a living. I believe in my heart that is the real thing. It would mean teaming up with someone who could really run a small farm.

Yet today's thought was perhaps a temptation – I can think of at least 5 of the scholastics who would be dying to go with me if I went to be a hermit. Some have already spoken to me about it. What they want especially is the simplicity of the Rule just as it was lived by St. Benedict . . .

Dr. Law – "Start a new order that is really contemplative . . ."

Fr. Paul Phillipe – "Stay in America."

It would have to mean a novitiate on my own in the woods for a year or two.

I am writing this – why?

To begin with, not as a book. It would be indecent to go into solitude all the while writing a book about it, although in fact I have a contract with Harcourt, Brace which practically demands it.

Writing this for myself because paper plays a definite part in the spiritual formation of a writer, even in the formation that will make him cease to be a writer and transform him into something else.

Because I believe this transformation is necessary.

For 37 years I have been writing my life instead of living it and the effect is vicious, although by the grace of God it has not been as bad as it might have been. But I cannot let myself become a hermit merely on the grounds that the thing looks credible on paper.

Which is why I don't like Doc Law's idea that I should start right now and "put the thing down on paper," i.e. the plan for the new kind of contemplative life.

The Rule St. Benedict put down on paper 1400 years ago is already quite enough. What I need to do is live *that* – something like the way he lived at Subiaco.

October 10, 1952

Made my private retreat (Oct 1st to 6th). The days of the retreat were beautiful and terrible. We husked corn in the bottoms in the mornings. In the afternoon I was in the woods, by the toolshed. The effect of solitude was to calm down, to some extent, the whole conflict, and I began to see more clearly something of what it has meant for me to be at Gethsemani these last eleven years. So that, when I came out of the retreat, there were still two sides to the question. Fortunately, because just then Rev. Father came home from the General Chapter. The letters from Dom Humphrey in Vermont and Dom J. B. Porion had been, of course, stopped and sent to him in Europe. I was worn out by the retreat and the inundated effect of everything that had happened in the last month (Fr. David's breakdown, the rejection of *Sign of Jonas* by Dom Gabriel[14] etc. etc.) and was in no mood to put up a great fight. In fact, I was very nervous and upset and Fr. Bellarmine told me to take some extra sleep and forget everything for a while.

The Carthusian letters were non-committal. Dom Humphrey told me to come to Vermont and talk it over. Reverend Father threw buckets of cold water on the mere suggestion and I was feeling too low to do anything more about it. Dom Porion said it would be difficult to be received into a Charterhouse, but that he would put in a good word to the General, if I wished. He strongly recommended going to *Camaldoli* in preference to the Chartreuse, but strongest of all was his recommendation to stay where I am and abandon myself completely into the hands of God.

Today, I got a letter from Dom Anselmo Gabbiani, Prior of the Sacro Eremo, at Camaldoli. It was the best yet. Very simply, said I could come if I wished and start right out as a hermit – everything about it seemed just as it should be – as Ann Wasserman said about her Cleveland Carmel "just right." Somehow it seems to me that this may be it, after all. And yet – I cannot do anything right at the moment. Reverend Father would do *any-thing* to prevent me from moving one step further in the affair. I am certain

---

[14] Merton was having problems with the censors of the Order regarding the publication of *The Sign of Jonas.*

that nothing is to be done at the moment. If God wills me to go to Camaldoli, He will show me when to take the next step and how. So I remain both certain and uncertain.

What am I certain of? If it were merely a question of satisfying my own desires and aspirations, I would leave for Camaldoli in ten minutes. Yet it is *not* merely a question of satisfying my own desires. On the contrary: there is one thing holding me at Gethsemani. And that is the Cross. Some mystery of the Wisdom of God has taught me that perhaps, after all, Gethsemani is where I belong because I do not *fit* in and because here my ideals are practically all frustrated.

At the moment I am able to face both alternatives with complete indifference – at least I hope it is with complete indifference. Because to me, desires and aspirations no longer really matter. They are so often deceptive.

The only desire that counts is to give yourself completely to God with Christ on the cross, in the renunciation of all human desires and aspirations, in order to live for God alone in sacrifice. It is to me quite clear that, if I stay at Gethsemani, all that St. John of the Cross demands for the purification of a soul can *easily* be fulfilled. The cross is here. I am sure it is also at Camaldoli. I would not go there seeking anything else. But since it is already here . . . The only thing that remains to be seen is whether God wills change or not. For that I am wishing, without excitement and without fever. His goodness and His love alone suffice. His cross is enough, for it is the sign of mercy.

October 22, 1952

Since my retreat I have been having another one of those nervous breakdowns. The same old familiar business. I am getting used to it now – since the old days in 1936, when I thought I was going to crack up on the Long Island Railroad, and the more recent one since ordination. And now this.

I think it is good to write it down, without asking too many questions as to why it is good. The writing of it forms part of a documentation that is demanded of me – still demanded, I think – by the Holy Ghost.

To begin with, I have left out two important elements in it – big events of the end of September. First, the General's refusal of the *imprimi potest* [let it be printed] for *Jonas* and second, Frater David's crackup.

Poor Fr. David! Big, dark, quiet kid, so completely good and simple, and so perfect a monk! He was one who loved the woods a lot. I have a sort of feeling that I led him over the cliff. But I know that isn't true. He was much nearer a crackup when he came out of the novitiate a year ago August than he was last winter, when he brought the novices out to cut down the trees I had been marking, and this Spring, when we went out planting seedlings together. Something beyond anybody's control brought on the strain that finally sent him to the hospital and now home. I hated to see him go and it worked on me very much.

I wrote to Dom Gabriel, but he left for China before my letter reached him, and since then I have heard nothing. He based his refusal of permission to permit the book on the report of a special censor – Dom Albert, prior of Caldey – who did not like the idea of a Journal or, at least, of such a Journal, filled with all the minute and trivial details of the monastic life. Dom Gabriel vetoes the whole thing, but Harcourt, Brace had already set it up in type, advertized it all over the country and got it accepted by several book clubs. Since Dom Albert thought the spiritual parts of the book were all right, I wrote asking permission to publish at least *part* of the Journal for Bob's[15] sake and to avoid making us all suspiciously grim – (as if the censors were trying to cover up some horrible scandal). Yesterday, Reverend Father got a wire from Bob saying Dom Albert had granted the *nihil obstat* [nothing stands in the way]. But Dom Albert is not the General.

Also, Dom Gabriel wrote a terrific letter about *Waters of Siloe*. He had just read the French translation. He told me with perfect justice – and great force – that I should have never written about de Rancé, Dom Augustin, Dom Urban, etc. He is absolutely right. Acting without guidance or control, I simply wrote the book that might have been written by some wiseguy outside the monastery. A monk *cannot* take the attitude I took towards great men who have shaped the destiny of the Order or, at least, he cannot make that attitude public with such a lack of restraint. In condemning them I have condemned myself. Perhaps they did have failings and limitations. God knows. But in publicizing their "limitations" I have publicized my own, and judged myself out of my own mouth.

It is always a relief to see the truth, and I find peace in confessing it. But it brings with it a shattering punishment – which is medicinal – the collapse of the condemned author. I mean the collapse of the "exterior man" who was too much in the book. The inward man is renewed from day to day, and arises anew from the fires of tribulation.

---

[15] Robert Giroux, Merton's editor at Harcourt, Brace & Company, was a friend from his Columbia University days.

Strangely, this condemnation of *Waters* and *Jonas* makes it seem even more evident to me that I ought to *stay* at Gethsemani. Why? Very simple. A man cannot go on to be a hermit until he has proved himself as a cenobite. I haven't been beating the air. I am not really a monk – never have been except in my own imagination. But it is a relief to *know* that. What exhausts me is the entertainment of all my illusions. At least let me get rid of the greatest illusion of all, and start to live all over again – or to die. For I feel sometimes as if, having admitted my complete futility as a monk, it would be decent to offer God my life and make preparation for everything by dying. No such offering would make sense unless it implied an equal willingness to live and be perfect, in obedience to Him – and to do *penance*. Whether we live or die, we are the Lord's. Life and death alike can be offered up as penance. I can make reparation for my impiety – not necessarily by imitating Abbot de Rancé (everything in me says that he is not supposed to be my model), but by living as perfectly as I can the Rule and Spirit of St. Benedict – obedience, humility, work, prayer, simplicity, the love of Christ.

The light of truth burns without a flicker in the depths of a house that is shaken with storms of passion and of fear. *Non timebis a timore nocturno* [You will not fear the terror of the night (Psalm 90:5 in the Vulgate)]. And so I go on trying to walk on the waters of the breakdown. Worse than ever before and better than ever before. It is always painful and reassuring when He who I am not is visibly destroyed by the hand of God in order that the simplicity in the depths of me, which is His image, may be set free to serve Him in peace. Sometimes in the midst of all this I am tremendously happy, and I have never in my life begun to be so grateful for His mercy.

Also – no more professional spirituality! Terrifically purged of ideas about prayer, and of all desire to preach them, as if I *had* something!

October 30, 1952

Yesterday we were raking leaves in the front avenue and burning them – nice quiet work under the sunlit trees. Cars came slowly through the smoke. I thought of the first Lent in the novitiate, when we worked in the avenue a lot. I even think that we raked leaves there my first afternoon in the community as a postulant. I realize more and more that the only thing in life that matters is our awareness of God and our desire to do His will – and yet sometimes I seem to be completely incapable of both, and incapable of *everything*. Yet I am aware of Him in the agony of knowing obscurely that I am paralyzed and know nothing.

When we came in, there was a letter from the General – written at Lan- · tao, the island off Hong Kong where the Chinese Trappists have taken refuge. He was very kind to me, reviewed the whole situation in which we got involved with *The Sign of Jonas*, said something about the relations of monks and publishers, and then granted permission for the book to be published.

Last Friday, Bro. Basil called me out of the High Mass to ask for a team of monks to come out and fight the forest fire which had been going on for the last 3 or 4 days in the knobs.

November 7, 1952

I was hebdomadary this week.

This morning I was preparing for Mass in the woods, as usual. It was cold but the sun came up and melted the frost. It was quiet, except for the crows. I sat on an old chair under the skinny cedars, with my feet in the brown, frosty grass, and reflected on the errors of my monastic life. They are many and I am in the midst of them. I have never seen so many mistakes and illusions. It should be enough for me that God loves me. For his love is greater than anything else. It is the beginning and end of all. By it and for it all things were created. Yet, outside His love, I am tempted to erect a cold house of my own devising – a house that is small enough to contain my own self, and which is easier to understand than His incomprehensible love and His providence. Why is it we must be afraid of Mystery, as if the Mystery of God's love were not infinitely simple and infinitely clear? Why do we run away from Him into the dark which, to us, is light? That is the other mystery of sin, which no one understands. Yet we act as if we understand sin and as if we were really aware of the love of God when we have never deeply experienced the meaning of either one.

November 12, 1952

The life of the foundress of the Little Sisters of the Poor was finished in the refectory today. Abbé le Pailleur (is that how you spell it?) – an imaginary mystic, made a real career for himself as the *imaginary* founder of the Little Sisters. Having put Sister Marie of the Cross in the shade and written volumes about her achievements being in reality his own, he came eventually to believe his story.

But that is one of the great and subtle temptations of all who aspire to sanctity. First, they imagine a sanctity which they feel to be appropriate to themselves. Then they imagine themselves (and contemplate themselves) striving for it in ways they deem fitting and efficacious. Finally, if they are sufficiently stubborn, they carry the story to the end and imagine they have achieved what they wanted. These are the saints who come in their own name and not in God's name – the prophets who prophesy without being sent. They are the clouds without water St. Jude speaks of: "They are fierce waves of the sea with shame for their crests, wandering stars, with eternal darkness and storms awaiting them . . . like the brute beasts they derive knowledge only from their senses and it serves to corrupt them . . ." (Jude 1:13 and 10). Yet all of us can be numbered among them. False humility is no protection against this vanity which turns the glory of God into a lie. And at the root of it is our forgetfulness of the fear of God. We talk of God when He has gone far from us (We are far from Him and His nearness remains to accuse us!). We live as if God existed for our sakes, figuring that we exist for Him. We use grace as if it were matter handed over to form according to our pleasure. We use the truth of God as material for the fabrication of idols. We forget that we are the matter and His grace is the form imposed upon us by His wisdom. Does the clay understand the work of the potter? Does it not allow itself to be formed into a vessel of election?

The truth is formed in silence and work and suffering – with which we *become* true. But we interfere with God's work by talking too much about ourselves – even telling Him what we ought to do – advising Him how to make us perfect and listening for His voice to answer us with approval. We soon grow impatient and turn aside from the silence that disturbs us (the silence in which His work can best be done) and invent the answer and the approval which will never come.

Silence, then, is the adoration of His truth. Work is the expression of our humility and suffering is born of the love that seeks one thing alone: that God's will be done.

November 20, 1952

Beautiful letter from the General, in Japan, about dark night of the soul.

The afternoon of the dedication [of Gethsemani's church] – clouds, dark green cedars – Jesus My Redeemer. Peace.

I am still exhausted by the very act of existing. Pleasure, waste, motion, blood coursing in the skull. And the repeated acceptance of sacrifice. To be without anything that I long for and to know that "This is it."

Yesterday Fr. Francis and I broke the new step ladder trying to get the top of a felled cedar out of an oak tree. It is a consolation to me that he is a saint and pleasing to God, and the thought that others are holy saves me from despair and fills me with a great joy which I cannot lay hands on because no joy is mine.

November 29, 1952

The annual retreat is ending. Father Phelan, who came from Toronto to preach it, was in the vault this afternoon, looking at the manuscripts and he was talking about Gilson and Maritain and how holy they both were. Gilson, after a lecture on St. Thomas, when being complimented: "Those things which I have to say are too high for someone like me – and to think I have to support my family by having to say them!"

I was very deeply moved by Fr. Phelan's conference on the Sacred Heart. Great depth of theology in clear and simple terms. It showed me how there really is an abyss of light in the things the simplest faithful believe and love and which sometimes seem trite to the intellectuals. Indeed, perhaps it is the simplest and most popular truths which are also the deepest after all.

For my own part, I think much has been done to me in the course of this retreat – in emptiness and helplessness and humiliation. Aware that I might crack up at any moment. I find, nevertheless, that when I pray, I pray better than ever. I mean by that – I have no longer any special degree of prayer. But simple vocal prayer, and especially the office and the psalms, seems to have acquired a depth and a simplicity I never knew before in *any* prayer. I have nothing but faith and the love of God and confidence in the simple means He has given me for reaching Him. Suspended entirely from His mercy, I am content for anything to happen.

I am beginning to know the meaning of St. Paul: *non plus sapere quam oportet sapere, sed sapere ad sobrietatem* [one ought not to think more highly of oneself than he ought to think, but to think with sober judgment (Romans 12:3)].

Yesterday – bright sun – I took seven scholastics out to burn cedar brush in the woods, allotted to us as our little portion. Today, after dinner, under a grey cold sky, I went out there and found the fire still smouldering under the fine silver-grey ash. I stirred up the ashes and sat by the fire with the wind blowing on my back and read about the humility of the Desert Fathers, and presently it began to snow. I had been praying to Our Lady for strength and perseverance.

The afternoon conference was all about Our Lady – how God willed her *fate* – not that He predetermined it, but her free choice to obey Him fulfilled His will. I could see, in the light of her presence, that my own choice would fulfill God's will in me and that the choice He willed was for me once again to forget about ever leaving Gethsemani. Our Lady of Gethsemani. Mary is, in a certain sense, the community which is my Mother. It is her love that has brought us here and keeps the community together. It is her love I have known out under the cedars, and working in the fields, and singing in choir. It is her love that has made me desire solitude, and she will fulfill that desire. She is my solitude and she is here. It seems I have to keep finding it out over and over again.

Maybe this time it is the end. I hope I have stopped asking questions. I have begged her for the grace to finish the course here and die as a holy monk in the monastery or in a solitude closely dependent on the monastery. I feel great peace and my heart has never been so free, so poor and so empty.

December 29, 1952. Feast of St. Thomas à Becket

A week ago I was reading the Christmas sermon from *Murder in the Cathedral* to the scholastics. I read them several of the choruses also. Today, after what has taken place in me since Christmas, I find I have lived through something of the same kind of decision as St. Thomas in the play.

You start by desiring something – an end, a vocation. You come to seek it with great imperfection, and there is a great danger of wanting the right thing for the wrong reason. And there is no decision possible. Suddenly occurs the "change of the right hand of the Most High" *(haec mutualis dexterae excelsi!)*. Now it is no longer we who question and plead and inquire and pray, but He who impels us. We feel the power of God suddenly upon us, and our desire is totally changed. It is objectively the same thing that we desire, but we see it in an entirely different light when we know that, by God's will, it is to be. For since in His intention it is already fulfilled, it is no longer a mere desire, no longer a wish we can *play* with. There is no playing with the will of God!

It is easy to understand why it is so easy and so pleasant to waste our lives playing with desires to which we unconsciously realize God is paying no attention. But what futility!

No – our joy is to be led by Him to the thing He desires, even though that thing be in some way terrible. As soon as *He desires* it, it ceases to be "our will." It becomes a sacrifice. It demands a gift of our whole being.

It was so with the priesthood. And now I think it will be so with solitude.

It is very serious. And very simple.

Yesterday, between two cedars, looking at the wagon tracks on the soft earth of the bottomlands and at the woods beyond, I knew that whatever

God will have granted me – whatever solitude – will be truly for the salvation of my soul. And I saw how much I need solitude for that reason.

Not solitude for the sake of something special, something exalted: solitude as the climate in which I can simply be what I am meant to be, and live in the presence of the living God. Solitude in order to be a simple Christian. Like climbing down from a mountain or a pillar and starting all over again to behave as a human being – I need solitude for the true fulfillment which I seek – that of being *ordinary*.

Life in the world was utterly abnormal.

Life in the monastery is not ordinary. It is a freakish sort of life. The freakishness is not St. Benedict's fault, but maybe it is necessary. In solitude, at last, I shall be just a person, no longer corrupted by being known, no longer creating myself in the image of a slightly unbalanced society. Living in the likeness of the God who is my life: that is to say, living as unknown. For a Christian is one whom the world does not know.

"Behold what manner of love the Father has bestowed upon us that we should be called the children of God, and such we are. This is why the world does not know us, because it did not know Him." 1 John 3:1.

In any case, the question of solitude is closer to a solution.

Christmas morning, after my three Masses, I felt sure Jesus wanted me to press forward and really ask for solitude. I had composed a letter to Rev. Father asking to be allowed to be a hermit, here or elsewhere, at the end of three years. But on Christmas day Rev. Father fell ill. I held on to the letter. Meanwhile Dr. Law came down and I saw him. He said don't wait three years: go *now*.

It means a gradual start. A week at a time in the fixed-up shanty. Both he and Fr. Bellarmine, who heartily agrees, will try to convince Rev. Father that this is *necessary* – if only to keep me from folding up completely.

The new bells sound wonderful from the woods.

The new decision makes me feel the way I felt when I finally made up my mind to become a Catholic.

St. John's day – Fr. Tarcisius and I walked all the way to Hanekamp's in the afternoon. Wonderful, quiet little valley! The silent house, the goats in the red sage grass, the dry creek and Hanekamp's vineyard. The beautiful silence of the woods on every side! Fr. Tarcisius looked about with such reverence you would have thought he was seeing angels. Later we separated to pray apart in the thinned pine grove on the south eastern hillside.

And I could see how simple it is to find God in solitude. There is no one else, nothing else. He is all there is to find there. Everything is in Him. And what could be more pleasing to Him than that we should leave all things and all company to be with Him and think only of Him and know Him alone, in order to give Him our love?

January 14, 1953. Feast of St. Hilary

One of the best of the scholastics died yesterday in the hospital. Fr. José came here in a wonderful way, like a homing pigeon, all the way from his island in the Philippines, where one day, in a minor seminary, he ran across our *Spiritual Directory*. He was a very simple and serious monk, and gave a great impression of solidity and coherence in his interior life. Like most Filipinos, he was small and wiry. Gave a great impression of quiet, humble fortitude and calm. I'll always remember the clarity and simplicity and the fundamental character of his questions – and the day when he came and said, as if quite by the way, "Jesus gave me a great desire for His cross." The next day he fell ill. That was in the Autumn. Today we bury him. I think the doctors finally decided that what he died of was Hodgkin's disease. For a long time they did not know what to do with him.

The Jesus on the walls of this hermitage is the *Devot Christ* of Perpignan.[16] I wonder if there is something truculent about my choice. Is this the Jesus of my prayer or the Jesus of my showing off?

There is one thing I must do here (and may I one day live here and do it all day long) and that is to prepare for my death. But that means a preparation in *gentleness*. A gentleness, a silence, a humility I have never had before – which seems impossible in the tension of the community where even my compassion is tinged with force and strain.

But if I am called to solitude it is, I think, to un-learn all tension, and get rid of the strain that has always falsified me in the presence of others and put harshness into the words of my mind. If I have needed solitude, it is because I have always so much needed the mercy of Christ and needed His humility and His charity. How can I give love unless I have much more than I have ever had?

[16] Perpignan is the city in France near Prades where Merton was born. The "hermitage" was a woodshed which Merton dedicated to St. Anne.

January 28, 1953. Weekly Day of Recollection

Fine ideas in Picard's *World of Silence*. (A train of the old time sings in my present silence, at St. Anne's, where the watch without a crystal ticks on the little desk.)

1. Foolish to expect a man "to develop all the possibilities that are within him." "The possibilities that are not fully realized nourish the substance of silence. Silence is strengthened by them and gives of this additional strength to the other potentialities that are fully realized." p. 67.

2. "There is room for contradictions within the substance of silence . . . A man who still has the substance of silence within him does not always need to be watching the movements of his inmost being." p. 66.

3. True solitude "does not derive from subjectivity. Solitude stands before man as something objective, even the solitude within himself. Solitude for the saints was not a result of great exertion like the 'inward' solitude of today." p. 65.

All this verified at St. Anne's, this month. Discovery and a gift. What the Carmelites got for me on New Year's Day! To be alone by being part of the universe – fitting in completely to an environment of woods and silence and peace. Everything you do becomes a unity and a prayer. Unity within and without. Unity with all living things – without effort or contention. My silence is part of the whole world's silence and builds the temple of God without the noise of hammers.

February 9, 1953. Feast of St. Scholastica

Evening. St. Anne's. I got permission to stay out here until collation.

It is a tremendous thing no longer to have to debate in my mind about "being a hermit," even though I am not one. At least now solitude is something concrete – it is "St. Anne's" – the long view of hills, the empty corn-fields in the bottoms, the crows in the trees, and the cedars bunched together on the hillside. And when I am here there is always lots of sky and lots of peace and I don't have distractions and everything is serene – except for the rats in the wall. They are my distraction and they are sometimes obstreperous.

Here there seems to be less and less need even of books.

[John] Cassian has become tremendous, in a site which makes him irritable.

If I were only here always! Cold mornings, hot afternoons. Came out the other day (Sexagesima Sunday) when there was thick frost on the ground but the sun was already warm.

The Spirit is alone here with the silence of the world.

St. Anne's is like a rampart between two existences. On one side I know the community to which I must return. And I *can* return to it with love. But to return seems like a waste. It is a waste I offer to God. On the other side is the great wilderness of silence in which, perhaps, I might never speak to anyone but God again, as long as I live.

(Back in the vault lies an existence that is already beginning to be remote and strange, a wayside station that I have passed in the desert, even though I still give direction there is the morning. The reviews of *The Sign of Jonas* lie under the typewriter table, stuffed into the first edition of the book that still awaits some more correction. But all that has nothing to do with the silence of St. Anne's.)

February 12, 1953

I am grateful to the scholastics simply because they exist and because they are what they are. And I am grateful to you, O God, for having placed me among them, and told me to be their Father.[17] But finally I am grateful to You, O God, because I am more often alone. Not that I run away from them. Yet sometimes I do not know myself with them. At other times I find myself in them and with them. Indeed, direction is sometimes an experiment in recognition: they recognize something new in themselves and I in myself: for God recognizes Himself in us.

February 14, 1953

Today we commemorate Blessed Conrad – one of the Cistercian hermits.

I might as well admit that in the novitiate I did not like the hermits of our Order. Bl. Conrad, St. Galgan, St. Firmian. Perhaps the stories of St. Albert of Sestri and Blessed John of Caramola were more congenial to me. The hermits, however, "never seemed to get anywhere." Their stories were inconclusive. They seemed to have died before finding out what they were supposed to achieve.

---

[17] Merton had been named Master of Scholastics in May 1951.

Now I know there is something important about the very incompleteness of Bl. Conrad: hermit in Palestine, by St. Bernard's permission. Starts home for Clairvaux when he hears St. Bernard is dying. Gets to Italy and hears St. Bernard is dead. Settles in a wayside chapel outside Bari and dies there. What an untidily unplanned life! No order, no sense, no system, no climax. Like a book without punctuation that suddenly ends in the middle of a sentence.

Yet I know that those are the books I really like!

Bl. Conrad cannot possibly be solidified or ossified in history. He can perhaps be caught and held in a picture, but he is like a photograph of a bird in flight – too accurate to look the way a flying bird seems to appear to us. We never saw the wings in that position. Such is the solitary vocation. For of all men, the solitary knows least where he is going, and yet is more sure, for there is one thing he cannot doubt: he travels where God is leading him. That is precisely why he doesn't know the way. And that too is why, to most other men, the way is something of a scandal.

Tomorrow: *Quinquagesima*

At the end of the Epistle St. Paul says "I shall know even as I have been known" [1 Corinthians 13:12]. In the Gospel: the blind man hears the crowd passing by and asks who is passing, calls out to Jesus, is rebuked by the disciples, calls out louder still, catches the Lord's attention so that Jesus asks him what he wants. "That I might see!" [Mark 10:51]. He receives his sight, knows as he has been known, and follows Jesus glorifying God. And Christ goes on his way with His face turned towards Jerusalem, ascending to His passion.

It is in the passion of Christ that God has proved to us that He has "known" us. That He has recognized us in our misery. That He has found His lost image in our fallen state and reclaimed it for His own, cleansed in the charity of His Divine Son.

It is on the cross that God has known us: that He has searched our souls with His compassion and experienced the full extent of our capacity for wickedness: it is on the cross that He has known our exile, and ended it, and brought us home to Him.

We have to return to Him through the same gate of charity by which He came to us. If we had to open the gate ourselves, we could never do it. He has done the work. It is for us to follow Him and enter in by all those things which go together to fulfill in us the law of charity, in which all virtues are complete.

In community: there is much material with which to build our charity. In solitude we seem to build it out of nothing. For in solitude, we have nothing: it is God Himself who creates our charity out of nothing.

The landscape of St. Anne's speaks the word "longanimity": going on and on and on: and having nothing.

February 16, 1953

It seems to me that St. Anne's is what I have been waiting for and looking for all my life and now I have stumbled into quite by accident. Now, for the first time, I am aware of what happens to a man who has really found his place in the scheme of things.

With tremendous relief, I have discovered that I no longer need to *pretend*. Because, when you have not found what you are looking for, you pretend in your eagerness to have found it. You act as if you had found it. You spend your time telling yourself what you have found and yet do not want.

I do not have to buy St. Anne's. I do not have to sell myself to myself here. Everything that was ever real in me has come back to life in this doorway wide open to the sky! I no longer have to trample myself down, cut myself in half, throw part of me out the window and keep pushing the rest of myself away.

In the silence of St. Anne's everything has come together in unity and the unity is not my unity but Yours, O Father of Peace.

I recognize in myself the child who walked all over Sussex. (I did not know I was looking for this shanty, or that I would one day find it.) All the countries of the world are one under this sky: I no longer need to travel. Half a mile away is the monastery with the landscape of hills which haunted me for 11 years with uncertainty. I knew I had come to stay but never really believed it, and the hills seemed to speak, at all times, of some other country.

The quiet landscape of St. Anne's speaks of no other country.

If they will let me, I am here to stay – unless there be some invasion of tractors and construction. (There is a jeep now in the fields before me. First time since the corn harvest there has been anything there.) And if there be some other place to go to, it need only be a mile or two away!

This is a different situation. The silence of it is making me well.

February 17, 1953. Shrove Tuesday

Lent, which begins tomorrow, is a sunlit season.

Today – *carnivale* – farewell to the flesh. It is a poor joke to be merry about leaving the flesh, as if we were to return to it once again. What would be the good of Lent, if it were only temporary?

Jesus nevertheless died *in order to return* to His flesh; in order to raise His own body glorious from the dead, and in order to raise our bodies with Him. "Unless the grain of wheat, falling in the ground, die, itself remaineth alone" [John 12:24]. So we cast off the flesh, not out of contempt, but in order to heal the flesh in the mercy of penance and restore it to the Spirit to which it belongs. And all creation waits, in anguish, for our victory and our bodies' glory.

God wills us to recover all the joys of His created world in the Spirit, by denying ourselves what is really no joy – what only ends in the flesh. "The flesh profiteth nothing" [John 6:63].

Looking at the crucifix on the white wall at St. Anne's – overwhelmed at the realization that I am a *priest*, that it has been given to me to know something of what the Cross means *(vobis datum est nosse mysteria regni Dei)*. [It is given to you to know the mysteries of the Kingdom of God (Mark 4:11).] And that St. Anne's is a special part of my priestly vocation: the silence, the woods, the sunlight, the shadows, the picture of Jesus, Our Lady of Cobre and the little angels in Angelico's paradise. Here I am a priest with all the world as my parish. Or is it a temptation, the thought of this? Perhaps I do not need to remember the apostolic fruitfulness of this silence. I need only to be nothing and to wait for the revelation of Christ: To be at peace and poor and silent in the world where the mystery of iniquity is also at work and where there is also no other revelation. No, there is so much peace at St. Anne's that it is most certainly the heart of a great spiritual battle that is fought in silence. And I who sit here and pray and think and live – I am nothing and do not need to know what is going on. I need only to hope in Christ to hear the big deep bell that now begins to ring and sends its holy sound to me through the little cedars.

This is the continuation of my Mass. This is still my Eucharist, my daylong thanksgiving, work, worship, hoping for the perfect revelation of Christ.

February 18, 1953. Ash Wednesday

Gruesome picture of the skulls in the Capuchin cemetery in Rome and three recently dead Capuchins rotting among them. It is posted in the little cloister. *Memento mori* [Remember death]. Ash Wednesday. I don't think we need anything so theatrical as this picture.

The ashes themselves bring the mercy of the blessing of Christ, in sobriety and bare-footed peace.

At St. Anne's the sun is as bright as the first day that it was created. The world is clean. There is sin in it, but Christ has overcome the world. Even on Ash Wednesday I begin to hear the silence of Easter.

Many birds, going North, were flying in the wind. They move slowly against the blue sky and looked like a school of fish in clear, West Indian waters. The sun shone through their wings and made them seem like red and orange fins.

Last night before collation, Fr. Anselm took me aside and said the Archbishop is supposed to be coming to ordain him deacon on the feast of St. Benedict. I am beginning to prepare his retreat – conferences on the martyrs. And I think of the unity of the Church in this her Lent (The lesson from Joel brings this out: *vocate coetum:* blow the trumpet and call the people together for the great fast! [Joel 1:14]). The whole church is called together and we realize that our Lent is united with the suffering of the martyrs and the fasts of the desert fathers and the good works and penances of all the saints. St. Anne's itself, beside my Mass and my office in choir, and the rest, is my contribution to the Church's Lents. In the morning, in the scriptorium, I have begun to review my moral theology on the Eucharist. Whatever I can give to God and to other men is only the effect and manifestation in me of the power of the Passion of Jesus. I would reply to his action and let Him show Himself in my life. This He will do in a way I have both expected and not expected; planned and not planned; desired and not desired.

My decisions do not anticipate His coming: they manifest that He has come, if they be His decision.

February 22, 1953. First Sunday of Lent

Eleven years ago to the day since I received the habit of novice. Once again the 22nd. comes around on the First Sunday of Lent. I received a Lenten book from the hands of my spiritual children, and in a short time I have become the spiritual father of many. Once again I am aware of the mystery of my vocation.

The greatest mystery is here at St. Anne's. Just as Baptism makes us potential martyrs, so also it makes us potential priests, potential monks, potential hermits.

I was clothed in this hermitage eleven years ago without even knowing it. The black and white house indeed is a kind of religious habit – and a warm enough one when the stove is going.

All this is to say that this silence is Christ's love for me and bought by His death and it purifies me in His sufferings and His Blood. I must receive it with great compunction and love and reverence lest His love be in vain.

Hortamur vos ne in vacuum gratiam Dei recipiatis. [We exhort you not to receive the grace of God in vain (2 Corinthians 6:1).]

I think the best way for me to receive His grace is with the utmost simplicity. When I am most quiet and most myself, His grace is clear and then I see nothing else under the sun. What else is there for us but to be tranquil and at peace in the all-enchanting wonder of God's mercy to us? It falls upon this paper quieter than the morning sun, and then, I know that all things, without His love are useless, and in His love, having nothing, I can possess all things.

February 24, 1953. St. Matthias

Struck by the text from *Acts*, in the Office and the Mass, that the apostles are "witnesses to the resurrection." Matthias is chosen by lot from among all the witnesses of the Resurrection to be the *witness* of the resurrection. This choice was the action of God. Vocation. All the succession of the Apostles, in a less perfect sense, continues this testimony. Our testimony is the Mass itself: not only a sign or token of the sacrifice of Christ, but the representation, the renewal of that sacrifice.

The priest bears witness to the resurrection by holding in his hands the Risen Christ – high over his head for all the people to see. And none of us see, except by faith. Faith itself is the light of the Resurrection, our sharing of the Resurrection. It is the effect of the Resurrection in our souls. By it we are buried and rise from the dead in Christ.

Father Green, a Maryknoll Missionary, spoke to us in Chapter (a few days after Ash Wednesday). In Holy Week last year, after nearly a year under house arrest and then solitary confinement, he was publicly tried by the communists [in China]. When he was on trial before the people, Easter

Day, I was in church, in Gethsemani, Easter Night. He stood before us now in a shapeless black overcoat. You could see right away that he was a man who had been in prison. He looked like a communist and talked with the intensity of one, but without any bitterness. The plainest thing about it all, to me, was that here was a man in whom Christ had visibly suffered. Here was another humble witness of the Resurrection. He described his own confusion and helplessness, and in so doing described the Passion of Christ without knowing it. The strongest point he made was his discovery, during his trial, that he was caught between Our Lady and the Devil, between her heel and the serpent's head, and that it had not proved to be a comfortable position to be in.

This made a great impression and when I heard it, I knew that all the Capuchin skulls in the picture were really relatively foolish. For God is the God of the living. He is not the God of dead bones, but of the relics of the martyrs.

Yesterday, began our Lenten book, *Je suis fille d'église* [*I Am a Daughter of the Church*, by P. Marie-Eugène, O.C.D.], about Theresian mysticism. Glad to get it but terribly oppressed by the necessity to read about mystical prayer. Noise of trucks coming through the window. Sunlight in the room. Very happy to be here, and yet feeling tense and ashamed and poor. Pushed ahead with the reading as a pure effort of obedience. And I mean effort. No help, no relief, except to look at the harmless titles of the books on the shelf in front of me, books that I will never have to touch. (*Jesus All Good; Méthode pour assister les malades*, etc.)

Gone are the days when "mysticism" was for me a matter of eager and speculative interest. Now, because it is my life, it is torment to think about. Like being in the pangs of childbirth and reading an essay on mother love written by a spinster.

In choir I am happier than I have ever been there, extremely poor and helpless, often strained, hardly able to hold myself in place. "Expecting every moment to be my next." Sometimes it is a great relief to be distracted. There is a "presence" of God which is like an iron curtain between the mind and God.

But here at St. Anne's I am always happy and at peace no matter what happens. For here there is no need for anyone but God – no need of "mysticism."

A fly buzzes on the window pane!

March 3, 1953

Heavy rains last night and this morning. At the end of the private masses the rain started coming in through the ceiling of the sanctuary (even though, with great noise and greater expense a new roof was put on the church last Fall). During Prime the sanctuary was peopled with a troop of large and small buckets, each one veiled in white cloth so that the drops falling from the high ceiling would not resound like gun-shots through the choir.

In front of St. Anne's a brook runs through the ashes of the fire where we burned cedar branches and the bones of a cow at the year's end. The bottoms are flooded. Now rivers decided to traverse in every direction, the plowed fields. A great white bird comes flying over these waters, as if it had suddenly found its way here, with the rain clouds, from some distant sea.

Mystery of a relic of St. John of the Cross solved. It came last Fall from a priest in Rome. Now I discover he is a friend of Lax.[18]

(Look at that bird hanging up there in the wind! I never saw such wings. Where did he come from?)

Then a letter came from Paul Hindemith, or rather from his wife, asking if I had anything he could use for a "Responsorial Chorus" for some youth convention. She had been evidently reading *The Sign of Jonas* and asked if I had something lying around "in the vault." Curious that now suddenly a lot of people know all about "the vault" – know more about it more than some of my brothers in the monastery. Will they have to find out about St. Anne's? Will I run from one solitude to another like Little Eva across the ice floes, with the public right behind me?

Here comes more rain.

Anyway, I have been writing something for Hindemith.

I got Fr. Chrysogonus to play me something from Hindemith's organ Preludes I, II and III yesterday morning. I sat in the back of the church and looked at the lenten curtain and the music sounded good. But it was hard to concentrate on it because novices were cleaning the church – making slow gestures of the most appalling solemnity. I finally prevented them from using a vacuum cleaner and they looked at me as if I ought to be thrown in jail by the Holy Office for listening to organ music during the time of work.

[18] Bob Lax, a close friend of Merton; they were classmates at Columbia University.

One thing is certain. Days of recollection and afternoons in St. Anne's, Mass and the Office, and the terror of the dark, are given to me for one thing: that I may find Christ and know Him, Who is "made to us power and wisdom from God" [1 Corinthians 1:30]. Not a question of examining myself, still less of planning work or how to be a spiritual director. Life is much more serious than that. Study has a serious place in it, too. *Non in persuasibilibus humanae sapientiae verbis.* [Not in the subtle words of human wisdom (1 Corinthians 2:4).] Not as if Christ could offer us an alternative wisdom to other similar wisdoms – as if He had a doctrine that was one of many! We have not yet sufficiently "learned Christ" and we do not yet know sufficiently what it is to find Him.

Another thing: I have discovered the penitential psalms.[19] You do not discover them until you know how much you need them. You do not know your need until you experience it. You do not experience your poverty when you tell yourself about it but when God tells you that you are poor. When God tells you of a sickness, it is because He means, at the same time, to provide a remedy. It is the Devil who tells us that we are ill, and taunts us for it, reminds us of our helplessness by making us even more helpless.

When I was a novice, I recited the penitential psalms at work every afternoon. Yet I did not know them and they did not know me. It was a wearying exercise. At St. Anne's I have found them and they have found me. Cassian, I think, was the go-between. Through Cassian I am getting back to everything, or rather, getting for the first time to monastic and Christian values I had dared to write about without knowing them.

Turbatus est a furore oculus meus. [My eye wastes away with grief (Psalm 6:7).] I did not know how much I ruined myself in eleven years, until, trying to recite a psalm out here, I discovered that the mere thought of a psalm makes me tense and hard, and I recite the words automatically like a nervous and well oiled machine. If I am still able, by some miracle, to pray the Office, it must be *in spite of* the way I recite Latin! That is part of the fury that has blinded the eye of my soul and kept it from being simple.

In the Penitential Psalms, Christ recognizes my poverty in His poverty. Merely to see myself in the psalm is a beginning of being healed. For I see myself through His grace. His grace is working, therefore I am on my way

---

[19] The seven penitential psalms are 6, 32, 38, 51, 102, 130, and 143.

to being healed. O the need of that healing! I walk from region to region of my soul and I discover that I am a bombed city.

While I meditated on the *Domine ne in furore* [Lord, not in thy fury (Psalm 6:1)] I caught sight of an unexpected patch of green meadow, along the creek, on our neighbor's land. The green grass under the leafless trees, the pools of water after the storm, lifted my heart to God. He is so easy to come to when even grass and water bear witness to His mercy! *Lacrimis meis stratum meum rigabo.* [I will water my couch with tears (Psalm 6:7).]

I have written about the frogs singing. Now they sing again. It is another Spring. Although I am ruined, I am far better off than I have ever been in my life, and my ruin is my fortune.

Saturday, I went around the Vineyard Knob looking for young maple trees to transplant. I found some beeches but no maples. It was the first time I had gone all the way to Hanekamp's by that road that runs along the South boundary of the monastery road.

More than half way there I stopped on a ridge, among pines. Vineyard Knob to the North. A small pine-topped ridge to the South and strange knobs like a school of dolphins over westward, or rather north westward.

I got into Hanekamp's valley and came to his house. He was spreading manure in his garden. I found out that, after all, his house has a front door. I doubt if he ever lets anyone in. I believe he also rarely goes into anyone else's house. He has more dogs than you can believe. A whole pack of skinny pups. I called one and he said, "You'll never catch them." Inside the front gate were the kids, meaning goats. Very small and pathetic. To get through the gate, he picked them up by the neck and gently thrust them aside. He came out the gate with two old cigar boxes containing letters and showed me a most recent letter from his niece, Thekla, back in the old country, Oldenburg. I suppose that's in Bavaria.

He has a great devotion to the late Fr. Augustine Arcand, a holy old priest of Gethsemani who died in 1941 a few months before I entered the monastery. He says he prays to Father Augustine every day. Got him to work a miracle – sudden cure of the wife of a neighbor, who was dying.

He described to me the rare occasion when he entered the neighbor's house to see the sick woman. He re-enacted his horror, clapping his hands to the side of his bearded head, like a creature in a Blake engraving, and crying out, "O, My God, Mabel! You look poorly!"

"That's all right, Herman. I got my appetite back."

It was the day of the miracle and when the Dr. came she said she was all well.

March 10, 1953

It is important, also, to be in conflict with the people you live with in order that the differences between you may be composed in sacrifice and without anger. This is less difficult than the weird struggle with nothing and with no one that goes on in solitude. It is a merciful relief to see *someone* against you and you come from solitude with an eagerness to be charitable, to be good, to give up your own self which is the thing you have grown most tired of.

Whereas, when you are alone, it sometimes becomes difficult to see how you are going to get rid of yourself. When you are with others, an opportunity soon arises. To be in opposition to another you have to return to yourself; you have to rediscover all the faults and weaknesses and passions which the "peace" of solitude had only seemed to lay to rest.

Dolor meus renovatus est. [My sorrow worsens (Psalm 38:3 in Vulgate).] Is it right or wrong for me to be alone? When I have no solitude, I am convinced I need it. When I am alone, I am convinced I have found the situation I need. Then I wonder if my need for it is enough to imply a right to it, even when my superiors think I need it. Can I face the fear of being thought eccentric? What is it that I really fear – the opinions of men or the fear of offending God? If they were not against me, I would not fear that I was not perhaps pleasing to God. How far do the opinions of men represent the values of God? Do I really know what they think of me anyway? Or do I imagine they are opposed to me, simply because I am afraid they will be? And if I am afraid of them, is it because my conscience tells me they *ought* to be opposed to me?

In any case, it is not comfortable to feel that you might be condemned by good men, holy men, for following what you believe to be God's will for you, the inspirations of grace, the judgments of your superiors.

Big fuss this week with the cellarer, Brother Clement. I did not answer his note in a spirit of meekness! He is tired of my solitude and I am tired of his machines. He thinks I am keeping the scholastics from working for him and I think, quite rightly, that he wants to wipe St. Anne's off the face of the earth, and build some kind of factory on the site. Yet, at the same time, the trouble is complicated by the fact that he loves silence to a degree, and is sensitive about his machines while I love work to a degree, and want to see everything done efficiently in the house of God and am self-conscious about being a hermit. We are both afraid of the names we might call each other in the name of our frustrated vocations. Anyway, he was full of dark allusions to people who "do their own will with permission" and openly stated that we were supposed to make our living by manual labor and not by writing books. He is quite correct. And also, we are supposed to live like monks, live lives of prayer, silence . . . etc.

And, as usual, the trouble is no trouble at all.

I find I have really learned that these "conflicts" are one of the *good* things of the monastic life: that they ought not to be feared but *faced* and negotiated with whatever virtue we have in us. We grow by making mistakes, individually and as a community. We must learn to profit by our own mistakes and by the mistakes of others. And the way to do it is to realize that no mistake, no fault, no weakness, can separate us from the charity of Christ when we realize that charity itself wipes out and makes up for everything else.

Consequently, I know that I have no right to fool around gardening out at St. Anne's on the pretext of making it a nice place for the kids to come and pray.

But I do have a right and even a duty to use the place for what it is for: recollection, prayer, solitude, study – justified in the minds of my superiors by the fact that they are the only thing that can keep me from cracking up, and that they are a good investment for the monastery – intended to bear fruit in direction, conferences, and books. Yet I certainly don't want to speak or write – *felix culpa* [happy fault].

One of the things that every monk needs to feel, for his own peace of heart, is that he is working for a living, and even making a living by the work of his hands. However, there are vocations within our vocation: it can always be a higher call to feel oneself to be, and actually to be, useless. Not however to be deliberately useless when you could be useful. Except on such terms as those of St. Benedict Labre. (I pray for the lady who sent me his relic – Br. Alfred has it.)

PART II

Master of Novices

July 1956–May 1960

July 17, 1956

It's necessary to write a book in which there will be a little less of first person singular, a little less dramatizing, and fewer resolutions.

Or rather, it is not necessary to write a book. Or anything else.

One is free to keep a notebook. That is sufficient.

One may write or not write. Therefore one may write.

Either you look at the universe as a very poor creation out of which no one can make anything or you look at your own life and your own part in the universe as infinitely rich full of inexhaustible interest opening out into infinite further possibilities for study and contemplation and interest and praise. Beyond all and in all is God.

Perhaps the book of life, in the end, is the book of what one has lived and if one has lived nothing, he is not in the book of life.

And I have always wanted to write about everything.

That does not mean to write a book that *covers* everything – which would be impossible. But a book in which everything can go. A book with a little of everything that creates itself out of everything. That has its own life. A faithful book. I no longer look at it as a "book."

How slender are the bodies of the young black oaks! With one stroke of the brush you could make them beautiful, on paper, but that would never be what they are.

The sun suddenly touches the woods beyond the cornfield, rapidly washes the hillside with a little pale light. Everything else is dark and wet, for the air is so wet you can swim in it.

It is time to do some exercises:

1.–We do not seem to wake when we are immortal.
     I dreamed this morning I had caught a young raccoon,
     Here in the South, where no raccoon dares to be tame
     We do not seem to be wild when we are immortal
     As I dreamed, this morning where no man dares to be caught
          inanimate with a tame raccoon.

Error: I woke up this morning dead in Alabama with a wild raccoon.
(We never seem so dead as when we are immortal.)

Home – Proverbs
1. We never seem so dead as when we are immortal.
2. Bishop Z is supposed to have a vivid imagination but this is not the case.
3. Some of the highest mountains of the world are under water.
4. Why pretend that you live around here, Goldfarb? You know you have no domicile!

PRAYER TO OUR LADY OF MOUNT CARMEL
What was it that I said to you, in the mirror, at Havana?[1]

Were you not perhaps the last one I saw, as the steamer left, and you standing on your tower with your back to the sea, looking at the university?

I have never forgotten you. And you are more to me now than then, when I walked through the streets reciting (which I had just learned) the *Memorare*. I have forgotten all the things I have prayed for to you. I think I have received them, but I do not remember, more important I have received you.

Whom I know and yet do not know. Whom I love but not enough.

Prayer is what you bring – for prayer is rather your gift to us than what you ask of us.

If only I could pray – and yet I can and I do pray.

Today, for example, it happened in the refectory that the vocation of Elias to hide at Kerith was read, from the Book of Kings [1 Kings 17]. It just happened to be time for it today. And I am going to the Woods because it is my day to pray. Before that, I find you here – in prayer.

And sacrifice then. But teach me what it means.

Teach me to go to this country beyond words and beyond names.

Teach me not to pray on this side of the frontier, here where the woods are.

I need to be led by you. I need my heart to be moved by you. I need my soul to be made clean by your prayer. I need my will to be made strong by you. I need the world to be saved and changed by you. I need you for all

[1] On a visit to Havana in 1940, Merton had a profound spiritual experience as he saw the reflection of the church of Our Lady of Mount Carmel in a mirror in his hotel room.

those who suffer, who are in prison, in danger, in sorrow. I need you for all the crazy people. I need your healing hands to work always in my life. I need you to make me, as your Son, a healer, a comforter, a saviour. I need you to name the dead. I need you to help the dying to cross their particular rivers. I need you for myself whether I live or die. I need to be your monk and your son. It is necessary. Amen.

July 18, 1956

Spender's *Collected Poems* – a most satisfying book.

He has done a better job of versifying than Auden.

No man should allow himself to publish so many poems in one volume as Auden did – and now, on top of everything else, the blurb on the back of the volume says "Auden . . . is the most impressive poet of his generation."

There are some individual things of Auden's I like better than anything in Spender – above all the poem about Freud.

However, I do not compare them.

For consistent perfection – I find Spender most satisfying. The cleaner, more austere, more controlled artist. Or rather (I said I would not compare) – a clean, controlled, austere artist.

Without looking at the book, I have in mind – ten schoolchildren (marxian) the war poems – Port Bou and the one for Altolaguirre, tremendous ones about London – moving ones about children, and often all the early ones are still the most impressive.

I like Spender's vocabulary.

It is not the single line that stands out. The poems are units. Each one is a whole – you cannot break it into anything.

There is one great religious poem at least

"An 'I' can never be great – man . . ."

Perfect choice of words – humility, perhaps feigned, but attractive in this:

> Different living is not living in different places
> But creating in the mind a map
> And writing on that map a desert
> Pinnacled mountains or saving resort.

Actually the word "pinnacled" is perhaps ill chosen, but expertly, because "saving resort" is perfect. Hence the *peu très* [little more] of the other choices is justified beyond measure.

Seascape – to name another wonderful poem! No, it is not strained. You accept everything from him. I do.

———————— . . . their eyes
Contorted by the cruel waves denies
Glitter with coins through the tide scarcely scanned
While above them that surf assumes their sighs.

[Straight lines indicate cancellations of words.]

Rich, baroque, controlled like Bach. Having fun too and fun for the reader. He plays grandly. Humble and magnificent. And if there are pretenses, one readily forgives him. It is one of the books I would like by me always.

EXERCISE

Does the wasp in the wall confess his sting
——or the defiled water regret the sky?
————Do the birds in the rafters
————repeat the same small messages?
——No one knows what they mean.
Only inertia
closes the forest.

[Short indecipherable passage.]

And the plane descends
—Sounding four dark horses
—the train whistles
The horses cover their heads with their hands
—And run backwards into the hills.

July 19, 1956

Importance, in the priestly life, of serious human and profane activities which are important instruments – essential in a particular case – for the apostolate. That is, for the formation of Christ in souls, for the Kingdom of God.

In some cases – sociology, politics in apostolate to the workers (in Europe – unheard of, I suppose, here).

In my case – psychiatry, psychoanalysis, Zen.

What is the function of these profane instruments in my work?

Tremendous, I think, though I have not seen it fully yet, of a solid article in *La vie spirituelle* (in this month. The one by Fr. Suaret).

Not to judge success in priestly life by narcissistic standards–success is not what makes me admired. Success of a priest is fruit in the lives of others. Real fruit, not a river of compliments.

July 20, 1956

Julien Green's idea that between the lines of what you write, say, in a _Journal_, is prophecy for your future.[2]

Reading a moment ago in my notes – the small notebook[3] with the dreams and resolutions – with Fr. Philip and several other _morts_ ["dead ones"] (instead of monks) outside the monastery going to an _enterrement_ [burial] (instead of entertainment).

So maybe the plane to Minnesota will crash after all!

Yesterday I told Father John of the Cross that if the plane crashed, and it went down, I would pray for him to be a good Father Master.

In order to live for others instead of oneself, it is necessary not so much to do different things but to be a different person. Even when he eats and sleeps, an unselfish person is doing it for others. But even when a selfish man gives away his money and works all night for others, he does it for himself. What, in any case, a priest must do is work for others and the Kingdom of God.

July 22, 1956. Feast of St. Mary Magdalene – in plane

Beneath us is savage country – Indiana.

We have just come up out of smoke and dust and the sun shines on the wings and on pure white clouds and now we see less of the forests which surprises me. Yet there is a lot of woodland and I spot the most solitary houses – the one you get to by little winding dirt roads.

Otherwise it is very much like something at a World's Fair.

There were small dirty lakes – and a big dirty lake full of grass.

Now, now, over there is a big clean lake.

We bump around a lot.

The plane, like a dumb bird, butts into the wind.

Not so smart as the buzzard I watched from the firetower.

---

[2] Julien Green (1900–), born to American parents in Paris, is a noted French author. He and Merton entered into a correspondence in the 1960s.

[3] Merton also kept, in addition to his journal, a reading notebook and a small pad for random jottings.

———

Big limestone quarries everywhere.

Indianapolis – "please do not forget any of your personal articles."
    The place is cleaner than Louisville.

I like to meditate on the little red and white house plumb in the middle of the airport. Ordinarily I would be able to say that it reminded me of something or someone – a forlorn vocation – to be left over from a bygone age (as it evidently is) with all the trees gone from around you, dedicated to some new efficient purpose which it never would have preseen, painted with broad red and white stripes so that it would not be bashed in by a plane – it is a house that has the same sort of vocation as a Pacific Island that is called on to be wiped out with an experimental bomb. This I feel is not my vocation.

(Indianapolis airport)
    The Gospel of Mary Magdalen
    I think the key to it is that the debtor, in a certain sense, is Jesus himself. He says – "Which debtor loves more?" "Him to whom much was given (forgiven)." But then right away: he lists all the things Simon has not given and Mary has given. Hence Jesus is the debtor and he loves more the one who has given him more.
    Yet – Mary has given him more because He has given (forgiven) her more.
    The mystery of this Gospel lies in the fact that both Jesus and Magdalen are debtors, indebted to each other.
    In the office of Sext. The antiphon *Maria unxit pedes Jesu.* [Mary anointed the feet of Jesus.] Then immediately the capitulum: *Manum meam aperuit inopi* . . . [He opened my hand to the needy.]

We go away from Indianapolis without seeing anything but cornfields and, oh yes, a junkyard, and a very straight railroad track.

(As we got out of Louisville I saw the Carmel there and blessed it – I thought of Mother Seraphim.)

———

The carpet below is definitely tacky. All the roads run at right angles to one another.

Again – we fly to the topmost level of the earth's dirty air. Clean air is above and beyond. We wander between them thoughtlessly. *si dormiatis medios cleros . . .* sleeping between two destinies.

Ha! archaeology – a very straight line through the fields – a former road or railway – lost under the grass – visible from here.

Meanwhile I make the Trappist sign for "food" to the hostess when she confessed she had no cold drinks but only coffee.

In this farm a murder was committed. In that lovers live happily. In this other it is an old German farmer who beats his children – in yet another, a fourteen year old boy who will one day be a bishop; soon he will come out with a hoe and hoe corn and never know that we superlative beings were in on his secret. Indeed, we invented it.

And this is the chief peril of travel by plane.

Now there is a little town half spoiled by the shadow of a cloud – an interesting parallelogram to which we will never go. We don't have to.

I could invent a name for it, of course, and pass on in the sky.

A last – a creek – a corkscrew.

Two rivers – one dirty and one clean. Both have islands.

We do not realize that the fields and the trees have fought and still fight for their respective places on this map – which, by natural right, belong entirely to the trees. We do not remember that these little clumps and groves are the fifth column of the aboriginal forest that wants to return. It is nice to think of, for a moment. But what could be more desperate than a journey, mile after mile, without hills, as rough as all those trees, and never know where you are going. But now it is wide open.

I do not commit myself, though. I am perhaps still on the side of the trees.

About 1:00. Chicago.

It is o.k. with me if the primeval forest comes back and takes over Chicago. The only appealing thing here, at the moment, is the wind (which made for a bumping coming in) – the rest is noise and machines and crowds and confusions.

Here we are in a big four motor busyness banging our heads against a black cloud, getting ready to climb high. Same landscape only forever.

Now she lifts and swings up. They made an announcement we would be at 7,000 feet and I believed it. Also I thought it was important – but we'll probably be no higher than the Eastern plane that brought us to Chicago. Beautiful looking back on the big cornfields.

What a wonderful thing, to ride in the sky and keep quiet and love God. It is indeed true that He asks this – not only the riding in the sky, but love, whatever it may mean for each of us.

We are a lot higher tunneling through the high cumulus clouds – last time we were below these – only seeing whispers of streams below as we came today into Chicago. The Wisconsin farms look neat and small and prosperous (with wide, wide fields).

Finally, and I suppose this was what we have been aiming to do – we are coming out on top of the clouds.

Prayer in a plane. You have to pray somewhat artificially because if you cease to connive with the "world" that flies you in its plane – where will you go? or will you? The problem of humility in plane travel. At the moment, I force the question, but have no ideas, here in these serious clouds. It doesn't seem to worry the little sunburned ladies who are hostesses.

There ought to be house exercises now. Instead, there are drinks.

(I remember suddenly the buzzing where I sit in the woodshed – with the sheep barn sun through a jab in the cedars. I have no doubt created for myself a problem of praying on idle machinery.)

Well here we are above them and I take everything back: it is a wonderful new world without fields or houses. The highest of them raise up thin cotton and can't touch us. I guess this is what they mean by 7,000 feet.

———

o.k. dinner away. Exercise. White Pastures
  1.–7 or 8 lines about being above clouds –

      "Pure Land" – God's Name
      These new pure pastures are called by God's own name
      There are no chimneys in them
      Soft land without fires, or houses, or fields or ways.

      Who walks in it? Silence (but for us)
      Would walk in it.

      Who talks here? No one (but us)
      No one but God and everyone
      Who calls His Name
      Or looks for his soft promises to wake in
      (and us but ours is different
      Talk. I for one have lost my voice)

  2.–What then shall we do here
      In this Elysium of upper air?
      Shall we get out and play
      our violins
      Walking about on the sky?
      Shall we surprise
      one another
      Mysteries of new slated lives-
      No! These are
      too hazardous
      Therefore it is dared
      That we shall do something
      Earthy lest we become
      too spiritual.
      We must eat.
      Yes here. We drink a thousand feet
      We eat the flesh of four footed animals.
      Clean animals (for there may be a Jewish passenger aboard)
      Shrimp cocktail (shrimp – permitted fish)
      Ice cream to entice the little ones
      who have come so far with us

Unto this unremarked, unlooked at
Heaven, so wonderful outside the porthole.

Nothing, merely more necessary
than, by eating in such a communion
With the discarded almost below:
Put in your mouth here, all of you
The food of earth
So graced with all that is true
The dull, distorting contact.

(The first poem I have written in or above clouds – here we are mostly in a cloud – and now I know where the Lord is and am comforted. Be humble enough to thank him for briefest 7,000 feet.)

New landscape through the clouds – far below, zig-zag roads, curved fields, terraces, no? The land is hilly and yes! Many lakes no – the Mississippi – wonderful Elsinore pattern of islands.

The town is LaCrosse.
I have crossed the Mississippi in a cloud – I doubtless misspelled it.

Going up the river – big hills, wooded valleys, isolated hilltop farms, the best yet. It is wonderful country. Also, I have yawned and recovered my hearing.

July 23, 1956. St. John's Abbey
I said Prime down by the lake. Quiet water, lined with thick woods, birch and pine and oak and fir trees around the monastery – and a great loon diving in the water.

The new monastery wing I find quite satisfactory, especially the grille at the entrance and the roughbrick floors. My room is very pleasant; a small porch looking out on the garden and the lawn shaded by fir trees. I see, however, a machine, which has something to do with levelling a new lawn and last night when I walked alone in the pasture swatting mosquitoes I saw the tracks of my enemy, the caterpillar tractor.

Last night spoke with a Moravian pastor less about psychiatry than about Isaias and the psalms.

Since Dom Augustine's talk at Gethsemani there is a temptation to give the visiting psychiatrists a "Why I became a Trappist" routine – very intense. Especially ones like Dr. Hastings who listens very intensely.

[Gregory] Zilboorg was there, I only spoke a moment to him.

Went to see J. F. Powers at St. Cloud.

Drove up with Fr. Cuthbert and an amusing old monsignor from Minneapolis.

This morning – Bishop of St. Cloud opened sermon with an intelligent and clear headed statement. I am very impressed with the real value of this workshop – as opposed to the silly generalizations for and against psychiatry made by some. A sense that something intelligent and sensible is being done and as best it can be done by people who are doing what God wants done.

Zilboorg – The will cannot be sick.

Psychological disorders not localized anywhere.

The whole person is sick.

I ask "How define the disfunctions of a neurotic"

He replies "Science does not start with a definition but ends with it."

We begin with an important phenomenological problem anyway in neurosis. The will is not directly affected, but blocked in its action by other processes.

Disfunction in thinking, willing, feeling? This division according to Zilboorg is meaningless.

Now to say Tierce, Sext, and None.

July 25, 1956

Many important things are welling up in the psychiatry workshop. And besides purely academic knowledge, I am also learning things most important for myself, my life, my work, my vocation.

1. *Phantasy of Omnipotence* – being a magic director. I have known this before but learn it better now and know – or begin to know – the urgency of the problem. It is a point where, for me, asceticism can be real and not artificial and formalistic.

2. Penitents seduce you into taking on a *role of omnipotence and omniscience* and in this situation while you are deluding yourself you also approve the things they want you to approve. Thus you get nowhere.

3. Prudence – one must know his true role – select the time and the place for the job to be done – not give direction irresponsibly.

4. Don't presume to act for the penitent when he should act for himself.

5. Don't let the whole thing immediately get intellectualized – to do this is to destroy your chance of doing good.

6. I had completely obscured and failed to see the difference between a character problem and a real neurosis.

7. Today – H. Rome was very good on dependence.

Failure to accept the difficulties, obligations, and loneliness of being a real autonomous person.

Not accept secondary gains.

The person who's dependent – regresses – retreats from freedom, sells out for secondary gains (support of something outside of himself) – but feels guilt. Guilt accumulates – he then tries to assuage guilt by seeking approval of a director – but the approval is never enough – always, wants more. Seeks to have another determine choice for his weakest request which he is spared to choose with full responsibility.

8. The dependent person – is really unable to collaborate.

9. He may well totally determine another individual and devour him – wants to use him – does not love what he is but what he has.

July 27, 1956

EXERCISE

Be still

Listen to the stories of the
Wall. Be silent, They try
To Speak your
Name.

Listen to the Living
Wall. Who are you?
Who are

silence are you?

O Be still, while
You still live
And all things live around you
Speaking to your own
Being, by the
Unknown that is in you and them.
"I will try, like them,
To be my own silence
But this is difficult. you? Whose
The whole world is secretly on
fire / the stones burn,
even the stones, they burn me
How can I be still then
When all things burn,
When all this silence is on
fire?"

Be quiet as these
stones are quiet[4]
not thinking of what you are, still less
of what you might be but rather
Being what you are, that is always thinking of your name
Doing
cannot know

July 27, 1956

Yesterday, feast of St. Anne, rowed over to Stella Maris chapel which I like. Reading Suzuki[5] and Diadochos of Photike under the birch trees and looking at the water. And today again, after the end of this week's workshop, spent most of the afternoon in the same place.

At the end of the lake what looks like a beach is really a stretch of shallows filled with lily-pads. All around the lake are swampy places full of birches that have been broken halfway up by storms.

The piano duets which are heard in the novitiate could indeed be more musical.

July 29, 1956

Yesterday, spent most of the afternoon in the quiet woods behind Stella Maris reading, thinking, and realizing the inadequacy of both thinking and reading. I believe what I saw was an otter. At that end of the lake also there is a great blue heron. The lake is so beautiful it makes me feel guilty. What is there in me that makes me feel I should not have so many good things? Or, rather, not only not have them, but not even see them?

A great loneliness is necessary, a loneliness and a detachment that nothing can comfort and no one can satisfy. Probably one of the most painful elements is the fear and indeed the risk, of illusion.

In this loneliness and peril one must move forward with inexorable desire. A desire that will finally take one over the precipice, into the fulness of peace – the leap into pure faith, pure prayer.

All the maneuvers of my conscious and unconscious life take me both towards this and away from it at the same time. On the surface I have my

---

[4] From the word *quiet* to the end, Merton drew a canceling line but the words are still legible in the text.
[5] D. T. Suzuki (1870–1966) was a Zen master and writer with whom Merton had a long relationship both by mail and through personal contact.

confusion. On a deeper level, desire and conflict. In the greatest depths, like a spring of pure water rising up in the flames of hell, is the smallness, the frailty of a hope that is, yet, never overwhelmed but continues strangely and inexplicably to nourish in the midst of apparent despair.

Friday night we went over to have dinner with Powers in St. Cloud. He reminds me in some ways of Brother Giles – a mixture of dryness and spontaneity, a thin, sensitive person whose vocation is to go through many unbearable experiences. His children are beautiful. And when we came into the small ancient red wooden house there was a procession of little girls holding up in their two hands large schooners of beer for the guests of their Father.

Powers, though poor, lives better than the rich people and we had a very pleasant and decent dinner by candle light on a small porch and drank Sauterne with our shrimps and salad, and laughed very much except that I was annoyed when Fr. Eudes began to tell Powers he ought to be living a life of prayer. Powers said, "But I can't pray" and Fr. Eudes kept insisting "Oh yes you can, if you try."

And the whole thing seemed to me to be foolish because Powers is a man with the hand of God on him – but one who is in no position to realize the prophetic character of his vocation.

Powers doesn't like Graham Greene, does not understand Kierkegaard – or my perverse interpretation of him – hates St. Cloud – says "we never see anybody." Didn't laugh much at my description of _Waiting for Godot_ – in fact, seemed a little disturbed by it. I am left with the impression that here is a man in whose life – forlorn and desperate – there is no place for facetious metaphysical extravagances. I am impressed by his humanism and his contact with reality.

I haven't yet talked privately with Zilboorg except about the article on _Neurosis in the Monastic Life_[6] which, he tells me, is utterly inadequate, hastily written, will do harm, should not even be revised, should be left on the shelf while I read – not Rank or any other analyst but Freud. And especially (this astonished me) Freud's books against religion. This is very interesting – they are the last things I would have bothered with.

[6] Published posthumously in the _Merton Annual_ IV (1991).

——

Diadochos – "the abyss of faith boils if you examine it, but if you look upon it with simplicity, it becomes once again calm. For being a river of Lethe in which evils are forgotten, the depths of faith do not bear to be looked upon with indiscreet reasonings. Let us therefore call upon the waters with simplicity of thought in order to reach thus the harbor of the divine Will." (Conferences – chap. 22)

"No one can genuinely love or believe unless he has within himself his own answer." (id. [Conferences] 23)

"The very act of our holy knowledge teaches us that there is a single material sense (knowledge?) of the soul divided into two activities as a consequence of Adam's disobedience; but another sense is simple – that which comes from the Holy Spirit and which no man can know but he alone who detaches himself from the advantages of this life in the hope of goods and who witness, by continency, all the appetites of his bodily senses." ([Conferences] 25)

(noon)

This morning before mass I talked an hour and a half with Zilboorg about my own troubles and a lot of things came out.

1.–It turns out *he* was the one who engineered my coming here – through Abbot Baldwin – partly because of the danger of the article being published and partly because he had sensed my own difficulties.

2.–It turns out also – as I know – that I am in somewhat bad shape and that I am neurotic – and that the difficulties handling it right is very considerable. He has his own ideas about that – God alone knows if they are feasible.

3.–Great extent of my dependence on vows – I would hardly have imagined I used them in the way he said – but anyway, I can get some details on it. As substitutes for reality?

4.–"You are a gadfly to your superiors."

"Very stubborn – you keep coming back until you get what you want."

"You are afraid to be an ordinary monk in the community."

"You and Father Eudes can very easily become a pair of semi-psychotic quacks."

"Talking to Dr. Rome (about Zen) you thought only of yourself using him as a source of information and self-aggrandizement. You thought nothing at all of your priesthood, the apostolate, the church, his soul."

"You like to be famous, you want to be a big shot, you keep pushing your way out – to publicity – Megalomania and narcissism are your big trends."

Things which I know and did not know. And I suppose that is just the trouble. I am quite capable of saying, "I am a narcissist" and yet it changes nothing and it has not helped me to understand.

While he said all this I thought "How much he looks like Stalin" but in reality I am tremendously relieved and grateful – and when I sung mass with the monks I was praying hard to know what to do about it.

Other things he said:

"Your hermit trend is pathological." "You are a promotor. If you were not in a monastery you are the type that would clean up on Wall Street one day and lose it all on the horses the next." (I thought – there must be a lot of Pop in me yet – Was it Pop that said "Don't think! Act on hunches"?)

When I asked what I had said wrong to Dr. Rome he said "You didn't say it. You conveyed it."

Then again he said: "These are not things you can foresee. They are traps you fall into as you go along and you don't realize it until you are hurt."

I was thinking again – that where I am most "verbological" is in religion. But that seems to be because what is real for me in religion is what I never even try, any longer, to express. However, that is wrong. And, in fact, I do mean and do hold and do believe what the whole church holds, means, and believes and it is real to me. Well – is it? Saying the Office by the lake, at any rate, I paid attention to the *things said* by the words. Can I say those things without meaning them? But it is true, I can say them automatically and often do.

Another thing he said – "It is not intelligence you lack, but affectivity" – meaning it is there but I have never let it get out – so that when the situation calls for it I either intellectualize – verbalize – or else go into a depression.

Again – "It will do you no good to be forbidden to write – you need some silence and isolation, but it needs to be prohibited in your heart – if it is merely forbidden, it will not seem prohibited to you – Yet your writing is now becoming verbological – but your words must be incarnate."

He said he had already told this to Bob Giroux.

August 2, 1956

The loons on the lake. To begin with they are two. They allow no others. They need plenty of room for themselves. They are seldom together. Once I saw them fly. They seemed to be chasing other loons away from the lake. They were filling the grey windy sky with their weird call.

The other day I tried to sneak up on one in a rowboat. He dived and stayed down I do not know long because I did not see him when he came up in a totally different part of the lake. There he sat calmly while I rowed away. Yesterday afternoon, walking under the pines of the point, I would see his white breast as he sat on the waters of the wave and sometimes laughed.

The loon, I think, is a very serious bird and I take him very seriously. To me it is not crazy but even, in a way, beautiful. It means: distances, wind, water, forests, the loneliness of the North.

August 3, 1956

In Minnesota, when there is thunder it is continuous. There was thunder last night and now it has been thundering again – softly, stubbornly, and without interruption, for fifteen minutes overhead, before the fall of the first drops or the first great blowing of wind in the pines and firs and maple trees.

It is evening and the lake is dark now. The monks are in choir chanting Matins. Everyone has gone, all those who were here all week, except four of us Trappists. Fr. Raphael Simon is staying until Wednesday but we leave early in the morning.

O Lord my God, where have I been sleeping? What have I been doing? How slowly? Awaken, once again, to the barrenness of my life and its confusion. You will forgive me if it is often that way – I do not mean it to be. How little faith there has been in me – how inert have been my hours of solitude, how my time has been wasted. You will forgive me, again, if next week it is all wasted and I am once again in confusion. But, at least, this afternoon, sitting on a boulder among the birches, I thought, with compunction, of Your love and Your Kingdom and again tonight by the boathouse I thought of the hope you have planted in our hearts and of the Kingdom of Heaven which I have done so little to gain for myself and for others. Forgive me, O Lord, by your Cross and Passion and Resurrection. Teach me to see what it means that I am saved by your Church, and as a priest to bring others to the knowledge of You and the Kingdom and to salvation. Teach me to live in You, with care for the purity of faith, with the zeal of true hope and with true and objective charity for my brothers, for the glory of the Father, Amen.

FROM [VLADIMIR SERGEYEVICH] SOLOVIEV

"The moral limit to the egoism of a given person is not the egoism of others, not their self-meriting will but only that which in itself cannot be exclusive and egotistic. That which in its nature is truth – love and self-sacrifice in their relation to men are possible only when they manifest the unconditional principle which stands above men; the principle in relation to which all equally represent an untruth, and all equally must recant that untruth." Lecture 1 on Godmanhood.

August 4, 1956. Plane

High above a low ceiling – very clear sky – very pure above us and ahead of us and below the strange woolly topography of rain clouds with occasional holes through which you see the farms in meadows.

The wonderful blue is right; for today is First Saturday.

Rev. Father has a seat up in front. I am here with Father Eudes and we ran into Fr. Giles, O.S.B., going back to N.Y. Fr. Eudes has been reading the copy of *The Presence of Grace* which J. F. Powers gave me with a humble inscription. For my part – there is no need to look at the clouds and the earth for it is evident. But also I think more and write that if you can be quiet in a plane it is a wonderful place in which to meditate.

Fascinating images of the Mississippi – the lagoons, islands, oxbows, channels, different shades of green, blue, yellow, brown – the dams and locks, the small geometrical towns in the middle of the luxuriant arabesques of the river and its channels – and there the inscape of the furrowed fields and crops. The designs never cease in this variety – one wonderful farm looked like a Picasso harlequin.

Men do not realize what they are doing, in the infinite, inexhaustible play of God's art – the playing of the Wisdom of Christ Child – "playing before Him at all times; playing in the world" [Proverbs 8:30–31].

———

Over Indiana – wonderful cumulus clouds – piling higher and higher as we go South over the steaming hot plains.

In the distance, coral reefs or coral mountains – or alps of rounded snow or palaces full of the light of sunset. Closer, we pass a great affable polar bear who stands outside our window stuffing his mouth with snow.

Perspectives through the cloud corridors – and always below, the earth, distant, unreal, sliding under the holes.

We are getting home now – over Southern Indiana – the wooded land.

August 7, 1956

On my arrival at Gethsemani two of the recent postulants were ready to leave. One, from the Carmelites of San Antonio, has already gone. The other (who was a novice here before) claims that if he does not get out of this monastery he will blow up completely.

Soloviev – The strength of a falsehood insists on the importance of a corresponding truth.

"The importance of a truth lies of course not in the truth itself but within us in our inconsistency by not carrying out a truth to the end, we limit it – and any limitation of a truth provides an expanse for falsehood."

"It is madness not to believe in God; it is the greater madness to believe in Him only in part."

He says, in effect, that consistency in truth means striving with pure and perfect hope to realize our "positive unconditionality" that is that we can possess in God the "whole content, the fulness of being, not as a mere fantasy – but as a real actuality." Also it is on this "inconsistency" that he bases his accusation of inadequacy of Catholicism – "it does not carry its faith to its logical end." He adds that modern materialism, struggling to overcome the Catholic tradition (and in this struggle according to him it will be successful) is a transition period between the inadequate spirituality of the past and the new, more perfect, spirituality of the future – "Godmanhood."

In this a tremendous challenge really *to live my monastic life.*

Compromises and approximations – how tedious and frustrating they finally become.

Equally tedious are those false "absolutes" and the unreal consistencies that do not furnish an antithesis.

God have mercy on me in the blindness in which I hope I am seeking you!

August 14, 1956. Vigil of the Assumption

For the first time in months – a quiet morning at St. Anne's. The weeds are very high outside. The young trees are all growing – but if the maples I planted two, three years ago had only lived, the cabin would be completely shaded by now.

The tractors in the bottoms would have exasperated me two years ago. I hardly notice them now.

The new schedule, voted by the Gen. Chapter in 1955, was finally approved – it has been approved for several weeks but here it was being "studied" and did not finally go into effect until last Monday – that is, yesterday.

A fine long time for reading after the night office this morning. In fact, it is most important to give the monks time to sit quiet and read. This is more important than extra sleep. I wonder how long it will be before all the reading time is again devoured by extra work, chanting of long offices, etc.

The Treatise on Prayer is the first thing of Origen's that I have really liked except perhaps the Homilies on Exodus and Numbers. It is simple and great. He really is a tremendous mind, although he often looks ordinary or even stuffy. But no, *The Treatise on Prayer* is great. One of the best things ever written on prayer – by its wholeness, objectivity. It is catholic and clear and close to the Gospel – Christ talks and speaks in it.

Julien Green's *Journal* has finally come to absorb me altogether in the sleepy time after dinner when I have to read something light to keep awake. The first two volumes were innocent and could be read like a magazine in a dentist's office with a certain detachment or, better perhaps, superficially. They do not invite the reader to commit himself. One is simply interested by the reappearance of Gide and by his bright sayings and by Green's struggle to write another novel. (I have never had any desire to read any of his novels.)

After the war years have begun it is another matter. Green, in America, had an imperious need for France, for Paris. Here there is no neutrality. I find I am in the same position – to some extent. Green challenges me to remember whether or not I am, as he is, French. Well, I am.

By the time I got to the 4th. volume (on returning from Collegeville) I could see that nothing matters except to reach the page on which he would mention the liberation of Paris. Everything else was also absorbing but of only transient importance. One waits for "The Day." It comes and goes.

There is not much said but one knows it reached the end of an epoch for at least one man.

To be completely dependent on a country, on a city . . . for a moment I was annoyed at Green and started finding fault with him as a bourgeois. But that is not enough. He may be a man of his (my) clan, but there is more to it than that. France is what it is and it is important to see this. Not to be able to see it is to have lived only a half-human life. Green's 4th. volume is very fine. It is a record of a civilized mind – perhaps one of the last. I am already, with my generation, far less civilized than he, far less able to see.

Also, no one should underestimate the powerful, though unassuming, intuitions about religious things, in which connection I appreciate above all his exactness and *refusal to pretend.*

On top of this, [Georges] Bernanos' *Last Essays* of which at least the last is fine (I have not touched any of the others) – again, the importance, the necessity of France. The fool might laugh at his intensity, but he is terribly right.

August 15, 1956. Assumption

Saddened in this morning's chapter – Fr. Francis, who has been very much overworked and who has been groomed for an exceedingly difficult job next year (retreat master) was so obviously in bad shape (he preached the sermon).

Most of the time he seemed to be terrified, yet consciously he was trying to appear informal and debonair. Result, a sermon he had not had time to prepare, was given in rushed, jumbled sentences, full of hesitations and repetitions, full of anxiety, and I would even say anguish – most of which was probably not quite conscious.

The worst of it was that I felt he was trying to imitate me in my "informality." I have done him harm, no doubt. But I know I have also helped him.

I certainly love the man and understand him and I think I am probably the only person in the community that is aware of his loneliness and helplessness. He is so good and so nice – such a quiet and charming and well meaning person and one with potential talents which have never become actual and he knows it – I can't do anything about it.

Perhaps I see in him the child in myself – no doubt I do. But I wish desperately I could help him – a poor kid, mutely stretching out his hand for help across the abyss which neither he nor anyone else can understand and which isolates him so terribly.

And so here is one who everyone in the community admires (except those who resent his enormous piety) whom most of the monks would canonize (and indeed I would too, for he is a kind of a saint) – and yet he is split in half by a conflict so terrible and so hidden that no one can even guess at it and he himself only realizes it very vaguely. That is – he sees the symptoms.

But what is going to happen to him, after they push him too far?

It doesn't seem to do much good to talk to Rev. Father. Fr. Francis is so admirable that no one will believe me (except Fr. Eudes and he, after all, is in a key position!).

And then, the three brothers making simple vows, paralyzed with terror when reading their schedules of profession – (one Bro. Nicholas who cracked up as a student and who is doing very much better as a brother).

All this is so important for my vocation. After all, why have I been brought into the middle of all this? And what is my responsibility towards the community, having brought so many others into it?

In other words, if I am the one who sees all this, it is because I am supposed to do something about it. The desire is to help and heal . . . To *want* everyone to be whole and find out how to help them!!

August 17, 1956

It is possible that a person with weak faith might lose his faith altogether in a Trappist monastery. In fact, I have seen it happen that a man supported by strict observances and the proper jargon has been insensibly emptied of all spiritual strength and ended up a husk, incapable of life as a religious or even as a good Christian.

Hence the monastery is not for the undecided, for those who doubt.

The toughness and integrity of Emmanuel Mounier[7] demands careful attention. Maybe of all of the men of our time he is the one we need most to understand and imitate. He is clever and hard with words. You cannot be comfortable with his language unless you think along with it, which is not all that easy. Hence he will make almost everyone uncomfortable – assuming they even listen to him at all.

---

7 Emmanuel Mounier (1905–1950) was a French philosopher, resistance fighter, and founder of the journal *Esprit*. Merton was reading his *Personalism* (London: Routledge & Paul, 1952).

August 18, 1956

The great harm done by complicated people in monasteries, and the great good done by the simple!

The nine ungrateful lepers may very well have thanked God in their hearts. Jesus who reproved the lack of faith of those who demanded his physical presence to work a miracle, commended the faith of the Samaritan who wanted to be physically present in order to thank him. There is need then, for simple external acts to bear witness to our faith in God. Interior acts are not enough – or at least not always.

August 19, 1956

There is great difference between spiritual reading and "pious reading" – in fact there are few things less spiritual than mere conventional piety. But the distinction is not one of mere subject matter. Spiritual reading is that to which and in which you are moved by the lifegiving Spirit, the Spirit of God who breathes where He wills, in order to love and pray in us more fully.

Reading that is nothing more than self complacent ruminations of orthodox ideas that have no more power to move or change us, can hardly be called spiritual – Notice that the ideas in themselves powerful and seminal may be, at any time, fruitless for certain individuals.

Spiritual reading puts us in contact not just with words, with ideas, but with reality – with God.

To seek God is to seek reality. And this must be something more than a flight from images to ideas. The interior life is not merely what is *not* exterior.

Thunder and rain during mixt. Curtains of mist hanging over the Knobs, pigs garrulous in the lush wet grass and a dove in the cedar tree – Enough for a *Haiku?*

Christ within us, says Origen, sits at the right hand of the power for which we pray.

Temptation – to put together a book the way one furnishes an apartment – to surround oneself with things and act as if one had made it all. The Braque on the wall, the T'ang vase, the persian carpet – A Cistercian should, no doubt, not even know such things. But a Cistercian on the point of going to New York cannot help but think of them. Caught between good and evil and sometimes not knowing which is which.

Julien Green was always asking himself, can a novelist be a saint, can a novelist save his soul? But perhaps the salvation of his soul, and even more, his sanctification depends precisely on taking this role. "He that would save his life will lose it."

EXERCISE

It might, perhaps, be pertinent
To write about the six horse wagon,
The huge public wagon,
(Save me!) The monks: their wagon with
Solemn flags sailing to the fair
Like Cleopatra's barge. This Trappist
Galleon of hams and cheeses comes, with serious music,
To the City and the Fair!
Six great nodding heads,
Six shining rumps, so brave
So brave the Belgian mares, so brave,
the flags, the harness, and the plumes.

But are there any plumes?
Though the outlandish harness shines
in the Kentucky sun, No plumes,
(Really!) No plumes.
One was tempted to see them, though,
Tempted to see the slow paced horses nod
In merry black with black cars creeping behind them
Full of serious ideas
Piled with flowers, going
Going to the Fair.

A woodpecker with a cry as sharp as a dagger terrifies the lesser birds while he is himself benevolent and harmless; and the beautiful kingfisher rattles like a bird of ill-omen.

Mounier says (in showing that the idea of person must be defined by the power to communicate – and showing how individualism bars communication –)

A kind of instinct works within us to deny or diminish the humanity of those around us . . . the lightest touch of the individual seems sometime to infect a mortal poison into any contact between man and man. *Personalism* p. 18.

I have had experience of that. I learned lately that one of the novices whom we thought neurotic and who was indeed disturbed, was disturbed largely by the bars and illusions that had arisen in his relations with me – he became very upset fancying that I demanded that he be a brilliant and complicated person (which is what he fancies me to be) and I enhanced that illusion by not giving him time to talk about himself but always delivering the diagnosis before he had even a chance to tell me all the symptoms. This, while beating him down and rendering him very insecure, also stimulated a desperate search for more "symptoms" so that I would deliver more and more godlike diagnoses. Finally, in a culmination of stupidity I even gave him the Rorshach Test (I had been encouraged in this by Dr. Kisker) and interpreted it all wrong. I will say this – I could see at once that my interpretation was useless. I hope I have learned a lot from all this. It was a great relief and liberation to admit my stupidity. I am sobered by the thought (again) of my great capacity to do harm as Fr. Master. And I see how much, really, depends on the grace of God to make up for our mistakes and draw good out of evil! What motives for peace and confidence and praise!

"The person only grows in so far as he continually purifies himself from the individual within him. He cannot do that by force of self-attention but on the contrary by making himself available." (Mounier – *[Personalism]*)

August 20, 1956

After None – the anointing of Brother Albert. We knelt for the first time on the terrazo floor of the new infirmary wing – Brother was very white and old, answered vigorously and inarticulately when Rev. Father asked if he knew what was going on. He still has energy enough to sit up in the middle of the night to wake the infirmarian with some imaginary problem, as his mind is free and he acts out his role of interior cellarer. "Shall we give them milk and cheese again tonight, Brother? Hurry, hurry, it is almost time for supper!"

A seven foot tall All American basketball player was asking about entering the monastery. Should he become a monk or should he get married? I did not encourage him to rush in.

___

Those of whom God denies the most perfect hope must look closely at their sins and this they do, not by hunting these out for themselves, but by having God suddenly shine his lamp on the dark corners of their souls.

I believe with Diadochos, that if at the hour of death my confidence in God's mercy is perfect, I will pass the frontier without trouble and pass the dreadful array of my sins with compunction and confidence and leave them all behind forever.

Lord, again, I do not doubt my call to holiness, even though I am not faithful. I do not doubt that you will fulfill your will in me in spite of my cowardice and lack of effort, in spite of all my unconscious and even conscious prevarications. You are God and You have destroyed my sins on the Cross before they were committed. Keep me from sinning again, keep me even from material sin, make me avoid even imperfections, although so often I cannot even guess at them.

Are we so sure we always know what God wants of us so precisely that we can easily tell the differences between what is and is not an imperfection?

Our glory and our hope – We are the Body of Christ. Christ loves us and espouses us as His own flesh. Isn't that enough for us? But we do not really believe it. No! Be content, be content. We are the Body of Christ. We have found Him, He has found us. We are in Him, He is in us. There is nothing further to look for, except for the deepening of this life we already possess. Be content.

From moment to moment, I remember with surprise, that I am satisfied, even though everything is not yet fulfilled. I lack nothing. *Omnino replet me.* [He fills me totally.]

Sapientia [wisdom] – *sapor boni* [the savor of the good] (3rd. nocturn – St. Bernard). To know and taste the secret good that *is present* but is not known to those who, because they are restless and because they are discontent and because they complain, cannot apprehend it. The present good – reality – God. *Gustate et videte.* [Taste and see.]

It is easy to say of every new idea one meets – "It is all in St. Bernard." It is very doubtful, for instance, whether Freud is "all in St. Bernard." However, Mounier's "Personalism" is essentially present in St. Bernard.

Hence to read Mounier with understanding is most profitable *spiritual* reading not only because it helps to understand St. Bernard but helps us to use him. We are paralyzed in our individualism and we turn everything to the advantage of sterile self-isolation (self centered) and we do this in the name of our contemplative calling.

I am more and more persuaded that our way of trying to be contemplatives by our individualism is utterly ruinous. But also, at the same time, what passes for community life and spirit can also be just as ruinous because the well-meaning neurotics who are its champions are themselves so completely individualistic.

What a disaster to build the contemplative life on the negation of communication. That is what, in fact, our silence often is – because we are obscuring it without really wanting it (yet needing it nonetheless) and without understanding what it is all about. That is why there is so much noise in a Trappist monastery. The infernal clatter and hullabaloo, the continual roar of machinery, the crash of objects falling from the hands of distraught contemplatives – all this protests that we hate silence with all our power because, with our wrong motives for seeking it, it is ruining our lives. Yet the fact remains that silence is our life – but a *silence which is communication and better communication than words!* If only someone could tell us how to find it.

The worse pity of all is that we think we know.

What we have found is our own noise.

No, that is not true. The Paradox is that in spite of all, we have found God and that is probably the trouble. Such a discovery is altogether too much and we beat a hasty retreat into any kind of protection.

August 22, 1956

A hope that is defeated is not good enough. Our hope is victorious.

Whether Emmanuel Mounier is a prophet or a siren . . .

At any rate I refuse to take him passively. But what he says about Personalism is for me a grace.

Have I ever examined my prejudice against machines? God help me if it is only a prejudice. I am discovering at any rate, that it is not strong enough to constitute real freedom. Hence it is perhaps only a prejudice. Another illusion.

I cannot afford such an illusion as that. All are costly and this costs more than the others.

——

The pitiful faith of this abbey in technics. It makes your blood run cold. What portent is behind it?

August 23, 1956. Vigil of St. Bartholomew

EXERCISE

THE EXPLOITS OF THE MACHINE AGE

They were dismayed by their own
Thin faces another morning. They
Hoped they would not die, again Today
They hoped for some light
Breakfast, and a steady hand.

To the protected house
They fled, to the unsafe machinery
They lived by. "It will go better this time.
We have arranged, at last,
To succeed. Better luck
This time."

So they went to their
work, muttering "better luck,"
('Til the chorus in the moon cried
"Then he struck!")
But no! Nothing was felt or heard! Once again the explosion
    was Purely mental. It shook them a little, though

The machines were still safe. But nothing,
Nothing at all had happened
Literally, nothing.

They came home again, exhausted by their nothing
Gathered in the street, faced the steadfast apartment
The globes, the windows, and even the moon.
Thus they made up their mind.

And so climbed homeward, grim
As yesterday and always muttering
"Better luck tomorrow!"

August 24, 1956

Last night, noise of people running up and down the stairs. Brother Albert was dead – 1:30. A forbidding new statue of Our Lady at the entrance to the cemetery makes the whole place suddenly look as if it were full of fantastic head stones instead of plain, ugly, uniform crosses.

The bright light, the dazzling skies of the last two cool days. Brilliant, yesterday afternoon working in the newly cleared fields at Linton's gathering up the refuse of trees destroyed by the machines that cleared the place of woods. Clear more land! Clear more land! We are acting out our own spiritual confusion! We will be saints by removing all forests. Then of course we will give the whole place to pigs.

Fr. Pedro, getting around to want to leave, wrote to his people in Hawaii to say that he might want to leave but . . . What can one do about the sea-change that goes on inexorably below the surface of a soul without consulting anybody? Only the surface of his soul consults me, since he doesn't even consult himself.

August 26, 1956

"Thou shalt remember all the ways through which the Lord thy God hath brought thee for forty years through the desert, to afflict thee and to prove thee, and that the things that were in thy heart might be made known whether thou would keep his commandments or no." Deut. 8:2.

(same day but *much* later)

Do you remember the old days with Tranche-chef at the Odeon?

I received a letter from him,[8] in the usual style, which reads, in part, as follows,

"I am again wondering how to think of myself as an artist. Strange, that an actor like myself, should be dominated by a fantasy of myself as a very modest person. Sincerely, it rarely, if ever occurs to me that I might be vain or proud. Am I really a proud man? And yet it seems I have actually *believed myself to be* all the characters I have portrayed. It is as if in exhibiting myself to the world in an endless variety of roles, I were saying (in my modesty) 'You see I am all those but much more too for the real "I" transcends them

---

[8] I have found no such letter; the name Tranche-chef may be imaginary. The Odéon is a famous theater in the Montparnasse section of Paris. The reference and the letter may well be one of Merton's "exercises."

all and gives them all life.' Now tell me, is this really pride. Or is it not after all a modesty of unimpeachable innocence?"

What are we to think of Tranche-chef? Can I call him a fraud? I have
sometimes been tempted to do so.

Program for a festive gathering. First, draw a noble personage –

Then, visit the livestock and the sick members of the household and
ride in the wagons. Make paper airplanes and finally, after the rosary
in common, a contemplative hug "What are you concerting in your private
home?"

I was very hoarse, I could hardly get that last word out.

August 28, 1956. Feast of St. Augustine

1. Is it true and salutary to say, as some spiritual writers say, that God is
our end but that in order to attain to our end, we must *first attain to perfection*, so that in practice, our aim is perfection?

2. And is it true, then, that perfection is attained only by a simple
minded concern for "spiritual things" seen as deeply marked off and separate from "temporal things"?

3. And then, are we to look at these "spiritual things" as in reality a set
of practices which are (allowing, of course, for grace) sure means of attaining to possession of God?

4. This being so, should we then apply ourselves very industriously to
the use of these means in order to attain to perfection very quickly and
thus gain possession of God?

All these statements may be perfectly true though 3 and 4 lend themselves to dangerous misunderstanding and the other two are already open
to much misapprehension. But after all – supposing each of these statements were faultless – the spiritual life would still be something quite different from that!

For we are perfect when we find God, or rather when God gains possession of us. And in a sense, from the moment we seek Him He has already
found us. And from the moment He has found us, all that is blessed by His
will becomes "spiritual" even though it may be a material thing like eating.

Is oversimplification a temptation which I must resist with the clear sighted
choice of a better course? If it is, I must see what I mean by a better course.

In the end, what does the Gospel say? To follow Christ. This is the spiritual life and the way of perfection.

"God is charity and he that abideth in charity abideth in God and God in him. In this is the charity of God perfected in us" [1 John 4:12].

Rev. Father complained to Fr. Prior about Fr. John of the Cross reading the *Brothers Karamazov.* "I don't see where he gets time to read 800 pages of a novel!"

There is the question in a nutshell. The *Brothers Karamazov* is a novel. Therefore a "temporal thing!" Therefore the time spent reading it is ipso facto without merit – a worldly and unreligious act. Whereas to read Tanquerey's *Spiritual Life* . . . that is another matter.

What if it turned out that the *Brothers Karamazov* were really a religious book? And what if reading it should open up new depths in our soul and make us see everything in a new light – and perhaps realize everything is not quite so simple as devoting oneself to religious practices . . . but that true life is in really loving God?

Dom Angelico wrote that he didn't like *Seeds of Contemplation* and did like *No Man Is An Island* and also said that Erik Satie was very much according to the mind of St. Benedict – and immediately added . . .

[Entry left unfinished.]

It would be so easy and consoling to say, at every moment: this thing I am doing is regarded by everyone as a sure means of attaining to perfection and to the possession of God. But would the peace and consolation I felt have anything necessarily to do with perfection or the possession of God? Might it not after all turn out to be the greatest of all illusions? A surrender to the authority of common opinion – "They say." How weak our consciences are! We give in and shut our eyes. We have conformed to "them." We are at peace. "They say" this is perfection.

Much more to the point: The prayer that struggles to get out of myself and reach God, in obscurity, in trial, fighting down the phantoms.

August 29, 1956

The great thing and the only thing, is to adore and praise God.

To seek Him is to adore Him and to say that He alone is God and there is no other.

We must lay down our life for His Truth. We must bear witness to what *is* and is the fidelity of God to His promises.

We must believe with our whole heart what God Our Father has offered and promised us.

We must leave all things to answer His call to us, and to reply to His grace.

When we have done this, we can talk of perfection but when we have done this we no longer need to talk of perfection.

August 30, 1956

What makes a feast day is not so much the exterior aids to devotion as the interior devotion itself. Indeed when there are too many aids there may end by being no devotion at all – everything is expended on keeping the aids to devotion going.

Today is not even a feast day of the lowest rank. It is a feria, with commemoration of mass of Sts. Felix and Adauctus. Yet devotion to these martyrs makes it, in passing, a great feast day. Not only is the mass very beautiful (Alleluia VIIth tone from one of the votive masses of June) but the martyrdom of St. Adauctus is glorious – and simple. He simply stepped out of the crowd and declared himself a Christian when St. Felix was being led to crucifixion. The soldiers took him along and killed him too. No one ever knew his real name. The faithful called him "Adauctus" because he was "added on" to the glory of St. Felix. A mystery of liberality and generosity and joy – of things we have forgotten – and yet we have not forgotten them either – witness the letters of those condemned to die under Hitler. There is in the act of St. Adauctus a great magnificence – in the sense of Aristotle and St. Thomas – a splendor of totality of giving which shines out all the more perfectly in the true simplicity of a story that tells nothing but the one essential fact, or two very important circumstances. He died for Christ. He gave himself up spontaneously while another was going to martyrdom – and no one even found out his name.

O great and unknown and nameless saint, whose name lives forever and forever in the secrecy of God, pray for me a sinner and far from the light of God, who nevertheless seeks God, groping in darkness. Bring me, by your prayers, light in darkness, and may the Lord Christ, the Risen Saviour, be glorified in my body also as He was in you. Amen.

August 31, 1956

A very small locust seedling, a few feet high, grows up triumphalistically out of the honeysuckle in the place where the wall is broken down. Beyond that, through a gap in the cedars, the old sheep barn with its plum colored roof, swelters in the noonday sun. A broken down mowing machine is stranded among the stones of the road and beyond, the wind moves the massive, light and dark foliage of the oak trees.

A tractor here, under the woodshed, picks up a piece of machinery with which to worry the soil and the latest postulant walks by, looking critically at the tractor.

I return to the small locust, whose slow dance in the wind is like that of a Japanese dancer – she turns up her delicate branches in the wind and the undersides of the leaves smile at the sun.

September 1, 1956

"A vigorous defender of the family, of freedom, or of socialism may be further from the spirit of those values than another person who may be opposing them, but, in fact, is only incensed against the hardened and decadent forms they have assumed." Emmanuel Mounier.

The sky is overclouded and look, there behind the hedge is a black cow with a white tail.

"Let us walk along here," said Tranche-Chef "And compose a number of sentences each one of which begins with the words 'You think you are a monk but . . .'"

The Cistercians of the 12th. century were forbidden to write not only rhyming verse, as Helen Waddell records, but any verse. And then, she has Serlo of Wilton always in a cowl, not only after his conversion, but before.[9]

Tranche-Chef interrupts: "But what are you *doing*?"

EXERCISE

Is there any law to forbid
Inventing a person? Or is every
creature of the mind another self?
Is not one self enough? Is it
Pride to make more of them?
To populate a whole world with

---

[9] Serlo of Wilton (1110?–1181) was a writer of erotic verse who later entered the monastic life, eventually becoming abbot of the monastery of L'Aumone near Chartres, France.

Oneself – I mean, of course, in a
novel. In a word, I ask –
Show me the law –
Show me why I
should feel, as I do feel,
Guilty when I invent a person?

ANOTHER EXERCISE:

When he went, he lost his balance
What he did he failed to repeat
Always
He took himself in hand
And kept his head before it was too late.
When he walked, they put him in prison. When he sang
(and all because his nurse hit him in the cradle) They paid
       him to shut up
He was no longer
steady on his feet
Later when he smiled
he showed a broken tooth.
And when he sat down
He lost face.

He called his dog to heel
And off they went
Along the canal.
Alone at last with his dumb friend
They ran and they walked and
They barked as they spoke.
It was a long night before he woke up[10]
In the field of hay
And many days before he made his way home
But his heart was in the right place
Clucking like a chicken.
Years had gone away

---

[10] The lines that follow below were written in a column parallel to the ones above but it is obvious from the page that Merton was only trying to "save paper" with this arrangement since these lines follow the sequence of thoughts and images of what is on the left-hand side of the page.

With his Mother, brother, and sister
No one called him to mind, only
Business men remembered
his name and his debts.
They came in by every door
They trembled as they sat
And he lost his voice
"You have," they said, "a serious problem"
And they took away his house.
He was found beside himself
When he came to his senses.
No one cared to have him around.

September 2, 1956

St. Antonin today.

Through the merits of thy martyr, O Lord, through the martyr in whose town I know thee,[11] whose sanctuary I did not enter, though, as a child, I danced as a child – through the great merit of thy ancient martyr, O Lord, bring me to the fulness of truth, to a great love and union with the truth, to a great fortitude with which to embrace and suffer reality which is, in fact, my joy.

Thy martyr, O Christ, has a deep green river, and a limestone bridge of unequal arches, reflected in the water.

Thy martyr, O Christ, has cliffs and woods and, as I understand, he no longer has a train.

Sometimes, O Lord, I pray best to the saints and best of all to this one, O my Lord, this martyr who had a clarinet, a gramophone (I was reproved for putting my head in the horn). The people of the town, O Lord! They have not changed. The Germans probably did not come. Wine barrels, berets, *tabliers*, *l'accent du midi*, singing in the stinking dark streets, walking quietly, walking slowly.

Thy martyr's town, O Lord, walks at the pace of ox carts.

Some charitable, some uncharitable, all of the houses smell of the same kind of cooking and of rabbits stewed in wine. How could I forget the people of thy martyr, laughing at table.

Or the dark skinned girl in the Hotel L'Enfant who told me: "Arnold Bennett slept here."

---

[11] Merton moved to St. Antonin (France) in 1925 with his father.

Today in chapter "Patience" by Fr. John Eudes.

He was not impetuous. He read calmly. The good ideas, very good, were over the head of the community which needed so badly to understand. Because they thought they did not need it, they looked for something that was not there – the platitudes for which there was no need.

He spoke of the impatience of the modern world, the cult of youth which is a disease, the fear of old age and death, which demand patience – call forth patience from us to be our crown. Patience with things as they are. Not protesting against reality and going crazy, trying to manipulate it – not Faust's "cursed be patience."

And in me? Impatience is not so much a vice as a full blown disease – hereditary. I have Pop's piles and his colitis. And literary impatience. Yes, it grows more frantic as I grow old and become less of a writer. (Perhaps, backwards, I became a real writer – but I do everything backwards pretending to do something else.) Perhaps impatience is, with me, after all, creative. I will be patient with it. Then: little else is to be done about it.

September 3, 1956

In the shows of the round ox
At the rabbit stand
They won themselves and gave all.

"There is no game like money"
(said the man with the hand)
So spend your brother?

To the tidy water
They are standing on
Waterwalkers owe
No genuine fortune.

"There is no game like homeward"
(From the flying show)
Drop a dime and grab all.

When they won they drowned
and swam to the mountains.

"There is no game like heaven"
Said the hidden outcry
"No dimes for this gate"
Said the hidden wall.

September 11, 1956

On Our Lady's day I baptized Fr. Cyprian's mother in the parish church of New Haven. Fr. John of the Cross and I drove over with Fr. Benedict in the back seat, delighted to be godfather. The car with the Texas license drove up the driveway and stopped behind us. They all got out and we talked a little about the brilliant weather and the hills. About how everything is green and how in Texas – is invaded by prickly pear. And how it was to be my first baptism since Trappists rarely get to baptize.

The church was empty and cool, at one o'clock in the afternoon. And Mrs. Williams, kneeling at the communion rail, quietly read the Profession of Faith which is quite long.

The others sat in the stalls behind and Fr. John of the Cross stood in the sanctuary and I sat in a chair and said the *De Profundis* ["Out of the Depths" – Psalm 130] and for her penance gave her to hear Vespers at the monastery.

Then we went to the baptistry and I said all the exorcisms and the prayers except the exorcism of the salt which was already exorcised.

At the anointing with the oil of catechumens she began to be very joyful.

She leaned sideways over the empty half of the font.

With a little cockle-shell made out of metal and kept on a chain – I dipped three times into the water and three times, made the sign of the cross, more or less, on her forehead.

Saying: *"Anna, si non es baptizata . . ."* ["Anna, if you are not already baptized . . ."] And the beautiful words of the form, naming the Father, Son, and Holy Spirit.

When I anointed her with chrism she was very joyful.

When with cotton I wiped away the chrism and somewhat dried the water on her brow, she closed her eyes like a very joyful child,

this mother from Texas who several times has been very ill.

Later we walked to the sanctuary and she knelt at the rail and prayed aloud and I was as happy as if I had been baptized myself and remembered the day of my baptism and the depths that opened in my soul.

Let her be faithful, O Lord, to her baptismal vows and love You with all her heart and open to You her whole soul and may the nourishment you promised be given her in abundance and may she enter into eternal life praising you and glorify your mercy forever. Amen.

September 12, 1956

Respect for mystery, sense of the mystery of God, veneration of the sacredness of mystery, awe, and humility in approaching the ineffable holiness of Him who can be known in Himself only by His own revelation of Himself – and these are essential virtues of a truly religious soul. To lose these characteristics is to lose our religious spirit. To grow in them is to grow in true interior life.

The gabby objectivity of a relationship in which familiarity has destroyed all sense of the reality of God's *Tremendum Mysterium* [Tremendous Mystery] is almost as bad as agnosticism.

Tuba mirum spargens sonum [the trumpet sends out a wondrous sound (*Dies Irae*)] – a religious line because full of mystery.

EXERCISES

1.–Went home
By car
(The long way
Sang in the snow)
Went home
To the door and wall
By a long lane of chances
I found, in each room,
Sounds, cool airs, holy pictures
The emptiness of houses.
When they were all away I praised
and defended the family.

2.–When a person's love makes a good darkness for another
      person to see in without light and without eyes
And reaches out to contain the whole universe
Each sees the other full of galaxies of great stars; then distances
Stretch from heaven to hell. There is no end
To Distances in love. There is no height
Too great, no world too far out of sight to be contained in it,
All time, all countries, all the geological epochs
All are held in the blinking of a person's eye

All things begin and end in the moment of dark when love
Stands and declares its proper name
As native as a volunteer.

A PARADE OF SUSPICIOUS VEHICLES
Youth and eye alike
Fight for the flag and with it
Rich and poor go side by side
With drum or trumpet
When the down wheel is in, the
other wheels are out. All chains
Hum together in the fury
Of six flags. The comrade
Pushing the pistons,
slaps his seat in his fun.
Drunken lords fling wide lists and diamonds when the rolling
    cars
Full of iron cops
Jig their niggardly promises
hiding their knees together
The streets run red with pennies,
O Feds! Catch as catch can!
Now everybody put on your helmets and we will have the
    parade over again.
Involved in
guns and dust
Tanks and flivvers mean
To do what engines must
Until the wheels fall off
So, so old Troy was won.
Tamer almost striding
Sideways as well as forewards,
Licensed in a meeker city
This omnibus of nuns
Has come to take all home
To their temperate rooms.
But no, there shall be guns and swords by Tory's flag
Our drunken state provides the gasoline
Happiness is well in hand!

Return, O muses, to silent and auspicious feats
Tracks are out in front

And herbs are in the lead.

1957

STATEMENTS

"As long as you don't feel, against reason and independently of reason, ashamed to be alive when others are put to death, and guilty, sick, humiliated because you were spared, you will remain what you are: an accomplice by omission." *[Arthur] Koestler.*

"*Etre fidèle à la Tradition, ce n'est donc pas répéter et transmettre littéralement des thèses de philosophie ou de théologie, que l'on se figure soustraites au temps et aux contingences de l'histoire. C'est bien plutôt imiter de nos Pères dans la foi l'attitude de réflexion intime et l'effort de création audacieuse, préludes nécessaires de la véritable fidelité spirituelle.*" ["To be faithful to Tradition does not mean that one hands on theses of philosophy or theology indifferent to the time and vagaries of history. Rather, one should imitate our fathers in the faith with that attitude of deep reflection as well as the effort of bold creation which are the necessary preconditions for true spiritual fidelity."]

H. Von Balthasar. Présence et pensée.

"*Lisons l'histoire, notre histoire, comme le récit vivante de ce que nous fûmes jadis, avec le double sentiment que tout celà est passé pour toujours et que malgré tout, cette jeunesse et chaque instant de notre vie reste mystérieusement présent au fond de notre âme en une sorte d'éternité délicieuse.*" ["Let us read history, our history, like a living record of what we once were, with the dual sentiment that all this has passed by forever and, despite that, youth and each instant of our life remains mysteriously present in the depths of our soul as a kind of delectable eternity."] *id. [H. Von Balthasar.* Presence et pensée*].*

"*Nous portons témoinage par notre prière et notre renoncement, mais si la prière se fait dans une sévérité qui dépasse ce qui est élémentairement moyen normal, pour le pauvre monde, il n'y a pas de témoinage.*" ["We witness through our prayer and our renunciation, but if our prayer is done with such astringency that it lacks elementary concern for the poor world, it is no witness at all."]

Abbé Pierre.

"*De rebus divinis cum sint supra nos non debemus judicare sed simpliciter ea credere.*" ["Since divine things are beyond us, we should not judge them but simply believe them."] *St. Thomas II II Q 60 a2 ad 1.*

"(Justice) The equality that characterizes justice cannot be finally and definitively established at any one time . . . it must be constantly reestablished, restored anew. The return to equilibrium which runs in *restitutio* is an unending task. The dynamic character of man's communal life finds its image in the very structure of each act of justice . . . The fundamental condition of man and his world is provisory, temporary, non-definitive . . . any claim to erect a definitive and unalterable order in the world must, of necessity, lead to something inhuman." *Joseph Pieper.*

"If political life is to regain its dignity a proper appreciation of the eminence of the ruler's task and the lofty human qualities required for it must be revived in the mind of the public." *id. [Joseph Pieper].*

"The dictatorship of the proletariat is the government of the proletariat over the bourgeoisie, a government which is restricted by no law and subject to no power." *Stalin.*

"Any of the most early recognizable characteristics of the temporary totalitarian constellation of power is expressly to cast suspicion on impartiality and objectivity and to declare that partiality of following the party line constitutes the very essence of true public spirit." *Pieper.*

"Because men must do without things that are due to them (since others are withholding them unjustly); since human need and human want persist even though no specific person fails to fulfill his obligation and even though no binding obligation can be constrained for anyone; for these very reasons it is not 'just and right' for the first man to restrict himself to rendering what is only strictly due." *Pieper.*

"*Il est dur de voir abandonné par les siens et vécu par d'autres ce que l'on croit, ce que l'on sent être la vérité, et de le voir vécu par les autres dans l'erreur.*" ["It is painful to see what one believes abandoned by one's own and accepted by others; what one feels to be the truth, and see it lived by those who *are in error.*"] *G. Rouget, O.P.*

April 4, 1957. F[east] of St. Ambrose
Both in Malraux and in Orwell it is there – the obsession with immortality. Orwell unexpectedly comes out with it in some articles, I forget which – first in passing; the "Great Question" or something like that. And then – the Ministry of Truth in *1984*. Then in Malraux's *Royal Way*, wanting to be immortal among the dead cities.

April 25, 1957
Bulgakov and Berdyaev are writers of great, great attention. They are great men who will not admit the defeat of Christ who has conquered by His

resurrection. In their pages, for all the scandals one may fear to encounter, shines the light of the resurrection and theirs is a theology of triumph.

One wonders if our theological cautiousness is not after all the sign of a fatal coldness of heart, an awful sterility born of fear, or of despair. These two men have dared to make mistakes and were to be condemned by every church, in order to say something great and worthy of God in the midst of all their wrong statements.

They have dared to accept the challenge of the sapiential books, the challenge of the image of Proverbs where Wisdom is "playing in the world" before the face of the Creator. And the church herself says this. Sophia was somehow, mysteriously, to be revealed and "fulfilled" in the Mother of God and in the Church.

Most important of all – man's creative vocation to prepare, consciously, the ultimate triumph of Divine Wisdom. Man, the microcosm, the heart of the universe, is the one who is called to bring about the fusion of cosmic and historic process in the final invocation of God's wisdom and love. In the name of Christ and by his power, man has a work to accomplish – to offer the cosmos to the Father, by the power of the Spirit, in the Glory of the Word. Our life is a powerful Pentecost in which the Holy Spirit, ever active in us, seeks to reach through our inspired hands and tongues into the very heart of the material world created to be spiritualized through the work of the Church, the Mystical Body of the Incarnate Word of God.

April 28, 1957

Yet one of Berdyaev's greatest mistakes is to reject the Gospel as incomplete and patristic theology as sterile. In wanting to free himself from limitations he fell into narrower limits. It is not a question of trying to find in the Gospel something that is not there. (*Le sens de la création* pp. 127ff.) If he had followed St. Maximus the Confessor he would have found indeed that what he sought was in the Gospel – the "Absolute" Christ in whom all is reintegrated. This is the Christ of St. John – and of St. Paul's Epistles, especially those of the Captivity.

It is not a question of being afraid to move forward unless every step can be fortified, by hook or crook, through Gospel texts. It is not a question of getting free from a "law of sin" and "Redemption" which is in the bible and finding some other law which is in man himself. If Berdyaev had looked more closely at the N.T. he would have seen that the New Law is precisely such a liberation. Christ having risen, death [is] no more. Man, once redeemed, is obliged to live in a new creation, according to the Law of the Spirit, the liberty of the sons of God – for such is the "law" of this new creation, *written in the heart of man* and not on tablets of stone.

Berdyaev is demanding – as Blake demanded – that man should truly find his liberty in Christ. He is aware that this indeed is the message of Christ. But has Christ some other messages than the gospel? Is it the gospel's fault if those who have preached the gospel have not always understood it?

He himself says clearly *"La création est la marque de la liberté par rend l'homme semblable à Dieu – elle rend – dans L'Esprit."* ["Creation is the seal of liberty which makes a person like unto God – restored in the Spirit."] True. But it is false or, at least, misleading to say *"C'est pourquoi elle dépasse les limites des écritures."* ["That is why it (the Spirit) goes beyond the witness of the scriptures."] The Spirit is the *fulfillment* of all the scriptures, hence beyond their limits. But the whole promise is contained in the scriptures and it is false to speak of the Holy Spirit as something given to supplant the scriptures and not talked about in the scriptures. It is in the scriptures that we receive the H. Spirit and it is totally false to speak of a "coming" or "anthropological" revelation which perfects the Gospel. What he is trying to say has been said better in the N.T. itself – by Colossians, Ephesians, etc.

If I can unite *in myself,* in my own spiritual life, the thought of the East and the West of the Greek and Latin Fathers, I will create in myself a reunion of the divided Church and from that unity in myself can come the exterior and visible unity of the Church. For if we want to bring together East and West we cannot do it by imposing one upon the other. We must contain both in ourselves and transcend both in Christ.

Against those who rejoice in every dogmatic definition as a *new limitation* which *restricts* the meaning of such and such a dogma to *what is contained in this formula* nothing more. Who desire to have more and more formulas, more and more limitations, so that in the end everything is narrowed down to a minimum of meaning which must be held. On the contrary, dogmatic definitions set limits beyond which error cannot pass, but does not set limits to truth, in the sense of forbidding a dogma to mean *more* than is envisioned in a given formula.

"Lorsque le concile du Vatican définit la possibilité en droit d'atteindre par la raison le Dieu Créateur, le théologien que trouvera dans l'écriture l'affirmation conciliaire de la création du monde et de l'homme y découvrira d'autres vérités que le magistère n'avait pas la mission de souligner en l'accurence, par exemple, le rôle dans la création de l'homme lui-même *image de Dieu, place pour y dominir sur les oiseaux du ciel et les poissons de la mer. De même tout ce qui fût défini sur la médiation du Christ ne peut oublier le rôle cosmique de cette rédemption si fortement exprimée par S. Paul."* ["The Vatican Council defined the possibility of attaining by reason the Creator God so the theologian will find in scripture the conciliar definition of the creation of the world and of man and the other truths which the conciliar definition *had no need to articulate, for example, the human role in creation where man* the image of God is placed to have dominion over the birds of the air and the fish in the sea. Furthermore, when one thinks of the mediation of Christ one cannot forget the cosmic role of redemption so forcefully expressed by St. Paul."]

P. Beaudoin, in Irenikon xviii, 3 (1954).

May 1, 1957

"Once, when the great 'we' still existed, we understood them as one had understood them before. We had penetrated into their depths, we walked in the amorphous raw material of history itself . . . At that time we were called the Party of the Plebs. What did the others know of history? Passing ripples, little eddies, and breaking waves. They wondered at the changing forms of the surface and could not explain them. But we had descended into the depths, into the formless, anonymous, which at all times constituted the substance of history and we were the first to discover the laws of motion. We had discovered the laws of her inertia, of the now changing of her molecular structure, and of her sudden eruptions. That was the function of our doctrine. The Jacobins were moralists, we were empirics.

"We dug in the primeval mud of history and there we found her laws. We knew more than ever has been known about material. That is why our revolution succeeded. And now you have buried it all again."

Rubashov in Koestler's Darkness at Noon.

Berdyaev, who is always so ready to offend pious ears with statements that are, as they stand, even heretical, had nevertheless profound insights into the real meaning of Christianity – insights which we cannot simply ignore.

For instance – the view of the cosmos which is incomplete (which he calls the cosmos of the Old Testament) –

1. In this view God *enclosed* the creature in a rigid, inert, static system.

2. Man broke out of this by sin; dynamism began with the Fall.

3. But all this must be stopped and Christ came to lead man back into the original inertia! What a horrible picture, and yet how common among spiritual men. It is the theology of Lucifer.

The real view – or, at least, what B sees is the real view.

1. By sin, man fell into the power of death, inertia, slavery to necessity.

2. Man is the image and likeness of God; man is supposed to witness the creative work of God – and how?

3. By union with God in Xst. God does not remain in heaven, a dictator and overseer. He becomes man in order that the creation should continue in God's manhood. *"Jésus le Christ Dieu est terrible et ne pas être expliquer."* ["Jesus Christ God is awe-inspiring and cannot be explained."]

4. The creation in 7 days of the O.T. must come out into the 8th. day of the New Adam, the new creation, in which God and man together continue the work done by the Father.

The *Incarnation* is absolutely crucial here (and here B is a real descendent of the Greek Fathers). It is in the Holy Spirit that man lives up to his true vocation as a Son of God and creator (contrary to what B says, this is the very heart of the New Testament if by creativity we mean the *power of charity* as a Source of life. B has not yet said clearly what he means by "creation" on man's part).

Reading such things one is struck with compunction. Look at us! What are we doing? What have I done?

May 13, 1957

". . . a clan in radical chains, one of the classes of bourgeois society which *does not belong to bourgeois society,* an order which brings the break-up of all orders, a sphere which *has a universal character by virtue of its universal suffering* and lays claim to no particular right because no particular wrong but complete wrong is being perpetrated against it . . . which cannot emancipate itself without freeing itself from all other spheres of society and thereby freeing all these other spheres themselves which, as it represents the complete forfeiting of humanity itself can only redeem itself through the redemption of the whole of humanity. The proletariat represents the disposition of society as a special order." *Marx – 1843.*

The perils of Marx's rhetoric.

The phrase about particular right and particular wrong, deeply poignant, has, in fact, become the cornerstone of a philosophy that denies the concept of justice.

And Marx's psychology – the bourgeois guilt and Jewish messianism . . . etc.

To attempt to *explain* Marx is by no means to dismiss him.

Marx is one of those who cannot be dismissed. For better or for worse, his influences are there and its effects are there and there is no getting around him.

But the big question is – how to interpret him, his place in history, his influence?

History is not ready for the answer. But we must know the answer before history is ready (thus taking a leaf out of Marx's own book). To ignore the problem is fatal.

Marx is, in some strange way, an heir of Ezechiel and Jeremias. Not that he is a conscious and willing instrument of God – but an instrument. We have to listen to his tune and understand it. Because it does not mean exactly what Marx himself thought it would mean or what the communists made it mean (for Marxism, in a sense, is dead. But the unintentional consequence of Marxism lives on and their work is terrible).

May 14, 1957

"To anyone whose constant subject of contemplation is the Mystery of the Church, nothing causes greater anxiety than the piety to which her innocence is exposed." *[Dom Anscar] Vonier.*

"But we must make a distinction between the Church's sanctity and her innocence. Sanctity is the abundance of the deeds of charity in the Church. Innocence is the absence of sins, at least of deadly sin . . . For many the wonderful and manifest fertility of the Church in every sort of good work is a spectacle for which they have no eyes. They pass it by as if it did not exist. On the other hand, sin, real or imaginary, in the members of the Church, scandalizes them in a way which is positively unhealthy . . ."

id. [Dom Anscar Vonier].

"When we speak of the Church's Whiteness we do not mean and cannot mean, angelic purity; to be exact, we mean human whiteness, the purity possible to man while he lives on earth." *id. [Dom Anscar Vonier].*

May 16, 1957. St. Gregory of Nyssa

De Hominis Opificio [On the Creation of Man]

Wonderful chapters on the dignity of man – the world formed to be his royal throne – His body formed like a musical instrument, for speech. If man did not walk upright, says Gregory, and use his hands for all manner of things, he would have to get his food with his mouth, he would have a snout and a tongue not apt for speech. But as it is, his hands also, and above all, help him to communicate his ideas.

May 18, 1957

Karl Marx refused to work for his living or to write "for money" (i.e. in order to make a living) but he made Engels write articles for him which he sold to the *N.Y. Tribune.* In addition, he got Engels to support him – Engels worked for his father's firm in Manchester, was one of the bosses.

Marx was a misanthrope, with piles, indulged in much scatological humor, understood very well the fetish character of money and the Jewish propensity to adore golden calves. He was a cynic, relentlessly purified the labor movement of all taint of brotherly love yet was a kind father. He was totally ignorant of machinery. "The simplest technical reality where intuition is needed is harder for me than the knottiest problems" (he said). He kept his room in a frightful mess and wore out the carpet walking up and down in thought. He made use of his own conviction that he was right, to permit himself to distort and amplify "history" in his own favor. His "objectivity" is to a great extent, a front – but, all the same, because he did in fact have a passion for penetrating the "front" of capitalism and its sham ethics. C. Wilson says of him "No one has ever had so deadly a sense of the infinite capacity of human nature for remaining oblivious or indifferent to the pains we inflict on others when we have a chance to get something out of them ourselves." Marx's great gift was in "diagnosis." He diagnosed the greatest evil of Capitalist society that "things" and "commodities" – especially money – takes the place of men and rules men. But he was fundamentally naive in supposing that under the proletariat "things" would again serve men. It has turned out quite the opposite. The dictatorship of the proletariat is more than anything else a tyranny of "things" and "commodities" over human values – everything must be sacrificed to production, but yet not to production that produces but to production that "proves" the a priori contentions of dialectical materialism.

Capitalism, with all its evils, at least produces something and distributes what it produces and production is not subservient to the demands of an a priori theory.

A genial statement of Marx, "All our invention and progress seems to result in *endowing material forces with intellectual life and stultifying human life into a material force.*"

It is ironical, though, that of all men in the last 200 years, he has done more than any other thinker in that direction.

The thing most significant about the genius of Marx is the ambivalence and internal contradictions which are bearing fruit monstrously in the world of our time. They too were and are prophetic.

Marx's subtlety of analysis – neutralized by the naivete with which he fails to apply his critical insight to anyone but the capitalist – the scapegoats on which he had unloaded everything he hated in himself. In the end, he was unable to make a real analysis of a society divided into classes.

Above all – *ambivalence on the questions of rights.*

Everything in his theory presupposes a vindication of the "rights" of the proletariat but he proceeds by a denial of rights and by throwing the idea of justice out the window as an "illusion."

May 22, 1957

"Only when a priest realizes that his life is not up to his ideal and cannot be, but that despite it all must keep faith with it and with God will any blessing for him and for his people grow out of his existential need."

Fr. M[ichael] Pflieger.

May 28, 1957

"*La vie spirituelle ne serait pas concevable sans le grand mystère de la pénitence. C'est sur ce chemin, semé de dangereuses embûches, qu'apparaissent les fruits spirituels de la meilleure vie. Pourtant le repentir n'est pas toujours fecund . . . Un repentir stérile épaissit en l'homme ses ténèbres intérieures, le conduit à l'auto-dévoration . . . Il ne reste alors qu'un chemin pour échapper à la mort spirituelle. C'est celui de l'ébranlement créateur de l'esprit. Mystérieusement et miraculeusement le repentir de l'âme se change en'élan vers la création, qui libère et fait tenaitre les forces humaines . . . Ceux qui exhortent l'homme au seul repentir de ses fautes, et lui défendent de s'exprimer par la création le condamnent en fait au désespoir et à une sorte de mort. En même temps que les ennemis de la créativité ils sont ceux aussi de la résurrection de l'esprit et de son acces à une vie nouvelle.*"

["The spiritual life is inconceivable without the great mystery of repentance. It is on that road, studded with obstacles, where the spiritual fruits of a better life appear. Nonetheless, repentance is not always fruitful . . . a false repentance creates an interior darkness in men, leading them to devour themselves . . . There is but one path to escape spiritual death. It is that of the creative force of the Spirit. Mysteriously and miraculously repentance of soul changes to power towards the creation which frees human forces . . . Those who exhort a person to repent only of his faults and forbid him to express himself through creation condemn him in fact to despair and spiritual death. At the same time, those who are the enemies of creativity are also enemies of the Resurrection of the spirit and access to a new life."] *Berdyaev.* Le sens de la tradition, *216–17*.

The beauty of the walnut tree at the end of the novitiate wall. More beautiful still because of the dead end of the branches that reach out, stark and black, from the rich foliage and gesture against the sky and the hills. The great leaves and the innumerable shades and patterns where they overlap. Inexhaustible beauty of design made more curious and fecund by the pruning two years ago that was not quite successful.

This is the year of the seventeen year locusts. They are almost silent in the woods now. The woods near at hand are almost entirely quiet. You can hear the locusts faintly in the distant forests. When they first began, about twelve days ago, I thought they were frogs or crows in the distance. Last week the din was enormous. The whole world throbbed with their love, which had taken over everything. Immense activity in the woods.

When they came out of the ground by the new lake they found the woods had gone which were there 17 (or 18) years ago. But they clustered in the leaves of the low stump sprouts and the suckers and we saw them there, black rubbery bodies, red eyes, and amber wings.

In a dream – people dancing – new dances and great gestures, like the Russian ballet. One of the dancers in a tight-fitting velvet of a beautiful leaf green, was a dark-haired woman with her hair cut close like a boy's. In the middle of the dance she bent over sideways and touched the floor with both hands in a curious gesture. I observed that the people dancing were elegant and serious and bored and the expressions of boredom were slightly different from what they used to be when I was in the world.

Men came into the room with straw hats: Kentucky politicians.

Governor Chandler – Happy Chandler – stolid and serious, standing on the front steps of the old guest house with his hat in his hand and the wind blowing his hair about his forehead, made a speech appropriate to the occasion, in which he mentioned "my young friend, Thomas Merton." He made several interesting syntactical errors which may or may not have a prophetic character about them. One of these was "You (monks) know you cannot be happy because you have material possession." (Instead of you monks realize that material possessions do not bring happiness.) I pointed this out to one of the monks who said immediately "Oh, but that is not what he meant." So true is it that everyone has the instinctive habit of paying attention not to what a politician says but what he seems to want to say.

In Theophane Zatvornik, a Russian bishop of the 19th. century, the asceticism of the fathers was revived, says Berdyaev, not to prepare for a new life but to "obey the consequences of sin" and to "fortify and preserve established (social) forms."

"Neither inside of man or outside of him is there anything perfectly free" said this Theophane. Everything being ruled by inexorable laws of God, God alone being free. "Order is above everything else" "Measure is everything . . . food, drink, clothing, furniture, work, rest, friendship . . ." Honor to corporal punishment: "evil cannot be expelled from the soul unless the body suffers." Tsar, governor, fathers links in a hierarchical chain coming down from God to bind us hand and foot. Submission to orders given! B. concludes: "He was a monophysite. He denied man. the God man and God manhood."

Later – in very important pages on genius and sanctity (in his contrast of Pushkin and Seraphim of Sarov) he points out the elements of sacrifice inherent in the work of genius and how the asceticism of convent life is perfectly well adapted to the positivist world and to the utilitarianism of bourgeois existence. But no more adaptation is possible in the work of genius.

He overstates the contrast and "incompatibility" of sanctity and genius – although he admits the correspondence in St. Francis. His contrast is overgeneralized and false just as the contrast and "problem" I made for myself between "Poetry and the Contemplative Life" is overbalanced and false.

But his statement of the problem *must* be faced. How many religious people are interested in facing it?

The solution lies in prayer. Prayer as creation. Not prayer as slavish and negative acceptance of frustration. Nor prayer as self-punishment and superstitious cupidity but prayer as the creative act by which love, moved by the love of the *Creator Spirit* Himself, reaches into the darkness of the divine mystery, or rather opens up the utmost mystery of our own being to God and finds the mystery within us. The act by which we give ourselves to God is by its nature *creation. Neque praeputium aliquid valet neque circumcisio sed nova creatura.* [Neither circumcision or uncircumcision counts but a new creation (Gal. 6:15).]

For jailer in the democratic primaries is running a man who has been in jail four times as a moonshiner. Happy's choice, I understand, and a "good Catholic."

May 29, 1957

Good writing and good art are coming to mean much in the salvation of Russia. It is sad that the cultural contacts that were beginning so suddenly ended. Even mediocre writing and art would have accomplished something once a dialogue was established. After all, it is not so much a selling them a theory, as of reaching some kind of human understanding with people who do, in fact, want nothing but that. One of the most terrible aspects of Stalin's fascism, – no, of all fascism – has been the complete confiscation of all that is original and positive and free in the human spirit, the negation of man's creative power, the representation of all artists and writers who are forced to meet not just the taste of the petty bourgeois bureaucracy, but the standards translated by their theory of what should be written. After all, if their taste is horrible, their ideals are even worse.

If at least they can read Dostoevsky . . . and fill their lungs with fresh air.

I knew the Reds would eventually declare Zoschenko the "scum of Literature." His *Russia Laughs* was a phenomenally good book. I do not even have to try to find out what may have happened to Kataev.[12] He probably went, with the others, in the Great Purge.

---

[12] It is unclear if Merton refers to Ivan Kataev (born 1902) or Valentin Kataev (born 1897)—both literary figures.

June 6, 1957

"*Malheureusement il a fait aujourd'hui que les ordres ne sont plus toujours capables de s'assimiler le nombre voulu des individus qui pourraient y trouver place de par l'élan de leur générosité et de leur foi, qui se voient rebutes par un certain esprit de caste. Les exigences posées semblent quelquefois ne ressortir qu'à la vertu de prudence. En fait, elles manquent de grandeur chrétienne, et nous sommes à une époque où ces élargissements sont un devoir grave.*" ["Unfortunately, it happens that today the Orders are not always ready to take in those who desire to find a place commensurate with the force of their generosity and faith but who find themselves stymied by a certain caste spirit. The demands placed on them are couched in the language of prudence. In fact, they (the religious orders) lack a certain Christian openness and we are in an age where such expansiveness is a great duty."] *Dom O. Rousseau.*

Notes for Two Plays in July

Prologue. First, I shall almost certainly write a play in which the four great rivers of France hold a discussion. This is not *that play* but another one. This is the play about a phoenix.

Characters: A, B, C, and a Phoenix.

Act I

A: First I shall almost certainly write a play in July.

B: About the four rivers of France?

A: [erasure]

B: I am concerned only with rewards and exiles.

A: Victor Hugo swims the lake.

B: When there was no money we remained pensive at home.

A: The scene is on an artist's stove.

B: With a view of Geneva.

(Enter C with a packet of letters)

C (reads aloud): The children were very thoughtful with their feet in the dust. They knew their own country was at war. They were also jealous of Mother, and did not believe in fruit – very tempestuous children, they were closed in on their own nature. In spite of every hesitation they were disinterested in the mirror. Then they were sent to bed for cutting their own hair. After that there were plenty of photos. Do you understand?

A AND B: You have explained two out of three recent wars.

C: Thank you. Any discourse is always in July.

Act II

A: Now we are in for a lavish excitement. Open up all the cellos!

B: Yes! They are coming in by every door with thirsty bundles!

A: It is the parish harvest. O the beautiful tumblers.

B: Every one an ace! Call Henry!

A: Yes! Let's call Henry!

B: Henry! Henry! Henry!

A: I cannot contain my joy at the forest of fiddlers.

B: (sings) –

> With cymbal trumpet and drum
> The Folios are out tomorrow
> Singed by the famous men
> Cocteau, Hugo and Racine.

A: We shall praise them in the square cathedral. How is the great piano tremendously hollow?

B: Here are prayers signed by the Loire and the Garonne.

A: Lord! I am out of breath.

C: Stop! Stop! Marshall Joffre.

(All cease. The personages fade.)

Act III

C: Darkness and Trouble – these are the only support of a sombre landscape.

A: (enters following B) – I was always jealous of your pretty English.

B: In my old age I was concerned with rewards. I lifted the penalties due to the rivers of France. I set everything aside in strict justice. Toulouse is forgiven!

A: I mean you to understand that I hate your confounded drum and the bankers and the axles!

B: Besides that, I gave away everything. I forgive you. Is there no hope?

C: Darkness and Trouble. These are the only support of a sombre landscape.

A: See my knife?

B: I am concerned only with tasks and duties. My rewards are noble.

A: I'll tax you to kill.

C: Darkness and Trouble, these are the only remorse of a loaded geography.

A: If the play only had a phoenix in it we could end happily. (He strikes, killing C.)

(Enter the four rivers of France, the Loire, the Rhone, the Garonne, and the Nile.)

Curtain

Explanation and Criticism. Frankly, one does not find it difficult to understand how the phoenix was not included in this play. True, his raving flame would have made a difference to A, B, and C but that would have been a rude bargain. In saving them he would only have set fire to the entire set and the audience – a most expensive theatrical production?

The children were always thoughtful. They knew above all that their country was at war today. It was a shame they were so suspicious for they did not believe in fruit. Tempestuous little ones, closed in upon their own natures. This was more than they could afford. After some hesitancy they were fully described in psychology. Remember, it only happened once but once was enough. After that, there were plenty of photos.

> *Le bon phoenix est mort*
> *Il s'était trop brûlé*
> *Les cendres (c'est dommage)*
> *Dans les grands fleuves de La France*
> *Se sont noyées.*
> [The good phoenix is dead
> too greatly burned
> the cinders (what a pity)
> drowned in the great rivers of France.]

Notes for play – cont'd.

(SPEECH OF C:) When I was born I was majestic in the cradle. I was born with silver teeth in my mouth, a rich child of rich parents. Already when I was only two and a half years old I could cut my own hair but didn't. I had servants. Where was the most expensive hotel? I lived in it, that's where. In the most elegant houses, I grew up, yes, in polished houses. Yes, dear, I am very rich.

B: When I was little I was smart but poor and so I had to work for a living. When I was six years old I taught Greek in a small but decent college.

A: Vampires! Prodigies!

C: Never, never, did I have holes in my stockings.

B: Is he exalted.

Scene II

> Sandy!
> What Sandy?
> Sandy all over.

c: I never had to exert myself in gymnasium since skill came natural.
>   sing us some of your jazz.
>   By all means. It is old, but a good tune. We call it "By myself."

> By myself
> How we got there altogether
> By myself
> We and they in ever larger numbers
> Yes, it's hell for leather
>> You and I
>> We are who? The People!
>> By myself
>
> once or twice
> I'll be everybody
> By myself
> Who told you?
> I found it out from everybody
> – There were a thousand pleasant roads to travel
> By myself.
> Is this what I wanted? This eggshell?
> All is already scattered.
> Good! Tell Henry!

a: Exaltation and cataclysm. I warn you to understand. Heaven only knows. What message. Here it comes. The longest part of the garden. That's home!

b: What precision! You deafen the orbs with precision.

a: I have always thought, Dear, death would be so humble. But it just comes natural.

Scene VII

> In the founts of the dells, where the lilies
> Yes, and trout also. Deer frequent the beechy shade. There,
>   yes, there.
> I was thinking of the same bygones.

It is the mood I was born for – I mean: swans.
Are you in earnest?
Then bury him right there.
It is a pity there was no phoenix in this play –
We might have had a happy ending.
Calm down everybody, I see trees.

[July 19, 1957]

A PRACTICAL PROGRAM FOR MONKS

1.

Each one shall sit at table with his own cup and spoon, and with his own repentance. Each one's own business shall be his most important, and providing remedies. They have however neglected
both bowl and plate.
Have you a wooden fork?
Yes, every monk has a wooden fork as well as a potato.

2.

Each one shall wipe away tears with his own saint, when these bells hold in store a hot afternoon. Each one is supposed to mind his own heart, with its conscience, night and morning. Another turn on the wheel, ho hum: and observe the abbot. Time to go to bed, in a straw blanket.

3.

Plenty of bread for everyone, between prayers, and saying the psalter and will you take another? Merci, and miserere [Thank you, and have mercy]. Always mind the clock and the abbot, until eternity. Miserere.

4.

Details of the rule are all solid and substance and what nun was first to announce regimentation? Yes, I dare say you are right, Father. I believe it, I believe it. It is easier when they can have ice water and even a little lemon. Each one can sit at table with his own lemon and mind his conscience.

5.

It is better to have sheep than peacocks and cows rather than a chained leopard says Dom'no in one of his proverbs. The monastery is owner of a joint rowboat. It is the antechamber of heaven.

6.

Each one can have some rain after Vespers on a hot afternoon. But *ne quid nimis* [not too much] or the purpose of the Order will be forgotten. We can send you hyacinths and a sweet millennium. Everything the monastery makes is very pleasant to see and sell for nothing. There is a sign of God in every petal when no one is looking. Woods all go calm at night, inside the cathedral. In Kentucky there is room for a little cheese. Each one shall fold his own napkin, and neglect the others. Have you a patron saint and an angel? Thank you, I have one of everything.

July 29, 1957

Bulgakov's explanation of his sophianology (*Du verbe incarné*, p. 16) seems to me clear and satisfactory.

The divine nature is distinct from the 3 Divine Persons, but is not therefore a 4th. principle superadded to make a "quaternity." No one imagines that it does. When the same nature is regarded as "Sophia" – why should that constitute a 4th. person?

Not quite sure I agree that the generation of the Son implies for the Son the "pain" of an eternal sacrifice – necessary for the beatitude of eternal love.

Very important for the understanding of Bulgakov – the idea that the Divine Nature constitutes for the Divine Person the "world" which they themselves are. Note the starting point of the whole conception – our own relation to our own nature as a world which is only partially in us and which we tend to become. (This would seem to throw light on Ruysbroeck, Tauler, etc. "*Grund*" [ground], "*Geburt*" [birth], "*Wesen*" [essence] names of God.)

"*La nature Divine n'est pas seulement la force de la vie, elle en est le contenu – le contenu absolu de la vie absolue avec toutes ses propriétés . . . Le propre de ce contenu est de comprendre Tout, puisque aucune limitation ne convient à la divinité . . . La vie de Dieu est cette Toute-unité positive, et La Toute unité est la nature de Dieu . . . La nature de Dieu en tant que contenu absolu de la vie de Dieu est ce qui est appellé par la Parole Divine (Prov. VIII).*" ["The divine nature is not only the dynamism of life but its content. The absolute content of absolute life with all its properties . . . the essence of this is total completeness apart from any limitation attributable to God . . . The life of God is this total positive unity and this total unity is the nature of God. The nature of God which is the absolute content of the life of God is that which is called by the Divine Word (Prov. 8)."] La sagesse de dieu, *p. 22.*

Divine Nature – explains the essence of God as Source of his life
" Sophia " " " " " without " "
same thing.

"*La Sophia est le plerôme, le monde de Dieu existant en Dieu et pour Dieu, éternel et incrée, où Dieu vit en la Trinité. Et ce monde divin contenant tout ce que le St. Trinité révèle d'Elle-même en Elle-même, il est l'image de Dieu en Dieu-même la propre Icone de la Divinité . . .*" ["Wisdom is fulness, the world of God exists in God and through God, eternal and uncreated, where God lives in the Trinity. This divine world, that contains all that the Holy Trinity reveals of itself and in itself is the image of God in God Himself, the icon of divinity."] La sagesse de dieu, *p. 23.*

Very important: the copula "is" is for us an indifferent means of joining subject and predicate logically. In God "is" means the union of love. To say God *is* his life, his Sophia, is to say that he loves it and it loves Him.

(Ah! Then it is a person! No. It loves Him in each of the Divine Persons. It loves Him in His creation and is loved by Him there. God loves in me His own wisdom. His own wisdom in one is love, uniting us to Him in the 3 Divine Persons.)

However – one must admit there is something unsatisfactory in this explanation. Precisely, what does it mean?

QUESTIONS ABOUT THE LONGEST CITY IN THE WORLD

Do tall white ladies still come to the sunburned wanderer upon the suspension bridges, in the small hours of the morning to fill his hands with coins and emeralds?

Do the blind daughters of the harbor startle the unfeeling night with their imbecile songs?

What of the detectives roaring for cash money in the cafeterias?

Once there was a lone boatman who suspended horseshoes over the unlucky doors of the poor. Has this altered their condition?

Every night the dead sit up in their graves and look around, when nobody sees them. They lie down again quietly after a few moments.

It is early in the evening. The law students drive away in borrowed cars and the streets are full of children looking for meteorites. Small girls run from the mud and thunder, and nun(s) groan in their underwear on deplorable fire escapes, as warm boys ascend from the rivers. On nights like these the entire city is attacked by bad language and worse morals.

They got lost in the halls looking for their own windows.

They heard the strangers in the night but did not wonder about other countries to the East and South. Though close at hand, the immense sea was unknown to them with its bells, its lights, its pilots, and its winds.

They were lost in the stairways looking for their own front door.

Japanese lanterns are torn. Fans also are torn. Screens are knocked down showing off what is behind them. But since the wires are not yet cut, everyone is uneasy on the telephone. The whole town is uneasy on a hot night when the power goes off and the naked ones are not arrested.

But the suspension bridges were closed and the pious ladies were brought to trial and there were no more emeralds.

These are a few questions I would like to ask about a long town.

July 30, 1957

The hope of a monastery in Ecuador.

Can such a hope be realized by anything except prayer?

Is it a hope or a temptation?

It could easily be done – a simple monastery like Toumliline in Morocco, like Cuernavaca (Moralos – Mexico).

To visit first Dom Gregorio at Cuernavaca[13] and learn from him how to make a small, simple monastery as unlike Gethsemani as possible.

With perhaps very few Americans in it.

(All the time my stomach is sick with the feeling that with Dom James nothing of the sort is possible.)

Can such a hope be realized by anything but prayer? St. Mariana of Jesus, you who prayed in Quito and loved God there and are venerated still and have power there still: give power to your prayers now and beg for a monastery near Quito or perhaps near Riobamba under Chimbarazo, a monastery in one of the large valleys.

We would not need so many tractors. But there would be some tractors, irrigation perhaps – or perhaps not. What would we grow [illegible] for? Make straw hats?

That was the first place in the world they grew potatoes. We could grow potatoes.

Can such a hope be realized by anything but prayer – prayer that burns out the heart, that fights despair, that comes up in flame and fights the cold darkness of despair.

---

[13] Dom Gregorio Lemercier, the prior of the Benedictine monastery at Cuernavaca, in Mexico, figures largely in Merton's life in the next few years.

Why should you want it so bad? That is the question.

We have to protest against something and it would be a protest.

We have to bear witness to something and it would be a witness.

(I have to lie to myself and maybe this is another one of my lies.)

The fact that it could be done and it needs to be done and it should be done.

A small monastery in the Andes, without too many machines.

A monastery that would mean a great deal in Ecuador.

To be a monk in a country where your being a monk would mean a great deal to everybody – to have one monastery that would help a whole country very much – And for the Indians – and because of our sins and the sins of all conquerors, particularly, of the conquistadores. And everyone.

Can such a hope be realized by anything but prayer?

July 31, 1957

"*En nous-mêmes, l'humanité est une réalité encore close, qui ne fait qu'aller se découverant et qui se découvrira alors seulement 'Dieu sera tous en tous' . . . La Sophie divine, pan-organisme des idées, est l'humanité surternelle en Dieu – Prototype divin et fondement de l'être de l'homme.*" p. 34 ["Within ourselves humanity is so close that one can seek to discover and will discover that 'God is all in all' . . . Divine Wisdom, the ground source of all ideas, is the eternal humanity in God – the divine prototype and foundation of the being of man."]

August 1, 1957

As I was coming back from a walk at the lake a green heron started up from the water in the culvert under the roadway where all the blackberry bushes are and flew up into some willows. I could see his beautiful mahoghany neck and his crest was up as he looked back at me. His legs looked bright yellow. Same heron as I saw the other day flying along in the right pasture, at a distance somewhat like a crow.

August 2, 1957

"*La Sophie est La Sagesse de Dieu, elle est la gloire de Dieu, est l'humanité en Dieu, elle est la Théanthropie, le corps de Dieu, le Monde Divin, étant en dieu 'des avant' la création. C'est là que se trouve 'le fondement suffisant' de la création . . . le fondement de sa sophianité.*" ["Sophia is the Wisdom of God, the glory of God is humanity in God, the 'theanthropy,' body of God, the divine world which was in God at creation. It is there that one finds the sufficient reason of creation . . . the foundation of Wisdomness."] *Bulgakov. p. 38.*

August 3, 1957

A Mexican magazine came for Fr. Lawrence (Cardenal) who has a poem in it, attacking the United Fruit Company.

The little Central American countries are all mixed up in one another's revolutions (for instance the dictator of Nicaragua got a dictator put in Guatemala and the U.S. backed them both because in this way the Reds pushed out of G. and now both dictators have been assassinated).

In this Mexican magazine *(Revista mexicana de literatura)* are some good French poets. Young ones.

Yves Bonnefoy in his picture is indeed a gentle poet. His poems are gentle and, I think, pure.

Aimé Cesaire, a Negro from Martinique, writes strong and improvised verse and has something to say and looks like a good guy. He has chased upon his woolly head the locomotive and the railway as well as the God of the commander, ever since Akhad and Elom and Sumer. That is one good poem.

"*Acaba de romper con el partido communista a raiz de los acontecimientos de Hungaria.*" ["He broke with the communist party because of the events in Hungary."]

Maybe the one I like best is Jacques Tupin, of whom there is no picture. Dry and rich at the same time. Austere, complex. I miss in him the directness of Aimé Cesaire, who has such a lot to say, such a lot to say.

Winged ants drop on me all the time.

Jacques Charpier good too. His picture looks distinguished. Compared with Cesaire he is precious. All the imitators of St. John Perse and Valery, no doubt, aim to surprise you every third line with the adjective "fine." It is no longer a surprise, nor is it anything else. It is just a word.

August 4, 1957

"*Proprement, l'acte créateur ne crée que la possibilité de l'auto-position qui s'effectue par le moi-même, prononçant son 'oui.' Cette liberté du moi se posent soi-même contient déjà l'image de Dieu, en l'esprit de créature . . .*

"*Dans la mesure l'homme voit Dieu comme son Prototype, il conçoit sa condition de crée, c'est à dire, son 'inoriginalité' metaphysique; il se connaît comme la réflexion du soleil dans une gouttelette de l'être . . . dans ce libre aveu de n'être que l'image d'un Autre, de l'Image Première, nait l'amour pour cet Autre . . . un amour qui est comme le sceau de la divine Filialité . . ."* ["Technically, the created act creates nothing but the possibility of self recognition which happens in the self through the self-articulating of its 'yes.' This freedom of the self within itself already contains the image of God in the soul of the created one. To the measure that one sees God as his prototype he sees himself as created, that is, his 'metaphysical unoriginality'; it knows itself like a reflection of the sun on a tiny drop of being . . . with the free acknowledgment of becoming the image of the Other, the foundational image, born of love for the Other . . . a love which is the seal of divine sonship."] *Bulgakov. pp. 66–67.*

But refusal to make this act of free recognition means refusal of *kenosis* hence "auto-position lucifereuse" ["a satanic self understanding"]. And man who refuses to empty himself and be all for and from God, becomes his own god.

The possibility of self-divinization springs from the fact that man is called to be an "I" who freely states his position and takes it up himself.

The true response *"Il a sa personnalité etc. etc."*

Also: *man is related to his nature as God is related to his Sophia.*

This is one of the basic concepts of the book.

Man's vocation is to *humanize* and *clarify* perfectly the potential "human" Sophia of creation which is entrusted to him. To make God shine in its charity.

(evening) Day of Recollection

> *Cur detestatus disciplinam*
> *et increpationibus non acquievit cor meum;*
> *nec audivi vocem docentium me,*
> *et magistris non inclinavi aurem meum?*
> *Paene fui in omni malo*
> *in medio ecclesiae et synagogae.*
> [How I hated discipline
> and my heart despised reproof
> I did not listen to the voice of my teachers or incline my ear
>   to my instructors.
> I was at the point of utter ruin
> in the assembled congregation.]

Prov. 5:12ff.

August 7, 1957

I think this morning I found the key to Bulgakov's Sophianism. His idea is that the Divine Sophia, play, wisdom, is by no means a fourth person or hypostasis, yet in *creation* spiritualized by the church, it is, as it were, hypostasized, so that creation itself becomes the "Glory of God." Man has frustrated this to some extent – "created Sophia" is "fallen" with man.

Wisdom has been corrupted into magic (i.e. magic hold of the cosmos over man who has subjected himself to it by trying to gain control over it).

Yet man remains the one who, in Christ, will raise up and spiritualize creation so that all will be "Sophia" and true glory of God.

For this man must be himself perfectly united and subjected to the wisdom of God.

August 8, 1957

Fr. Aelred (Walters) who was in the air corps in Newfoundland tells of a man who dropped dead in a restaurant on the outskirts of St. Johns.

The restaurant is crowded. Four people, two women and two men enter, and look for a table. There is none. As they are going out, the man falls on floor near the doorway. He falls in the only open space, near the desk where you pay – between desk and the door. Everybody looks at him. No one thinks of anything to do or say. The women (one is his wife) are already outside the restaurant when he falls. They return, take one look at him lying on the floor – say nothing – show no sign of any emotion whatever. They turn around and walk out – disappear. No one knows where they have gone. The other man stands there mute, doing nothing. People sit at the tables eating and looking down at the unconscious man.

Walters leans over him, thought he was trying to whisper something, but it was the death rattle. He prayed, said Hail Marys, and thought of the man's soul "rising up and standing before God in judgment."

He called up the hospital and after a brief time the ambulance came and took the man away. By that time he was dead.

He had remained lying there in the entry to the restaurant with the customers carefully and respectfully walking around him on their way out.

Lately – after the copy of South American books.

Reading some Pound in the woodshed. There is no more uneven poet. No one who can move so rapidly from the best to the worst and back again.

Some of his epigrams are marvelous. (How is it that I seem to have forgotten them all? Yet I used to own *Lustra* in the 1st. edition.) Generally I like the Cantos. Fascinated even by the Rock Drill cantos. He was best it seems in the Twenties. It was when China got into him that he really matured – when the Chinese poets pushed out a little of the Browning. A marvellous cross between China and Rome. If Pound had not written I would never have realized that China and Rome had so much in common.

Finally got the rest of Green's *Journals*.

Their climate is wonderful. I am really at home in it – he is an honest mind – and dishonest too, like all of us, but simple about it. And he loves France. I am more fascinated by his days than anything I can think of.

His moments of despair are important to me, because, above all, he clings in desperation to the reality of the religious life. It is most "edifying" to look at religion through his eyes – which are honest ones. For edification does not mean delusion. He sees religious as they are – with their limitations.

And I have those limitations too. To what extent have they crippled me? I ask that as if there were an answer. But I will probably never know.

Why don't I write about something besides books?

A habit of priestly evasion.

Working in the woods – cutting brush and trees for an electric line to the firetower. Yellow jackets everywhere. One postulant got stung 5 times. A yellow jacket even went up the leg of his pants and stung him on the thigh. I got stung on the left eyebrow and it was painful for a long time – even until night time when it helped to keep me awake.

Trees coming down everywhere. I ran madly to avoid one, down the washed out road on the steepest part of the hill worsened by an "inspiration" which got me over all the ruts and stones without breaking my ankle or at least falling on my head. A very strong feeling of the power of instinct which had awakened within me to run over that impassable ground in safety. As if held up by an angel. Is it any less from God if it is an instinct? Or is it both "instinct" and "angel"?

Maybe it was all angel. Have I any instincts left?

August 10, 1957

"*On peut dire que Dieu créa le monde pour S'y incarner, qu'il créa à cause de cette incarnation. Celle-ci n'est pas seulement le moyen de la Rédemption, mais elle est son couronnement suprême . . . En s'incarnant, Dieu a montré Son amour pour la création.*" ["One can say that God created the world to incarnate himself; that He created for the sake of the Incarnation. This is not only the means of redemption buts its supreme crown. In incarnating Himself, God shows his love for creation."] *Bulgakov. p. 94.*

It has always been difficult for me to see how a Christian would possibly think otherwise. The Sophianism of Bulgakov is built on this idea. And, of course, Proverbs 8 (cf. epistle – F of Immaculate Conception) makes it seem obvious. But of course a theologian can always approach the mystery of Christ from some angle which leaves Wisdom out in the exterior darkness. Then, of course, one can take a different view. A matter of law and justice etc. Yet how separate Law from wisdom if you really know the scriptures?

As far as one who has the question "Would the Incarnation have taken place if man had not sinned" one opens the way to much nonsense and doesn't lead to a solution. B wisely says that the solution is to *"rayer la question même en tant que casus irréalis."* ["Negates the question itself as a misplaced one."]

"Le casus irréalis consiste ici à admettre que Dieu aurait pu ne pas S'incarner, si l'homme n'avait point péché." ["The misplaced question consists in asserting that God would not have incarnated Himself unless man sinned."]

A neat turn. To understand it one must remember all the anthropological perspectives of B and perhaps, a Thomist would say he was simply begging the question. But for B *"L'Incarnation exprime la raison la plus fondamentale et déterminante de Dieu avec le monde et non point un événement particulier de la vie de ce dernier . . ."* (96) ["The Incarnation expresses the most fundamental determining reason (of the relation) of God to the world and not some particular event in life afterward."]

A letter from Fr. Bruno James about his new book on St. Bernard.

"You see, I am certain that the Cistercian life is quite dead, has been dead for generations. I don't think it survived the first generation of Cistercians. I believe it died because the contemplative spirit was out of it, the contemplative spirit which gives liberty. Its place was taken by "observance" and the whole thing took on the rigidity of a corpse. Because the great Truth was lost sight of that the whole life is a life of prayer . . . I think the Trappists missed the boat even more completely than the old Cistercians . . . I think the church is going through a more dangerous phase."

All this, he said, would be reflected in his book but I have not found it there – an occasional dig. For instance the Trappists would have been scandalized to know St. Bernard countenanced the reading of Ovid – at least by Rainald [of Bar]. He does say something about the whole thing having "died" after St. Bernard.

He exaggerates.

At the same time, he does not say enough. If the sickness is a sickness and if it is really there, it goes right down to the root: all the squabbling about observance, with the Benedictines.

Is St. Bernard right in saying that he himself would not have been saved at Cluny? Since he says it himself, we all believe it. But is a man to be believed in everything he says about himself? If St. Bernard was wrong on this point, it is certainly a monumental error. But the statement has had tremendous effects. I am convinced he was utterly wrong. All one can say is that he probably thought he was right.

For my own part I confess that the whole Cistercian question has lost all meaning. There is *no solution* as far as I can see and all one can do about it is to save his own soul as best he can.

It makes more sense to frankly ask oneself an idiotic question: "What is the noise made when one claps one hand instead of two?" It is the same question out in the open. It is a Koan – and has, somewhere, a solution, but not an intellectual or an ethical one.

A spiritual solution is beyond the depth of thought. Very simple – if only you can make it. "Contemplation" is not enough of an answer. It suggests an illusory object to be obtained – and more waste of time and energy.

At Mass precisely (before the letter came) I was praying, almost in agony (for a moment) for spiritual liberty. I wonder if anyone has ever had less.

To have that, I must let go of what I "need" most – the advantages of my present situation. Or should I say, all secondary gains.

A question of *disciplina*, I suppose. I wonder if anyone has talked more about listening and himself listened less.

The important question is: not how "contemplative" is the Cistercian Order, but can one practice charity in it? Everything hangs on that. In its essence – the life is perfect for charity. *Per accidens*, since the end in *esse* has been observed, there is much that obstructs the one thing necessary.

The best of Pound is in *Hugh Selwyn Mauberley*

> His true Penelope was Flaubert
> He fished by obstinate isles;

> Observed the elegance of Circe's hair
> Rather than the mottoes on sundials.

I know of few lines I like better anywhere!

> Charm, smiling at the good mouth
> Quick eyes gone under the earth's lid . . .

And this – whether quoted or not – is perfect in the setting.

> When our two dusts with Waller's shall be laid.

Sometimes as much like Ogden Nash as he is like Auden.
Pound found marvellous words everywhere.

One feels that the most fruitful moments in the life of Julien Green are those which he spent looking out of his window, not thinking anything, just looking at the buildings and the trees of Paris.

August 14, 1957
Fly catchers shaking their wings after the rain.

The reader in the refectory each day announces the title of his book – "A Right To Be Merry" it is called. He drops his voice ever so slightly on the word "Merry" as though to say "No! God forbid! Not a right to be merry!"

If he ever reads anything about eating or drinking he drops his voice ever so slightly with the same pious fear (Eating! O Mercy! A sad necessity of our fallen nature!).

But when he reads the words "die" "Death" "dead" he lays them down squarely in the middle of the refectory with satisfaction and with finality. A truly Trappist mixture of piety, rigorism, and totally unconscious self-righteousness.

I have noticed how one of the most austere members of the community – at any rate, one who insists most on austerity, eats his food very slowly after mashing it all up like the food of a baby.

Bobbie A, a boy who came yesterday for two weeks – during his vacation. Is about 15 with all the seriousness of 15: but serious about lizards, snakes, salamanders, birds, butterflies, all living, creeping, and flying things. We were out in the woods a little on my day of recollection and talking to him about these things was as good as praying.

He walks along through the long grass looking seriously ahead of him and catching things as he goes along and talking all the time about them. I wonder if he is not the best material I have yet seen. He has absolutely no pretenses, no artificiality; he is purely and simply a 15 year old boy. Not pious, not anything. I wonder if he will be so completely good when he is 18 and enters the monastery.

At present he comes swinging into choir at the wrong end after the office has started and gets adroitly to his place with no concern for monastic gravity. Which I will have to tell him.

Frankly, Ovid had terrible taste. Yet in the *Metamorphoses* there are some wonderful things mixed up with ponderously comical lapses into crudity. The goddesses who are able to sustain their nobility for twenty lines and then break down into slapstick and hit someone in the face with a dead fish. Followed by the inevitable change into a plant, a brook, a newt, a frog, a tree. But I ought to keep quiet and look at it again in Latin.

August 20, 1957. F. of St. Bernard

> If you call one thing vile and another precious,
> If you praise success and blame failure,
> You will fill the world with thieves, lawyers
> And businessmen.
> I have praised the saints and have told at what cost
> They surpassed lesser men.
> What folly I have preached in sermons!
> Because of my saints and their virtues
> My brother has become
> A thief, a lawyer, or a businessman.

August 29, 1957

I do not read enough. I only pretend to read.

All morning, a tractor has been worrying that little triangle of land down by the road – a plot scarcely big enough to turn around in. The dust clouds get bigger and bigger and the fury of the tractor is almost hidden from view. It must be fun for somebody.

"La Théanthropie est une forme particulière de la connaissance que la Divinité a de Soi-même à travers la humanité, et que la humanité a de soi-même à travers la Divinité; elle est la fusion du Créateur et du crée, laquelle apparait ensemble

comme la kénose de la Divinité et la divinisation de l'humanité, et s'achève par la glorification parfaite du Dieu-Homme." ["Theanthropy is a particular form of knowledge that divinity has of itself in relation to humanity and humanity has of itself in relation to divinity. It is the fusion of creator and creature which appears as kenosis (emptying) in divinity and divinization in humanity and expresses itself through the perfect glorification of the God-Man."]

Bulgakov. p. 169.

LATIN AMERICAN FOUNDATION

A letter from Fr. Lawrence's friend Kinlock (who grows ipecac root in the jungle by the San Juan river in Nicaragua) spoke of the island of Ometepe in the great lake of Nicaragua as the best place for a Cistercian foundation.

Mark Twain saw the island of Ometepe and compared it to a circus tent – with one volcano higher than the other.

Fr. Lawrence flew over Ometepe in 1954 and saw the active volcano in eruption. The other volcano is inactive.

We could grow coffee and sugar cane and oranges and lemons and papayas and everything done on the side of the inactive volcano.

Colombia There would be a wonderful place near Medellin in Antioquia or in the Cauca Valley. Not too high for work. High enough for cool weather and coffee, etc. Bogota too high? or Tunja? Or the mountains between Bogota and Tunja?

The great problem of every South American project – entering a country where the hierarchy in fact always supported conservatism, injustice, and tyranny. And in that environment, without silly politics and without going outside the limits of one's vocation, being on the side of progress and social justice. For instance, something for the Indians in the Sierra region of Ecuador.

Clinic. Cooperative. Reunions of intellectuals, such as they have at Toumliline in Morocco.

In a word – the great problem of justice and truth and humility.

Venezuela – Perhaps the best country for us to start in. More our speed. Better chance of a good beginning. Transportation no difficulty. Probably more able to use machines – break them down and repair them with our usual abandon. We should use machines but wisely and not extravagantly.

Near Caracas or near Valencia or near Maracay.

Or in the mountains overlooking the lake of Valencia.

Or on the other slope looking at the sea.

Or near Barquisimeto – a most fascinating name.

It gets better and better when I think of the Andes around Merida.

I am fascinated by the pictures of the Gran Sabana of Venezuela, but come on, lets be practical.

Paraguay – I weep to think of it. No abbot I can think of would risk starting in Paraguay. It would be a medieval foundation with lots of mosquitoes. Fr. Bede says the Brazilian ambassador to Asuncion worked always in a cape of mosquito netting.

There have been 19 postulants since May, not counting the kids who came for a week or two, or for a few days, but who went to choir and to work with the novices.

September 3, 1957

A phenomenal weekend. It was 100 on Sunday, Sept. 1, in the shade of the cedars by the cemetery. Still that hot today.

Sunday afternoon, depressed, reading Job with great satisfaction in the woodshed.

I had come across, in a pious book, a statement of one Msgr. Hulst who before his death is reported to have said something like this: "I have never denied God a moment of my time. *I hope He will take that into account*"!!

In other words, God had better take the good works of the Monsignor into account or else . . .

Later I was comforted to find the same thing, more or less, on the lips of one of Job's friends. Right at the beginning, Eliphaz, mildly shocked, asks (B de Jerusalem)

> *Ta piété, ne te donne-t-elle pas confiance,*
> *ta vie integre ne fait-elle pas ton assurance?* (4:6)
> ["Is not your fear of God your confidence
> And the integrity of your ways, your hope?"]

What's the trouble, Job? Aren't you one of us?

I am thoroughly committed to the position that the words of Eliphaz are a blasphemy – Even if I had good works to trust in, I wouldn't dare trust in them.

Departure of F. Berchmans who finally laughed and laughed all day long.

And one to California – Richard Ranger who for some purely coincidental reason associated in my mind with Nicaragua – and with Peru. One day in direction he sang me some fantastic thing that was sung by an Inca woman somewhere – a series of jungle calls!

Then F. Amadeus to the brothers. I will miss him but everything will be quieter and *it has to be quieter.*

In Julien Green.

"La religion est mal comprise. Elle rend stupides ceux qui se veulent pieux afin le pouvoir s'admirer dans cet état. Il faudrait se perdre complètement au Dieu, il faudrait le silence parfait, le silence surnaturel. Les pieux discors ont quelque chose de revoltant." ["Religion is not understood. Those who wish themselves pious, in order to admire themselves in this state, are made stupid by religion. What is needed is to lose ourselves completely in God; what is needed is perfect silence; supernatural silence. Pious talk has something revolting about it."][14]

Beautifully quiet and cool in the novitiate conference room – everyone so good. For once it is like paradise. It hasn't rained yet (not for weeks).

September 10, 1957

Rained all night. Rained the day after Our Lady's feast.

I was on the night watch. Sat half asleep under the shelter in the *Preau* and as I nodded the rain became like a huge aviary full of parrots and I woke up again.

In Louisville last Friday. Yvo (the workman) drove me in. He went to see his "kinfolks." Talked volubly after his visit to them and drove madly, jamming on the brakes in traffic just in time to avoid climbing up on the car ahead.

Some statement of Yvo . . . "When Father Gettlefinger works in that field he works like he was killing snakes."

About an accident of Joe Carroll (family brother – brakes of dump truck full of cement went out on the hill going down to High Grove. Joe landed in somebody's frontyard covered with cement). The lady of the house said: "He tried to whistle and he couldn't whistle. He tried to sing and he couldn't sing. He tried to talk and he couldn't talk. He couldn't do nothing and he looked like a nigger with that cement all over him."

Yvo expressed contempt for those who follow a golf ball around a golf course. One way in town we passed the golf course in Bardstown (on account of a detour) and he said "When we come back tonight this way,

[14] This is Merton's own translation as he published it *Conjectures of a Guilty Bystander.*

they'll be there" and when we came back in the evening, he said, "See – there they are!"

The Baptist preacher walking around in the cathedral.

Went to Terrell Dickey about layouts for a postulant's pamphlet. Bembo for body type if they can get it and Venice for headings but don't tell anybody. He kept kidding me about wanting a modern layout. And gave me a huge magazine called *Holiday* all about South America written mostly by "that ass" V. S. Pritchett (Waugh called him that). So for all I know about it is that for Pritchett, South America is a "body blow." Well, for me too. Even the magazine is that.

Reading John of the Cross again, fundamentals in the *Ascent* to avoid getting too many such body blows. "When you live by your eyes and ears as I do . . ." says Pritchett. Hungry for experiences, which is what he accused me of being.

Is it more damned hypocrisy to wonder if I ought to refuse to let 37 meditations[15] to be published? Because I will probably end with my right hand publishing it without my left hand knowing what I am doing – and leaving the sorrow until afterwards, when it won't do any good.

No easy generalizations about Job and Zen. Job is a big koan. So is everything else.

Best book yet about Ecuador – Bemelman's – *The Donkey Inside* – which I got in the Louisville library.

September 11, 1957. Protus and Hyacinth, Eunuchs and Saints
A picture of Rimbaud. Verlaine shot him in the wrist and had to go to jail for two years. Deeply moved by the story of Rimbaud and his character – and his exile in Africa, etc.

A satanic theology (some of which Rimbaud had to learn somewhere and France is full of it) – hides Christ from us or makes him vanish or makes him too beautiful, too remote. He was man like us. "Oh yes! But he was God, He was *not like you.* He suffered; well, he seemed to suffer. But he knew he was God. He knew *he was not like you.* All his life long he was

[15] Eventually published as *Thoughts in Solitude.*

looking around at the men he had come to save knowing that he *was not like them*, death could not hold him, and he did not really have to pray. He just prayed for show." Satan has made Incarnation into a monumental hypocrisy. And that is the tragedy of Rimbaud's gospel meditations – the despair of one who feels that to be poor and miserable is to be damned and excluded, who feels that the "beautiful" Divine Master is sent to save one or two and drive the rest deeper into despair. Christ is never on that side of the fence. Rimbaud, with only a little less contempt in his life, would have the face of a saint and who will say that the bitterness was his fault?

Docetism, Jansenism; the revelations of the Sacred Heart did not use these heresies; some of the "faithful" used them to make things worse.

If Christ is not my brother, with all my sorrows and all my sufferings and all my miseries and *with all my human limitations*, then there has been no redemption. Then what happened on Calvary was only magic and the miracles were magic without purpose.

September 13, 1957

Letter of the general on poverty. How little we understand it, especially in America. How little *I* understand it. And I remain uneasy after reading and hearing all the more or less exterior presentations on Religious poverty. Some more strict, some less so. Strictness, by itself, is not the solution.

Sure, you have to be *poor*. Poor with Christ.

Even Charles De Foucauld does not seem to have the satisfactory answer. There is something wooden about it.

Where poverty really makes sense is in the Gospel and in Jesus. And in St. Francis and St. Benedict – Poverty by itself is not poverty. Poverty sticking out like a sore thumb is not poverty. Poverty is only true when it is integrated in everything else – when it is saturated with humility – and can no longer see itself.

It works the other way too.

We have to be humble to be poor, poor to be humbled – we have to face the humiliation of poverty and transcend it.

Dom Alexis Presse – "*A l'école de St. Benoît*" ["In the School of St. Benedict"] has some very nice things – a good sense of balance everywhere. But not in his chapter on the office. Defending the Opus Dei on a kind of aristocratic basis – Opus Dei, in Latin, sung is far above what the base ordinary faithful would ordinarily like. All the rest – sentimentalism etc.

More and more I agree with Dom Gregorio. We need the psalms in *the vernacular.* We need a public prayer that can be appreciated without college courses in Latin, history, liturgy, etc. etc. A prayer that the *people* can understand. Useless to say that they are a bunch of fools.

September 15, 1957

St. John of the Cross on the desires. Easy is read, easy enough to understand the words, easy to misunderstand in practice. If one only knew beforehand, by experience, the freedom that is really meant by the saint. Not every desire hinders union with God although he says every desire does this.

But it must be a desire that is *voluntary* and contrary to God's will.

If we do not read him carefully, he seems to say that every desire is contrary to God's will.

Every desire is for a pleasure.

If we read him wrongly, we seem to hear him say that no pleasure is willed for us by God. Every pleasure prevents union with God.

Every voluntary and *sinful* pleasure . . . Yes.

But if God wills no pleasure, every pleasure is sinful.

No. There can be pleasures that please God.

"Every pleasure that presents itself to the senses if it is not purely for the honor and glory of God must be renounced . . ."

(Hence there can be such a thing as a pleasure which is *purely* for the honor and glory of God.)

How can we tell?

"If there presents itself to a man the pleasure of listening to things that tend not to the service of God . . ."

"If there presents itself the pleasure of looking at things that help him not Godward . . ."[16]

What things tend to the service of God – keep us "Godward"?

That is the whole heart of the matter.

If I say categorically in advance, without qualification, that this refers only to things in themselves pious or *considered pious by pious people* etc. . . . or considered holy by third rate "holy" books – then, disaster.

---

[16] These sentence fragments come from John of the Cross's *The Ascent of Mount Carmel*, Book I, chapter 13, 4–6.

One immediately seeks the living among the dead.

And this is what happens to people with *a priori* notions of what pleases God or "ought" to please Him. (Eating always displeases Him, fasting always pleases Him etc.) They end up by disobeying in everything or almost everything. The true will of God for us as Christ has taught it to us and St. Paul. Making void the law of God for the traditions of man.

St. John of the Cross himself leads readers into this misapprehension.

Where he says, "Strive always to choose not that which is easiest but that which is most difficult," he seems to be saying that the difficult is always the most perfect, the most pleasing to God and the easy is always imperfect – always less pleasing to God, always displeasing. The perfect equated with the hard and unpleasant. To say this is sometimes true is correct, To say it is *always* and necessarily so is FALSE! And that is the trouble.

We have got to remember that certain desires and certain pleasures are willed for us by God.

That is humility to accept this fact and pride to refuse to take it.

That it is often more perfect to do what is simply normal and human than to try to act like an angel when God does not will it.

I think it is impractical for me to fly from "every desire" and "every pleasure" that is not explicitly pious or religious.

I think that in my own life and in my own experience it has been shown that for me, the pleasure of reading and writing poetry within certain limits "helps me Godward" and refraining from doing this altogether on the pretext that it not according to the ordinary notion of what a Trappist ought to do – or a contemplative ought to do – does not "help me Godward" or helps me to be a monk or a contemplative.

The same goes for reading – for me it seems to be better to read almost anything and everything.

It certainly does not seem to me that what goes on in my head when I am being purely and totally "pious" and "mortified" gives any glory to God. Because then I am not totally human, much less a saint.

For others who are human enough to be saints without losing any of their humanity it is alright to do things that seem inhuman. For one as deficient as I am the ordinary ways are safe – I mean they are a safer and surer way to *sanctity*.

I mean the ordinary ways of religious *men* – not for what at present is beyond the normal for a monk. What may be good for me might be very bad for another.

September 16, 1957

In the refectory "The Western Fathers." Soon get tired of Sulpicius Severus and the miracles of St. Martin, but on the other hand the life of St. Ambrose is severe and impressive. Wonderful picture of the world of sober and efficient priests in which Ambrose lived and of which he was the center. His energy and sense – one has the feeling of reading about the kind of person we need in the world today.

Father Linus reads well. Serious and businesslike and no striving for any kind of effect. For once I leave the refectory edified.

September 17, 1957

Colombian coffee, brought by Fr. Restrepo, finally got to us in the (infirm) refectory. Even though it was not hot coffee or iced coffee but just came cold or half cold, without ice or cream, it was still the best coffee I had ever tasted.

As for Fr. Restrepo – a gay person – he has gone to Boston to take his little brother Javier, who is ill, to see a specialist.

Having seen something of the Restrepos and read a little more about the subject, I think that all around Colombia would be the best place for a foundation (though Ecuador in itself might be more interesting). All I have said about Venezuela I take back as having probably been quite crazy.

Near Medellin or near Cali or near Papayan.

Probably near Medellin.

If it were not to satisfy my own desires, near Papayan and thereby near Ecuador.

If wishes were horses . . .

September 22, 1957

I wonder if it is a sin against poverty to read the poems of St. John Perse. They are magnificent. Immensely rich. To read such poems is to be a millionaire, to live in splendor. Your heart becomes a palace, full of all that is fine in the world.

Exile, the first that I read, my discovery, months ago, I still like the best.

More perfect and spontaneous delight in *Crusoe* – moves one more personally, more intimately. Such joy in reading it.

Only *Stages* has let me down a little so far – it is halting and does not have the sustained grandeur of the rest.

I write this in the woodshed, surrounded by charred and sweet smelling wood of broken up whiskey barrels. Not ours, naturally!

Rev. Father writes from General Chapter. The two superiors from Yugoslavia were there. Which made everything around much more serious. Dom Walter and Dom Anthony, my fellow novices, there for the first time. Dom Robert still in Paris but recovering.

The general's letter on poverty. Long and exhausting. Though it said *everything* one could possibly say about religious poverty – is practically a textbook on religious poverty – I felt that something was missing. Maybe what was missing was not something in the letter but something in myself.

Anyway, I begin again the usual, inarticulate, helpless stock-taking.

In advance I know it is alright – that though I don't quite know what is coming off in my "spiritual life" God knows and has everything in hand. What is poverty? What is love?

Not to be talked about; that is certain.

Perhaps you begin to possess them when you are no longer able to speak of them (knowing that you have never possessed either).

Maybe what was missing in the General's letter: the realization that none of us will ever really be poor – or that we are so poor already that no attempt to forget our poverty in monies and possessions makes us anything but poorer.

God help the man who seriously thinks that he will be able to reach the point in "stripping himself" at which, as a result of his stripping he will suddenly "become a contemplative."

Tremendous religious power and purity of St. John Perse's *Rain*.

Four lines like the prophetic books of Blake, but a sane and ordered Blake in communication with the world.

I mean the lines: "*Dressez, dressez, à bout de caps, les catafalques du Hapsbourg, les hauts bûchers de l'homme de guerre, les hauts ruchers de l'imposture etc. etc.*" ["Raise up, raise up, at the end of promontories, the Hapsburg catafalques, the tall pyres of the man of war, the tall apiaries of imposture."]

St. J. P. writes like the prophets of the Old Testament and like the Greeks at the same time. But never copies them, never mimics them, never borrows their expressions. It is all new and his own. A great effort of sincerity and detachment.

September 29, 1957

Mark and Dorothy Van Doren[17] were here yesterday on their way to Illinois – long enough to walk to the cowbarn and back and for me to show Mark the novitiate.

I was happy to have him stand in these rooms, so wise a person and lean against the bookshelf in the scriptorium and talk about some things that had come up when he was at the Hampton Institute the day before. The English professor there complained that his students had no preparation to face Shakespeare and Mark said that everyone is prepared to read Shakespeare by the time they are 18. They have been born, they have had fathers, mothers; they had been loved, feared, hated, been jealous, etc.

At the cowbarn we looked at brushfires being lit along the hillside of St. Bernard's field and Mark talked about his love for fires and mine. We decided that everybody loves fires and those who admit it are not pyromaniacs, but just love fires reasonably.

Lax has been ill – somehow paralyzed for a couple of months (?) but better now and going to stay with the Van Dorens in Connecticut.

He knows and admires St. John Perse who lives in Washington.

St. John Perse had always thought of Cape Hatteras as a legendary terrible place like Cape Horn and the first thing he wanted to see when he came to Washington years ago was Cape Hatteras. Sure enough, the day he was there, a terrible storm raged, ships were destroyed, etc. You see.

A doctor was called out one night and came back exhausted after working with the patient the night long. "I have had a terrible time with the delivery of a child called Victor Hugo." (It is a story [illegible] I had never heard.)

When I talked a moment about Bulgakov Mark quoted the wonderful lines at the end of Dante where he sees in Christ the face of man and the Face of God and they are one face "but to explain it is as hard as to square the circle."

They were pleased that both their sons had married Jews this Summer and I too.

---

[17] Mark Van Doren (1894–1972), professor of English at Columbia University, had been Merton's mentor and close friend.

And we talked of this crazy race business in Arkansas and everywhere, a problem that has been created by politicians.

October 5, 1957

Dom Robert died in Paris on the 3rd, when they thought he was getting well enough to take the plane back to America. Rev. Father full of contempt for the French hospital. (He also remarked that no one he saw in France had a dehydrator for hay. We have one. He is very proud of it.)

I try occasionally to read the French translation of *Ascent to Truth* in ms. P. François de St. Marie has done much to clean it up and put it in order; it is still an abominable book.[18] Almost no theological insight and no spirit. Tedious and stupid and a waste of paper. And nothing can be done short of rewriting it. Or burning it. And I can no longer do that, after all the trouble so many people have taken to get it published. Yet I don't feel honest in letting it be published either. Another stupid compromise. Saying so, doesn't help much.

I tried to say something about Dom Robert to the novices and could not think of much except generalities: "He was kind. He was a man of faith. He loved the Bl. Sacrament." In truth, he was a very plain person. The adjective "plain" is sometime used as a condemnation of a person. He was not plain in that sense. But he was a long time in the Order and had a lot to do with a great many people in it. And the longer a person lives in the Order the less there is to say about him and his life. What one says becomes more and more vague, more and more general. Perhaps that is at it should be. Certainly it is, at least on paper.

I need not say, for instance:

"Well, he had a big chin. He talked rather slowly."

One thing that impressed me about him – I don't know why. When he was here a year ago, showed little or no interest in anything about the house, least of all in the renovated novitiate. Yet he had been novice master here for about 25 years.

The warblers are coming through now. Very hard to identify them all, even with field glasses and a bird book. (Have seen at least one that is definitely

[18] Published as *La montée vers la lumière* (Paris: Albin Michel, 1958). Merton supplied an introduction.

not in the bird book.) Watching one which I took to be a Tennessee warbler. A beautiful, neat, prim little thing – seeing this beautiful thing which people do not usually see, looking into this world of birds, which is not concerned with us or with our problems. I felt very close to God or felt religious awe anyway. Watching those birds was as food for meditation or as mystical reading. Perhaps better.

Also the beautiful, unidentified red flower or fruit I found on a bud yesterday. I found a bird in the woods yesterday on the feast of St. Francis. Those things say so much more than words.

Mark was saying "The birds don't know they have names."

Watching them I thought: who cares what they are called? But do I have the courage not to care? Why not be like Adam, in a new world of my own, and call them by my own names?

That would still mean that I thought the names were important.

No name and no word to identify the beauty and reality of those birds today, is the gift of God to me in letting me see them.

(And that name – God – is no name! It is like a letter. X or Y. Yawheh is a better Name – it finally means Nameless One.)

October 7, 1957

The last chapter of Baruch, the first chapters of Ezechiel.

And a marvelous article by Evdokimov on *Ikons*. The best spiritual (or any other) reading I have done in ages. New perspectives. They are rare and hard to come by. This article deeply moving; I want to read it over and over. How rare it is to find such theology! And it moves one to a deep examination of conscience for my escape into secularism. (Still the South American reading has its place, unless I am totally deceived. It will mean something some day.)

October 11, 1957

"Whoever seeks Christ without the Church, putting his trust in his own insight and what goes by the name of criticism, deprives himself of all possibility of finding the living Christ . . . The Christian Community is nothing more than Christ's power of resurrection working on in history, Christ eternal unfolding Himself in history, the fullness of Christ . . . The Church would have been able to give the living image of Christ to us even without the bible because the content of faith is, to such a vast degree, this very image . . . Christ is as near to us today as He was to Peter . . . The source of my faith is to be found where the Pentecostal Spirit breathes – in the community of the Holy Spirit, in the company of the Saints, in the Church as the Pentecostal congregation." *Karl Adam.*

Beautiful and deeply moving preface to Eugenio Zolli's autobiography in the refectory. Father Augustine says that the rest of the book is not so good. Fr. Bede said he met Zolli at Rome when they went down from San Anselmo to visit the Synagogue. The life of St. Germanus was good but on the whole everyone seemed glad we were done with "The Western Fathers."

Bright Fall weather today, brilliant blue sky, leaves beginning to fall – one begins to be glad of a little sun to sit in.

Read St. John Perse's poem on his childhood in Martinique again – it is one of his greatest.

> *Ici les fouets, et là le cri de l'oiseau Annao – et là encore la blessure
>   des cannes au moulin.*
> *Et un nuage*
> *violet et jaune, couleur d'icaque, s'il s'arrêtait soudain à couronner
>   le volcan d'or,*
> *appelait-par-leur-nom, du fond des cases,*
> *les servantes.*
> [Here the whips and there the cry of the Annao bird – there
>   again the wound of the sugarcane at the mill
> And a cloud
> violet and yellow like the coco-plum if it stops suddenly to
>   crown in the gold the volcano,
> called by their names out of the cabins,
> the servant women.]

Thought for a moment of Marx and writing a poem about Marx. Maybe I am not big enough, deep enough, have not meditated and thought enough to attempt any such poem. It would have to be serious and not a flippant exploit since, after all, on his account, we are going to enter into our most terrible and perhaps last war. This is NO time for kidding.

October 13, 1957

"The real root of every heresy is to be found not in the sphere of revelation but in the pagan philosophies." *Karl Adam.*

October 22, 1957

Mirum est quod homo potest umquam perfecte in hac vita laetari, qui suum exilium et tam multa pericula animae suae considerat et . . . . [It is a cause of wonder that anyone who thinks about his exile and the dangers to his soul could be happy in this life.] *(Imit Xt)* *[The Imitation of Christ].*

Wrote to Dom Leclercq probably much too late about 37 *Meditations.*

Interviewed Fr. Linus' brother in the guest house about vocation. Thinks and talks slowly and maybe that is very good. Anyway, he seems smart.

Beautiful churches in a valley in Andorra, in an issue of *Zodiaque* which came yesterday.

Fr. Enrique Aguilar, a Franciscan at St. Bonaventure [University] has sent a long poem, a dialogue of creatures about beauty and love. It turns out he is from Cali, Colombia.

Fr. Restrepo still in Boston.

Fr. Girald, at the Javeriana in Bogota, invited me to stop there in case I am sent to Colombia prospecting for foundations at Ogala!

Rev. Father in Georgia for the election of the new abbot today.

Waiting for proofs of the postulants guide.

And for something from Frank Kacmarcik[19] about the other booklet we are printing in St. Paul.

During high mass thought for a moment, with horror – what if I should be elected abbot in Georgia and what if, in spite of everything, the election was confirmed? Thought of that huge white elephant of an unfinished church – and the cement burial vaults reserved for abbots in the crypt. And all of the rest of that enormous building. And the huge reservoirs of restlessness and conflict which I suspect to be present in that (or any other) community but perhaps most especially that one. Everyone from there seems to be living under a terrific strain – at least the ones I have met lately. Fr. Joachim seems to thrive on it, of course and he is the logical one for abbot or Dom Augustine.

A thrilling and terrifying and fascinating book – *The Third Eye* by a Tibetan lama who calls himself Rimpoche Rampa. Life in the lamasery and their religion in general sounds like something out of ancient Egypt – the

[19] A noted liturgical artist with whom Merton corresponded; the booklet was *Monastic Peace.*

Old Kingdom.[20] Everything centered on death. Getting the monk to the other shore by telepathy. Or rather, to their next incarnation. Astrology. The fascinating names of the years. I forgot what this one is – "Firebird" I think. Fr. Sebastian suggests we play Stravinsky's "Firebird" in honor of the year. Next year what? Wood dog or Wood hog. I suspect these are bad years – the dull demands taking the dull animals. The Iron Ox, 1961 – which may turn out to be the year of the foundation and 1984 – fire Dragon – the year, he says, of the cataclysm.

The indifference to human life. The nun flying in kites (a breath taking chapter). The fantastic training. I like the Dream karma and the opening of the "Third Eye" which enables the monk to see the aura of others. Everything complete with secret passages and an underground lake. But in the end his astral travels were, I fear, a bit too much to swallow.

And now for Dom Marmion.[21]

October 24, 1957

One has either got to be a Jew or stop reading the bible. For the bible really cannot make sense to anyone who is not spiritually a "Semite." The spiritual sense of the Old Testament is not and cannot be first an emptying out of its Israelitic content. The New Testament is the fulfillment of the Old, not its destruction. The fulfillment of the promises made to Abraham, the promises Abraham believed in.

Hence, the last chapters of Ezechiel – his Torah – the dimensions of the Temple, The City, etc. far from being meaningless are the most successful part of the book. It is not that they refer to "the church and not to Jerusalem" – for the Church *is* Jerusalem. The Jerusalem which is above is not Jerusalem. The City of David is all the more the City of David for being the city of David's Son.

Hence, the terrible mystery of the persecution of Israel in our time. *Salus ex Judaeis.* [Salvation comes from the Jews.] Christ crucified again in His people "according to the flesh." Israel remains the Servant of Yahweh even though Jesus has fulfilled the type in Isaias. Israel is still His people even though Israel has denied Him.

Is Job, perhaps though a pagan, something to do with Israel? The One who seems to deny God in his tribulation? At the same time, Job is Christ, who does not "come down from the cross."

[20] Merton notes in margin, "This turned out to be a hoax."
[21] Traditional spiritual reading; Dom Marmion was one of the "approved" authors.

Dark, rainy autumn day. Loud rain in the night brought great joy after long drought. The dark clouds are joyful also.

Novices tear out the dead tomato plants killed by the first frost.

We have planted dogwoods and maples and redbuds and pines all over the hills and in the worthless lot by the woodshed.

Fr. Lawrence (Cardenal) struggles with the Spanish translation of 7 *Storey Mountain*, trying to correct it. It is crawling with absurd mistakes.

Zolli in the refectory is sometimes dull but in general deeply moving. Sometimes the mysticism is a bit vapid but when he gets back into the concrete, it is fine again.

How can we sing the psalms, or understand them, if we are not Jews?

Psallite sapienter [Sing praises with a psalm (Psalm 46:7)] – in the Spirit, not in the flesh. Yes, but one can get too far away from the suffering and yearning of Israel in the flesh and these are inseparable from the Spirit. I think for example of Koestler and the Zionists. His work *Thieves in the Night* which is tremendous. And very loyal to the truth.

October 25, 1957

Fr. Restrepo arrived today, tired, in the bus from Boston. Was glad to see him. It is, he says, as cold here as it ever gets in Bogota. He brought a copy of *Seeds of Contemplation* autographed by Archbishop Cushing who called him crazy for entering here.

How mortally ashamed I am of those 37 *Meditations*. Dry verbiage. What you should do, what you should do. Here is the answer. This and this and this. The mind and the will and the instincts and the emotions and the passions and the imagination and the desires and the appetites and the conscience and the virtues and the law of God and every man is a heap of abstractions. Phooey!

Let's begin reading Isaias and get serious for a change.

Have got to make an entirely new start, as a writer – or stop writing except for fun. Stop dogmatizing, anyway.

Yesterday Rev. Father said the abbot of Martories, who is a Uruguyan, has received an offer of a property near Medellin, Colombia and that he could not take it. But that he would refer the offer to us. Maybe he has forgotten.

The ending of *Thieves in the Night* is something of an anticlimax. A very useful book for monks who can read such books. Insights on community life. Joseph the cellarer. The Psalms – they are something special when read through Zionist glasses. As I say, one has to sing them as a Jew, or not at all.

October 26, 1957
"Ten years of my life have been consumed in correspondence and litigation about my book *Dubliners*. It was rejected by 40 publishers; three times set up and once burnt. It cost me about 3,000 francs in postage, fees, train and boat fare for I was in correspondence with 110 newspapers, 7 solicitors, 3 societies, 40 publishers and several men of letters about it. All refused me except for Ezra Pound."   *Letter of James Joyce to John Quinn. 10 July 1912.*
[The whole first edition of *Dubliners* was burnt.]

Cold rain and snowflakes, in a wild wind.

And in the woodshed with the communal raincoat over my shoulders and was very happy, full of coffee, after Tierce. The wailing wall, blacker and blacker, and the weeping willow standing at the corner. This morning I went to the vault to go through the mss. I had left there and found the original mss. from which 37 *Meditations* had developed. But the original is not bad. With the disorganized spontaneity it had when I wrote the stuff out in St. Anne's in the Winter of 1953 mostly. I think the original left as it is, will be all right. Quite different from my edited and tortured version. It is the writing and pretense of system that makes it doctrinaire.

This morning there was a theological conference in chapter. F. Alphonse came out with a dignity befitting his age and after a very long silence began reading what he had written on the back of envelopes about Holy Communion and the Mystical Body. As the general tittering subsided and gave way to patient expectation of the finish, Fr. A went out persistently and almost unintelligibly to develop his theme. I for one practiced a little deep breathing five or six *pranayanas* and some square breathing – concentrated on the stream of air entering the nostrils. The time passed pleasantly with this and the Jesus prayer. At the end, the usual atmosphere of strain was intensified, as questions were asked for. Fr. Arnold complained that "Father might have brought in some quotes from the Fathers of the Church." Fr. Anastasius quoted something from Mersch's "Theology of the Mystical Body" and Fr. Vianney read two declarations – one from St. Teresa and the other, I think, from the present gloriously reigning pontiff. Fr. Timothy as moderator said, as usual, that it was a very good conference and even added that it might have been a little long. Everybody, I am sure, heartily disagreed with this last suggestion.

As usual, I felt extremely uncomfortable, with the sense of the complete falsity of the situation. Or rather, the complete inadequacy of the words and the talk and the total incomprehension of their connection with a present existential reality. The community itself in its pathetic tongue-tied witness to the discomfort and the glory of struggling to be one when we are the people we actually are!

Koestler says, "Poenitentiaries, concentration camps, monasteries, artist's colonies, ethnic minorities, tuberculosis sanatoriums, political and religious sects, all develop into little ghettos with a hot house atmosphere, a peculiar jargon, a private walled-in universe."

That's it. Fresh air.

My interior life has become a passion, perhaps a guilty passion, for fresh air.

Not just to break out of the ghetto, however. Not just to get fresh air for myself but to stay and let the fresh air in.

Perhaps the great Temptation is to think that if I entered another monastery in Colombia, in mountains, in a new place, it would not be a ghetto.

One reason why it is so hard to read Bernanos' *The Diary of a Country Priest* is breaking this ghetto wall. Don't mind the Jews in their ghetto – But *we* in *ours* – ! That is harder to stomach.

But Father! Our ghetto is so truly refined, it is a veritable paradise!

Fresh air!

October 27, 1957. Day of Recollection

There is nothing whatever of the ghetto spirit in the Rule of St. Benedict.

That is the wonderful thing both about the Rule and the saint. The freshness, the liberty, the spontaneity, the broadness, the sanity and the healthiness of early Benedictine life.

The same healthiness and sanity in the early commentaries – Smaragdus, Hildemar (and therefore Warnefaid).

But closed in on itself, interpreting interpretations of interpretations, the monastery becomes a ghetto.

Reforms that concentrate too excessively on a return to *strictness* do not in fact break the spell. They tend to increase the danger of spiritual suffocation. On the other hand, fresh air is not the air of the world . . .

Just to break out of the ghetto and walk down the boulevard is no solution.

The world has its own stink too – perfume and corruption.

The fresh air we need is the air of the Holy Spirit "breathing where He pleases" which means that the windows must be open and we must expect Him to come from any direction.

The error is to lock the windows and doors in order to keep the Holy Spirit in our house. The very action of locking doors and windows is fatal.

What about enclosure? What about the world?

St. Benedict never said that the monk must *never* go out, *never* receive guests, *never* talk to anyone, never hear *any* news – But that he should distinguish what is useless and harmful from what is useful and salutary, and in all things to glorify God.

October 30, 1957

"The 'People' are regarded through the Socialist Bureaucracy's eyes as a target for propaganda, not as a living reality whose interests, tastes, foibles must be understood and shared if you wish to change the face of the world. The Socialist party bosses or most of them come from the people but were not of the people; they tried to control or manipulate man without identifying themselves with him. Their voice was the voice of the pamphlet or the lecturer at the evening school – not the voice of a new humanity."

Koestler.

October 31, 1957

"The man who does not in his heart protest against obvious baseness and does not passionately try to suppress it whenever he can is not a moral man." *K. Adam.*

However I do not accept at all the context from which this statement comes – K. Adam's portrait of a "choleric" Jesus.

November 2, 1957

Some seem to want to make of this a feast of death, with much rattling of bones and lots of skulls. The cult of cemeteries. In piety towards the dead more than in everything else the lack of taste and of religious feeling comes in to corrupt the true Christian spirit. And with great satisfaction we make of All Soul's Day a day excessively devoted to gloating over the punishment of our Dead.

They rest in Christ. The cemetery is a symbol of Christ. To rest in Christ is to live (hence the evergreens. Cypresses are not supposed to suggest melancholy thoughts but just the opposite). But they do not yet live fully in Him. What Purgatory is we neither know nor understand, but why regard it as a supernatural reform school?

The procession to the cemetery was quiet and beautiful – a slight haze in the air and sun shining through it and shining on the hills, all the trees yellow and dirty bronze for in Kentucky they tend just to dry out rather than change color. Coming out into the air from the Chapter Room, singing the *Libera,* the voices suddenly deadened and hushed by the open space (no more echo).

Over under the cedars stood pathetically that little boy, a family brother, who was dismissed from the Brothers novitiate for being weak-minded. He watched the procession and as we passed handed a note to someone.

And so we came back into the building, chanting the penitential psalms.

I must get to know something of modern physics. Even though I am a monk, that is no reason for living in a Newtonian universe, or worse still, an Aristotelian one. The fact that the cosmos is not quite what St. Thomas and Dante imagined it to be has, after all, some importance. It does not invalidate St. Thomas or Dante or Catholic theology. But it ought to be understood and taken into account by a theologian. It is futile to try and live in an expanding universe with atomic fission an ever present possibility and try to think and act exclusively as if the cosmos were fixed in an immutable order centered upon man's earth. Modern physics has its repercussions in the monastery and to be a monk one must take them into account, although that does nothing whatever to make one's spirituality either simple or neat.

One must get along without the security of neat and simple ready-made solutions. There are things one has to think out, all over again, for oneself.

November 5, 1957

Douglas Hyde says the missionaries in Asia are the shock troops of the Church, which I am perfectly willing to believe. Fr. Philip Crosbie, the

Australian Columban Father, who was a prisoner in Korea, a case in point! Yet Fr. Columban here, who came from the same society and was formed in the same place in Australia, says they receive little or no spiritual training. Seminary discipline (under Jesuits) and intellectual formation, yes. But . . .

Yet, at the same time who, among the Trappists here, would be capable of bearing up under persecution as Fr. Crosbie??

"Of course he had a special grace."

An answer which is, in fact, an evasion. Or is there an answer at all?

To be trained spiritually is to be trained in cooperation with grace. Or does training matter after all? God is master of these gifts. And is that an answer?

Do we receive, need I give, a spiritual training?

November 6, 1957

Very satisfied with Karl Adam's Scotist solution of the problem raised by Christ's statement that not even the Son knows the hour of the last judgment. Distinction between natural and *habitual* possession of *scientia visionis* [the knowledge of the (beatific) vision]. Christ would know all Truth necessarily and as He applied his mind to it, according to the will of the Father, and He had not yet looked to see this one thing which the Father had not yet willed Him to know and reveal.

This really fits the text and spirit of the gospels.

Perhaps we are really now on the eve of a most terrible war – the worst one of all.

Everyone who can crawl will be in on it, said Fr. Henderson who is colonel in the Chaplain's Corps and ought to know.

It is now (or so it seems) to the Russians' interest to start a war. They think themselves strong and probably are. They think us to be unprepared and no one doubts for a moment that they are right. It is in a sense greatly to our credit that we are not prepared and in another sense it is great folly because this is no longer the kind of world in which good will and good intentions have any political significance.

Our helplessness to read and understand the Signs of the Times. It is not comfortable to realize that we are now the ones who have eyes to see and do not see, ears to hear and do not hear. The political language of the world has been taken over by somebody else and what we say no longer means anything. There have been new words coined, new kinds of meaning, oriented not to thought but to political pressure. Opportunistic symbols and signals for action different from our kind of action. The Capitalist world is terrified and inert. Yet it will eventually do and say something, no one knows what. And the others, with their incantations and whatever may be behind their rituals. No use talking about it. What do I know anyway? I of all people.

What strikes me most is the lack of communication with Russia and what is outside the Russian sphere. Communists and non-Communists. The advantages and tragedies of segregation. Millions of soldiers with a completely illusory idea of the enemy they are called upon to fight. It is fantastic and yet perhaps it is a very old situation – Christendom vs Islam!

No use thinking much about it.

Dark morning, low clouds, wild rain, wind and silence.

Will it happen before Christmas?

I look at the big sycamore by the mill and wonder if I will end up a chaplain or what – the enormous work that is to be done.

It seems today that my life as a writer and even as a monk is almost over. And the last job that needs to be done, before I die, makes its approach and its urgency – a job outside all monasteries.

Perhaps this will all go away again like the clouds or the hawks. Now, again, at last, I see and appreciate this silence I have been living in. This afternoon is very quiet, at least in this valley in Kentucky.

November 6, 1957

"The history of philosophy is the history of human inquiry and human error, not the history of Truth. Truth has no history. It is an eternal present, the Word of Jesus." *Karl Adam.*

November 11, 1957

Yesterday and today in the refectory first a news article about the two sputniks and the dog in the second one. Then Eisenhower's speech about science and defense – a fantastic future which, I suppose, we have to take for granted from now on.

It has been unusually cold – down to 20 at night. Very cold in church with Summer cowls and no heat. But warm in the novitiate.

If there is one place where an altar facing the people would be justified it is the novitiate chapel. Yet it is not enough for people to "feel like" having such an altar. (The one in the crypt, for example, tucked away in a corner under the stairs, certainly does not make much sense, although the Brothers go to communion there.) Would it be right to give the novices here and get them used to it, "form" them for that kind of outlook and then let them loose in a community where they would never see such a thing again, most probably?

Joyce's *Letters* (sent them back to Louisville today) – a very fine book. Especially enjoyed his letters to his family – Lucia, Giorgio. A great and good person, hounded by a lot of narrow minded idiots. That generation and that world have almost vanished now. The picture of Joyce and family, as if they were all going to step out together in a fantastic dance. Joyce's passion for singing and singers. I want to read *Finnegans Wake* the way I want to hear good music. Patience, man. Mortify yourself in something. The quiet in the cannery this afternoon was, for once, as good as music and more healing to my soul.

Joyce's *Letters* were better than all the mail I didn't get at All Saints.

November 12, 1957

Necessity of the Bible. More and more of it.

A book like Gillet's *Thèmes bibliques* fantastically rich and useful. Every line has something in it you do not want to miss. Opens up new roads in the Old Testament.

Extraordinary richness and delicacy of the varied OT concepts of sin – very *existential* concepts, not at all mere moralism! For instance sin as a "failure" to contact God. *Peccavi tibi.* "I have failed Thee – I have failed to reach Thee." And all that follows from that!

Importance of reading and thinking and keeping silent. Self-effacement, not in order to be left looking at oneself but to be "found in Christ" and lost to the rest.

Yet – not by refusing to take interest in anything vital.

Politics vital – even for monks. But in this, due place and with right measure.

To live in a monastery as if the world had stopped turning in 1905 – a fatal illusion.

November 14, 1957

Rain all night and a heavy wind out of the South. Buffeting the novitiate chapel during Mass, running headlong into it like a large, soft, live thing, sweeping and brushing all the walls and pounding all the windows. When day came the wind was already gentler and it was good to see all the fields washed with rain and the grass deep in puddles of rain after so many dry weeks. The wind tore off and smashed a shutter of the postulant's room in Hogan's alley.

Koestler, who gives an impression of great frailty, writes two pages a day or perhaps four in some eight hours of work. [Graham] Greene the same. And Julien Green's difficulties too. I view my frailty with alarm. Or rather, I ought to be content to work a little harder and a lot more patiently when I write. The fact that I have to revise a line does not mean that I have come to the end of my rope. Or should not.

The things a religious person needs to think about. One of them is Communism. Absolute necessity to understand the Communist mentality. To ignore all this is not only dangerous but irreligious, for here is one of the keys to the mystery of Providence in our time. History is the place chosen by God for His revelation of Himself. (In practice, for the Communists since Stalin, "history is bunk" – that is to say it is a pure Communist creation – History is alive for the Communist as long as it has not taken place. Afterwards – it is dead, a corpse that is cut up and rearranged in various ways and even exhumed and rearranged all over again after burial.)

Thought of writing a book on Colombia under Spain, for instance. To study the "closed system" in the light of present day events.

After all, one of the most interesting things about Marxist-Stalinist authoritarianism is the likeness to our authoritarianism.

It is important to realize to whatever extent I am subject to the mental gymnastics of a good Communist following the Party line. Of course, my case is much simpler, my real freedom is incalculably greater, and no fear of a real Siberia. Yet plenty of threat of a moral Siberia in community. To what an extent the existence of a monk can be subject to the hazards of politics. How much depends on "right thinking."

When all is said and done we are much closer to the old liberalism.

J. Laughlin had two books by Machado de Assis sent down for me. At least I was able to enjoy the titles. *Epitaph of a Small Winner* and *Philosopher or Dog*. Unfortunately Fr. Abbot would not pass them on because, as he said "There was kissing" in one of them.

I had no doubt there was more than that.

Fr. John of the Cross received the new Gilson book on painting – with all the nudes torn out.

Was profoundly moved by news, in a letter of Dom Leclercq that Dom Winandy has resigned as abbot of Clairvaux (Luxembourg) and gone to be a hermit in Switzerland.

This, too, is taboo with us. Not to be mentioned or thought of.

We remain well meaning blind men and nobody yet knows how blind. We think our blindness is a virtuous refusal to look, but perhaps we no longer even have eyes to see with. If we have eyes, we have forgotten how to use them, it is much more convenient not to see.

Was Jeremias, perhaps, speaking only of the Jews?

"Go about through the streets of Jerusalem and see and consider and seek in the broad places thereof, if you can find a man that executes judgment and seeks faith; and I will be merciful unto it. And though they say, 'The Lord liveth,' this also they will swear falsely, O Lord. Thy eyes are upon Truth. Thou hast struck them and they have not grieved. Thou hast punished them and they have not received correction. They have made their faces harder than a rock, they have refused to return . . .

"The prophets prophesied falsehood and the priests clapped their hands and my people loved such things. What then shall be done in the end thereof." (Jer 5)

November 15, 1957. Feast of the Dedication of the Church

This always turns out to be a feast of anguish, as well as one of joy.

Nothing could be more beautiful, nothing could make me happier than the hymn *Urbs Jerusalem* [City of Jerusalem] – and to sing certain verses of that hymn in the evening looking at the sacramental flame of the candles upon the wall where the building was touched and blessed by Christ and made into a sacrament of Himself.

Disponuntur permansuri sacris aedificiis [They shall stand forever within the sacred walls].

I too *disponor permansurus*, placed in a permanent position. I am glad, I am truly happy, I am really grateful to God – for it means eternal salvation.

And yet it raises again the unanswerable question: "What on earth am I doing here?" I have answered it a million times. "I belong here" and that is no answer. In the end, there is no answer like that. Any vocation is a mystery and juggling with words does not make it any clearer.

It is a contradiction and must remain a contradiction.

I think the only hope for me is to pile contradiction upon contradiction and push myself into the middle of all contradictions.

Thus it will always remain morally impossible for me simply to "conform" and to settle down and accept the official rationalization of what is going on here. On the other hand it in no way helps matters for me to replace the official statements with slightly better rationalizations of my own.

But a great deal of the trouble comes from the fact that I look for a formula and expect to find a good one. If you want to find satisfactory formulas you had better deal with things that can be fitted into a formula. The vocation to seek God is not one of them. Nor is existence. Nor is the spirit of man.

Obviously there is a certain amount of truth in the fact that my psychology is that of a bourgeois intellectual partly predetermined by economic influences. That is not the statement of a problem for which there is implied (in the very statement) a solution. It is merely a challenge: can I not prove by action that I can get free from this supposed determinism and rise above it?

That already throws a new light on my struggles here: it is a struggle against the determinism of what is socially "given" – what everybody else is in fact stuck with – the attitudes, the mores, the points of view, the sets of values which we all more or less inherited from their class background and which they cling to all the more peacefully because it all hides under a surface of religious formulas.

It is certain that I have no quarrel whatever with the formulas – (though I generally think they can be stated more clearly and more specifically) my real struggle is with the psychology, the attitudes, that are implied, that are so clearly printed between the lines. It is this psychology that really speaks, not the formulas.

Guilt and resentment at myself for having fled to America, to a country whose culture I secretly despise while loving it and needing it. The country of Pop's optimism – an optimism with no foundations, merely a facade for despair. All this, Father laughed at – and I have identified myself with it out of cowardice perhaps. Yet at the same time I despise far more the more decadent and hollower values of the European bourgeoisie. Where then do I stand? Have I the courage to stand on my own feet or do I have feet to stand on? And what has it meant to stand on them?

All this has to boil up from time to time. This boiling is part of my life. Thank God for it.

There is no solution in withdrawal. No solution in conforming.

A Koan! What sound is made by one hand clapping against itself?

That is where I think Zen is smart: in its absolutely fundamental psychological honesty. This honesty is inseparable from the interior poverty and sincerity which Christ asked for when He said: "Can you believe? All things are possible to one who can believe."

And faith is infinitely more than blindly defending yourself with a few catchwords!

I do want Truth and will pay any price for it. And yet I know that I have found it already. Is it presumptuous to want to see and enjoy what you possess? Or to trade with the Talent you have been given?

(To trade with it is not yet to enjoy it!)

November 17, 1957. 24 Sunday After Pentecost
Da pacem Domine [Grant peace, O Lord].

Tomorrow to Doctor in Bardstown to get my guts looked at. Perhaps an operation.

Have had a cold the last few days. It is not asiatic flu, or I think not. I had a shot three weeks ago. All this adds up to something or other. Interesting dreams which I forget.

Found the original notes of 37 *Meditations* more spontaneous. Still too much verbalizing but they can make a decent book nonetheless.

Koestler's experience "at the window" of the prison in Malaga. Communism and the life of the Spirit incompatible. False, demonic "mystique" of communism. Must study the real *ratio* of this.

Rain again. Looking at maps – Hungary, Russia, Siberia. All the "cities" above the Arctic circle – cities of prisoners.

Reinhardt[22] finally sent his "small" painting. Almost invisible cross on a black background. As though immersed in darkness and trying to emerge from it. Seen in relation to my other object the picture is meaningless – a black square "without purpose" – You have to look hard to see the cross. One must turn away from everything else and concentrate on the picture as though peering through a window into the night. The picture demands this – or is meaningless for I presume that someone might be unmoved by any such demand. I should say a very "holy" picture – helps prayer – an "image" without features to accustom the mind at once to the night of

[22] Ad Reinhardt, an abstract painter who had been a classmate at Columbia University, sent Merton one of his "black on black" cross paintings.

prayer – and to help one set aside trivial and useless images that wander into prayer and spoil it.

He deserves the Molotov-Zukhov medal as the artist who has gone farthest from "socialist realism."

FROM KOESTLER'S INVISIBLE WRITING

"Their mentality (of party intellectuals in 1930s) was a caricature of the revolutionary spirit . . . the seeds of corruption had already been present in the work of Marx in the vitriolic tone of his polemics, the abuse heaped on his opponents, the denunciation of rivals and dissenters as traitors . . ." 29

"The liberals in Germany and elsewhere have clearly understood that there are situations in which caution amounts to suicide . . ." 38

Quote from Bert Brecht *Punitive Measure:*

"He who fights for communism must be able to fight and to renounce fighting, to say the truth and not to say the truth, to be helpful and not helpful, to keep a promise and to break a promise, to go into danger and to avoid danger, to be known and be unknown – He who fights for Communism has of all the virtues only one: that he fights for Communism."

(In the play villain falls into 4 traps – "pity, loyalty, dignity, righteous indignation") p. 41ff.

Quote from a Communist in Bruckberger:

"We manufacture gods and transform men to believe in Order. We will create a universe in our image without weaknesses . . . in which man will attain his cosmic grandeur . . . We are not fighting for a regime, or for power or for riches, we are the instruments of fate."

Faktionspolitik [Factional Politics] "It is difficult to explain to people used to thinking of political activity in terms of parliamentary debates, etc. (But) entirely different techniques initiated by M. himself . . . Delegates at Party conferences did not represent interests of constituents . . . The factions were alliances among individuals temporally held together by a common concept of strategy or more often by a conscious bid for power. The internal history of the various CPs is a story of struggles between the various 'factions' which in the absence of democratic procedure could only be waged by means of intrigue, the springing of traps, etc. . . . The final decision rested with Stalin. Principles and ideals, gifts, etc. . . . grasp of reality . . . originality, initiative, and personal integrity, all these were not merits but liabilities to the Comintern politician. 'Politics' for him meant the acquisition of techniques and skills . . . the direct opposite of those qualities first mentioned – (Stalin's) lack of any attributes of greatness . . .

the deadly tedium of his writings . . . absence of principles, ideals, original-ity – his treacherousness, deafness to suffering, gross falsifications of his-tory – all of this would have made him a grotesque outsider in the H. Commons and made his – incomparable greatness as a *'Faktionspolitiker.'*

"*Exact timing* is one of the secrets of *Faktionspolitik* – Inside a closed universe whose heroes are periodically unmasked as traitors and which re-quires in a jagged zig-zag of policy reversals, everything depends on mak-ing the proper shift of personal allegiance and political orientation at exactly the proper time. The Comintern's politician's fate is not unlike the trapeze acrobat whose life depends on letting go of the swinging bar with split-second precision." p. 259.

(From *Darkness at Noon*) "The Party denied the free will of the individual – and at the same time exacted his willing self-sacrifice. It denied his capac-ity to choose between two alternatives and at the same time it demanded that he always choose the right one. It denied him power to distinguish be-tween good and evil – and at the same time it spoke accusingly of guilt and treachery . . . etc.

"With our training in dialectical acrobatics it was not difficult to prove that all truth was historically class-conditioned, that so-called objective truth was a bourgeois myth and, 'to write the truth' was to select and em-phasize those items and aspects of a given situation which served the prole-tarian revolution and were therefore historically correct." p. 387

"The realisation of the real truth about the regime which now rules one third of the world: that it is the most inhumane regime in human history and the greatest challenge that mankind has yet encountered, is psycholog-ically more difficult for most of us to face as an empty universe was for Gothic man. The difficulty is the same for the illiterate Italian peasant or for a highly literate French novelist like Sartre . . ." 390

November 24, 1957. Last Sunday After Pentecost – Bardstown Hospital
The horrors and peace of the last week.

The combination – operation for piles, extraction of an impacted molar, all within two days – turns out to have been more traumatic than I ex-pected.

Last Monday, in torrential rain, sitting in the dentist's chair in the middle of Bardstown, waiting for the business to begin, listening to ancient jazz, stuff that I had forgotten I once listened to with pleasure. "Lady, play your mandolin / Lady, sing your song of sin . . ." Gradually overcome with a sense of immense hopelessness and defilement. The song has haunted my sleep, I woke up in a cold sweat with it going around and around in my head.

Not only the inanity and tastelessness of the song but the fact of having one after another, like that, poured over your head in a dentist's chair while they are breaking pieces of your jaw!

When they finally got down to business they were playing either a *paso doble* or one of the more conservative Spanish American numbers. I prayed, without conviction, for the foundation.

The operation and its effects, on Tuesday, seems to have let loose some kind of subconscious terror. Sense of despair and brittleness for two days. Allergic to the morphine they gave me and vomited all night. The horror when I discovered I could no longer pee. They had to put a tube in me for that. But fortunately the skill came back and I revived.

Happy with hot water, which became my best friend. The hot packs and the sitz bath.

Happy with fresh air when I could go out into the Sisters' orchard.

Happy above all with Communion, in my total poverty.

Happy with the Office. The psalms, the lessons. Saying them in the sun, under the little apple trees, or in the wind of the grey days that looked like rain. Saying psalms with the stink of mash, from the distilleries, in my nostrils. The awful stink of this whiskey country! The operation has brought a new revulsion against everything that is not church or monastery. Revulsion against all that is cheap and empty and vain and noisy in the world.

Even revulsion against many good things. I brought Bemelsman to do some "light reading" and got sick of Bemelsman and "light reading."

The screams of the girl they brought in at 11 the other night, in labor pains with her first child. The crying of the baby with the broken arm. The enormous hullabaloo made by the gent who came in with a badly broken hip (it sounded like a murder). The complete silence next door where a man is dying – he first came up from a ward. He is being anointed. All around the radios yap in the other rooms.

The great grace came with the present of the book on Ikons from Bob Rambusch. Lossky and Ouspensky. A marvelous book – great Theology and great spiritual reading, full of light, full of glory. Exciting and challenging and satisfying. So many things one must study there and weigh and think about. This question of Ikons is *decisive* for Christian mysticism. It is the very heart of the whole question of contemplation. A mystical theology that leaves out all these things and fails to consider them is not fully Christian because it has never really grasped the Church's faith in the Incarnation.

November 26, 1957. Leaving today

The man next door did not die but gets better in his oxygen tent – I saw him for a moment. He deals with the monastery – the pig end of the monastery. Is a monumental face of a farmer called – with a family of thirteen children.

A man robbed the New Haven bank Saturday and was caught yesterday morning coming out of the woods without shoes.

Have mercy on our blindness and our poverty.

Our inability to grasp the infinite riches of God's mercy and His Kingdom. Immense sorrow for those who seek to alleviate man's misery by an earthly parody of the Kingdom. The vicious lie of communist messianism which can still appeal to the hearts of so many great men. Neruda – wonderful poet – his faith in that lie breaks my heart. He and his poetry will of course be destroyed by what he has chosen to serve, for there is really in him nothing in common with Stalinism.

Inability above all of Christians, of priests, to realize the objective immensity and power of the Kingdom that is established, in mystery and of the great unknown liturgy that goes up to God from the darkness of the world in which the Kingdom is denied. Its citizens perhaps do not even know for sure of what Kingdom they are citizens, yet they suffer for God and the Word triumphs in them, and through them man will once again be, in Christ, the perfect Ikon of god. (Man is, already, in Christ, that ikon – but even we who should know it best and be overwhelmed by it, are constantly forgetting.)

Subjective faith, personal spontaneity, ascetic good will, devotion to duty – these are not enough. Yet they too are necessary. But they are only the beginning.

Wonderful Brazilian poets. A whole new world. Radically different from other Latin-Americans (except perhaps Carrera-Andrade in Ecuador) – No hardness, sourness, artificial attitudes. Great spontaneity, great sense of human values. Difference between someone like Manuel Banderia, whose love is for men and the Marxists writing in Spanish whose love is for a cause – (and very easily leads to hatred for men). The fallacious exaltation with which each string of verses end with "But the brothers will lift our heads and march into the future." It has become a mechanical gag – a final pirouette performed out of habit.

Yet the bitterness must be and it is part. Deeply moved by Alfonso Reyes. And of course Neruda (but Neruda is not a poet of party line theses).

Above all, Jorge de Lima, a profoundly exciting poet perhaps the one poet writing today with whom I feel myself in deepest personal contact and sympathy (like Lax – tomorrow I write about him at once).

December 3, 1957. A week since I got back

Rain today. Dom Anselm, from California, spoke vigorously in Chapter and Rev. Father was mightily consoled at the success of his California foundation.

The Postulants guide came. Disappointed in the second color and in my compromise which led to our using Garamond as the body type. I should have kept on looking for something better when it turned out that Binny was a monotype.

Again – satisfied reading through the now typed copy of *37 Meditations* (now *Thoughts in Solitude* – back to the original notes).

At the same time – sense of the futility of the work I have ever done – because of the human motives. And why care? I may have lost a human reward which was impossible anyway. But I have God. This is sometimes very evident in an obscure way. Otherwise – things seem close to despair and that too is all right. Total bankruptcy of everything earthly in my life – no assurance of anything else – only hope in the mercy of God. In the end, that alone is real.

December 10, 1957

"*Propter nomen meum longe faciam furorem meum et laude mea infrenabo te ne intereas.*

"*Ecce excoxi te sed non quasi argentum. Elegi Te in camino paupertatis.*

"*Propter me faciam et non blasphemer, et gloriam mean alteri non dabo.*" *Is.* 48:9–11.

["For my namesake I defer my anger for the sake of my praise I restrain it for you that I may not cut you off. Behold, I have refined you but not like silver. I have tried you in the furnace of affliction; for my own sake I do it for how could my name be profaned? My glory I will not give to another."]

Deeply moved by these lines in the refectory the other day, sought them out again today. Everything is in them. Nothing more needs to be said.

Solemn profession of Fr. Bede on the Feast of Our Lady. Happy with his new crown and cowl and his mother and sisters from Brazil. His sisters are very Danish and they all shout instead of talking and are, like Fr. Bede, interested in everything. In Washington they wanted to walk in the snow.

Letter from Fr. Theodore, Jesuit novice master in Quito, brought tears to my eyes the other day – wants to help us make a foundation near Ambato or Riobamba, says he has long dreamed of our coming. Rev. Father says not yet. Fr. Crisanto knows him. I will write tomorrow.

But I am resolving to think no more about going, that is entertaining no more desires of it on purpose. I have a vow of stability. God can take care of the rest and of my going, if He will it. Study Latin America but give up the desire to go. Prayer is the most important thing.

December 14, 1957

    "Qui benedictus est super terram benedicetur in Deo amen; et qui jurabit in terra jurabit in Deo amen; quia oblivioni traditae sunt angustiae priores et quia absconditae sunt ab oculis meis. Ecce enim ego creo coelos novos et terram novam et non erunt in memoria priora et non ascendent super cor. Sed guadebitis et exultabitis usque in sempiternum in his quae Ego creo." ["So that he who blesses himself in the land shall bless himself by the God of truth and he who takes an oath in the land shall swear by the God of truth; because former troubles are forgotten and are hid from my eyes. For, behold, I create new heavens and a new earth; and the former things shall not be remembered or come to mind; but be glad and rejoice forever in that which I create."]

                                                       Is. 65:16–18.

How I need the *novitas* [newness] that will come with the *nova per carnem Nativitatis Domini* [the new things through the flesh because in the birth of the Lord]. Longing for the renewal of the whole world "grown old in sin."

The other day when it was very cold, decided on the spur of the moment that we had time to take a truck load of Christmas trees to Bardstown when we didn't have time. The truck was very slow, the detour was very long, the man gave us coffee, and we ran out of gas, besides which I ran into Dr. Sonne and he examined the healing wound. It was dark when we got back. Wonderful sunset over the cold country – the bare woods and the fields full of snow and the low hills (knobs in the distance) – open and bare land, poor dark land, wild land, my home. Fr. John of the Cross came and I thought of the time we were over on the Holy Cross road (which is the way we came home) the afternoon of his solemn profession and of the *Urbs Jerusalem* and that we are stones placed together in this Church by the Providence of God.

The man who gave us a couple of gallons of gas at Holy Cross was very kind and laughed a lot at the monks being out late. Got home at 5 and Father Prior said we had incurred neither excommunication nor censure.

Frs. Vincent and Alcuin freezing in the back of the truck.

Today in the refectory, beautiful homily of St. Maximus of Tours on the fact that we do violence to God when we pray for mercy as He cannot resist such a prayer, especially if we are merciful. "We are indeed thieves."

December 17, 1957

"A hundred times every day I remind myself that my inner and outer life are based on the labors of other men, living and dead, and that I must exert myself in order to give in the same measure as I have received and am still receiving. I am strongly drawn to a frugal life and am often oppressively aware that I am engrossing an undue amount of the labor of my fellow men. I regard class-distinction as unjustified and in the last resort based on force . . ." *Albert Einstein.*

Beginning my first contacts with this beautiful mind and person who is Einstein.

Note in him what was good in Marx, the true social conscience and not what was bad, the neurotic violence.

A great prophet of the dead Age of Liberalism – with the disconcerting kindness and innocence of the liberal, emerging from his political muddle into his little moment of clarity. We can no longer afford to look down on that sort of thing. In the same way I have been impressed by the probity and sincerity of Eisenhower, in his moments (what I know of them).

Yet there is the inevitable disappointment, the philosophical vagueness of life based on abstractions "Kindness, Beauty, Truth."

Here, however, is a paragraph which I can and ought to make my own:

"My passionate sense of social justice and social responsibility has always contrasted oddly with my pronounced lack of need for direct contact with other human beings and human communities. I am truly a 'lone traveller' and have never belonged to my country, my house, my friends, or even my immediate family with my whole heart; in the face of these ties I have never lost a sense of distance and need for solitude – feelings which increase with the years. One becomes sharply aware, but *without regret,* of the limits of mutual understanding and consonance with other people. No doubt such a person loses some of his innocence and unconcern; on the other hand he is largely independent of the opinions, habits, and judgments of his fellows and avoids the temptations to build his inner equilibrium on such insecure foundations." (*Ideas and Opinions,* p. 9)

His religious views are to me not insuperable obstacles to sympathy. I agree with him that he is a fundamentally religious man. I think the core of his philosophical difficulty is the concept of freedom. He has not *thought* much about the nature of God because he has not felt the need to do so – has perhaps felt it was more honest not to do so. (The ancient Jewish fear of this – an emotionally healthy fear.)

December 24, 1957. Christmas Eve

A grey, cool quiet afternoon. Lots of water falling over the rocks in the creek and this is the only sound. The Christmas preparations in the novitiate have been happy and less crazy and turbulent than they might have been. As usual everything ended up more elaborate than it had been planned. The tree is, once again, too big and every time someone goes by more tinsel falls on the floor. Fr. Placid wanted it set up last night and was grieved when I told him to wait until Christmas. "Everybody lights up their trees before Christmas," he complained.

Long letter from the Abbot General as to why *The Secular Journal* cannot be published.[23] Reams of paper from four censors who are very good at wasting paper and time, theirs as well as other people's. Two censors see "nothing wrong" with the book, one of these two thinks it is "not good enough" (from a literary point of view) to be published. The other two pick up lots of statements which are criticisms à la Leon Bloy of the "good" average Catholic. Well, perhaps they are right on that. I have enough experience of my ability to hurt people uselessly and have no desire to make such a fetish of "frankness" that I will go on hurting them even more. I will

---

[23] It was eventually published in 1959.

write a dutiful letter to Catherine and Farrar, Straus & Cudahy can cry in their beer.

Nonetheless I wish not to be too sarcastic about F.S. & C since a pile of books came from there, one being a diary of a woman in Brazil, then John Jay Chapman, Eliot (on poets) and Edmund Wilson's *Classics and Commercials* which looks to me interesting. Bob also sent Bernanos' *Dialogue des carmélites* one of the first things I read after coming over to the novitiate.

I keep liking and sympathizing with Einstein's opinions. What a muddle he is in about religion. Nothing strange, just the ordinary muddle of all "cultivated men." A really religious man who thinks it weak to be "religious" in an integrally social manner. He has long ago left behind the physics of Aristotle – and has kept the god of Aristotle. The pure intelligence, the unmoved mover, perhaps not that, either but I must study him.

I have said so much about Christmas and so much has been said about Christmas everywhere in the monastery and this morning Fr. Gerald in his usual grandiloquent conference tried to say everything in 45 minutes of close-packed theological errors and self-contradictions . . . Enough talk about Christmas. Utterly sick of the chapter from Fr. Farrell's *Only Son* that was read at table on the subject. Evident that a bourgeois attitude makes a man totally blind to everything, to all values, human or divine. Pure, empty verbalizing.

Fr. Crisanto set up the crib with Bro. Benet's balsa wood figures, light as air, and Fr. Lawrence helped with the moss and cedars and Fr. Crisanto made everything come to life with "existentialist stars" (so he called them). He took the habit today.

If I could ask for anything I liked and if I had first of all assumed it and taken for granted that I asked to be saved and to be a saint, then I would put it this way – that I would ask for the grace in every case and in all cases to be perfectly consonant with God's Will and that if it were His will, that I become a saint by making a monastic foundation in Ecuador and that the community there would be a very happy and simple one that would do much good in that country and everywhere else too. Said that we would truly discover there how best and most genuinely how the monastic life could be lived in our time and in short that there I might fulfill all that God has destined for me, and find myself completely in Him, and bring Him many holy souls, and make that monastery a great spiritual force in Latin America.

And, if not Ecuador, then where Our Lady has found the best place for it.

I think and I believe – that this prayer is going to be answered though perhaps not exactly as I have said it for there are better ways of doing such things.

In the meantime I will continue "not thinking" about it, that is trying to refuse the satisfaction of wondering about it, or cherishing any desires about it.

There are many, now, praying for this foundation in S.A. and I think it natural that the prayers of those in Ecuador should be the strongest with ours and everything else in my heart. I will kneel at Christ's crib tonight.

December 27, 1957. St. John's Day
A cold night and a beautiful frosty morning.

Rainy Christmas. Christmas night was as wonderful as ever. I was assistant priest. While the community was receiving communion and filing around the altar it was like being enveloped in a procession of seraphim. *O altitudo divitiarum sapientiae et scientiae Dei.* [O, the height of the riches of the wisdom and the knowledge of God.]

Christmas morning, in the novitiate chapel, after the 3 masses, with the rain pattering on the roof, unutterable peace.

Christmas afternoon, still raining. Sit in the straw in the loft of the sheep barn and forget my glasses there. Rain coming down on the cedars.

This year they seem to have given me all the cards that came and this takes up time. But a monk *should* have something to do with the world he lives in and should love the people in that world. How much they give us and how little we give them.

My responsibility to be in all reality a peacemaker in the world, an apostle, to bring people to truth, to make my whole life a true and effective witness to God's Truth.

Moving words of Einstein – (with whom I agree that Gandhi has been in reality the most effective and trustworthy political thinker of our time).

"We must revolutionize our thinking, revolutionize our actions, and must have the courage to revolutionize our relations among the nations of the world. Cliches of yesterday will no longer do . . . To bring this home to men all over the world is the most important and fateful social function intellectuals have ever had to shoulder. Will they have enough courage to overcome their own nationalities to the extent that is necessary to induce the peoples of the world to change their deep-rooted national traditions in a most radical fashion."

Love is the only answer. But medieval talk about love solves nothing. What does love mean today? What is its place in the enormous dimensions of the modern world? We have to love in a new way and with a new attitude and I suppose perhaps the first thing to do is to admit I do not know the meaning of love in *any* context – ancient or new.

December 29, 1957

Preparing notes on first epistle of St. John for the novice's conference.

I ask myself, *is it possible, in a capitalist economy to live up to the doctrine of this epistle?*

"In this we have known the charity of God because he hath laid down his life for us and we ought to lay down our lives for the brethren. *He that hath the substance of the world and shall see his brother in need and shall shut up his bowels from him, how doth the charity of God abide in him?*

"My little children, let us not love in word nor in tongue, but in deed and in truth." 1 John 3:16–18.

Certainly, there is no lack of good will and good intentions. There are men and women in the world who try, even heroically, to live up to this.

Lack of good-will is not the fundamental problem.

We no longer live in a world in which "the substance" (riches) is what it used to be: – land, buildings, crops, money.

In a world with a complicated economic structure like ours, it is no longer even a question of "my brother" being a citizen in the same country. From the moment the economy of another country is subservient to the business interests of my country I am responsible to those of the other country who are "in need." In what does this responsibility consist? To what does it obligate me? Who can answer? Is Marx right in saying that the Capitalist world does not and *cannot* seek an honest answer? I am bound to agree with him.

Hence the problem of cooperation with those who exploit. A frightfully difficult problem. What have moral theologians done so far to open up these new horizons? Nothing as far as I know.

Hence – *my obligation to study questions of history, economics,* etc. in so far as I can.

This obligation is by no means in conflict with my "contemplative" vocation?

Until my "contemplation" is liberated from the sterilizing artificial limitations under which it has so far existed (and nearly been stifled out of existence) I cannot be a "man of God" because I cannot live in the Truth, which is the first essential for being a man of God.

It is absolutely true that here in this monastery we are enabled to systematically evade our real and ultimate social responsibilities. In any time, social responsibility is the keystone of the Christian life.

In no time more than in ours has this been so urgent – and too poorly understood. But I admit that what Dom Louis[24] etc. have said about manual labor in our life reflects a real practical approach to the question for us as monks and that is the first step, without which other steps only lead further into illusion.

Perhaps no monastery is at a greater disadvantage on this issue than Gethsemani.

The unrest in the community springs from a dim awareness of the awful contradictions under which we live.

We are supposed to be poor and we have all our needs satisfied and live on a higher economic level in many ways than even the well to do in some countries – perhaps not as individuals but as a community.

We are supposed to be monks and the mental attitude of the community is frankly that of a business concern. What matters is not the value of the product but how it can be sold, for how much, with what advertising.

A little medieval paternalism towards the neighbors does not take care of the situation.

And as for me – to what extent have I allowed myself to become, without knowing it, implicitly a propagandist for capitalism, militarism, etc.?

N.B. No question of the *graver* responsibility of those who foolishly cooperate with communist materialism which is certainly worse and more nefarious than anything we have in America.

What is the answer?

My ignorance is practically perfect. But something has to be done.

December 31, 1957

Dom Desroquettes arrived last evening and spoke in chapter this morning. A monk, very welcome. One feels very much at home with him – and he assured us it would be something besides a lot of *arsis* and *thesis*.

---

[24] Abbot of Melleray – the Father Immediate for Gethsemani at that time.

Ended this year with Habakuk. The theophany in *Bible de Jérusalem* is terrific, but still I have gone a little way on the prophets. But fell by chance into the "sacrifice of jealousy" and the trial by ordeal of the suspected adulteress in Numbers 5 and was overwhelmed by it. The first time the Law had ever hit me that hard. We are wrong to be supercilious about the Torah and even about its ceremonial. It is full of meaning, just as full of meaning as the Prophets. But we have lost the power to grasp that kind of meaning.

Pictures of the University of Mexico. (Aztec liturgical decor very much in the spirit of the Torah – the color of earth, the mountains, the lava – like Sinai and the Arabian desert. Mood of Aztec art is the mood of the Torah, fierce, liturgical, absolutism.) The library astounds me – I mean the outside of it for I have no pictures of the inside.

Augustin de Iturbide the make believe Emperor.
   And Santa Anna.
   Hidalgo and Morelos and their Indian armies.
   Viceroy O'Donohue who quit. Material for Cantos à la Pound in Mexico!!
   (Book about New Mexico in refectory over Christmas, *A Supernatural Christmas Eve*. Very charming. Everyone ate popcorn and listened to the story of the St. Christopher statue.)
   Bobbie A. is back over the holidays and his little brother also with a blue and white jacket and "Central Catholic" on the back in letters big enough to be read all over Kentucky. Two such good kids were never seen.
   Fr. Sebastian during meditation fiercely noting down all the faults of the choir on small pieces of paper.
   Got to read more Spanish. Thought the house was full of Spanish books but find there are not too many that I want to read. Do I for instance want to read Fray Luis de Leon? Maybe Bover on St. Paul. In any case a thin book on the spirituality of lay people by Lili Alvarez who, Fr. Lawrence tells me, is a tennis star.
   Postulants Jesus Enrique, the Marist Brother. I admire the neatness of his letters and his courage as well as his patience with the slings and arrows of outrageous fortune. So now he goes to Tepatitlan for a year!

Padre Hugo, in Costa Rica, who reproaches me today for not answering his last letter.

Antonio Canedo, the Bolivian seminarian in La Plata, who is so smart and seems to have a lot of character and whom I already like very much though I have never met him.

And Fray Jaramilo in Bogota – our letter to whom went astray at the most crucial moment.

What of Padre Amayo at Iquitos? And the solemn Garcia boy in B.A.?

And Fr. Crisanto's friend Josue Gangon (whom he calls Genghis Khan!) and Gomes in Rio de Janeiro whom I have sent to Don Marios Barbosa – and Ferman, the school teacher in a village in El Salvador? and Padre Alacion of Cornientes Argentine who has vanished into oblivion? And the new one in Villa del Mar, Chile? called I think, Sourain?

January 6, 1958. Epiphany

A beautiful sentence at the end of Evdokimov's article on the Nativity ikon in _Bible et vie chrétienne_. (Concerning the angel in the ikon who comes up over the side of the mountain of God and leans towards men.) This is the angel whom we hear when we are silent and when we get to heaven his voice will be the most familiar of the voices to us and will be like our own voice. Too good for comment.

New Year's Day – dark and cold in the pasture behind the sheep barn looking at the dark pine trees and at the valley. It is very satisfying. Yesterday – cold but sunny – The grey dead tulips all over the tulip poplars. Trying to read Gabriella Mistral, to whom I am much attracted – her poem about Mexico and about women.

There is always much grace in being hebdomadary – a very important part of our contemplative life. (Yet – I do not believe in taking one's turn when one is snowed under by so many other things that he cannot fulfill the Office well.) Once again, I begin my week with a High Mass for the brothers.

It is this week that we are making the changes decreed by the General Chapter and it does not seem to me that they are all good. All right for the secular clergy to drop the _Pater_ and _Ave_ before each office but for us it is a good way to get your breath and get re-collected. I also will miss the antiphon _Spiritus Sanctus_ and the prayer _Laetifica_ which is so beautiful. I am the last to have recited it in the house here, yesterday at Prime.

January 11, 1958

"On provoque inévitablement un malaise, quand on ne regarde que la fonction sociale. Celle-ci n'est un fin en soi ni en général ni dans l'église, car la communauté est un définitive au service des individus, et non inversement." ["Inevitably a crisis arises when one pays attention only to the social function. It is not an end in itself neither in general or for the church because the community is fundamentally at the service of the individual and not vice versa."]

Pope Pius XII – Oct. 5, 1957.

(the lay apostle) *". . . des hommes constitués dans leur integrité inviolable comme images de Dieu; des hommes fiers de leur dignité personelle et de leur saine liberté; des hommes justement jaloux d'être les égaux de leur semblables en tout ce qui concerne le fond le plus intime de la dignité humaine; des hommes attachés de façon stable à leur terre et à leur tradition."* ["Persons constituted with their inviolable integrity as images of God; of people proud of their personal dignity and of their sane liberty; of persons justly jealous of being equals in their likeness in all that concerns the most intimate depth of their human dignity; of people rooted in a stable fashion to their land and their tradition."] (quoted in above talk from another talk of 20 Feb. 1946)

"Le matérialisme et l'athéisme d'un monde, dans lequel des millions de croyants doivent vivre isolés, oblige à former en eux tous des personalités solides. Sinon, comment resisteront-ils aux entraînements de la masse qui les entourent?" ["The materialism and atheism of a world within which millions of believers must live isolated lives obliges us to form in them solid personalities. Otherwise, how will they resist the traps of the majority which surround them?"]

January 12, 1958

It is sad it is not the Sunday within the Octave of Epiphany.

The new changes in the Liturgy seem to me to be in many ways bewildering and senseless – a matter of juggling with words and manipulating the rubrics rather than a real vital adjustment.

So the Octave of the Epiphany has, for some reason, been abolished, yet the office remains essentially the same. Tomorrow, the Liturgy of the Octave Day will be what it always has been. But it will be the "Feast of the Commemoration of the Baptism of the Lord"! This is the mouse which our mountain is bringing forth. We are all wrapt up in our liturgical red tape.

Brothers singing the office with the choir for the first time officially today – The Community as a whole is bewildered. As a whole: happy. But there is a fringe of perplexity and unrest – as if we did not quite know what to make of it.

January 14, 1958

When the Brothers came to None on Sunday it was very good. The singing was strong and full of enthusiasm.

However I hope they will take advantage of the great opportunity that has been opened to them now that the G. Chapter has voted to let them say their offices (outside choir) in English. This is still not approved by the S. Congregation. I hope it will be.

For the Brothers to come to choir seems to me to be somewhat equivocal and of little importance relatively, since they do not know Latin. Neither for that matter do some of the choir monks, really.

January 14, 1958

The fantastic theocratic cities of Central America – to me more impressive than Egypt – a different kind of intensity.

I have [Miguel] Covarrubias' new book *[Indian Art of Mexico and Central America]* from the Louisville library.

Great Olmec heads in the jungle – this not so interesting. Football players with helmets.

But the fantastic little pre-classical figurines of clay.

A lovely slate mask of Teotihuacan style – the style I like best. Classical and pure and full of spiritual light. (Toltecs)

According to the latest tests, clay figurines of the Zacatinco and Tlatilco type (the earliest) go back to 1400 B.C. This is fabulous. (Very close to Olmec style, however.)

The lovely Tlatilco mask may be as old as that. The *realistic* and completely Chinese figure from Morelos – one wonders if the date is not mistaken. Can it possibly be so early? After that, the big breasted, three eyed, two nosed ladies, amusing but not so beautiful.

The Tlatilco material – is above all *spontaneous and free* – with a spontaneity lost in later formalizations. Covarrubias remarks on the absence of religious themes – which could be significant – Primitive *monotheism* and knowledge of a spiritual god.

Tlatilco figures – the most ancient and the most modern. They fascinate me – they represent a state of mind that I can appreciate, an outlook that I can sympathize with fully. After that, Mexican art gets further and further away, until the Aztec, dead and repugnant, yet fascinating too.

What a wonderful world, South and Central America!

January 16, 1958

Had a talk with Dom Desroquettes.

The Chilean Benedictine foundation at Santiago from 1938–1948 (Taken over by Beuron).

Founded due to intervention of Dom Pedro Supercazeaux – Chilean barrister.

Solesmes very slow to take it up, Quarr abbey made the foundation.

French monks went there not knowing Spanish.

The superior was in poor health and passive.

There were almost no postulants for about 10 years but by that time the monastery was nevertheless beginning to catch on.

They left at the suggestion of abbot of Solesmes.

The Chileans who were there wanted at all costs to save it for Benedictines – monks came from Beuron and Maria Laach but the mixture has not perfectly "gelled." Etc.

He knows the Colombian Benedictines from Monserrat, founded at Medellin. Was at Guam during the war.

FROM GANDHI'S LETTERS

"Why should rest not be taken in the spirit of service? Of course it can be easily abused and often is. But that is no reason why honest people may not honestly give themselves to rest so as to fit themselves for further service. I regard it as self-delusion if not worse when a person says he is wearing himself away in service. Is such service preferred by God to service steadily and detachedly to be performed?" (28.9.30)

"If you work with detachment you will refuse to be rushed and you will refuse to let anything get on your nerves. Having put one's whole heart into the thing entrusted or undertaken one can leave the rest to God. Then there can be no rush and no hurry." (19.10.30)

January 19, 1958

Dom Eugene Boylan is preaching the annual retreat here. Energetic, red-faced, lean, a good Cistercian, in the slightly disorganized and disoriented way Cistercians have, today, of being they know not quite what.

Good conferences so far on the only thing that matters – not basing our hope on ourselves but on God. The more our hope is based on our own virtues and resources, the less we are able to face the truth – obviously. This is the Gospel, God has saved us, but we are still "men of little faith."

I see it so clearly in myself. And that is good. I still do not see it clearly enough – haven't the courage, I suppose.

He read a splendid passage from Bl. Guerric about humility making up for any other virtue we may lack (if it is united with confidence in God).

I have two teeth apparently abscessed, which will probably have to be pulled out tomorrow.

A letter from Gregory Zilboorg saying he wants to talk to me about something.

All the Communist techniques of spying and bullying are simply the exaggeration of tendencies that are at work in all social groups practically all the time and their reduction to an extreme conclusion:

Conformity to accepted ideas – refusal to see unacceptable truths – constant check on deviationist tendencies – punishment of those who deviate, who have a tendency to see things otherwise, to see them in an unacceptable manner –

And, at the other end – in the individual himself – the tendency to protest or to criticize by not-conforming. Non-conformity is an attack on the group. The Reds are in a sense logical when they take away any non-conformity and dress it up as open hostility and subversion. What the deviationist "would have done" if he dared or had the chance.

But, what is the point? A vital society *preserves differences,* and conformism kills a society. Communism is the absurd reduction of a ridiculous idea that you can make things what you want them to be merely by forcing all to concur in your own thought. If all *think* a thing is so, and *act as if* it were so, then it *becomes* so.

Conversely – for the individual – the duty is to keep up with what "They" are all thinking and act as "They" are all acting.

No one can be allowed to spoil the game and say it isn't so.

Koestler, I think, applies to this situation the tale of the King's new clothes – and someday the child will inevitably point out that the King is after all naked and no amount of pretending will cover him with garments.

The Reds are carrying *our* error and sins to their logical conclusion.

It will not help us a bit to think that they are the only ones that are deluded.

More from Gandhi (quoted by Regamey in *Vie spirituelle*).

"... *il faut avoir de courage pour résister à la violence ... il faut avoir vaincu la peur. Il n'y a pas de plus grand péché que la lâcheté ...*

"*Dieu est l'intrépidité. Comment sans intrépidité peut-on chercher la verité et l'amour?*

"*Nous voulons enseigner aux masses l'intrépidité.*" ["One needs the strength to resist violence ... one must overcome fear ... there is no greater sin than cowardice ... God is fearlessness. How can one search for truth and love without fearlessness? We must teach fearlessness to the masses."]

January 23, 1958

Had a good talk with Dom Eugene walking briskly up and down the front avenue on a very grey, very cold evening – a bit of wind and drops of rain. I accused him of bringing us Irish weather.

Caldey must be a strange place. They have very few brothers. Only seven, of whom two are almost incapacitated. Result, the choir monks and priests cook, bake, etc. Cannot be at all of the Offices.

He thinks, as I do, that we have gone to extremes here in this business of getting brothers into choir. Last evening for instance they were in there not only for Vespers but for Vespers and a Nocturn for the dead. During this retreat week they have been crowding in for all the Offices except Vigils and Lauds.

It seems to me that this is going to have a bad effect on the interior life of the Brothers and of the whole house. The simple fact is that the Brothers are not choir monks and if they try to be choir monks they try to be something they are not and are not meant to be. They will lose the graces (great ones) that belong to their own vocation and will not get the graces that belong to ours. I think that they have made the great mistake of missing the point of their vocations and not seeing its advantages. Or rather, they are now in great danger of doing so. Of course most of them are not at fault at all. They are passive and perfectly pure in their intentions. I don't know if as much can be said for the moving spirits, who have influenced the whole trend, but it seems to me that those are the men who do not know what it means to be brothers and do not really appreciate the brothers' vocation.

___

When all that is said, I must confess that perhaps the same can be said of me, in regard to the S. A. foundation. Perhaps it is a matter of restlessness, of not appreciating my opportunities here, of not giving myself sincerely to contemplation (if that phrase really means anything).

Yet still I think it is in some way God's Will.

I am struck by a phrase Dom E. used. "When some men are not willing simply to love God, He is content to let them serve Him."

It is better to love Him purely and simply than to serve Him by active works. All this I believe.

Yet, in the concrete, it seems to me that I have greater peace and am close to God when I am not "trying to be a contemplative" or trying to be anything special, but simply orienting my life fully and completely towards what seems to be required of a man like me at a time like this.

I am obscurely convinced that there is a need in the world for something I can provide and that there is a need for me to provide it. True, someone else can do it, God does not need me. But I feel He is asking me to provide it.

January 24, 1958

At the consecration of my Mass I suddenly thought of the words "If you love me, feed my sheep!"

The other day a wonderful letter came from Monsenor Ricaurte in Bogota. He is the spiritual director of a boy who is coming to us from the Franciscans – Guillermo Jaramillo who left them 3 days before solemn vows, to come here.

Mons. Ricaurte is very interested in our foundation idea. He wrote giving suggestions. He had talked to the Bishop of Tunja who was already to get out the necessary documents and start things moving.

1. The abandoned Dominican monastery of *Ecce Homo* near Leiva or rather 20 km. from Leiva in Boyaca. High, dry, plateau land which does not hold water. They used to grow olive trees. It was, I think, their novitiate. I spoke to Rev. Father of the advantage of getting a whole monastery all built and ready. He said "There would be no running water." As a matter of fact – there would be no water at all. That is the catch.

2. The church and convent of Moniquira. This is also in Boyaca, near a weird place called Sagamoso (Something in Colombian history?) and near

the Lago de Tota, a lake which Fr. Crisanto says is very beautiful. Terrible: it is a parish church and a place of pilgrimage to boot. Mons. R. says it has many 17th. century paintings by one of the great native artists of the time.

3. There is a new bishop in Medellin, Mons. Salazar, who turns out to be from Manizales, is a friend of Fr. Crisanto, was formerly bishop of Zipaquira where the salt mines are. He is going to be installed in Medellin Feb 2. Mons. R. had a long talk with him about the foundation and he is very enthusiastic – says there are many beautiful farms, belonging to *gente rica y piadosa* [rich and pious people]. No question that Antioquia would be, naturally speaking, an ideal place to start. We will see what happens.

I wrote a long, happy letter to Monsenor Ricaurte.

And resolved not to think about the place anymore, but the resolution was fruitless.

Now that suddenly real people are talking about real places, the whole idea becomes more sober – it is no longer a mere dream, with all the lawlessness of a dream. It is no longer just something private, that you can think about as you like (though to your own cost).

It is now something which, when thought of, begets responsibilities.

One's thoughts must now be true. They must seek a true road and must meet reality all along the road.

Now one begins to remember that there will be difficulties.

For a moment I was afraid – and also I thought "How will I ever leave the woods, here?" – and other things like that. Later I thought of taking a vow to go.

In any case, the whole thing has a new aspect. I am convinced that Rev. Father now really intends to make the foundation and that barring unexpected events, it will take place.

The wonder of being brought, by God, around a corner and to realize a new road is opening up, perhaps – which He alone knows. And that there is no way of travelling it but in Christ and with Him. This is joy and peace – whatever happens. The result does not matter. I have something to do for Him and if I do that, everything else will follow. For the moment – it consists in prayer – thought – study and above all care to form the South American postulants as He brings them here.

January 28, 1958

Dom Eugene has left – He went Sunday.

Dom John, the new definitor, came Saturday evening. Spoke to him for a few moments when Fr. Hilary brought him around to the novitiate. He is the former sub-prior at Spencer and has also been Superior at Berry-ville. He spoke in chapter this morning – A childlike little man with ruddy cheeks and horn rimmed glasses, not at all as solemn as he looks. It took them about fifteen minutes to catch on to the fact that he was very humorous.

And Fr. Joachim from Georgia is here too.

So those are the people who have been, or still are, here, in this grey weather.

Woke up in the middle of the night with feelings of insecurity, wonder-ing, if indeed, I would really get the two books I have asked for from the Library of Congress.

One a book on Ecuador published in Sweden, though it is in English.

One a "political biography" of Stalin.

(Dom Eugene agreed with me and, separately, with Fr. John of the Cross, about "reading everything.")

Fr. Lawrence's cousin has written a book about the Somozas, the blood-thirsty dictators of Nicaragua.

Somoza enters strangely into the wonderful story of Fr. L's vocation.

Fr. L was delayed in coming here because after his cousin was let out of jail where Somoza's son had presided personally over his torturing and in-terrogation, he was exiled to the jungle of the Rio San Juan. A seaplane from Costa Rica came down on the river and took him away. Fr. L delayed coming here long enough to make arrangements for this.

In a letter, the cousin says "We will probably move in this February or March . . ."

Newspaper reports of the abortive revolution against Perez Jimenez (Venezuela) are read in refectory.

37 Meditations – Thoughts in Solitude – Les chemins de la joie reads well in French.[25] The man who translated it – A Benedictine in a poor monastery of the Andes has it full of all the silence and simplicity I intended and felt when I wrote these things. Now that the fog has lifted I see it in this new perspective. I feel it is not a bad book.

A curse on letters!

[25] It was not published until 1961; Merton must have been reading a typescript of the translation.

Another grey day. There has been some snow. It never stays on the ground. The novices work in the woods. I hope to get out tomorrow. I cannot get enough reading.

January 31, 1958

Rain. Pouring all afternoon. A flu epidemic may perhaps be starting in the community. If it goes on raining like this the novices will certainly get lots of books done in the bindery.

Said Mass in honor of St. Mariana (of Quito) for the foundation, and for those who should follow. It is my 43rd birthday.

It is most important that people of our time know well the lives of men like Hitler and Stalin, and of their rise to power. Particularly Stalin. Men who in a strange way intuitively kept touch with what was always ready to happen in the society which they to some extent typified.

How in so many ways they shoved aside, out of the picture, men more brilliant than themselves. Trotsky more brilliant than Stalin. This is not an age in which great things are to be done by brilliant men, but one in which blind forces work in and through men who are in many ways stupid, blind, yet terribly shrewd in their opportunism – and, above all, *tireless in working* for what they want.

Whether we like it or not, we have to study such men.

There is no question that what is important, to history and ideas, in Stalin is the fact that he is not exactly a Robespierre, still less a Nero. He is something else. Certainly a very different kind of lunatic from Hitler.

And there is something very significant in the fact that to be ignorant of Russia, now, means to be ignorant of all the rest of the world besides. The most fatal of omissions, in political life, a failure to know through and through the Communist mentality and all its varieties, orthodox or otherwise.

In an age of politics it is fatal to know nothing of the chief politicians – contrary to all I may have said about this before.

The violent industrialization of Russia was marked by the same abuses and defects which Marx observed in the more spontaneous industrialization of England. Primitive accumulation – Land grabbing – blood, discipline, pressure, etc. Probably expect the same in S. America?

———

Dreamt the other night that I was in a general store somehow connected to the monastery. In the store were Soviet manufactured articles, dreary and tawdry, which were being thrown away or destroyed – in particular, cheap desk lamps. I remember gathering up some of those things to appropriate them, thinking that though they were useless, it was "against religious poverty" to let such things be thrown away, particularly since they symbolized the tragic suffering of millions of nameless people. The keeper of the store disdained my choice. These articles had been taken in "the days when Fr. Placid was cellarer."

Beautiful book on Ecuador – modern Ecuadorian art – faces of the Negroes of Esmaraldas and some of the Indians – views of the volcanoes, the plain simple church of El Carmen in Cuenca.

February 3, 1958

Purification today – Yesterday was Septuagesima.

Quite a lot of snow and cold weather for the last 3 days.

The infirmary is full. On Friday Fr. Sebastian went down with the flu and had to go to the dormitory with it. Saturday we fixed up a bed for him in the novitiate typing room. That evening his temperature was over 102. He got up during the night and passed out, but came to and got back to bed. In the morning his temperature was down to 100. We got him in the old wing of the Infirmary yesterday after much diplomacy and strained relations with Bro. Wilfred and now he is getting better. Blessed the throats with candles and St. Blaise's blessing after conference yesterday evening.

One thing anyone can learn from Stalin is – to keep one's mouth shut most of the time. Stalin got the power he got because he was *not* an easy-going intellectual – more than that, because he was as much Asiatic as he was European. Perhaps if Trotsky had taken over, Russia would have been swamped by Germany . . . ? Or perhaps if Trotsky had taken over, Hitler would have never risen to power in Germany.

Perez Jimenez is out of Venezuela and has gone to Santo Domingo and Peron is there with him, said Rev. Father today in chapter. (Later it turned out Peron had only taken refuge in the Dominican Embassy in Caracas.)

———

Meadowlarks singing in the snow, along the road from the cowbarns. Cold water of the stream, full of sun, over green watercress between banks of snow. Blue water of the lake, very blue, and blinding with sun, along the edge of the sheet of melting ice, covered with snow.

Most inspired by the example of Pére Monchanin, priest of Lyons who went to be a hermit in India and died last year. First attracted to him by the article on the *"Spiritualité au désert"* in *Dieu vivant* 9 years ago. Above all, he was interested in everything. Even in his Indian ashram he kept up with all that was going on in thought, art, politics, in Europe. I cannot conceive things otherwise – and for me to try to be other than that would be a falsehood. I am glad of his providential example. It has been written of him

"... *il considérait en effet l'événement du prolétariat comme le point d'impact le plus important en notre age de civilisation, de l'essentielle et constante tension de l'univers vers sa plénitude théandarique.*" ["He considered the rise of the proletariat as the most important point of impact on civilization in our age and the essential and persistent tension of the universe toward its divine fulness."] (*Vie spirituelle,* Jan. 1958, p. 7).

"... *le mystère de Dieu se manifeste aussi, pour qui sait l'y soi, aux synthèses des philosophes, aux découvertes de la science, aux mouvements de l'histoire, aux connections grammaticales.*" ["The mystery of God manifests itself, for those who sense it, in the synthesis of philosophers, in the discoveries of science, in the movements of history, in the structures of language."] id. [*Vie spirituelle,* Jan. 1958, p. 7.]

At the same time – Monchanin was an authentic mystic, contemplating God in darkness and emptiness. *There is no contradiction* here – once one is called by God.

February 4, 1958
Beauty of the sunlight falling on a tall vase of red and white carnations and green leaves on the altar in the novitiate chapel. The light and shade of the red, especially the darkness in the fresh crinkled flower and the light warm red around the darkness, the same color as blood but not "red as blood," utterly unlike blood. Red as a carnation. This flower, this light, this moment, this silence = *Dominus est* [the Lord is here], eternity! Best because the flower is itself and the light is itself and the silence is itself and I am myself – all, perhaps, an illusion, but no matter, for illusion is nevertheless

the shadow of reality and reality is the grace that underlay these lights, these colors, and this silence.

The "simplicity" that would have kept those flowers off the altar is, to my mind, less simple than the simplicity which enjoys them there, but does not need them to be there.

February 9, 1958

More sick. Fr. Vincent left the night Office. Fr. Aelred sleeps in the typing room. Fr. Basil still in Hogan's alley – all these have been moved to the front wing, in the old guest house.

Reading Ciro Alegría's *"El mundo es ancho y ajeno,"* walking up and down the stonepath in the cold. It is a beautiful book, garrulous but simple, about an Indian village in Peru. Good reading for after dinner. Good to read a novel in which there is still respect for life, unlike the dead stuff that has been coming out of Europe and the U.S.

February 11, 1958

Hundredth anniversary of the apparitions at Lourdes – there will be a solemn votive mass of the Immaculate Conception. I said a mass for the sick. Still more novices are getting the 'flu – a postulant (Jim Hinchey) arrived in the midst of the plague.

Bro. Wilfred complains that "all Reverend Father thinks about is temperatures and eggs. Well, I could go and set the henhouse on fire and that would take care of both."

Fr. Vincent hasn't had much of anything to eat for 2 days, walks up and down the room in the guest wing where there is 6 beds. In one of them Fr. Lawrence, covered up to the chin, asked how he feels, smiles broadly and says "Very good."

Everyone says the Northern Lights were seen all over the sky early this morning – I did not see them (they appeared between 2 and 5 when we were in choir or saying Mass).

Brother Alexander says that the last time the Northern Lights were seen by the monks (in 1938) a war followed and maybe it would be the same this time.

It is still very cold – there has been no let-up. Slightly warmer today – it is above 20.

Perhaps *The Secular Journal* will be published after all. The General has consented to reconsider it, if I make *all* the corrections (although the censors said there was "nothing against faith or morals").

Letter from Fr. Fernandes, Redemptorist Superior in Lima. He wants to come and we have accepted him (He wrote first in November and December), Padre Pablo Gusman in Lima definitely thinks Fr. F. should enter here.

February 15, 1958. Saturday

Heavy snow. The cold weather continues, though there was a warm moment the other day after dinner and I heard a song sparrow out in the fields beyond the wall, and looked at the sunlight on the dead, yellow grass of the mill bottom.

A curious view, across the mill bottom, and across the road, to the big dirt dam, with yellow grass all over it and the two walnut trees in front of it, and behind all the wooded barrier of the long forty acre knob. Somehow, seen from down there, the view suggests to me something I have never seen in Peru or Mexico.

More are sick and some are getting sick over again for a second time.

Room 5 in the old guest house has been full of novices, full of dissipation, pillow fights, useless signs, and even breaks of silence (by Fr. V.).

Bro. Patrick and Bro. Guerric push a little wagon up the long hall of the old guest house bringing soup, fruit juice, and crackers to the sick.

While the novices live in comparative decency the professed are in abject squalor, at least in room 4 where I saw them for a moment, unshaven, in various stages of dress and undress from complete cowl (Fr. Michael) to robe with a heavy flannel shirt over the outside, to underwear . . .

In the bishop's room – Frs. Prior, John of the Cross, Flavian and Marion sit around a table eating oatmeal and hot biscuits while the snow falls interminably outside.

The other night – Fr. Eymard got in a room with two others and started snoring. The others moved out – Fr. John of the Cross to the third floor of the new guest house and Fr. Innocent – to the floor of the professed scriptorium.

Have been editing the *Secular Journal* – still like it. Have written to Fr. Irenaeus at St. Bonaventure's for the original mss. To add more. The cuts suggested by the most critical of the 4 censors have, perhaps, been wise.

In the midst of all this, a letter from Mons. Urrea, of the Diocese of Santa Rosa de Osos in Colombia, offering us a property of a hundred hectares.

Fr. Crisanto knows him. He is well to do, and very anxious to have a contemplative Order come to Colombia – offered this property first to the Carthusians at Venta de Banos (Spain) who refused saying they were not prepared to come to a "Mission Country" (loud laughter from Fr. Crisanto).

The country around Santa Rosa de Osos is high and mountainous, 8,000 ft.

Grow corn and frijoles.

Hydroelectric plant at Rio Grande – plenty of power in the region.

On the highway between Medellin and the Caribbean ports.

Rev. Father was at first very hesitant, but I talked to him yesterday morning and I think he will look into it further. I arrived late for the novice's conference.

The Bishop of Sta Rosa de Osos is a great figure in the Church of Colombia. *"Muy batallador!"* ["A great fighter!"] An arch conservative and a fighter who has lots of enemies no doubt. Everyone I have met from Colombia, talks about him. He has founded a congregation to work in the jungle missions.

Curious novel of Bioy Casaris, *Plan d'évasion*, about a governor of Devil's Island experimenting with certain prisoners to put them in a different, schizophrenic sort of a world by various operations and "adaptations." It ends up by being a very good and very original mystery story, in which, entering this new dimension created by the governor, four or five men are murdered by a mad priest – in a repetition of a murder he had committed when shipwrecked on an island. In trying to help his prisoners to be "perfectly happy" the governor puts them all into the weird dimension in which the priest committed the crimes for which he was imprisoned. Book starts slow and ends well, with a slow, progressive complication of threads. A kindly Argentinean Kafka, but clear and Latin, without Kafka's brooding and darkness. In the end, I like this curious book which was sent down by New Directions.

The novel fits strangely into the context of our plague here.

Sterility of Bioy's escape – political background??

Vocation of Fr. Lawrence and its connection with the dictator of Nicaragua, Somoza. Must read his poems, "Zero Hour" – Zero hour for Somoza and for himself. Somoza murdered and he himself "dies to the world" – there is much to investigate here. First, to read the book of Pedro

Joaquim Chamorro, tortured by Somoza's son in prison. L. writes to Chamorro of finding Somoza in the psalms – Og, Sheol, etc.

Suddenly, saw, this afternoon, the meaning of my *American* destiny – one of those moments when many unrelated pieces of one's life and thought fall into place in a great unity towards which one has been growing.

My destiny is indeed to be an American – not just an American of the U.S. We are only on the fringe of the True America. I can never be satisfied with this only partial reality that is almost nothing at all – is so little that it is like a few words written in chalk on a blackboard, easily rubbed out.

Never so keenly felt the impermanence of what is now regarded as American because it is *North* American – or the elements of stability and permanence which are in *South* America. Deeper roots, Indian roots. The Spanish, Portuguese Negro roots also. The shallow English roots are not deep enough. The tree will fall.

To be an American of the Andes – containing in myself also Kentucky and New York. But New York is not, and never will be, really America. America is much bigger and deeper and more complex than that – and A is still an undiscovered continent.

Waldo Frank has said many silly and callow things, but I agree with him on the deep and fundamental point: the *Great Vocation of America*, a hemisphere that is called and chosen.

America has her own vocation and no one else can help her to find it – least of all Russia (but Russia can perhaps place some bit of ferment in her, that will start things working – but no ferment is needed. It works mightily!).

The vocation of America is the vocation of men who are called and chosen from amongst the peoples. It depends on them.

Men like Bolivar, who have seen and understood something of it.

My own vocation – it would have been dreadful to have returned to Europe, to Italy, to Camaldoli. It would have been fatal.

My vocation is American – *to see and to understand and to have in myself the life and the roots and the belief and the destiny and the Orientation of the whole hemisphere* – as an expansion of something of God, of Christ, that the world has not yet found out – something that is only now, after hundreds of years, coming to maturity!

The problems and the dangers (who cares about the dangers?).

Possibly, to be able to reach out and embrace all the extremes and have them in oneself without confusion – without eclecticism, without dilettantism, without false mysticism, without being torn apart.

No one fragment can begin to be enough. Not Spanish colonial Catholicism, not 19th. century republicanism, not agrarian radicalism, APRA, not the Indianism of Mexico – but all of it, everything. To be oneself a whole hemisphere and help the hemisphere to realize its own destiny.

Back to Bioy Casaris' *Plan d'évasion* – as a symbol and a symptom.

It is about French people. The death rattle of Argentina's dependence on France. The frustration of the American intellectual who can't get along without a Europe that can no longer sustain him. (Yet – he is sustained, without knowing it, by his own latent vitality.) This has been to a great extent my own frustration as a writer – from which I escaped temporarily "upward" – into spirituality – but that was not enough, because it is not a matter of escape, but of incarnation and transformation. (Like Dick Whittington turning again at the sound of the Bow bells, because London was his life and vocation and fortune. I have "turned again" at the voice of the Andes and of the Sertao and of the Pampas and of Brazil – again, the voice of Jorge de Lima! As if they were my own voice – but not yet the Sertao by any means!)

Evening – cold winter wind along the walls of the chapel; not howling, not moaning, not dismal. What is there mournful about the wind? Its innocence? What is more innocent than the song of the strong child who is the wind, enjoying his play, amazed at his own strength, gentle and inexhaustible and pure? He burnishes the cold dry snow throwing clouds of it against the building. The wind does not mourn, yet the chapel is very cold and two die-hard novices (Fr. Denis and Luke) are there, alone, and still, no longer even pretending to enjoy it or to understand.

February 16, 1958
Land Problem in Latin American foundations

Would it be regarded as an injustice for monastic community to acquire a property of 1,000 to 2,000 acres (400 to 800 hectares) in Latin America?

On the basis of redistribution of land in the agrarian reform of Mexico.

Richer lands – in central part of Mexico, were distributed at the rate of some 8 to 12 hectares per person in the *ejidos* that received land. 14 hectares per person in Guerrero, 12 in Michoacan, 15 in Aguascalientes, 10 in Jalisco, etc.

10 hectares or 25 acres per monk, in a foundation of 40 monks, would equal 1000 acres – not allowing for growth of community. For a community of 80 monks to over 2,000 acres of richland would not be an injustice if they cultivated it themselves (2,000 acres are more than we can cultivate ourselves, even in a large community).

Mixed lands – *arable + pasture* – were distributed at the rate of 30, 35, 40 hectares per person in states like Coahuila, Chichuahua, Tamaulipas, etc. In Durango they got up to 60 hectares per person. In this case only 6 hectares were arable. In a department like Boyaca or Cundinamarca, Colombia, it would certainly be just and necessary for a colony of monks to occupy a farm of 2,000 acres or more if much of the land was poor.

N.B. Church cannot own any land in Mexico.

The minimum plot to be granted to each individual member of the ejidos was 4 hectares – 10 acres = 400 acres for a foundation of 40 monks, 800 for 80, etc. 1,000 for a hundred. It is legitimate to suppose that 1,000 acres would be a minimum size for a monastic farm whose community would be supposed to number, nominally, about 100.

The *pequena propriedad* [the little holding] left to the haciendos after expropriation of 100 to 150 hectares (250 to 375 acres).

Note – a *hacienda* implies usually absent ownership, a resident manager and force of workers – peons held by a system of unpayable debts etc. A hacienda is normally over 1,000 hectares (2,500 acres) often up to 20,000 hectares or even bigger. In 1940 there still remained in Mexico over 11,000 haciendas, a few of which (in cattle country) had more than 40,000 hectares.

The normal rural property is the *rancho*, below 1,000 hectares.

February 17, 1958

Colder still. About o this morning and still that low by Prime.

Because of a cold (in reality not very bad) I have spent the last couple of days in the novitiate, only going to church for mass and vespers yesterday. Better get back into the swing today, since it does not seem to be turning into flu.

But I cannot deny that it was a great joy to say the office in private, Lauds and Prime especially with the sun coming up slowly and shining on the sunny pastures and on the pine woods of the dark knobs which I see through the Novitiate window. Lovely blue and mauve shadows on the snow, and the indescribably delicate color of the sunlit patches of snow. All the life of color is in the snow and the sky. The green of the pines is dull and brownish. The dead leaves still clinging tenaciously to the white oaks are also dull brown. The cold sky is very blue, and the air is dry and frozen so that for the first time in years I see and breathe the winters of New York and not the mild or ambivalent winters of Kentucky.

The strength of the cold, the austerity and power of the landscape, redeem the snow colors and delicate shadows from anything of pastel shading. I can think of no art that has rendered such things adequately – the 19th. century realists were so realistic as to be totally *unlike* what they painted. There is such a thing as *too close* a resemblance. In a way, nothing resembles reality less than the average photograph. Nothing resembles substance *less* than its shadow. To convey the meaning of something substantial – you have to use a sign which is itself substantial and exists in its own right.

(N.B. Man is the *image* of God and not the *shadow* of God.)

February 19, 1958. Ash Wednesday

Things were quite upset yesterday – Bro. Amedeus left and Fr. Sebastian came in with a broken heart about it. Later Fr. Tarcisius went down with the 'flu – he is on the third floor of the new guest wing which is where they are putting them now. The Infirmarian rarely gets around to see them up there. Fr. Tarcisius seems contented though – leaving me without an undermaster. Fr. Sebastian fills in – at least for the parts of the job that involve conversation.

It is getting slightly warmer. About 10 again, at Prime, and now much warmer.

No shoes were taken off at the distribution of Ashes this morning. The singing was very sad. I don't know what Dom Desroquettes felt about it.

I say so many foolish things I don't mean and yesterday I was forced to think a lot about my real inability to be spontaneous with Fr. John of the Cross who is the person I most like and admire in the monastery and who is my confessor since Fr. Timothy left for California the other day.

In trying to be natural with him I am so natural that I am unnatural and in trying to be super-sincere I say things I don't mean to say, as if I were somehow expected to make the most outrageous possible statements about everything.

It is a curious situation, because in the past when I was his director there wasn't any of that.

I suppose that the situation is just so anomalous we both feel embarrassed about it. I expected myself to be able to handle this perfectly gracefully and really got myself insecure instead. Oh well. I suppose in a way it is a kind of Zen relationship after all – words certainly get to be meaningless with all the mental slaps in the face we give each other at every new statement – and all the uncomfortable silences.

This is the first time that my confessions have been anything other than strictly business, short and sweet, and strictly detached and to the point. Here – I want to be perfect, I want direction, I want response, I want to be appreciated, I suppose. And it is no go. So be it. He seems incapable of saying anything to me, probably because I don't let him – as soon as he opens his mouth I take the words out of it, compelled to be always so smart. I am not, after all, a really humble penitent. May God reward the poor guy for bearing with me.

What I should really do for Lent, among other things, is stop saying the things that embarrass me so much – the smart, casual, half-comical statements about everything, statements which I don't mean, and which are, perhaps not even intended as communication and which express nothing but my insufferable pride – Hey, don't say it, but convey it.

I suppose this is really a very good situation and I pray that I may use it.

Summary: When I talk to Fr. John of the Cross now I act like a complete phony and he is aware of it and I guess embarrassed by it, for my sake as well as for his own. Because, after all, that is what I really am.

But the phoniness comes from over-anxiety and impatience. On paper I have time to compose myself, and I can be more "real." With another person I am thrown into confusion and do not foresee the consequences of the next statement and am too busy trying to avoid a crisis that I do not really listen to the other person. This is only fully true of my relations with Fr. John of the Cross. With other persons I am disinterested enough to be more detached, more serene, and relatively normal. But John of the Cross I love and admire and his affection is something I value very highly and I am very insecure about it. I fear to lose it and imagine that I already have.

Reading proofs of *Thoughts in Solitude*. I wonder what on earth I was objecting to in this more "edited" version.

February 21, 1958

Yesterday by surprise Guilliermo Jaramillo arrived from Medellin. I had just received some signed and sealed papers from Columbian consul NY – papers which were thought to be necessary for him to get a visa. I was preparing to send them off to the consul in Medellin when, lo, he arrives. Bro. Alexander at the gate couldn't tell who he was and Rev. Father didn't know who he was, but called me and said, "There is someone over there talking Spanish, go see if it is Jaramillo."

He had an enormously heavy suitcase full of philosophy books, and I found him talking to Dom Desroquettes in the dining room.

He seems a very good boy, simple and dutiful and sincere – and I don't always find the accent of Antioquia easy to follow. He has reddish hair and hardly looks like a South American – more like an Irishman.

Jaramillo brought a letter from Mons. Ricaurte who has found *another* hacienda – this time a very fertile one near Altan, in Cundinamarca. I found it on the map halfway between Bogota and the Magdalena river – pretty well down the mountainside where it is warmer, and coffee and sugar cane and oranges grow plentifully.

It is very obvious that Colombia is where we will have to begin.

I still like the idea of Antioquia.

J. brought three newspapers from Medellin – all dated Feb 1. All had front page stories and pictures of the new archbishop, Mons. Botero Salazar – in *El Colombino* I read a long moving account of his life. The arrival of a famous and rather handsome little Colombian matador called Pepe Caceres was pushed into the back pages by the new archbishop. (Pepe Caceres who has already killed bulls in Seville, says he is going back to Spain to get right to the top of his profession.)

Mons. Botero Salazar has for his motto the words of St. Bernard *"Respice stellam, voca Mariam"* ["Look at the star! Call on Mary"] and in the revolution of April, 1948 he was nearly mobbed as he rescued a ciborium full of hosts. He seems to be a true bishop and I hope he will one day be my ordinary – or the suffragan of my ordinary!

El Obrero Catolico was the best, though the smallest, of the three papers. It seemed very much alive and on the ball – the Catholic Action paper of Medellin. Strong lucid editorial on attempts at economic penetration into Colombia by the Soviets.

Everything I see makes one get more engrossed in South America.

Jaramillo also brought, as a gift from Ricaurte, the works of Sor Francesca Josefa de la Concepcion, a Colombian mystic in Spanish times.

It is warmer and most of the snow has melted, but the epidemic continues – Some getting sick for the second time.

February 27, 1958

I suppose I have heard it before: that the moment in a bullfight when the matador is to kill the bull is called "the Moment of Truth."

Today – was suddenly struck and powerfully moved by the religious implications of this. It presupposes a fundamentally religious attitude towards life, a sacrificial attitude. (Religious origins of the bullfight – which is a ritual ceremony.)

Zen resonances in this expression, the "Moment of Truth" when the bull, the Koan, is killed. (Zen sees life itself as a spiritual Bullfight. Spaniards simply externalized it.)

Jaramillo has the plague. At the moment he is sleeping or trying to sleep in Hogan's alley.

The weather is warmer. Have made beautiful brushfires behind the sheep barn, with great tides of flames swimming from side to side in the warm wind. Fires of cedar brush, where we cut down trees this Winter. Less luck in burning the old wet piles of oak branches left two Winters ago by Bro. Bruno behind the lake that leaks – massive, sodden piles of wood and wet mulch. The leaves on the top catch and the whole thing is briefly washed in fire, then the fire dies and nothing is left but blackness and smoke.

It rained again early this morning, soaking everything nicely.

The other morning I heard the wrens back, singing in the sun while I was up in chapel. The wren houses are ready but they have not made as if to look at them yet.

February 28, 1958

Yesterday turned into a day of frustrations – minor ones, anyway.

First of all I was discontented with the mass ticket I got – there are already an enormous number of masses to be taken care of by me and it seems to me the secretary is now putting on the ticket masses that could easily have been said by somebody else. However – a simple matter to correct this.

The Hammers[26] were coming in the morning but arrived late (No matter – we had a good talk in the afternoon, of this more later).

It was my day to see Rev. Father – I have been upset by the condition of the forest which is in an awful mess and asked once again if we could have or at least sometimes have a jeep – answer negative. No jeep.

Then Rev. Father spent most of the time talking on the telephone (I am used to this and it doesn't bother me much).

Worst of all, he seemed to say definitely that I will *not* be sent to South America, and that the whole idea of the Foundation is at present premature.

Then a lot of silly by-play about names for the new novices. As soon as anyone comes in who is a little fat, Rev. Father insists on calling him Aquinas, because Tho. Aquinas was reputedly fat. This I find extremely silly – but it is one more thing I am finally getting used to.

In the evening one of the novices came in and talked at considerable length about nothing, when I wanted to do something else. But here I have no right whatever to complain since the novices come first even when they talk about nothing. Also the new postulant seemed to me, in his infinitely long direction period (lasting until the middle of the conventual mass) to be talking for the sake of hearing himself put forth all the familiar platitudes about our life. I told him rather curtly that I did *not* think Cistercian monasticism was a panacea for all the ills of our time.

At collation, everyone else got something appetizing and I got something I do not like. Etc. etc. I am ashamed to write all this down because it is after all so usual, and the life is made up entirely of such things. I do not ordinarily notice them and if I feel annoyed I am not surprised at myself and soon forget it.

But, after all these things, I had a dream. It may have had no connection with them whatever.

---

[26] Victor and Carolyn Hammer, friends of Merton, were from Lexington. Victor Hammer printed limited editions of some of Merton's works.

On the porch at Douglaston I am embraced with determined and virginal passion by a young Jewish girl. She clings to me and will not let go,
and I get to like the idea. I see that she is a nice kid in a plain, sincere sort
of way. I reflect "She belongs to the same race as St. Anne." I ask her her
name and she says her name is Proverb. I tell her that is a beautiful and significant name, but she does not appear to like it – perhaps the others have
mocked her for it.

When I am awake, I rationalize it complacently. *"Sapientiam amavi et
quaesivi eam mihi sponsam assumere"* ["I loved wisdom and sought to make
her my wife"] – Sophia (it is the *sofa* on the back porch . . . etc. etc.). No
need to explain. It was a charming dream.

March 4, 1958
Dear Proverb,

For several days I have intended to write you this letter, to tell you that I
have not forgotten you. Perhaps now too much time has gone by and I no
longer exactly know what I wanted to tell you – except that though there is
a great difference in our ages and many other differences between us, you
know even better that I that these differences do not matter at all. Indeed it
is from you that I have learned, to my surprise, that it is as if they never
even existed.

How grateful I am to you for loving in me something which I thought I
had entirely lost, and someone who, I thought, I had long ago ceased to be.
And in you, dear, though some might be tempted to say you do not even
exist, there is a reality as real and as wonderful and as precious as life itself.
I must be careful what I say, for words cannot explain my love for you, and
I do not wish, by my words, to harm that which in you is more real and
more pure than in anyone else in the world – your lovely spontaneity, your
simplicity, the generosity of your love.

I think what I most want to say is that I treasure, in you, the revelation of
your virginal solitude. In your marvelous, innocent, love you are utterly
alone: yet you have given your love to me, why I cannot imagine. And with
it you have given me yourself and all the innocent wonder of your solitude.
Dear, should I ask myself seriously if I will ever be worthy of such a gift?
No, I am not – not because I could never probably be worthy, but because
of my own love for you. And so, I give you everything.

Dearest Proverb, I love your name, its mystery, its simplicity and its secret, which even you yourself seem not to appreciate.

I know enough not to put my hopes vainly in this South American foundation! What do I expect to accomplish – even supposing I am sent? (I still believe I will be sent.) What great good will be done by a group of people living as more or less frustrated contemplatives? Or else keeping a Rule for the sake of a Rule?

Someone else can do that. Surely, it is not my mission in life.

But if I would attempt the thing I think I really ought to do . . .

I still do not clearly know what I think and there is no point in struggling to make it clear. The hour has not yet come and I cannot hasten it. I wait in peace for a clarity that will perhaps never be fully clear until after the work is done.

I am no longer in doubt – yet I am not yet certain.

A great stage, this – into the peace and darkness which is between doubt and certainty. This, in fact, is another kind of certainty, a higher kind – the certainty of what you do not know.

Jaramillo – telling of Rojas' troops firing tear-gas into the church of the Portiuncula at Bogota – the tanks in the crowded street, the people surging out of the church into the Friar's enclosure and everybody, of course, "weeping." He was in the monastery there, on the 6th. of May.

Fr. Crisanto – first great emotional crisis – his vocation is not too solid. Will it last?

March 6, 1958

Am convinced that Fr. Crisanto will leave. Another blow to the foundation project. His vocation to this life was too negative.

Sore throat kept me awake part of the night.

Letter from Jaime Andrade, the sculptor, in Quito, the other day. I am thinking of getting him to do a statue of the Bl. Virgin and Child for us. I wrote telling him very seriously what my idea would be: a statue that would tell the truth about God being "born" Incarnate in the Indians of the Andes. Christ poor and despised among the disinherited of the earth. The Christ of the Poor who are to inherit the earth. Today, Lazarus and Dives in the Gospel. Not hard to understand and apply. The mystery is always there and so obvious that nobody can see it. I am not fortunate to have lived such a "fortunate" life. Yet it is not really a question of having and not having: but of having what belongs to somebody else. How do you know? It is not a matter of accounting and justice. But of giving whatever you have.

The fact remains that few people here will want such a statue and few will want it to be explained to them.

Still haven't written a word about the Hammers' visit last Thursday. Most impressed by Victor Hammers' complete and religious acceptance of the fact that he is the kind of artist that is really out of fashion. I like them both, they are wonderful people, with great integrity and great love for honest work in art and anything else. Hence their printing. They are doing *Prometheus*[27] for me and it is my favorite kind of project. Nice printing and no one inquiring about publicity or money or sales or anything. Doing something good for the sake of its own worth and therefore for the glory of God. 250 copies *"pro manuscripto"* [limited edition] in which I say something which I firmly believe.

The usual horrible Lenten reading in the refectory. Another French author of the early 20th. or late 19th.

Where the Gospels say the youth clad in a sheet fled away from the soldiers in the garden naked, this monster says he fled away "in a nightgown or at least in a loincloth." Falsification of the Word of God in favor of middle class decency. God is not enough of a prude for the pious people of our time. He must be made to conform.

The same writer – absolves the Apostles for deserting Christ – only complains of the fact that they *ran* away. No, they should have walked off in a dignified manner!

Still, it is not as bad as that frightful whine by Fr. Perroy which we had last year.

March 10, 1958

Poor Fr. Crisanto!

In the middle of High Mass, just before the consecration he left his place in choir and started for the sanctuary.

So I left my place in choir and started after him.

He knelt on the sanctuary step with a rapt expression, during the consecration. I came after him when the bell rang for the end of consecration and said: Come we will go together to the novitiate.

[27] *Prometheus: A Meditation* was printed in Lexington in a limited edition in 1958.

In the cloister he knew I was displeased and he said, "They all think I am crazy."

In the novitiate I said "The time has come for you to return to Bogota."

And he said, "Thomas, did you see the Little Flower conducting in the choir?"

So he went to the guesthouse and while he was there he scalded his hands in boiling water and got into the shower with all his clothes on and when I arrived he was saying in a loud voice, "I have committed many sins."

After that – Bro. Odilo got oil and put it on his hands.

He said, "Is it not true that friendship can work miracles? Cure my hands!"

And I said, "You have caused me sorrow."

Also I told him he had lacked prudence.

His hands waved in the air, as they hurt bad, and were very red and full of blisters.

And he said, "It is true, I have lacked prudence."

And then Bro. Marcellus and Bro. Bertrand brought the car and took him to Our Lady of Peace[28] and I wrote to his provincial in Bogota on the events of the day.

March 11, 1958

My day of recollection. Went to confession to Fr. John of the Cross in the vault, as usual. Had to wait a little for him and took down Gabriel Marcel's *Homo Viator* from the shelf as "spiritual reading" – haven't done much lately (except for my Lenten book, Ramon Lull, whom I find at times impossible, although on the first day I was exhilarated).

In Marcel's book came at once upon the Essay on "Obedience and Fidelity." I am sure I had read it before but without too much attention.

It clarifies much of my present struggle and confusion.

Really, under the surface, there is very little struggle. I am content to go the way I am going, which is not a special way at all. But – intellectually and emotionally there is a struggle to justify what I am doing. There is so much here that I cannot accept. And I know in the depths of my heart really that it is not supposed to be accepted, and it is better not to accept it. That if I accept in the sense of "conforming" I would be *unfaithful* to my real vocation.

[28] The psychiatric hospital in Louisville.

I agree with Marcel that the obedience of a child is unworthy of a grown man and I do not think that this is the ideal of religious obedience. Many here *do* think so – and so no doubt do many theologians. I certainly don't believe that St. Benedict thinks so, except perhaps in the case where the monk accidentally remains a child.

Confusion between obedience (owed to the chief as chief – to his function) and fidelity (owed to *persons* to whom, rarely, we bind ourselves) leads to servility. We do not owe "fidelity" in this deep, personal sense, to all the chiefs we must obey. Doubtless it is a very good thing when it is *deserved.*

– When there is a vow like ours, there is obviously a relationship that implies fidelity to one's abbot as well as obedience. Not just a matter of personal obedience. *Abbatem suum sincero corde diligant.* [They will love the abbot with a sincere heart.] But this stops short of the special self surrender and self-consecration which I have never been able to give to any man or to any institution, even to my own Order. I hope I believe I have consecrated myself thus to Christ.

The big question – is it possible to consecrate oneself to Christ without a complete self-dedication to his human representative? I would say *yes.* Most people in the Order would probably say no. I think it is enough to obey and respect them and to love them as Superiors who are also friends. One owes fidelity to his friends. Yes. But one is not married to them. One does not become a replica of them.

Basic fidelity – fidelity to myself.

G. M. says: the artist who labors to reproduce the effects for which he is well known is unfaithful to himself.

Fidelity to myself is response to an "inner call" to transcend what I have already done "to get clear of it, to go on living, to find renewal."

Danger of uncritically assuming that fidelity to oneself means acquiescing without changes to fixed principles, adopted once for all.

Growth of the "profane self" alienated from the mystery of the true inner being when one does have the right to bind himself by oath to another? Sometime, one must do this. "The gratuity of a being can be recognized and found by the fidelity of which he is capable."

It is the basis of any true code of ethics – it reveals man's desire for the unconditional and for the absolute.

If one makes vows in an Order, this presupposes that he has seen that in that Order he will surpass and fulfill himself. Obviously his vocation is a call to be true to his vows in the deepest sense – not by "conforming," not by mere obeying, but by living out one's personal consecration.

Obviously my vows did not consecrate me to the abbot or to the Order, but to God Himself in Christ.

Difficulties, for me at any rate, come only from not seeing this clearly enough.

March 13, 1958

All that was written there two days ago is only a vain attempt to say something. It does not say what I mean, it misrepresents what I mean and makes it appear foolish. I will not try over again, to say what I mean except that in all fairness I do not think I am bound to narrow my spiritual life (if any) and my ideals (if any) down to the narrow, rather rigid concepts of this Order of Strict Observance with which, as ideals go, I agree less and less.

I have no desire to correct anyone or reform anyone or make anyone think differently from the way in which they seem to think. I can be a monk in this Order without making my own spiritual life a carbon copy of Dom Gabriel's latest letter. I will certainly obey what he lays down – and I will read whatever I can get permission to read and I don't believe that solitude can any longer mean, for me, indifference to or separation from what is happening to the rest of the human race.

March 19, 1958. Feast of St. Joseph

In St. Anne's. It is so long since I have been here – I can hardly tell how long.

The peculiar peace and sweetness of St. Joseph's afternoon, the gentleness of the divine mercy, the silence of the air – eleven years since solemn profession, fourteen years since simple profession! How fantastic. A red shouldered hawk wheels slowly over Newton's farm as if making his own special silence in the air – as if tracing out a circle of silence in the sky.

How many graces, here in St. Anne's, that I did not know about, in those years when I was here all the time, when I had what I most wanted and never really knew it. Which only shows that solitude alone was not exactly what I wanted. How rich for me has been the silence of this little house which is nothing more than a toolshed – behind on the hillside for two years they have tried without success to start a rock garden.

Yesterday, in Louisville, at the corner of 4th. and Walnut, suddenly realized that I loved all the people and that none of them were, or, could be totally alien to me. As if waking from a dream – the dream of my separateness, of the "special" vocation to be different. My vocation does not really make me different from the rest of men or put me in a special category except artificially, juridically. I am still a member of the human race – and what more glorious destiny is there for man, since the Word was made flesh and became, too, a member of the Human Race!

Thank God! Thank God! I am only another member of the human race, like all the rest of them. I have the immense joy of being a man! As if the sorrows of our condition could really matter, once we begin to realize who and what we are – as if we could ever begin to realize it on earth.

It is not a question of proving to myself that I either dislike or like the women one sees in the street. The fact of having a vow of chastity does not oblige one to argument on this point – no special question arises. I am keenly conscious, not of their beauty (I hardly think I saw anyone really beautiful by special standards) but of their humanity, their woman-ness. But what incomprehensible beauty is there, what secret beauty that would perhaps be inaccessible to me if I were not dedicated to a different way of life. It is as though by chastity I had come to be married to what is most pure in all the women of the world and to taste and sense the secret beauty of their girl's hearts as they walked in the sunlight – each one secret and good and lovely in the sight of God – never touched by anyone, nor by me, nor by anyone, as good as and even more beautiful than the light itself. For the woman-ness that is in each of them is at once original and inexhaustibly fruitful bringing the image of God into the world. In this each one is Wisdom and Sophia and Our Lady – (my delights are to be with the children of men!).

Dear Proverb, I have kept one promise and I have refrained from speaking of you until seeing you again. I know that when I saw you again it would be very different, in a different place, in a different form, in the most unexpected circumstances. I shall never forget our meeting yesterday. The touch of your hand makes me a different person. To be with you is rest and truth. Only with you are these things found, dear child sent to me by God!

Marvellous books for a few pennies – including *The Family of Man* for 50 cents. All those fabulous pictures. And again, no refinements and no explanations are necessary! How scandalized some men would be if I said that the whole book is to me a picture of Christ and yet that is the Truth. There, there is Christ in my own Kind, my own Kind – "Kind" which means "likeness" and which means "love" and which means "child." Mankind. Like one another, the dear "Kind" of sinners united and embraced in one only heart, one only Kindness, which is the Heart and Kindness of Christ. I do not look for sin in you, Mankind, I do not see sin in you anymore today (though we are all sinners) there is something too real to allow sin any longer to seem important, to seem to exist, for it has been swallowed up, it has been destroyed, it is gone, and there is only the great secret between us that we are all one Kind and what matters is not what this or that one has committed in his heart, separate from the others, but the love that brings him back to all the others in one Christ, and their love is not our love but the Divine bridegroom's. It is the Divine Power and the divine Joy – and God is seen and reveals Himself *as man*, that is in us and there is no other hope of finding wisdom than in God-manhood: our own manhood transformed in God!

March 23, 1958. Passion Sunday

Karl Stern was here the other day and I am glad that after all he did not speak in Chapter for he would perhaps have disturbed some of the Fathers. I am glad he did speak to the novices for although he was mostly over their heads, they liked whatever they could get out of it. Fr. Denis made profession on St. Benedict's Day and looks most innocent and holy in his new crown and clean cowl – but I wonder if he will survive his studies!

It rains very slightly and a song sparrow sings in the rain.

I wonder when the wrens will begin to take an interest in their little houses – they are very late because it has been so cold.

Fr. Pedro (Jaramillo) cannot sleep because of the cold and I have put him in the warm room in the guest house. But I think he was badly shaken by the Crisanto incident and will not last. There goes our second Colombian, then – and perhaps with him the hope of the Colombian foundation. But Rev. Fr. prefers, he says, to make a South American foundation with North Americans. And everywhere I see the horror from which there is no escape – the monotony of good, empty headed, generous, rather dizzy American monks who are not horrified by commercialism, who accept Franco, who are utterly dumb and impervious to all the sources of real corruption capable of ending their monasticism in one generation. And I, with my resentments, my weakness, am full of the same corruption only in a slightly more subtle form. That is the source of all my agonies – they are only sullen attempts at evasion.

March 25, 1958. Annunciation

This morning's chapter: I have just fled to the woodshed in the rain to recover. I do not mean that it was any worse than the usual feastday chapter. Or that I was more upset by it. I think at last I really don't care. I used to be utterly unnerved to think that somehow I have to defend myself, justify myself, because the morning chapter has been so absurd and I have been sitting there, as it were passively cooperating. In the old days I regularly renewed my resolution to become a Carthusian as the feast-day chapter drew to a close. And yet if I wrote what I really felt about it I am afraid the things I would say would be only a series of silly gripes, and I know I should not waste time by saying them – they would not be what I really mean.

(Andy Boone over there just started up his buzz-saw with a whoop I heard one half mile away.)

Well, what for instance.

A rather tedious first sermon. Yet the preacher is a good kind man and everybody likes him. One feels that his sermon could have been otherwise if what? If he did not imagine he was a young priest preaching a sermon. That is where the trouble starts. We are so darn convinced that we are very holy monks and priests, very important people, and men of great spirituality and faith, and there begins an infinitely complex set of pretenses and verbalizations which of course are enough to make a sincere man lose his faith forever! What a horrible and constant stumbling block. And yet I must admit that of all of us there could hardly be anyone more sincere than the good young Father. Perhaps it is I who am insincere. Yet I have to be at least sincere enough to realize that I cannot say Amen to everything in our feastday chapter.

The infinitely complicated nonsense about our chant – the ever more intricate arrangement for placing the schola now one way and now another – there are five or ten new rules promulgated every week, on solemn occasions. The cantor's schola moves up and down during vigils, Tierce, and Vespers, then, the schola stays put. And Rev. Father makes it clear that the brothers not only "may" come to choir but *should*. (The G. Chapter seemed to indicate the brothers could *occasionally* come to choir on Sundays etc. – but they are in choir for the little hours every day – except Tierce.)

Now when the schola stays in a fixed position, the man at the South end of the schola moves North with a preoccupied and gentle smile to alert the non-schola man who is next to the schola at the North end, to move to the South end, if there is an empty stall. (I would gladly furnish one myself without the slightest hesitation.)

This is just one new rule out of a million. Or rather an old rule that was dropped wisely several years ago because it was found to be ridiculous.

The revival and creation of ridiculous rules has gone up 100% since Fr. C. was appointed choirmaster. He and the abbot abet one another in their madness.

Why can't they just let the poor brothers be brothers and live in peace?

The ones among the brothers who were most anxious to be "like the choir in everything" are now wandering around very miserable since they got what they wanted.

No use listing everything: the news of the earth-satellite launched at last by the navy (this was the other day) – the statistics about how many boys from Catholic schools end up in jail – or fail to do so – the pleas for prayers from friends of the monastery who have lawsuits or are being investigated for invasion of income tax – prayers of thanksgiving for a novice – it is the sixth month since he entered the monastery and his little brother aged 6 already wants to become a monk – etc. etc. These are typical examples rather than today's specials.

Today's final special – The Bl. Virgin had Christ in her womb for 9 months. Well, someone has figured out that if the Host stays in us 15 minutes, then if a man receives Holy communion every day for 63 years, he will have Christ in him for 9 months in all. This, we are told, is "very beautiful."

Oh yes. It was also announced today that on March 25 Adam and Eve ate the apple.

Today's question: perhaps I am not *supposed* to sit through it with complete indifference. But what then should I do? Write an exposé and send it to the press? That is where the anxiety begins, because one is not yet able to see anything but the false choice between a "fidelity" to nonsense and an infidelity which would be a betrayal of love and truth, under the pretext of stating a truth.

It is a constant and diabolical dilemma – excuse the expression, but in its own silly way it is I believe quite correct. This is a torment the devil has devised for monks, to mock their efforts at loving the Truth.

The great thing is to go on, miserably, honestly, recognizing one's dishonesty and one's cowardice, not covering it with either kind of sham, betraying nothing and faithful to one's search for the real truth that does not need either kind of declaration.

Because all along, when one is quiet and listens to the song-sparrows and the crows, he knows very well that the real truth that he has come here to find is not contained in these declarations, it cannot really be stated, it is lived and grasped in the depths of the heart and one must be very careful of words, for words betray it. And that is what goes on in our chapter: we use words to defile the Truth we recognize in the silence of our heart.

March 30, 1958. Palm Sunday

Fr. John of the Cross is really the only one here who has anything to say and his sermons are a tremendous contrast to anything else that gets said in our chapter. He preached this morning, and what he preached was really the Gospel, not words about the Gospel – or about something more or less remote from the Gospel. He preached Christ and not himself – or someone else who is not Christ. And I think this is the reward of his integrity which does not come without cost, for he has to suffer in order to be true to the love that is in his heart. And because he is true to the love and does not betray it in favor of formulas and human respect, he is able to speak the words of Christ. I doubt if I could reproduce his words without distorting his sermon, so true is it that sermons do not consist simply of the words in which they are preached.

Speaking of friendship with Christ – he said that in all friendship there is first a stage in which we see the acts of the other and come, by them, to know who he is. But after that we know who He is, we see his acts in the light of who He is. And even acts apparently dubious in themselves, or ambiguous, are understood or at least accepted in the light of who he is. And that the transition point comes when we clearly see the inmost desires of our friend's heart. And that the inmost desire of the Heart of Christ was to love the Father and to be about the Father's business. He said, too, that we do not have to know and understand all about the Kingdom or lead the way to it, because Christ knows and does that. He alone knows and is, the way we do not fully understand.

All this was strong and consoling in several ways – because also it gave me great light and peace about my own love for Fr. John and, since there is no doubt that we really know the desires of one another's heart and accept everything without question as a result of this.

What a precious thing is this confidence which is not scandalized in one's friend. This must be our confidence in Christ and our knowledge of Him – but if we do not know and trust our earthly friends how shall we know and trust Him?

Wrote several things this week and I think they were good (the new Sacred Art article and the preface to the Sudamericana volume – [29]) but was afterwards keenly aware of the despair and megalomania which formed part of the doubtless good idea of writing these things. A salutary shame and acceptance: certainly graces! Painful ones. But the wound that bleeds will be a clean one.

One reason I am so grateful for this morning's sermon is that my worst and inmost sickness is the despair of ever being truly able to love, because I despair of ever being worthy of love. But the way out is to be able to trust one's friends and thus accept in them acts and things which a sick mind grabs as evidence of lack of love – as pretexts for evading the obligation to love.

So much evasion in this dream of South America! If it were really love, how strong I would be! And how soon there would be a foundation! But there, right away, is the ambiguity for I do not really love my Order as it is, I am suspicious of its inmost aims and desires, I wonder if they have anything to do with Christ and with love. I seriously wonder, all the time, the fault is probably mine. But in my case there is so much I do not (cannot?) accept and understand.

Rev. Father closed the Chapter with "Yes, Jesus must be our real pal, our most intimate buddy, intimacy with Him is everything."

Good Friday – April 4, 1958

Yesterday evening, after the Mass and collation, I was standing out in the garden looking at the grey skies and the birds and Fr. Pablo (Jaramillo) came along with a knowing look and said that the view of the hills certainly offered much poetic inspiration, did it not? After that we talked a little about climates, earthquakes, and whatnot and about the "terrible cliffs" along some of the roads in Colombia – in Caldas, he was talking about.

Most of the day yesterday I was sad at my own bitterness and lack of charity but things perked me up after the Mandatum [the ceremonial washing of feet] (where I was one of the foot-washers and kissers) and above all after communion.

[29] "Sacred Art and the Spiritual Life" was published in 1960 in *Sponsa Regis*. Merton was also writing a preface for a Latin American edition of his writings published by the editorial hous Sudamericana.

This morning the psalter was something tremendous – with the system we now follow of letting everyone go off and recite it by himself after the first hour.

I had been reading Dom Leclercq's new book *L'Amour des lettres et le Désir de Dieu* which is very fine, and I spent most of the time in a *meditatio* of psalms 85 and 86 saying them over and over by heart in the depths of my being.

These were the ones I have recited scores of times before without ever seeing them.

How long it takes us to discover some of the psalms.

In particular:

Confitebor tibi Domine in toto corde meo et glorificabor nomen tuum in aeternum / Quia misercordia tua magna est super me et eruisti animan meam ex inferno inferiori. [I give thanks to Thee, O Lord my God, with my whole heart / And I will glorify Your Name forever. / For great is your steadfast love towards me; / you have delivered my soul from the depths of Sheol (Psalm 85:12–13).]

I will have to return more often to this kind of *meditatio* it is absolutely essential, one of our great failings here is that we have neglected it totally (not even heard of it – we think meditation on the psalms means "thinking about" certain lines – no doubt with thoughts suggested by one of the "scientific" commentators. And we wonder at the futilities and aridities of our prayer!).

After the discipline this morning – a Bewick's wren singing like mad on the clothesline in the twilight of dawn. Are they finally going to build their nest in the bird house?

Antonio Canedo – Fr. Francesco Solano – a bright and dreaming young man, seems to be turning out very well. From La Plata seminary in Argentina – a very resourceful type indeed – Begged well over $300 to get here in grand style – *all* the way by plane, no bus from Miami. The only thing was that they forgot to put his suitcase on the plane and it still hasn't arrived. In it are some copies of *Sur* which he got for me (free of course!) at their office, by producing my letter asking him to bring one issue. When he was going the rounds begging he went to the provincial of the Franciscans who said, "Ah! You know our poverty. I cannot give you any money but still I will give you something for the good of your soul" and he presented him with a discipline. But not one of the iron ones which Fr. Pablo showed me yesterday and which they use in Bogota.

Read a little of G. Marcel's essay on "Value and Immortality" but am not sure I know what he is talking about. Caught a few intuitions here and there, but out of context. The Truth is, that I am ill-prepared to understand Marcel as a philosopher but at the same time I am temperamentally disposed to see things his way. When I follow him, it is more or less by instinct.

In any case, I ask myself – do I really put up the necessary fight against pseudo-truths and pseudo-values or [Line breaks off here.]

Holy Saturday – April 5, 1958
Whatever I was going to say (when I was interrupted by Fr. Francisco!) I have forgotten but it was probably useless. I mean, my words would not have said it. Perhaps I can say it today.

Not so much a matter of "putting up a fight against pseudo-truths and pseudo-values" as, rather, knowing and seeking real truths and real values.

Well, what are the real truths and real values, I seek?

If I had a clear-cut answer, then I would certainly be insincere – or else an angel.

It is of course a dishonest answer to say glibly "God" and leave it at that. This is the dishonesty characteristic of monks. And what do you mean by God?

We can string plenty of words together to answer that one. But are we saying something, or are we playing with words? Is it honesty enough to add word upon word until you get half a page of them and sign your name at the bottom and take an oath that you believe it?

I do not think it is perfectionism in me to be utterly dissatisfied with any such "honesty" as that. It is the dishonesty of breeding false values and hiding the True. It is what hides God so that no one can ever find Him. Belief in "propositions" is only the beginning. Full belief must imply some *grasp of the reality* expressed in the propositions, and that grasp goes beyond propositions – it attains to "something more."

Another approach.

Yesterday I was sitting in the woodshed reading and a little Carolina wren suddenly hopped on to my shoulder and then on to the corner of the book I was reading and paused a second to take a look at me before flying away.

(Same wren just came back and is singing and investigating busily in the blocks of the wall over there.)

Here is what I think.

Man can know all about God's creation by examining its phenomena, by dissecting and experimenting and this is all good. But it is misleading, because with this kind of knowledge you *do not really* know the beings you know. You only know *about* them. That is to say you create for yourself a knowledge based on your observations. What you observe is really as much the product of your knowledge as its cause. You take the thing not as it is, but as you want to investigate it. Your investigation is valid, but artificial.

There is something you cannot know about a wren by cutting it up in a laboratory and which you can only know if it remains fully and completely a wren, itself, and hops on your shoulder if it feels like it.

A tame animal is already invested with a certain falsity by its tameness.

By becoming what we want it to be, it takes a disguise which we have decided to impose upon it.

Even a wild animal, merely "observed" is not seen as it really is, but rather in the light of our investigation (color changed by fluorescent lighting).

But people who watch birds and animals are already wise in their way.

I want not only to observe but to *know* living things, and this implies a dimension of primordial familiarity which is simple and primitive and religious and poor.

This is the reality I need, the vestige of God in His creatures.

And the Light of God in my own soul.

And God in man's history and culture (but so mysteriously hidden there and so strangely involved in the Passion which He must suffer to redeem us from evil).

The wren either hops on your shoulder or doesn't.

What he does – this he is. *Hoc est* [That it is].

And our ideas of Nature etc.? all very well, but *non est hoc, non est hoc* [it is not this, it is not this]. *Neti, Neti* [Neither this nor that].

Do no violence to things, to manipulate them with my ideas – to track them to strip them, to pick something out of them my mind wants to nibble at . . .

April 9, 1958

I think the only country in which the history and intellectual movements of the 19th. century really interests me is *Russia*. Only there do I find thought that really seems to me vital and promising, literature that I really want to read. Want very much to get hold of Khounniakhov of course. Also Chandaev. Soloviev, the "Russian Newman" is to me a thousand times more interesting than Newman even though, perhaps, he was not a Newman.

The tremendous interest and faith in the destiny of Russia shown by the intelligentsia of the 19th. century is deeply significant.

April 11, 1958

Had a couple of good talks with Dr. Kerekes who was here visiting his son Bro. Fidelis.

It is more or less definite that I am to get to work on a book about Soviet Russia – from the religious viewpoint. Or at least begin the necessary research (I have already been reading about it). I like the idea of his Institute for Ethnic Studies at Georgetown. How much we talk about working to unite the world and how little we really do about it. People will move mountains in Africa for business, but won't kick a clod of earth out of the way of charity.

The mania for making everyone else like oneself – this is the apostolate of alienation and hatred.

If I am to write on Russia I must first of all understand it and that is one of the hardest things in the world. But really understand – which means love. But the starting point is love of America, oddly enough – But not a prejudiced and jingoistic love. I must unite in myself all that is good in both Russia and America, see all that is vain and false in both, in myself, purge that out of myself. I pray that my book will be discreet and wise and full of deep understanding so that all can recognize the Truth in it and be ashamed of any error they have embraced before.

April 20, 1958. II Sun After Easter

The wrens built their nest last week.

The linden leaves are beginning to come out and this week we will see beech leaves, which are the loveliest things in creation when they are just unfolding.

Censors passed *The Secular Journal*.

I was wise to come here to the woodshed instead of getting under the cedars outside the wall, for now rain is falling.

A big four motor army transport just flew over very low – about three or four hundred feet.

What struggle we have to put up, in order to find the Truth and stay with it.

The Truth is a Way and a Person – and a Way and a Person have to be found and followed. Truth is to be lived. There are, in fact, no simple formulas that will suffice once for all. True, there are principles. But a principle is worthless if it is usually known and not applied and when we supply it, we have to have regard for circumstances which make the principle true in a unique way in this unique case – or which, perhaps, call into action some entirely different principle which gives the lie to the first.

How hard it is to be loyal to the Truth when most of the time you do not see any of it! Thus loyalty demands constant criticism, constant rejection of empty formulas, of words used to evade the struggle and to allay anguish, rather than to find Truth, or express it. And can we use words simply to *find* Truth? Is not this an illusion?

There grows in me an immense dissatisfaction with all that is merely passively accepted as truth, without struggle and without examination. Faith surely, is not passive, and not an evasion. And today more than ever – the things we believe, I mean especially the things we accept on *human faith* – reported matters of "fact"; questions of history, of policy, the interpretation of wants – they should be *very few*. In great spheres we should believe little or nothing, except what is obviously and incontrovertibly true – that the atomic bomb was dropped on Nagasaki, for instance.

Same plane came over again, a little further to the North, but only a little. The stink of pigs come up to the woodshed, and I can hear the peaceful racket of Nally's chickens, over there on the hill. And how many birds, especially a mocking bird!

Buber's *I and Thou*, in an execrable translation, very difficult to follow at first. An important book, in which I am confronted with the hollowness and falsity of my own life – yet the comfort that right here, this writing is an "I-Thou" writing – isn't it? But so much other writing which is nothing but a closed door. I close the door on Thee by giving Thee too many standard names, and hiding Thee with concepts – Then inviting everyone to stand in front of the door I have closed in their face.

Article on Tillich in *Theol. Digest.*

What do I mean by untruth? I would be untrue to myself and to God and unfaithful to Truth if all I took from this article were to be such words as "his epistemology is a mixture of Kant, Schelling, positivism, and existentialism." It is very easy to look for signposts such as these and be satisfied with them – and never to go any further. In point of fact there is much in Tillich – It is useful to remember that as far as Catholic theology is concerned he is perhaps a "betrayer of ontology" and this is not just a matter of words.

The value of someone like Tillich for us is that he can take risks (thank God!) which we cannot take, and he can come up, as a result of the risks, with insights that are of great value to us and are not in themselves risky.

So the thing for a priest to do is, it seems to me, is to take note of the risks, and use his head, and then go ahead and read Tillich. The sermons in "The New Being" offer no "danger" for one who knows a little of our theology: he will feel the ground go out from under his feet whenever T's Christ turns out to be Nestorian. That is not the important thing. What is important is the clearing of the way for contact with God, however you may explain it.

Fr. Pablo who, I think, has no vocation to this life, buttonholed me in the sun the other day among the daffodils and said "Has Your Reverence ever thought of leaving here and starting a new order more adapted to the needs of present-day man? Your Reverence's mission here is accomplished and it is time to go on to other things."

"How foolish and hopeless would be the man who turned aside from the course of his life in order to seek God; even though he won all the wisdom of solitude and all the powers of concentrated being, he would miss God. Rather is it as when a man goes his way and simply wishes that it might be the Way; in the strengths of his wish his striving is expressed."

Buber's I and Thou, *p. 80.*

Later – Day of Recollection resolutions.

I know that the hour of Truth must come for myself and for the whole world.

And I know until this hour I also, like the others, have not used the key I found and have not opened the door to the whole world. But this was to be expected for no one had told us what this key was, that opens a door that cannot afterwards be shut, and lock a door that cannot afterward be opened.

Before the Bl. Sacrament, I know now that this door must be opened, and that its name is dangerous to mention. It is better not mentioned.

The people of the whole world, in poverty, oppression, confusion, frustrated by rich empires or wracked by violent empires, are waiting in despair for what has been refused them. The despair of those mocked and exploited by Russia and the despair of those used and sold out by America, a whole new world in despair waiting for the hour of Truth, which the degenerate fascist marxism of Stalin has delayed for perhaps another hundred years. And yet perhaps that was unavoidable, and has its place.

Meanwhile – what is my position?

Thank you. I know my position. I begin to see it. And there are many to whom I have no business giving any account of my position. Too much is said about positions. Here are the relevant points at the moment:

1. My lot is cast with the future which I do not yet know. The future of the whole of America, North and South.

2. My job is to shut up and avoid political mysticism and other forms of false mysticism and apply myself to learning and to open my eyes, and see what is going on.

3. And learn to help to "go on" to where it is going. And to help myself from joining those who one way or another, want everything stopped dead and kept that Way – or everything to run the way they think it is supposed to be running.

4. But can I take a leaf out of the marxist book by keeping my mouth shut and my eyes open and to watching for what is to happen.

Why in God's name can't people like Silone get organized? And Koestler and Auden, Spender, and the rest?

Who are the people who are able to *do* something – how can I ever contact them?

How wrong I have been to spend my life in passivity and negativism and confusion writing only things that could so easily be used *against* freedom and salvation!

The bloodiest crime of our day has been perpetrated by all the innocent ones who have been made dishonestly "safe" – and have flung themselves into futile works that mean nothing and were only an evasion.

". . . cleansed from dead works to serve the Living God."

If History is in God's hands, then what in God's name are we sitting on our fat rumps for, doing nothing, blind, deaf, and dumb, waiting for God to prevent history from happening? . . .

You know, all of a sudden, I begin to understand those Essenes by the Dead Sea – and the prophetic importance of their apparent folly.

The business of being "on neither side" – first of all is it possible?

It has to be possible.

But then, the big thing: to work for the creation of *another* order = the real one. The side of the people who are hungry united with the people who want freedom, in order that all may have both bread and freedom (cf. the end of Spender's article in *The God That Failed*).

April 22, 1958

Charmed and fascinated by everything Berdyaev says in "The Russian Idea" until suddenly I am brought up with a jolt by his statement that Proust is "France's only writer of genius!" An intuition that might possibly, from a certain point of view, have truth in it. And yet is not true.

His insights, then, are brilliant and right but one must remember they are not always meant to be "true" in the sense of "definitive." They are always tentative and that is a good thing. Perhaps this makes them in their way truer than those judgments which are sound and "true" "for all men at all times."

April 24, 1958

Fine climax to Buber's *I and Thou*

"Meeting with God does not come to man in order that he may concern himself with God, but in order that he may confirm that there is meaning in the world.

"All revelation is summons and sending. But again and again man brings about instead of realization, a reflection to Him who reveals. He wished to concern himself with God instead of with the world. Only in such a reflection he is no longer confronted by a Thou, he can do nothing but establish an It-God in the realm of things, believes that he knows of God as of an It and so speak about him . . .

"*God remains present to you when you have been sent forth; he who goes on a mission has always God before him: the truer the fulfillment the stronger and more constant his nearness.* He cannot concern himself directly with God but he can converse with Him. Reflexion on the other hand makes God an object. *Its apparent turning towards the primal source belongs in truth to the universal movement away from it . . ."*

These are among the wisest religious truths written in our century.

Ten years ago I would have been perplexed and scandalized by them, but in the depths of my heart I realize how true they are. And I realize how monumentally we fail, in this monastery, to understand this!

I do not know how these words would sound to a technical theologian, and don't much care. I feel no need to juggle with them and manipulate them and make them "theologically acceptable" – they are words drawn from experience. They can certainly be controlled by theology. That control is not my business. My business is to verify Buber's experience with my own. And that is easy. Also, for the moment, that is enough. If I come to say the same thing in my own words, I will perhaps say them in a way that will not scandalize those who do not understand. But I do not write for those who do not understand.

In these matters we have greatly magnified the problem of scandal and misunderstanding. When was there ever a problem in the fact that a report of religious experience lends itself to misunderstanding, even among religious people?

April 25, 1958. St. Mark

Mark Van Doren, D. Marcos Barbosa, and the postulant in Brazil (Peru) P. Marcos Fernandes – May God bless them on this day.

What a beautiful Spring it has been. A late, cold spring, sometimes rainier than usual. Sunday morning after Mass, sitting in the quiet novitiate chapel, with the sun coming in through the East windows and a warm dark rain blowing up against the West windows and embracing the whole building in a great rumor.

The lovely leaves of the young linden we planted two years ago, fresh green against the dark hills, yesterday, when it was cloudy.

The new shrine of St. Fiacre, and the laburnum we planted near it. The laburnum already begins to be full of promise.

The maple we planted down the hill, beginning to flourish in virginal splendor. And all the other young trees that God planted down there, stretching out their arms with joy – and the small leaves coming out all over them.

The great wind that blew on the building all the other night, rattling the doors in the darkness. The goldfinch that flew across the garden. The titmouse in the woodshed with a short ebony beak, and very soft grey plumage and the inexpressible rose tint about the belly, if a titmouse has a belly. It came within three feet of my foot as I sat on the saw-rig. Very friendly, or rather, that is wrong: the wonderful unpredictable curiosity of birds which we desecrate by reading into it motives from our own psychology.

I am deeply moved by John Collier's book on *The Indians of the Americas.*

Have we ever yet become Christians?

The duty of the Christian to see Christ being born into the whole world and to bring Him to life in all mankind.

But we have sought to bring to birth in the world the image of ourselves and of our own society and we have killed the Innocents in doing so, and Christ flees from us into Egypt.

Have we ever yet become Christians?

April 29, 1958. St. Robert

Fr. Barnabas, trembling, tense, and apparently furious, made his simple vows in chapter. He has assured us that he wanted to.

Fr. Sebastian is in the hospital for a nose operation. He has assured us that he wanted to have it. He suffers continually with an allergy. And with philosophy. Is a touchingly good and simple person, and another one of those for whom there appears to be no special place anywhere. The kind who are always here as it were provisionally and who nevertheless stay. I hope. What he loves: birds, the garden, the brethren, chant. What he hates: philosophy, Trappist spirituality and *all* spirituality, probably some of the brethren. But I doubt if he would hate a *person.*

The 3rd. Sunday after Easter (the day before yesterday) always stirs me strangely and I will never forget the day in Havana, 17 years ago – it was the 3rd. Sunday in Paschal time.

In John Collier: the shattering record of the treatment of the Indians in the U.S. – and S. America too (but that is all too familiar).

Until the beginning of the century it was assumed that the Indian problem and the harm done to the Indians arose from *corrupt individuals* in the government. But after 1900 the individuals concerned were honest and upright – and things went on as before for the policy, the system, the philosophy and the laws were themselves corrupt. Collier says "It was not individual corruption but collective corruption; *corruption which did not*

know it was corrupt and which reached deep into the intelligence of the nation . . .
collective corruption is more effectively carried into deed through agents not per-
sonally corrupt."

April 30, 1958

Tanagers in the woods yesterday – vivid scarlet against the young green leaves and the fresh blue sky. Lots of little warblers which I could not see to identify, not having field glasses.

A beautiful, simple letter from Jaime Andrade. About his life and his work and his plans to go ahead with our statue and that he is not related to Carrera Andrade – but he gives me the poet's address in France.

Pablo Antonio Cuadra is supposed to be coming here Friday, to see Fr. Lawrence. In connection with this visit I have had some correspondence with the Governmental Affairs office in Washington and they sent me the itinerary got up for him.

April 25 – 7:32 A.M. – Get up, shave, wash your face, put on your pants, meet our representative in the lobby, have breakfast. Please take a taxi to the fairgrounds, if you haven't already received an accolade from Carl Sandburg you will receive one at the fairgrounds . . . etc. All ending with a big, jolly injunction "Have a pleasant trip!"

Letter from Lax in Flushing hospital, blood poisoned. He sent a clipping about some old ladies who are waiting in car outside the Old Folk's Home to go for a ride. The car all by itself ran down a slope into a lake and they were drowned. The newspaper report had about it the insane, inhuman factuality such things have, and so I wrote a poem about the old ladies.

There is so much death in the newspapers that no one dies in them anymore and no one lives in them. There are neither lives nor deaths in our press, only a stream of words passing over the living and the dead without ever touching them.

Fr. Pablo, who does not sleep, is going to have to leave and return to Colombia. He doesn't mind leaving but is making difficulties about returning to Colombia. Today he read me long passages he had copied from Unamuno, doubtless before Unamuno got on the index.

And tomorrow is May.

May 2, 1958. St. Athanasius

The long martyrology, the powerful Epistle and Gospel of his Mass. The power of his own writing. Athanasius was a mighty bishop and his might needs to be understood. How long a time I had last year penetrating into his mind and history of his age – gave it up. I am busier now and more profitably so, with my own age. Yet it is very much like his.

We speak and think as if the Reds were the only ones who had ever falsified history – but *everybody* falsifies history! *Omnis homo mendax!* [Every man is a liar!] You have to seek truths laboriously by pitting one lie against another – or many half-truths together – until you can make your own mendacious guess as to what the truth was.

"The disciple is not above his master nor the servant above his lord. If they have called the good man Beelzebub, how much more them of his household!" (Matt. 10. Gospel of the Mass.)

In the monastery, or at any rate in choir, I have been forgetting how to think – and only in the past few days have I woken up to the fact that this is very dangerous! I mean the constant, habitual passivity we get into. No matter how honest the surroundings and how clean doctrine believed in them, no man can afford to be passive and to restrict his thinking to a new rehearsal, in his own mind, of what is being repeated all around him.

But we are not as honest as we think, and our doctrine is not as pure as we hope it is. I least of all can afford to be passive in this place.

One must constantly be asking himself – "What do I mean by this? Am I saying what I mean? Have I understood what this implies? Have I some notion of the *consequences* of what I am saying? I am particularly bad on the last question, because usually I think on paper, that is I often do not really know what I think, until it is set out before me in black and white: then I can agree or disagree.

May 3, 1958. Holy Cross

Why, of all the 19th. century political thinkers, did Marx come to have such success?

Because his system is built on the most powerful and most universal emotion of man in our time – *resentment*.

A He diagnosed, with the intuition of genius, the source of this resentment, *alienation*.

B He rationalized this resentment as a "good thing" in the dialectic of class struggle. Class hatred becomes a dynamic force which will solve all problems and build the new society. It is therefore justified and praise-worthy.

c Present resentment can be glossed over and forgotten by dwelling on all the good effects it is going to have. One already imagines that those good effects have begun to be attained – etc. Marxism – a religion of resentment.

Pablo Antonio Cuadra arrived with his wife last evening and left this afternoon.

Read me some very fine poems – his latest – *El jaguar y la luna*[30] – after showing me some Indian ceramic designs by which they were inspired.

Fine short poems with a very high degree of mystical quality and power.

Was deeply moved by dialogue of two stars (Indians believed warriors and mothers became "stars" in heaven because of their suffering). The warrior says he died that the future might be born and that he has not seen that future. This was what most moved me, because perhaps this also is my own destiny.

All the poems had very impressive titles.

Were at once very Asiatic and very American. This is the voice of the true America.

We talked of the Island of Ometepe again – he and I and Fr. Lawrence.

They have driven to the airport – this is Derby day. I hope they will avoid the crowds.

May 5, 1958

Thinking of the new and necessary struggle in my interior life.

I am finally coming out of chrysalis. The years behind me seem strangely inert and negative, but I suppose that passivity was necessary.

Now the pain and struggle of fighting my way out into something new and much bigger. I must see and embrace God in the whole world.

(It is all very well to say I have been seeing God in Himself. But I have not. I have been seeing Him only in a very small monastic world. And this is much too small.)

Said the Mass *Ad Tollendum Schisma* [For the removal of schism] – one of the most beautiful.

[30] "The Jaguar and the Moon"— Merton would later translate this poem.

Cool again this morning. Many birds singing. The tops of the hills still hidden in mist. The lark still sings "Dr. Zhivago" – (which I very much want to read).

May 8, 1958

It rained and became cold after having been warm and I caught a miserable cold by coming in a sweat out of choir and giving out work in the draughty novitiate cellar. So now on a wonderful bright May day I am sitting in bed in Hogan's alley in one of the blue rooms painted last year by the postulants. But a mocking bird sings brightly in the *Préau*.

Fr. Pablo left on Sunday asking for this, that and everything: money, books, a statuette of the Bl. Virgin, some more clothes, and finally "some wine and fresh eggs," which, he thought, were good for a journey. The desperation with which he wanted to acquire things in his moment of crisis! For some reason the return to Colombia seems to have been for him an unacceptable humiliation. He had told his parents never to write to him again – they had not written one letter even though he wrote and pleaded to hear from them.

Rev. Father secretly learns Spanish and this makes me angry because it means that he has no intention of taking me to South America if and when the time comes – if he can help it. And I have no doubt he will be able to help it.

He does not trust anyone else to do anything important – except Bro. Clement, and there, too, it is a strange relationship. The last thing in the world he would want would be a foundation that got out of his own hands and did not faithfully strive to copy Gethsemani in everything. Any foundation in Latin America made by him will have to be made by yes men – North Americans over whom he will have full control, men without originality and not too inclined to be Latins or to understand Indians. That is why the whole thing will have to wait indefinitely – though I learned he wrote to the Bp. of Medellin that he would come to Colombia next year.

Meanwhile I come more and more to admit the utter folly of my wanting to run a Cistercian foundation in Latin America – freedom to apply ideas that I really don't have anyway. Or rather, freedom to resist despair by trying to put into effect ideas that would necessarily explode all Cistercian limitations.

The things I want to say can be said more simply and powerfully in books than in monastic foundations.

Nevertheless – what is it that moves me? The thirst for stimulation? The need for a new country and wider horizons? I don't pretend to know what is really eating me. Partly temptation, and partly something immeasurably more solid than that.

May 9, 1958

Yesterday Victor and Carolyn Hammer came from Lexington and I sat sneezing in the back of their station wagon and we talked of various things, notably about the proofs of *Prometheus* which they are printing. And his crucifix for the grunelius chapel at Kolbsheim.[31] And the booklet I am doing for *Art and Worship*.

Victor said at one point: "*Must* one read Heidegger?"

I said I thought not.

Rev. Father said there had been an election in Colombia but that he did not know who was elected. I asked if it were Lleras and he said he thought it might be.

May 13, 1958

Yesterday – a white eyed vireo playing in the dry sumacs in the hill before you get to the old lake. And a pine warbler in a little elm, standing on his head to get down under the leaves at the end of the branches.

A possum sleeping in the fork of a hickory sapling, with his hand hanging down.

And just now, two little siskins, the tamest things I ever saw, busily working on some dandelions on the ground almost under my feet, where I was reading and walking about below the retaining wall. Lovely birds, very small.

May 18, 1958

Sunday morning. Outside the wall, facing the sheep barn, in the cool morning air – across the blue sky the tracks of a long departed jet plane.

There, in the sycamore to the right, a Carolina wren.

Directly in front, in the willows, a song sparrow.

Over there to the left beyond the cedars a cat bird or a mocking bird sings. Yes, a catbird.

---

[31] The chapel of the chateau where Jacques Maritain lived; the crucifix now hangs in the infirmary chapel at Gethsemani.

———

In Louisville to see the doctor who appears to have a successful way with my complaining and irritated rectum.

Bishop Maloney spoke of nine gypsies he had confirmed near Elizabethtown at a place called Cecilia. These gypsies come from Georgia where they all gather for the Winter and here in the Summer they go about painting the roofs of farm houses and doubtless also the sides of barns.

We spoke also of sacred art (since I had brought the sacred art mss. for censorship) and he said that Archbishop Floersh was reluctant to "give permission for one or other of those old statues to be taken out and buried" as one must leave certain people in their invincible ignorance. A comforting principle, which will excuse many unpleasant things!

In the library spoke to ex-mayor Farnsley, who is an extremely pleasant person. Had bad luck with the record music piped up from the cellar – Couldn't get Hopis and Navahos as I wished – but a little Art Tatum (yes) and later, with Fr. Sebastian, some Villa-Lobos and Fr. S. who is exceedingly sensitive to music, liked it.

Decided not to bring home a Silone novel right away. Later, yes!

Book on Indian art, with a fine Navaho poem which I must find again.

The lovely locust trees blowing around all the farm houses in the country, especially around Holy Cross. The irises everywhere – the beautiful Spring day. Fr. S. showed me an azalea hedge which, he said, had been "beautiful last week" (he had a nose operation and goes in often).

Read some modern Greek poems, from the War years – some of them very moving. Why am I suspicious of Greek poetry, as if they would never be poets again, as if one had to compare them at all times to Sophocles and reject them? They were good poems.

Above all, this year has marked my discovery of Pasternak.

First, in the copy of *Encounter* which came by chance with a review of *Strange Islands*.

Then, in last month's *Partisan Review* clandestinely acquired.

I have just finished his marvelous story "The Childhood of Lovers." This is a great writer with a wonderful imagination and all he says is delightful – one of the great writers of our time and no one pays much attention (now no doubt they will, with *Dr. Zhivago* – coming out in English in the Fall). He is so good I don't see very well how the Reds can avoid killing him.

Coming down the chapel steps and praying for his soul, a great one, a man who is spiritual in everything he thinks and says!!

May 29, 1958

Marvellous brilliant day. The most brilliant day of this or of all years, amazing one by its wonderful clarity ever since morning.

A day of grace and of blue sky. Of definitiveness, of freedom. of certitude, of new found ways of open doors.

Admired the young linden in the morning.

The terrible insights of Hannah Arendt's *Origins of Totalitarianism*.

Wrote notes here under the pine trees in bare feet.

Finished Pasternak's *Safe Conduct* and felt as if I must at once begin to read it again. A magnificent book, one of the great ones.

The fabulous descriptions of the flower store in Leningrad – the incidents in Marburg and Vienna – trains – the Urals – his devotion to Scriabin and Maiakovsky – Maiakovsky's suicide, his piteous lamentation over him and the cryptic conclusion.

I have thought several times of writing to Pasternak. How absurd – as if I could contemplate the writing of such a letter.

But perhaps I could send him "Prometheus" – And need to send the "Tower of Babel."[32]

A titmouse came with a new clear whistle I had not noticed before and darted from one dry branch to another in the big pine above me there. O admirable friend, singing, as I think "True, true" (and not just "Tee Vee").

Fr. Sebastian went to Louisville again, shyly leaving poems on our desk to read – as if he waited to get as far away as possible while I was reading them.

May 31, 1958

An admirable book from the Louisville library. Berdyaev's *Slavery and Freedom*.

I think it is useful to know what one man one tends most closely to sympathize with, to "agree" with in a general way (though by no means with all his individual statements) – to agree with in the whole of his doctrine though not in each particular fact by itself. He says, among other things:

"The self-realization of personality presupposes resistance, it demands a conflict with the enslaving power of the world, a refusal to conform to the world . . ."

[32] Poem first published in *Jubilee* (October 1955).

Repeatedly, since last year, two years ago, this thought comes to me with all the power of a "message."

And I still don't quite know what to do about it.

In a sense, this was the reason for my entering the monastery, but that only shifted the problem to another level.

It was not a solution.

June 2, 1958

"It is very easy to see fanaticism in other people but difficult to spot it in oneself." *E. M. Forster*

Another cool day. They (we) are all planning Corpus Christi designs. It rained in the night. I do not know what happened to the wrens but the nest in the wren house is abandoned and they sing somewhere else.

Bro. Clement came in with a cheese ad, again, and I worked on it, God forgive me.

June 10, 1958

I had forgotten to put down anything about Spencer's foundation in Argentina. But it is a fact – at least the plan is a fact. From Fr. Segura, at La Plata, I have very unimpeachable information that they have been offered a place near Azul, South of Buenos Aires in some low hills (not plain pampas) and they will very likely accept it.

We had been wondering who were the four Trappists of whom we had heard reports first from Argentina, then from Chile.

Quiet morning – I am hebdomadary and sit in the cool garden, smelling honeysuckle and wet grass and earth, listening to crows, larks, bobwhites, doves, titmice, wrens, and sparrows. Seeds from the sycamore fall on this page. Dew shines on the sheepbarn roof.

The more I read about Russia the more I think it is better to be silent about what goes on in the world and not mix oneself up in it. Except, too, that I think one ought to make some kind of a statement of one's position – when one had an intelligent statement to make, which perhaps I do not yet have.

"It need to be said that politics are always based on lies . . . (we ought to) demand the reduction of politics and of their fictitious power over human life to the very minimum. Politics are always an extension of the slavery of man. The astonishing thing is that politics have never been an expression even of intelligence, to say nothing of morality, or of goodness. The so-called great among statesmen and political figures have said nothing wise and intelligent. They have usually been men of ordinary, current ideas, of banalities adapted to the average man." "The majority of these great figures are distinguished by the same criminality, hypocrisy, craftiness, and intolerance . . . An exception must be made in favor of social reformers who emancipated man from slavery." *Berdyaev.* Slavery and Freedom, *p. 143.*

June 12, 1958

In town yesterday to see Dr. Ryan again and Terrell Dickey about designing "Art and Worship."

In the library – a good article in *Kenyon Review* on Dostoevsky's women characters. Listened to Prokofiev's Sonata for 'Cello and Piano, and a sonata for flute and piano. The first began well but they both got dull – evidently due to his efforts to produce something that Zhanov and Khrushchev can whistle in their bath.

Got a special number of *Atlantic Monthly* on France – and read about DeGaulle business in other magazines. The whole thing seems to me confusing and sad. I don't believe DeGaulle has that much to offer. We'll see.

June 22, 1958

Wonderfully cool. Never saw such a June. Bright blue sky. Birds singing everywhere. Not a cloud. Sunlight falls on this page through the branches of the cedars outside the wall and is not oppressive, but pleasant, like the sun of May or October.

The fine top of this strange table rescued from the tailor shop before they ripped out the innards of the Northeast wing.

Tearing down the mill or part of it. Bro. Wenceslas hurls down bricks of the chimney one by one. Fr. Sebastian and I wonder where all the chimney swifts will go. The chimney swifts – remember one I rescued on the night watch, picked him off a screen in the cellar and let him go out the door he could not find – and it was when I was thinking of going to Camaldoli. And a good thing that I didn't.

The other day – the novices found a bat in the conference room, and brought him out into the garden in broad daylight in the middle of the morning. I took him back inside and let him hang upside down in the tool closet. The wings are a bit repellent (why?) but the bat himself is a beautiful thing. Clinging blindly to our notebook and trembling all over. His long ears, small eyes, "peaceful expression." (There we go again. Rank subjectivity.)

Very good book on Fr. Matthew Ricci in refectory. Admired his jesuitical technique immensely, until the strange vision on the boat outside Nanking, at which I began to wonder.

The battle against inertia. In the life and in myself. This is the great thing. The constant struggle to break through illusion and falsity and come to Christ and to freedom. And how often we fail. I am convinced there is something in our long offices and formal prayers which induces inertia and stupor. Am I just? Or is this more subjectivism? Be honest in seeking the answer.

Letter to Fr. Lombardi (Rome) who wrote with an enthusiasm I do not altogether trust; perhaps not sufficiently enlightened. Yet I took it as coming in the name of Christ in all Truth – replied frankly, Telling of my boldest and most "reprehensible" projects. (Reprehensible from the viewpoint of the O.C.S.O.)

Wrote of the same to Fr. Segura at La Plata – who can get all the Argentine bishops behind me any day!

The conviction that I have not yet even begun to write, to think, to pray, and to live and that only now I am getting down to waking up. And that, by God's grace, this comes from finally trying, with great difficulty, to be genuinely free and alone, as humbly as I can, in God's sight, without passively accepting all the standards and the formulas which have been adopted by others – or, at least that I am now exercising a wider choice in my sources of inspiration.

June 25, 1958

"Henceforward I must take up a position even more antagonistic to my contemporaries than that of a mere critic of the mechanistic system. I must take a position antagonistic to the very basis of their organization. And I must appear antagonistic even to the Church itself. Of course that is all nonsense, but that is how it must appear. For the Christians everywhere have committed themselves to the support of Capitalist industrialism and therefore to the wars in its defence, mechanized war to preserve mechanized living, while I believe that capitalism is robbery, industrialism is blasphemy, and war is murder." *Eric Gill.*

July 22, 1958. F. of Mary Magdalen

The other day, taking the discipline while thunder crashed and rain poured down outside . . .

We are remodelling the novitiate chapel (in part). Tore out the two crazy booths that served as "sacristies" – moved back the so-called "sanctuary step." There will be only two altars. Getting paint, fabrics to hang behind the altar, Kentile. Hope we will be finished by Assumption.

No reply from Lombardi. Dreamt that Rev. F. was angry about my letter. Tried a *"sortes"* [random opening] in Scripture and got:

Go not into the way of the Gentiles nor to the cities of the Samaritans But go rather to the lost sheep of the House of Israel.

Wait – and if in time the thing develops – tell the General or someone like that. Wait perhaps a few more years.

While I think of going to the intellectuals, Rev. F. wrote a contemptuous letter from Utah about the arty people of Aspen Colo calling them "playboys" – and some hot air phrase about them which made me indignant – especially in the context of all his talk about bulls and chickens.

Letter from Jaime Andrade and ideas about the statue.

Camus' *La chute [The Fall]*. I admit is too long.

Purity of Faith. The need to struggle with Truth – and my inability, *unwillingness* to do so. To go out every day and face the same mental wall. But this Truth is not far away from me. I do not mean the Truth of the whole world – just my own Truth. I both am and am not the Truth that I seek and there lies the difficulty.

Read an article of Jung which Fr. Matthew tore out of something or other. A good one, but full of ambiguities. One wonders if he knows just what he is talking about when he tries to talk about religion.

Howard Gold here. Ad Reinhardt in Afghanistan. And all this trouble in Lebanon not Ky. – but the Near East.

July 25, 1958

I suppose I have to face the fact that most of my South American projects are absurd.

Why are they absurd? Hard to say. Largely perhaps because I do not really know what I mean by them. More and more they get pared down to nothing.

Now the vocation of Fr. Francisco (Canedo) is falling apart.

To found a Trappist monastery in South America would be to found a nest of discontentment and predatory neurosis.

I have come to the conclusion that if there is anything I want to do it is NOT to attempt a Trappist (O.C.S.O.) foundation anywhere, but precisely something quite different.

Having what characteristics? Avoiding what faults?

Easy enough to say "greater simplicity" – poverty, etc. No point in planning anything special – let Ecuador take care of those details. Live as they live and you will live poorly enough.

A small monastery.

1. Without a "program."

2. Without a special job to do. Monks to *live*, not to be "monks" as distinct from every other kind of being, but to be *men* – sons of God.

3. Without a special future. No drive for postulants.

4. Without a special reputation or renown for anything.

5. A hidden monastery, not well known, perhaps, as a monastery. Perhaps not even wearing a special habit. Without observably distinctive buildings.

6. But certainly isolated, cloistered and cut off.

7. With hermit types – i.e. possibilities for personal solitude for a certain portion of the year. Special solitude in certain seasons. Advent, Lent.

8. Made up of a nucleus of *mature* monks, each one able to decide for himself in fasting, etc.

9. Taking an interest in art, music, Literature, politics, etc. of our time.

10. Manual labor of course. Maybe some teaching. *But care to keep the life from getting crowded with works and projects.*

One sensible thing – I can begin to live now, as far as possible, the life I would like to live in such a monastery, and with the same spirit.

Rule? A return to St. Benedict – or an application of St. B.

Rise between 2 and 3 – *Recite* Matins – 1 1/2 hr interval for reading and prayer.

About 5. Lauds – *Conventual* mass – and private masses.

5:30 Mixt – odds and ends (shaving etc.).

7. Prime – Work (Chapter + distribution of work, announcements, etc. regarding the day. No formal daily sermon). Work until 11. (Break about 9. for tierce). Manual work in a.m. as far as possible.

Sext. Dinner.

12:30–2:30 Rest, reading.

2:30 None, Work or study (intellectual work in p.m. or work with guests or in clinic. (Can be 4 hours straight for intell. work or study with break for None.)

4:30 Vespers. Supper. Informal chapter (not reading).

6:45 Compline.

7–7:30 Meditation in church or in cell. Lights out at 7:30.

A private room for each professed. One or two hermitages. Fish and eggs allowed in refectory.

August 3, 1958

On the Feast of St. Ignatius (last Thursday) before mixt, Fr. Urban was going around getting everybody's blessing. He was sent to O[ur] L[ady] of the Genesee. I was his guardian angel 16 years ago. The only one here who was a novice with me and who is still at Gethsemani is Fr. Hilary. Fr. Bernard entered just before I was professed. He is still here – made me a sign about it this morning.

Novitiate chapel may turn out well – yet have doubts about the color on the walls and serious doubts about the brown on the benches, with which we are hiding the grey that got on in Fr. Urban's regime. If only they had left the natural white oak – it was very beautiful!

Went to town Friday, in more rain, to work on the art with Terrell Dickey. He keeps kidding me about my "modern" taste. The job is complicated but I think it will work out all right.

Why does this have to sound like a letter to one's grandmother?

Came out of chapter slightly angry as usual on Sunday.

Doing violence to myself to read Regamey's book on non-violence because I need it. A lot of it is arid and plodding but here and there one comes across good stuff. Gives the impression that he is saying more than is necessary in order to make it all "acceptable" and ends by being diffuse and trite. He would have done it all much more effectively in 50 pages of aphorisms – but who ever heard of a Dominican doing that?

[Louis] Bouyer's book on Newman, in the refectory, is very good – especially interested in the parts about Oxford. If I could have lived my undergraduate life over again – if I could do it now I mean! But I cannot and am glad in the end. What is done is done and my life is what it is – and the mercies of God have been very great.

In Chapter – heard that a Russian had mapped out the springs and irrigation canals of our monastery in Utah.

Rev. Fr. announced with relish that the U.S. Army now has a sputnik flying over Russia. Felt like vomiting.

In Louisville picked up a magazine called *Dissent* – mostly left people – nothing very striking in it, but a breath of my own kind of climate, for a change.

"The very substance of my philosophy is to have nothing at all to do with the thoughts of times which, so far as I am concerned, are over and done with. I look to the thought of a world which is to begin – the world of a new Middle Ages." *Berdyaev.*

Always very fine ideas in Guardini on Providence.

For instance that the will of God is not a "fate" to which we submit but a creative act in our life producing something absolutely new (or fail to do so) something hitherto unforeseen by the laws and established patterns. Our cooperation (seeking first the Kingdom of God) consists not solely in conforming to laws but in opening our wills out to this creative act which must be retrieved in and by us – by the will of God.

This my big aim – to put everything else aside. I do not want to create merely for and by myself a new life and a new world, but I want God to create them in and through me. This is central and fundamental – and with this one can never be a mere Marxian communist.

I must lead a new life and a new world must come into being. But not by *my* plans and *my* agitation.

August 14, 1958. Vigil of the Assumption
Fr. Francis wants to go to a smaller monastery (perhaps Utah) out of what seems to be a legitimate desire for more poverty and austerity. It must be admitted that there is less and less real austerity here and that unless one does continual hard manual labor there ceases to be much penance in this

life. Those who complain of lack of penance are sometimes those who (perhaps through their own fault) do the least real manual labor.

I must confess I feel the lack of hard work. Enjoyed sweating and getting tired with a scythe in the weeds yesterday (fighting the jungle between the novitiate and the old mill). But it seems to me that I am obliged also to study and put in as much time as I reasonably can in studying – in this I run the risk of being wrong and I am at last simply running the risk for better or for worse. I am a writer and though I don't intend to write so much, any more, I feel I must know something about the world in which we live and in which we are supposed to fight for the Kingdom of God.

There are things I will not know about my faith and about my vocation if I fail to understand Communism. This I have to do for myself and for others as well. It is part of my solitude which, as a matter of fact, is now very real.

This shelter where I sit, looking over the mill bottom and the enclosure wall, under the sycamores, is one of the better projects that, as it were, built itself this Summer. Tile flooring in this afternoon in the chapel (I like the walls all right).

August 15, 1958. Assumption

Huge jamboree in finishing the chapel, in haste, in contradiction of my express orders. Just wrote Fr. Tarcisius a strong note about it. This Trappist disease of running wild with projects, especially decorative projects. They were up at least until 8:30 last night (1 1/2 hrs after bedtime). I was down at 8, which probably stopped them staying up another hour wiping up the adhesive that was all over everything including the door.

Concluded that the only really good thing about the chapel is Fr. Lawrence's crucifix. The altar is very slick, and looks good, but with the Kentile floor, the drapes and the gladioli the place looks like a middle class living room. The light fixtures I chose in a hurry (God forgive me) will work and cap it all and make the place look like a semi-genteel cocktail lounge.

I was angry all morning.

Chapter – Dom Vital on Martha and Mary. Our wonderful contemplative vocation, how much better off we are than the active orders. Utterly unable to swallow the mass of half-truths and delusions and good middle western complacencies that made up the usual feast-day chapter (Not Dom Vital more than anyone else. He was only part of it).

Then Rev. Fr. saying "You know we have made ourselves responsible for Fr. Francis in giving that affidavit" – wants to push him over the border into Canada or Mexico and leave him to float. "We can't have him in this country... he may leave Utah and then... etc. etc." Mepkin won't take him.

No letters whatever this morning, only a visiting card of someone in Italy selected from the pile I didn't get and given to me as a joke to keep me "detached."

Good talk with Fr. Lawrence after conference. The story of C. who wanted to know if monks exorcised their farm machinery before using it. C. also (a poet) who in New York as cultural attache in the Consulate where the consul, a creature of Somoza, treated him as a lackey. In order to have a certain independence he went out and got a job – as an office boy!! – in a business firm. One day he was sent out with a package to the Consul of El Salvador. But this was an acquaintance who he met several days before at a diplomatic function. "I can't be seen delivering a package, he'll think Nicaragua has fallen apart" etc. etc.

A wonderful novel could be written about a character with all the features of a recent Latin American Dictator. The things they have done are stranger and sometimes more terrible than a novelist would likely to invent. And generally funnier, also. Hopelessly comic as well as blood thirsty. They are portents of our time.

August 17, 1958. Sunday

Sounds of rain in the night – I lay in bed appalled by the weight of water falling upon the earth, it seemed, in a solid mass. Wonder what happened to the crops.

Our tobacco this year is early because of all the rain and we shall start cutting it tomorrow.

Fr. Bede yesterday, in my Portuguese lesson, told me Brazil had won the World's soccer championship in Sweden. I was happy to hear it. The abbot in Sao Paolo wrote him to "*instigar*" [instigate] me to make a foundation in Brazil. I am already instigated but nobody else is. More and more I realize it is a good thing we are *not* trying to make an ordinary foundation, or rather that I am not involved in one. It would finish me, to have to work my head off with all the limitations we work under, and to produce a community whose value I most seriously doubt. So much falsity and hollowness in our life – so much of it a pure verbalizing about nothing. Self-delusion.

August 20, 1958. St. Bernard

Problem of feast-day chapter scenes to be solved by a little strong coffee. Took some today and found the whole business not only tolerable but gay – ("St. Bernard didn't come to the monastery with his head full of baseball, football, and track – No! He knew nothing but the Bible and the Imitation of Christ"!!)

Yesterday good day of recollection in the woods. Read the part of *The Possessed* about the mad Saint Symeon and something clicked – a strange light on Bernard's *"fiducia"* ["trust"] and one he might perhaps have repudiated, but the root of my problem remains fear of my own solitude – imagined solitude – the fear of rejection, which I nevertheless anticipate – as if it mattered! I should be more bravely real – it is what I need, and no one would be surprised at it in me – I think even my vocation requires it. In passing Fr. Hilary quoted in sermon: "How great should be our confidence *when we recognize in ourselves the image of God!*

Serious need to give the "folly" of God a predominant place in our very serious and seriously insane world! It is perhaps the most valid reply if not the *only* reply.

The answer of apparent wildness is the providential and divine criticism that is demanded of us and I have not been nearly as wild as I need to be – it is a reply also to the serious stupidity of our misguided "holiness" here.

I am really a monk when I can let go completely of "being a monk" (self-consciously) and I think I have let go of that long ago. Now I face the terror of being, by the same "letting go" a Christian? And a writer and myself.

How crazy it is to be "yourself" by trying to live up to an image of yourself you have unconsciously created in the minds of others. Better to destroy the image if necessary. But even this is not serious, or to be taken seriously.

After Mass – faced seriously the question of Ecuador and could only pray to go there – in what way I don't know – certainly not as a Trappist founder. But have no idea of pushing anything – on the contrary!

August 25, 1958. F. of St. Louis

The grip the *present* has on me. That is the one thing that has grown most noticeably in the spiritual life – nothing much else has. The rest dims as it should. I am getting older. The reality of *now* – the unreality of all the rest.

The unreality of ideas and explanations and formulas. I am. The unreality of all the rest. The pigs shriek. Butterflies dance together – or danced together a moment ago – against the blue sky at the end of the woodshed. The buzzsaw stands outside there, half covered with dirty and tattered canvas. The trees are fresh and green in the sun (more rain yesterday). Small clouds inexpressibly beautiful and silent and eloquent, over the silent woodlands. What a celebration of light, quietness, and glory! This is my feast, sitting here in the straw!

At Mass, sad inmates of Dachau, Auschwitz, Vorkuta, Solovki, Novolsk, Karajanda, stood triumphantly by the altar at the commemoration of the dead.

Kacmarcik and J. D. Robinson and a seminarian (O. Gentry) who drove them – here yesterday. Lecture and lantern slides for the novices. Tremendous pictures. We talked about many good things. Not the least, of my monastic idea – and I met with nothing but agreement and support.

Mother Benedict of Regina Laudis talks to the nuns about Marx and that is what started me going. This is the way *it should be*. Our contemplative life must be rooted in our time. I see it more and more clearly. It involves at least an interior dialogue with what has been said that is most challenging and crucial. *Not* an apologetic. Real consideration, understanding, grasp. A contemplative life that takes cognizance of all that is articulate and is able to see, understand, judge – not a contemplative life which "bends" blindly, hesitantly, in fear – and decides nothing. *Spiritualis judicat omnia.* [The Spiritual (realm) judges everything.]

Bro. Mathias received extreme unction after None, sitting in a brown chair at the head of the choir. He is dying of cancer. Again, the mystery of the present. Wasted and changed by illness he is still Bro. Mathias, in fact, more Bro. Mathias than ever – his life is crowned by his patience and goodness in his suffering, so that this will be the definitive Bro. Mathias – and I am sure he no longer knows anything about this and has lost sight of himself. He just suffers, and the days go by. How strange it would be to say he received the Sacrament "with great faith." Which, of course, is true. How true to say he received it with the earnestness and the depth of feeling which we know in him and which is his very self to us. He received it as Bro. Mathias – as one loved by Christ, and chosen by him. This is the real heart of the mystery, so obvious and simple. *The presence of Divine Mercy in the midst of us, in Christ.*

The lights for the chapel came today and I dread to think what they will do to it, though they are all right in themselves (i.e. all right for a clubhouse!).

September 7, 1958. Day of Recollection

September Day of Recollection is always for some reason the most beautiful in the year. (Yet, as I look back, last year I was tired and depressed – but with the climactic struggle at the end of the noisy Summer.)

Summer explodes, Rev. Fr. goes to the General Chapter, and I frantically send away novices and postulants.

Fr. Tarcisius to France, at his own request, with nebulous and strange ideas of some impossible vocation.

Fr. Paul of the Cross – Rome, or to Benedictines, or somewhere where his emotions will be quieter. (Later – he decided to stay on.)

Fr. Vincent to the professed side, with his signs, his dissipation, and his despair. Yet I like him and am one of the few who understands (?) him and tries to have confidence in his vocation.

Fr. Cuthbert thinks he can squeeze into a Camaldolese hut with Dom Agostino on the California coast – that Camaldolese foundation for which I had prayed so much. What will come of it?

This beautiful day, with the quiet sun shining on the bronze paint of the Garden-Virgin and on the marigolds and the weeds and the hills. Crickets everywhere. Nothing moving in the garden but the wind, a butterfly, and my pen.

Fair day of recollection in the new chapel, and I was happy in it and accepted its imperfections, and accepted everything. That is all that is needed. When you accept what you have you see all you have received more than enough and you are overwhelmed. I desire other things because I fear to be content with what I have – I fear it is inglorious. In the last few days I have seen what matters is to be humble enough to admit I am content with just this. Leave the rest to God.

September 9, 1958

For the last 5 days or so – reading *Dr. Zhivago* which finally came. Deeply moved by it. Not being in the habit of demanding absolute structural perfection in a novel, I can call it great. Wrote to Helen Wolff at Pantheon about it and she wired asking permission to use what I said. Later sent a tepid review of the book clipped from the *NY Times* as a specimen of the kind of reception it is getting. I would like to write something about Pasternak. Wrote a letter to him but don't know if it will get through. Sent him "Prometheus." Books on Le Douanier Rousseau from library of U. K. Work on them now. Mark Van Doren's autobiography coming some time soon, he writes.

September 13, 1958

On the 11th. Fr. Francisco left – he will go to Spain. I have not much hope for his monastic vocation and I am surprised how great was the relief I felt at his going. He was a load on my mind – a silent, offensive, manipulative "dependence." Immense complications and, I think, evasions. The day he left, there came a deeply moving letter from Victoria Ocampo[33] – as if the confusion and mystery of his being here were resolved and clarified. I had asked him to bring copies of *Sur* and he went to the editorial offices in BA to get some (free, of course). I sent her an article and "Prometheus."

Of Pasternak, Helen Wolff (at Pantheon) says that he twists the tail of the Soviet tiger as if it were a mouse and sends out messages on unsigned postcards expressing his defiance.

September 16, 1958

Hot weather – and now we have the cowls on.

Galley proofs of *Secular Journal* make it clear to all that my best writing has always been in Journals and such things – notebooks.

Fr. Romanus, sailing next week for Rome, thin, shaggy without a haircut, came in to talk about his worries – afraid of the jealousy of other monks. He goes to get a degree in scripture. The first we have sent in years. Again, the other monasteries, including our own foundations, are far ahead of us. Two from Genessee, Two from Utah, one from Mepkin.

September 22, 1958

Fr. Peter came into the infirm refectory last evening with a small snake in a glass jar, and this morning I saw him walking down the cloister with a cigar box. I guessed from his smiles that the snake was in the cigar box.

Baudelaire's prose poems – in a very thin volume from the Louisville library.

Faubus in Arkansas: the curse of God must be on this country!!

[33] Founder and editor of *Sur* as well as publishing house of the same name.

R. de Leon, a Filipino postulant, objected yesterday when I spoke of Gandhi. Said non-violence was "not-natural." No, I guess maybe it isn't. And yet without some more of it, what is going to happen to human nature?

Ps. 38 – Psalm of Satyagraha (*dixi custodiam vias meas*). [I said that I will guard my ways.]

Psalms in woods yesterday (Sunday)

A card from Rev. Fr. – another of the *Cloître des copistes* at Cîteaux.

Yesterday, said mass for France, etc.

September 26, 1958

Very hot weather – as hot as any we have had all Summer.

Secular priests, ending their retreat, singing in the church.

Yesterday in Louisville. Saw Fr. Romanus off at the airport – afraid of the oriental languages he will have to study at the Biblical Institute. He and some others left their pen too early, started for the plane and were driven back. He stood with his black hat on, looking unsteadily at the enormous bird. Later in the library I picked up the *New Yorker* and there was a full page ad of the American Export Lines (He is going on the *Independence*) – and it said "*You* can still sail on the *next* trip." Oh, I can, can I??

At Terrell Dickey's – the *Graphics* manual. And they hunted for ten minutes trying to find me a picture of St. Patrick's Cathedral in the Penrose Annual. (*Graphics* always fills me with wonder. It has softened me – I believe that advertising art can be civilized after all!)

Then I went to the Chancery to talk to Bishop Maloney about the pictures in *Art and Worship*.

After that, had a good day in the library. Some C. F. Andrews on Gandhi (the concept of *svadharma* [personal service] important for me!). A book on Etruscan painting; some Latin American prints (good ones by Portinari). Looked briefly at Kierkegaard's *Either/Or.* Tatum, St. [an] Getz, etc. on record. *New Statesman and Nation* – special number on American Lit. with a tender essay by V. S. Pritchett on the Beat Generation, and what seemed to me a very good, or at least readable, poem by Lowell about his father.

Last time I was in town – we had to drop something at the G.E. plant – Appliance Park. We came at the enormous place from the wrong side and had to drive miles all around it. Surrounded by open fields with nothing whatever in them, not even thistles, marked "Property of General Electric. No Trespassing." The buildings are huge and go on forever and ever, out in the midst of their own wilderness. Stopped by guards, we signed in at the appropriate gate and promptly got lost in the maze of empty streets between the buildings, finally came out right. What struck me most was the immense seriousness of the place – as if at last I had found what America takes seriously. Not churches, not libraries. Not even movies, but THIS! This is it. The manufacture of refrigerators, of washing machines, of tape recorders, of light fixtures. This is the real thing. This is America.

It is for this, then that we are to fight Red China over Quemoy?

I am afraid I lack faith. I don't like it. I do not find it in myself to lay down my life for General Electric or anything it represents.

Oddly, Rev. Father staying with a G.E. man in Paris!

September 27, 1958

It is a bright afternoon: what am I going to do? I am going to work with my mind and with my pen, while the sky is clear, and while the soft white clouds are small and sharply defined in it. I am not going to bury myself in books and note-taking. I am not going to lose myself in this jungle and come out drunk and bewildered, feeling that bewilderment is a sign that I have done something. I am not going to write as one driven by compulsions – but freely, because I am a writer, and because for me to write is to think and to live and also in some degree even to pray.

This time is given to me by God that I may live in it. It is not given to make something *out of*, but given me to be stored away in eternity as my own.

But for this afternoon to be my own in eternity it must be my own this afternoon, and I must possess myself in it, not be possessed by books and by ideas not my own, and by a compulsion to produce what nobody needs. But simply to glorify God by accepting His gift and His work. To work for Him is to work that I myself may live.

How else shall I study Pasternak whose central idea is the sacredness of life?

September 28, 1958. Sunday Morning

The Chapter was over early – thanks to Fr. Prior. That is one of the good things about Rev. Fr. being away. (The election at Melleray is apparently over and we have a new Father Immediate.)

The decisions of the General Chapter become, for me, more and more disappointing. The changes constantly made seem to me to be foolish and irresponsible – and evasions of *real* action. Instead of doing something valuable and important, they do silly things – abolish the Lenten curtain, which could perfectly easily have been kept. It was a very ancient custom, oriental in origin, and we were perhaps the only ones left to have it. And now it is gone. Utterly senseless! What good will its absence do anybody? Its presence had a beautiful and special significance, and paradoxically the fact of having a Lenten curtain is of more value in reminding us of the participation of the faithful in the liturgy, than taking it away! The fact that the curtain was there in Lent broke the normal and *reminded* everyone of our participation since the altar was closed off from viewing temporarily! What a lack of liturgical sense!

Suddenly, during the Chapter during the prayers of Prime, this thought struck me: In monasteries where the priests have some active work to do – v.g. the Benedictines, they expend their energies on *others*, who are receptive and grateful. In our order – the active drives are frustrated in some: in others, they are turned full on to the *community* itself. We do not effectively preach to others, we preach ineffectively to ourselves. I think especially of campaigns to improve the chant, etc. Another paradox! a room full of frustrated contemplatives, many of whom are neither contemplative nor active, who resent the frustration of their capacity for activity, are forced to suffer the impact of the zeal of one of their number who has been let loose and turned against them. They bear the full weight of all *his* frustrations as well as their own. They increase the weight by reminding him openly of their resentment, and of his own anomalous condition. His guilt expands itself in them . . . etc. We wonder why our grandiose projects go nowhere! And we are unaware of our vanity and hypocrisy, as we look down on "active orders," not realizing that with a little less activity within the community we would be a lot better off. Failing that, if we must be alive, let us turn it into channels where it might do a little good! And above all let us be honest about it.

October 2, 1958. F. of the Guardian Angels
Brilliant and gorgeous day, bright sun, breeze making all the leaves and high brown grasses shine. Singing of the wind in the cedars. Exultant day, in which even a puddle in the pig lot shines like precious silver.

Finally I am coming to the conclusion that my highest ambition is to be what I already am. That I will never fulfill my obligation to surpass myself unless I first accept myself – and if I accept myself fully in the right way I will already have surpassed myself. For it is the unaccepted self that stands in my way – and will continue to do so as long as it is not accepted. When it has been accepted – it is my own stepping stone to what is above me. Because this is the way man has been made by God – and original sin was the effort to surpass oneself by being "like God" -i.e. unlike oneself. But our Godlikeness begins at home. We must first become like ourselves, and stop living "beside ourselves."

The charm of Origen – entranced by his commentary on Numbers with its inexhaustible fertility of ideas (which only later became stereotyped in the writings of others, who were so much poorer!).

I no longer care about a foundation – The idea is done with – unless some one brings it upon me. If there is a "work" I think I should do, then let it be done here. And the first thing is to get uncluttered so that I can be free to write if I have to. I have been living under an enormous heap of books from libraries – Louisville, and the U. of Kentucky – some useful, many useless. No matter – there were things I had to read up on. Now to take time and digest it all.

Everything adds up to these two points:

A My instinct to regard as an evil and an oversimplification the thought of "losing oneself" in total identification (submission in) with *any group* as such – this instinct against such, as correct, it is good.

To be a man of the church I have to be fully myself – and fully responsible and free before God – not a "unit" or a mere "member."

B My vocation and task in this world is to keep alive all that is usefully individual and personal in me, to be a "contemplative" in the full sense – and to share it with others – to remain as a witness of the nobility of the private person and his primacy over the group.

October 5, 1958. Day of Recollection

Last night – ran into a snake in the dormitory, on the way to the john, when every one was asleep.

Father Peter now has five snakes and a turtle in his infirmary room.

Frank Dell'Isola[34] here. I am pleased to see him looking better. The first day he was in bad shape – his wife died recently of cancer after eleven terrible months.

Read a little of Dom T. Verner Moore's *The Life of Man with God*. It has some good things in it but the whole approach is naive and misleading. I

---

[34] He was to compile the first full bibliography of Merton's writings.

remember the questionnaire I filled out for him and came across something like it – but ascribed to a "she."

One thing is certain – I am not leading a conventional religious life at all and perhaps it is a bad thing – or perhaps it is a good thing. In any case, it is not easy. Perhaps I am being lazy and selfish, perhaps I am being honest and free, perhaps I am a very great fool.

Certainly, I must get rid of all implicit rebellions and refusals, of which there are many and which have a bad effect (though I am not conscious of them all).

For instance how often the thought of some job I might have in the future rises before me and I harden my heart and my guts and my whole being against it in rejection! All this is my pride. I pretend I don't want to compromise, to do something I do not believe in, etc. To be what I am not, to stand up for something that seems to me to be false. I don't know if I am speculatively right or wrong, but in practice there is violence and spite in my refusals and repugnances, and this is very bad.

As long as I have such things in me, how can I really be honest about the life I am living?

At Benediction I tried to tell Our Lord that I would accept anything – realizing in my bones that I would probably never have to.

In any case I want to try and make a little retreat of my own for a couple of days next week – I really need it.

October 7, 1958. F. of Holy Rosary

A day of spiritual fires, quiet fires, warm skies. Pink beasts in the field (pigs).

Angry kingfisher rattles over the foul creek and swings upward, to head for the clean lake.

Wrote a perhaps useless article on Spiritual Direction[35] yesterday because I had to write something fast – and almost finished it in the afternoon work. Agreeably distracted by the thought of changes. Took the thought of articles for nuns to direction – Is it better to write fast, easy (useless) articles for nuns or slow, difficult, important articles on Le Douanier Rousseau, Pasternak, etc.? Fr. John of Cross said "What do I know about it?"

He spends all his time in the woods. Meanwhile, I'll write all articles – both kinds.

---

[35] Later published as *Spiritual Direction and Meditation* (Collegeville, MN: Liturgical Press, 1960).

—

Reading Vallejo. *Oye a tu masa* a terrific poem which I will translate.

Fr. Fernandes came last night. How he has worked – everything from a college to a chicken farm all together and all in Lima. I think he is solid and ought to stay. Was rector of a seminary at [illegible] do Campo. Again talk of a foundation came up – my principal vice. This time – near Petropolis. (Fr. F. is a Brazilian.)

October 12, 1958. Sunday

These are the most beautiful days of the year, except for days in May.

Sun every day now, and very bright sky, clear, dark blue. The leaves of the trees change though not all changes into bright colors, as in the North. The sweet gums do well, though – there are some small ones coming up in the novitiate woods. Some good young poplars in the wood of the former piglot we are clearing (thinning out) along the Bardstown road.

Wednesday we worked up by the lake. Wednesday night, deep, peaceful sleep – and woke up in the morning with the rain falling. Pope Pius XII was dead. I did not see the notice until after Mass but I had said a requiem mass anyway for the community in which of course he was included.

Then on Friday Mark Van Doren's autobiography came and I have begun it, getting with him as far now as the army in World War I and the Negroes. The world of Illinois and of his childhood is very much the same as the world all around us and yet I suddenly find it hard to believe in such peace and such security. That only means that I have finally realized such peace and security have never been normal for mankind as a whole. They have existed, but as an anomaly. But they should be normal.

And who, above all, Thursday afternoon Rev. Fr. gave me a letter from Pasternak inside an envelope from New Directions – air mail, registered, but unopened. I explained with vehemence to Rev. Father that Pasternak was a great and basically religious writer and I could see he did not believe me – or, if he did, a little, it was against his will to do so. The letter was brief but very cordial and confirmed my intuition of the deep and fundamental understanding that exists between us. And this is the thing I have been growing to see is most important: *Everything* hangs on the possibility of such understanding which forms our interior bond that is the only basis of true peace and true community. External juridical, doctrinal etc. bonds can never achieve this. And this bond exists between me and countless people like Pasternak everywhere in the world (genuine people like Pasternak are never "countless") and my vocation is intimately bound up with this bond and this understanding for the sake of which also I have to be solitary and not waste my spirit in pretenses that do not come anywhere near the reality or have anything to do with it.

October 15, 1958. F. of St. Teresa

Finishing up a very good two day retreat. Spent it all under the five or six pine trees near St. Teresa's field in the calf pasture – the part that is now "ours." could hardly think of a better place and was not tempted to look for one.

Barefoot most of the time. Read little. Some psalms. Some of the new Bouyer book *(Le trône de la sagesse)*, some Symeon the New Theologian, some Zen. Whatever problems I have are on the level where Zen can hit them squarely. They are matters of psychology and disorganized living – wrong attitudes, "conflicts" more than an anything else. And because of them I have been failing to face the issue – have been getting away from the big job of my life, the fighting out of the inner battle for freedom, and losing myself in exterior plans – and in useless writing. Mind cluttered with lumber and dust. All ready to cut back on foolish but easy, writing projects for "quick results." That is, only apparent results.

The novices were very sweet about the whole thing (my retreat) and tip-toed around the novitiate giving me knowing smiles and acting as solicitous as if I had broken a leg.

Interminable articles on the way a Pope is buried in 3 coffins are being read in refectory. The symbolism of Roman ceremonial looks very queer in the jargon of newspapermen.

October 18, 1958. F. of St. Luke.

Two letters have arrived from Pasternak – my letter and Prometheus got through to him and apparently quite easily. He commented on Prometheus, saying that he liked especially sections IV and VII – and that the last had some "fine individual Christosophic touches." I was very pleased. Will write to him again. He keeps insisting that his early work is "worthless." His heart is evidently in *Dr. Zhivago* – to which he does not refer by the full name. Only as "Dr Zh" or "the book published by Pantheon."

Talking to Fr. Lawrence about it and remarked on the strange and marvelous fact of this apparently easy and natural communication between a monk in a strictly guarded Trappist monastery and a suspect poet behind the Iron Curtain – I am in closer contact with Pasternak than I am with people in Louisville or Bardstown or even in my own monastery – and have more in common with him.

And all this while our two countries, deeply hostile to one another, have nothing to communicate between themselves – and yet spend millions trying to communicate with the moon!!

This simple and human dialogue with Pasternak and a few others like him is to me worth thousands of sermons and radio speeches. It is to me the true Kingdom of God, which is still so clearly, and evidently, "in the midst of us."

October 23, 1958

Very busy and I think uselessly. Various short pieces – vg. on Spiritual Direction – and a new one on *Christianity and Mass Movements*.[36] I think it would be a lot better if I were working steadily and quietly on a large book, instead of this kind of journalism.

Especially – *Art and Worship* is in confusion. Our production plans have changed again. Perhaps finally we will give up trying to publish it ourselves. I have written to Bob Giroux about this.

Bro. Mathias died Tuesday just before the High Mass of St. Ursula. They took away the red vestments, lit more candles, and there was a Pontifical Requiem.

Yesterday learned "by accident" from Rev. Father of a letter from Mons. Ricaurte in Bogota which he would not give me. (It was addressed to me, of course.) It sounded provocative and interesting – of course, a foundation project. Something of which Rev. Fr. highly disapproved of and which sounded great to me. I was bitter and depressed for a while and even woke up in the night thinking about it, and about the frustration of all my ideas and hopes for something sane in monasticism. But no! to be always a prisoner of *vanitas monastica* [monastic pride] and its crudities, incomprehensions, and falsities! Brought back face to face with my vow of obedience – and the paradox that this is what matters most. And it must matter not only on paper but in life. Yet I refuse to make the great melodramatic gesture of false acceptance – which would include the acceptance of things God does not want me to accept. I simply obey. But I still never lie down and accept this monastic situation as inevitable, definitive or "right." At the same time, once again – how can I be sure that I have something better to put in its place?

---

[36] Published in *Cross Currents* 9 (Summer 1959): 201–11.

And it is quite true that my evasions are dangerous, both for myself and for others. But if I remained content with negativism and compromise with truth I could never have a good conscience either.

Peace, not in what ought to be, not in what is officially declared – but simply peace in the reality of my own inner life which has nothing to do with all the rest.

Novices moved out of dormitory today. Tearing out the floors and stairs.

Book from Alberto Girri. I like the new development of his verse.

Community angry with Bouyer's book on the Cistercians (his chapter) because he thinks he finds neurotic trends in St. Bernard. Doesn't sound altogether unreasonable to me! But heresy to so many who have fled to the idea of sanctity as a cure for all anxiety. If there is neurosis even in the Saints, then all is lost!! More of our monastic vanity and perhaps the very root of it.

October 26, 1958. Sunday

Angry kingfisher flies up the rock creek in the rain swearing and scattering the other birds in all directions.

The cardinals are in conclave. Rev. Father thinks it is "Red Propaganda" that Montini has little chance because he is no friend of the Jesuits. All I know of Siri is something he said about religious poverty in the Congreg. of Religious. A religious should not have a watch (?). Or will it be Lercaro *pastor et nauta* [shepherd and sailor]? Or Roncalli, a "compromise candidate" they say. Cardinal Mooney died in Rome an hour before the opening of the conclave.

From the Library of Congress I got Bulgakov's *Wisdom of God* which is tremendous, particularly his last chapter on the Church. I wish it were possible to get more of him. This has to go back too soon for me to think about it but I will get Fr. Bartholomew to copy the best pages and I will have them. It is certain that his teaching that the Church is the Revelation of God's Wisdom has a strong basis in Ephesians III 9–11.

"The Church is the heart and essence of the world, its final cause."

"God – manifested in history."

Fine rain falls on this page and spoils this writing. The shelter does not keep it out.

Drawings of [Norman] Laliberte from St. Mary's College, Notre Dame. Very fine – sacred apocalyptic character. Room for development – an artist of promise.

October 30, 1958

The other day Fr. John of the Cross heard over Hanekamp's radio that Pasternak had won the Nobel Prize in literature and that the Reds did not want him to receive it. A great fuss about this – Yesterday I decided, perhaps in a crazy moment, that I might perhaps be able to do some good if I wrote a letter of protest to the Union of Soviet Writers, which I did. Sent copy to Helen Wolff at Pantheon – afterwards felt very strange, as if I had sent up a rocket into a sky of which I know nothing. And I wonder about my motives, too. Consciously, they were good enough. Unconsciously, maybe they were crazy.

Cardinal Roncalli has become Pope John XXIII – This happened Tuesday. Yesterday in the woods, Fr. William cut himself in the foot with an axe.

To what extent is jazz spiritual? A question I find it impossible to answer intelligently. But I think it is a question that makes sense, and not altogether absurd. Hard to judge because things which remind us of the past are accidentally disturbing. Anything at all sweet is disturbing. The more "hot" it is, the more spiritual it seems to be. Something hot and abstract like "Fifth Dimension" (Mary Lou Williams) strikes me as quite spiritual . . . I can abide all Boogie Woogie with relative comfort. It remains good. But none of this can be played long, or make sense for more than a few minutes, anywhere near the monastery.

Now to translate the Desert Fathers. Their silence, without boogie, makes plenty sense.

October 31, 1958

By the time I had written my letter of protest about the treatment of Pasternak he had already, under pressure, refused the Nobel Prize. Perhaps my protest in union with many others, may keep him at least alive. The general opinion seems to be that he will be forced into complete isolation.

A wonderful letter from Pasternak to Kurt Wolff, in German, was forwarded to me from Pantheon – most of it is concerned with his reaction to my letters and to my "perfect" understanding of all that was most important to him in his work. *"Die Richtigkeit seines Verständnisses, das Wunder seiner Einsichts [sic] unglaublich scheinen."* ["The aptness of his understanding and the clarity of his insights is beyond belief."] – and he picks out especially my reaction to his Hamlet poem and the Business about the Red Sea and the Bl. Virgin – and about God-manhood.

That I have been able to give him the consolation of understanding and appreciating what he most wanted to say is also to me a great consolation.

Later in the letter, a most important point, and one which came back to me this morning after my Mass:

". . . *einmal möchte man nicht da stehen bleiben, wo die politischen und aestatischen [sic] Braüche und Moglichkeiten steckenzublein gewohnt und gezwungen waren, einmal sollte man sich die Mühe gegeben haben, einen weiteren Schritt zu tun.*" ["One cannot remain immobile where the political and aesthetic customs and potentialities are so conspicuous and so compelling; one must take another step."]

This again I agree with perfectly, and I see that this is the very heart of my own personal vocation.

I must, in my writing, in my prayer, in my life – take this further step and go beyond my limitations and the limitations of thought, art, and religion of our time. And this requires effort and suffering. I simply cannot sit down and *accept* my limitations – that is impossible. But I must take care most of all not to be content with merely a fanciful transcendence – going beyond my limitations in thought and imagination only. It must be a real transcendence.

Pasternak is convinced that in the very structure of his novel, he has been going beyond modern limitations.

"*Die Uberwindung der Dekadenzzenge [sic] und modernistischen Beschranküng ist hier auch nicht Nebensache der Form?*" ["Is not the overcoming of decadence and modern constrictions also a by-product of form?"]

His letter was written Oct. 18 – which, in the light of my thoughts and my entry that day, is to say the least arresting.

November 9, 1958. Sunday

My week as hebdomadary. This morning had to talk in chapter about the Psalms of Sext. "to help the brothers," said Rev. Father. I am not so bored in chapter when I am the one talking and come out full of the spirit of family life!!

John XXIII seems to me to be a most wonderful Pope and I love him already very much – he is a kind of simple person with a lot of good sense and all of a sudden he seems to me, for this, for his simplicity, to be a great man and I cannot help feeling right away that perhaps he is a saint. My kind of a saint – who smokes a cigarette after dinner. (I have got over the idea that this would immediately disqualify him – that went out ten years ago.)

Helen Wolff at Pantheon sent more clippings about Pasternak, almost all a week old now. But there has been a statement attributed to him, about the "present glories" of Soviet Russia. Which makes no difference to me one way or the other except that I am sorry for him more than ever.

H. Wolff, thinking I know Russian, offered me the poems of Pasternak for translation. I wish I could do it!

They are all very upset and wanted to know if Kurt Wolff sent me by mistake his private annotated copy of P's *Essai autobiographique* in French. He had not.

Have been reading Tu Fu – a very fine poet – one of the greatest.

Neruda's works came from Argentina – a tremendously influential volume.

And a whole spate of books from Ecuador, including Jorge Carrera Andrade – a most charming poet. If that is the spirit of Quito that speaks in him, then I understand why I am so mightily attracted to that place!

Alberto Girri's book, a few weeks ago. I sent him a poem. I like his terse style and his "metaphysical," but disciplined subtlety. A fine poet and a religious one.

Meanwhile – nothing left but to give up Pasternak and let him rest in peace. H. Wolff spoke touchingly of how much they missed his letters and cards.

It is really not a political question at all. Or rather it did not become a political question until the Reds made it one. Before that, it was simply a spontaneous human happiness at finding someone in Russia who could understand, who seemed to be speaking sincerely, and not parroting a part – one with whom communication was possible. Instead the Reds burst in and set up once again the artificial barrier, and gave out their screams that they were being attacked. Any expression of spontaneous human feeling can constitute an "attack" on communism and its rigid falsity.

November 10, 1958

Reading Mabillon's wise and delightful book on monastic studies.

Among other things – this beautiful quotation from Seneca:

"*Si te ad studia revocaveris, omne vitae fastidium epurgeris, nec noctem fieri optabis tardis lucis, nec tibi gravis eris, nec aliis superacuris.*" ["If you will give yourself to study, you will ease every burden of life, you will neither wish for night to come or the light to fail; neither shall you be worried or pre-occupied with other things."]

It appears that one of the great powers in the Church in the last 20 years has been Mother Pasqualina, Pius XII's housekeeper.

Warm sun, quiet morning. Pigs bang the lids of their feeding troughs. Fr. Placid madly at the honeysuckle. I sit on the very low bench under the cedars, outside the wall. John (of the Cross) told story of Bro. Clement and "his men" trying to "capture" Bro. Colman and a local farmer to whom Colman was selling pigs. They thought the farmer was stealing pigs because Bro. C., zealous for poverty, did not put on the lights. One brother rushed upon Bro. Colman in the dark crying "This one's all for me!" Nobody was hurt, but the farmer was paralyzed and speechless for five minutes – and said he would never come to buy pigs here again.

Reading Czeslaw Milosz *The Captive Mind* – a *really* interesting book. When you read something worthwhile in these days, you know it right away – and this is worthwhile – every line of it. The challenge it presents – very clear and sober. Who is there in the West that can write a book that will really be appreciated by someone who has lain on the cobblestones of the street with the machine gun bullets whizzing by him and re-arranging a pattern of upturned paving stones? I have got to write stuff that will be *worthy* of the public in Poland, Hungary, Czechoslovakia, Russia, even though it never reaches them. I mean worthy of those who know the falsity of Dialectical Materialism and look for "something" undefined from "somewhere" else. (What one of them does not, in his heart?)

November 13, 1958
"The whole of political life seems to be ordered with a view of attaining the happiness of contemplation. For peace which is established and preserved by virtue of political activity, places man in a position to devote himself to contemplation of the Truth."

> St. Thomas in Eth. quoted in Pieper's lucid Happiness and Contemplation, *p. 94.*

Failure of materialistic society in US and in Russia – the lack of all sense of *what to do with* the time that has been saved by techniques, to fulfill one's practical life spontaneously seek fulfillment in contemplation but the wrong kind. TV etc. "The greatest menace to our capacity for contemplation is the incessant fabrication of tawdry, empty stimuli which kill the receptivity of the soul." *Pieper. p. 102.*

November 18, 1958

Rain. Sitting in woodshed. Rev. Father is away for the blessing of the first abbot of Berryville – Dom Hugh. Dom Anselm from Vina was here over the weekend.

Aldous Huxley's article on drugs that produce visions and ecstasies has reached me with the protests of various Catholic women (sensible ones). I wrote to him about it yesterday and the article is on the notice board in the Novitiate conference rooms.

Fr. Anchieta (Fernandes, CSSR)

A long and good letter came from Jaime Andrade from Quito. First he is happy about the way the statue is going. Then he speaks at length about my foundation idea and says I would be caught in the middle between an extremely reactionary clergy and ruling class and a red intelligentsia and would be fired at from both sides, which I think is true. And that is going to be necessarily a part of anything loving and useful I may do – because I cannot produce anything good if I identify myself too closely either with the Reds or with Capitalism. The vocation of a very good writer and spiritual man today lies neither with the one or the other, but beyond both. Heartily agree with Milosz's conclusions at the end of his very fine book.

What matters is *not to line up with the winning side* but to be a true and revolutionary poet.

The struggle to keep awake on this island of Lotus Eaters.

A prospect of huge rotten logs; wet barrels with rain falling on them. A smashed gate. The thin cedars with patches of rusty autumn pasture showing through them. The warm straw and the rain on the roof.

November 21, 1958. F. of Presentation

Praying this morning during meditation to learn to read the meaning of events.

First of all the meaning of what I myself do and bring upon myself and then the meaning of what all mankind does and brings upon itself. In the middle is this monastery – what it does and brings upon itself.

Before one knows the meaning of what happens, he must be able to *see* what happens. Most men do not even do that – they trust the newspapers to tell them.

(Aidan Nally tried to tell me the other day that Spellman had been chosen Cardinal – news that is at least ten years old. He meant Cushing.)

The meaning of this integration business in the South . . . That would be something worth understanding. It is important and prophetic.

November 25, 1958. Day of Re[collection]

My Zen is in the slow swinging tops of sixteen pine trees.

One long thin pole of a tree fifty feet high swings in a wider arc than all the others and swings even when they are still.

Hundreds of little elms springing up out of the dry ground under the pines.

My watch lies among oak leaves. My tee shirt hangs on the barbed wire fence, and the wind sings in the bare wood.

The meaninglessness of any life that is not lived in the face of death.

This has struck me very forcibly, reading a passage from a Zen Samurai writer and warrior of the 17th. century quoted by Suzuki.

Our great dignity is tested by death – I mean our freedom. There is no ordinary death. But there is all the difference in the world between flying from it interiorly and facing it with a man's freedom – with a man's acceptance. When the "parting of the ways" comes – then to set one's foot gladly on the way that leads out of this world. This is a great gift of ourselves, not to death but to life. For he who knows how to die not only lives longer in this life (as if it matters) but lives eternally because of his freedom.

Never has man's helplessness in the face of death been more pitiable than in this age when he can do everything except escape death. If he were unable to escape so many other things man would face death better.

But our power has only strengthened our illusion that we can cling to life, without taking away our unconscious fear of death. We are always holding death at arms length, unconsciously trying to think ourselves out of its presence – and this generates an intolerable tension that makes us all the more quickly its victims. It is he who does not fear death who is more ready to escape it and when the time comes, he faces it well.

So he who faces death can be happy in this life and in the next and he who does not face it has no happiness in either. This is a central and fundamental reality of life, whether one is and or is not a "believer" – for this "facing" of death implies already a faith and an uprightness of heart and the presence of Christ, whether one thinks of it or not. (I do not refer to the desperateness of the tough guy, but only to the sincerity of an honest and sober and sensitive person, assuming responsibility for his whole life in gladness and freedom.)

November 29, 1958

Yesterday *prima nix* [first snow] and I shortened the conference to get tonsured before Sext.

Wet snow and heavy ice bows down all the evergreens and I am afraid of it ruining the loblolly pine sapling in the garden – I am attached to it. We tied it to a stick and I shook it, to try to loosen the ice, but shook off many needles and a small branch, so one must leave it alone.

Thanksgiving Day and I finished a twenty two page article on the Pasternak affair.[37] It is clear that he is a Christian anarchist, if any political label at all can be attached to him. Certainly the Russians want no part of a Christian anarchist. Writing the article – after the usual hesitation to attack the subject – was enlightening for me. But it is too long.

Went out into the snow yesterday afternoon after finishing the last page and walked under the icy branches of the big sycamore with Fr. Alcuin's work shoes on – looked into the black sky of the West and thought of Pasternak in solitude at Peredelkino.

Today walked there again after dinner. Now everything is blinding and bright so I had on dark glasses. Going down the steps conquered a scruple that by wearing them I was not seeing things "as they really are." Who says I would see them as they are with the naked eye? Anyway the glass trees were brilliant and fragile in the sun and great halos of light whirled in the sycamores – the land was transfigured like St. Seraphim of Sarov, full of the Holy Ghost (yet I remain suspicious of its coldness and its appeal to the maker of Christmas cards).

Read remarkable pages of Suzuki on the tea-ceremony.

I scolded Fr. Alberic (Prendegast) yesterday for not eating his cereal (as a child he must eat his cereal). He complained saying it was plainly the fourth degree of humility for him to obey me and today as I came though the refectory he hid his empty bowl under the table to see if I would scold him but he explained before I got there that he had hidden it to fool me. The kids this year are charming as one's own children and I never get tired of them.

November 30, 1958. 1st. Sunday of Advent

The simplest, easiest, and most enjoyable work I have done this year has been the translation of some Sayings of the Desert Fathers – from the

---

[37] Merton finally published two articles: "Boris Pasternak and People with Watch Chains," *Jubilee* 7 (1959): 17–31; and "The Pasternak Affair in Perspective," *Thought* 34 (Winter 1959/1960): 485–517.

Verba Seniorum [Sayings of the Elders].[38] I would do a page or two whenever I had time left over from preparing the novitiate conferences and every time I read them over my soul is filled with the fragrance of their simplicity and I want to be as humble as those men were. Their words are all full of sunlight and they are like children, yet they could only be so by being very strong.

Much the same atmosphere as the *Wabi* that Suzuki talks about.

December 2, 1958

Plan

To begin Russian – Mon-Fri pm's. Thursday and Saturday pms – reading of Latin Americans – work on Jorge Carrera Andrade, etc. Keep up with Pasternak on Mon and Fri also. Thursday morning – free for correspondence or revisions of ms. – Saturday – idem – or Portuguese. Wednesday p.m. all out walk in woods. Tuesday – day of recollection.

December 7, 1958

Maybe what is wrong with American Catholicism is that it is in large measure *Protestant* rather than Catholic. Whether this be true or not, one would look in vain for any of the trace of the spirit of Medieval Catholicism in America or in this monastery – its broadness, its universality, its all-embracing compassion, its joy, its understanding of man and his nature, its cosmic outlook, its genuine eschatology; its asceticism; its mysticism; its poetry.

Asceticism? – Yes, we have it here all right – but it is protestant self-discipline, dour, individualistic, puritanical.

Protestant features of our life – and Catholic life as a whole.

1. Distrust and rejection of emotional symbolism of art, of poetry, of contemplation.

2. Distrust of what is interior, distrust of joy, of happiness. (At the same time an all-American cult of good-humor, as "a sign that one is among the elect" – as a defense against anxiety, rather than true inner joy. Pragmatic joy, for efficiency's sake. A good humorous Christian fits in better and accomplishes more. He belongs.)

3. Cult of energy, of efficiency, productivity, prosperity – again as "signs of election."

---

[38] Later published as *The Wisdom of the Desert* (New York: New Directions, 1960).

4. Stern, practical, legalism. Man face to face with demands of the divine will.

5. Harshness, aggressivity.

6. Artificial separation of "body" (evil) and "soul" (good – divine). Splitting up of life into compartments, disintegration. Resultant abstraction or abstractness of the spiritual life. (Our contempt for "flesh" is in reality a contempt for aristocratic luxury.)

7. Respect for comfort and ease, *together with self-discipline* characteristically Protestant. *Gemütlichkeit,* rather than real spirituality or taste.

8. All deviations tolerated – primacy of economics tacitly admitted, provided one is energetic about self-discipline and *obedience.* This too, belongs to the totalitarian spirit of Protestant groups not to the broad tolerance of the Middle Ages.

Why this? Because in the South, in Latin America the Spaniards who were too medieval were able to succumb and go native mixing with the Indians. But in the North, we have exterminated the Indian, and brought nature under despotic control, because we were *not* medieval. Hence, obviously, we fear and despise what is meant by the Middle Ages.

We are much more akin to those new Puritans, the Communists, than to our Catholic forefathers (except, of course, in theory).

Fr. Alberic got up to get a mop in the refectory and Fr. Anselm took one of his eggs and gave it to Fr. Walter to hide, but Fr. Walter ate it. Consternation of Fr. Alberic. Wanted to know "Is it all right to take your neighbor's eggs if he isn't looking?"

December 9, 1958

Hans Urs Von Balthasar. *"Dieu et l'homme d'aujourd'hui"* [God and Man Today]

December 11, 1958

The other day Norman Laliberte, an artist, was here with a philosophy prof. called Perrilat, both from St. Mary's, Notre Dame. Laliberte had some good drawings, illustrations to Genesis, naive, original, primitive and sophisticated at the same time, a very good sense of line, the decorative effect of many thin lines creating a plastic and fluid "Thing." And very appropriate for Genesis – a contemplative treatment. They brought many huge art books from Sister Rosanne at St. Marys and since then I have been reading about Flemish primitives and Josse Wyd (the donor in the Van Eyck altarpiece of the Adoration of the Lamb) haunts my dreams.

On the feast of the Immaculate Conception, tired and dry in the long Mass (Fr. Linus made solemn profession) I bore up by asking myself: "What am I here for?" and discarding all the conventional answers. The only satisfying answer is "for nothing." I am here *gratis*, without a special purpose, without a special plan. I am here because I am here and not somewhere else. I am not here because of some elaborate monastic ideal, or because this is "the best" (which it probably is not) – but simply this is where "God has put me." I live here, I work around here. The people who live in New Haven or down the road don't have to have some special answer to the question "What am I here for?" I know I have answered this differently in print, and what I have said about it in print still stands. But for myself, the only intelligible answer is an existential one – I am here gratis, for no special purpose, with no strings attached, freely. I have no serious reason for wanting to be elsewhere, though I might *like* to be elsewhere at times. The fact remains that elsewhere is not where I am, or where I am likely to be. The point is not that this is a sublimely wonderful and special place. Not at all. To try to convince myself of this after 17 years would be madness and insincerity. The point is that it does not much matter where you are, as long as you can be at peace about it and live your life. The place certainly will not live my life for me, I have found that out. I have to live it for myself.

It amuses me to think of my relations with my undermaster, Fr. Tarcisius – a prim, quiet, devout, and deeply self-willed person. How deeply I had never realized until these last few months. He will do anything, take any initiative, reverse my orders or turn plans upside down, as long as it concerns something domestic – especially decorations in the chapel, what is to be done around the house, where this or that is to go – etc. Things, I admit, which are usually profoundly indifferent to me. But I get annoyed when he had novices working late at night for the Assumption, when he ordered a vesting table and ruined a set of the St. John's altarcards by cutting them down, etc. all without consulting me.

What it amounts to is that he is possessed of a deeply feminine need to run a house. It is remarkable how much of the young mother is in him. We are practically husband and wife, father and mother. And we are getting all the classic problems of a middle class home. I the successful professional man, engaged in my career, my wife – highly social minded, quietly efficient, getting her hands on everything in the family, not without a basic, but interested, loyalty to father. A most political wife, who would probably dress quite smartly (but not smartly enough in New York and would keep me constantly humiliated by a determined and prim provincialism). So it is one of those businesslike efficient, marriages, a working partnership, a definite *do ut des* [I give that you give (i.e., strict)] contract in which there is a certain air of overlapping and encroachment and certain subterranean hostilities and tensions, smoothed over at all times by the correct expressions of tenderness, forgiveness, and patience. Under cover of this nobility we are both resolutely selfish.

I resolve to be a good husband because my selfishness is probably greater and more fundamental – maybe it is my solitariness and lack of love that have finally brought all this on. The maneuvers of my spouse in the household are perhaps in part a protest against consistent coldness and lack of attention, lack of interest in things domestic.

Husbands, learn from my predicament and follow my example.

"Christian humanism, which preserves the development of all the creative capacities of man, may be understood as a new comprehension, a new revelation of Christianity. It is no new Christianity, it is only its new comprehension." *Bulgakov.*

Yesterday – selecting poems for a paper backed collection, to be issued by N[ew] D[irections].

Saw that my best ones were the early ones, and that I cannot go back to that.

The fervor of those days was special and young. It can inspire me to seek a new and different fervor, which is older and deeper. This I must find. But I cannot go back to the earlier fervor or to the asceticism that accompanied it. The new fervor will be rooted not in asceticism but in humanism. What has begun now must grow but must never seek to become spectacular or to attract attention to itself – which is what I unconsciously did in those days, proclaiming that I was a poet and a mystic. Both are probably true, but not deep enough, because then it was too conscious. I have to write and speak not as the individual who has cut himself off from the world and wants the world to know it, but as the person who has lost himself in the service of the vast wisdom of God's plan to reveal Himself in the world and in man.

How much greater, deeper, nobler, truer and more hidden. A mysticism that no longer appears, transcendent and ordinary.

December 13, 1958. St. Lucy

Going in town yesterday was a kind of "retreat" for my seventeenth anniversary in the monastery: impossible to think, without immense qualifications, the things I wrote the other day about being here for nothing. Really I am here for everything. Being out "in the world" would really be nothing and an awful waste. The "waste" of one's life in a monastery is the fruitful thing; or at least it is for me.

The overwhelming welter of meaningless objects, goods, activities – The indiscriminate chaotic nest of "things" good, bad and indifferent, that pour over you at every moment – books, magazines, food, drink, women, cigarettes, clothes, toys, cars, drugs. Add to this the anonymous, characterless, "decoration" of the town for Christmas and the people running around buying things for no reason except that now is a time which everybody buys things.

And I myself bought things – a pile of paper-backed books, the *New Republic*, *Dissent* and even, with shame, *Time* (because of a long cover article on Pasternak).

Met Clifford Shaw, a musician, who for some reason admires me and we had lunch in the Brown Hotel.

The rest of the time I was milling around in the library – read part of a good article on Mount Athos in the *Yale Review*, listened to some piano music of A. Berg and Bartok. Looked up some books to take home. Then while waiting for George and the station wagon – looked at marvelous bird-books (photos of Arctic loons, quails, bobwhites [my totem bird], warblers, woodpeckers, all kinds of ducks and grebes). (We saw a great blue heron on the way to work the other day, I looked it up to make sure and that is what it was) – at an old fashioned tree book and I was sinking to such depths that I had begun to look at jet planes when George arrived at 3:30.

The reason for going in was to see Terrell Dickey and get all the pictures for *Art and Worship* off to N.Y., for Farrar, Straus & Cudahy must do it. Too big a job for us.[39] I like the people in the library, smart and friendly and patient with my requests. Gave them a fruitcake which George had left

---

[39] *Art and Worship*, over which Merton labored long, never did get into print as a book.

over. One of them dragged out some drawings by Pasternak's father, which were in *Life*. Clever and lively *fin de siècle* stuff.

George had a load of cheese and fruitcake and said he got rid of $700 worth. That is a lot. We were stopping all the way in and all the way out and got home so late that I had supper at Bill Jones' place in Bardstown with a lot of kidding because the girl tried to give me pork instead of fish in a sandwich and it was Friday. (Delighted laughter of the Colored guys and girls back in the kitchen looking through the serving window.)

Walking up and down in Bardstown outside Krogers, in the cold, saluted by man, woman, and child. I thought that never, never could I make sense of life outside the monastery. I am a solitary and that is that. I love people o.k., but I belong in solitude.

It was so good to get back and smell the sweet air of the woods and listen to the silence.

December 19, 1958

The other day, providentially received an offprint from *L'Orient Syrien*, an article on the ashram founded in Southern India by Fr. Francis Mayhieu of Chimay and Dom Bede Griffiths. Fr. Francis is still canonically a member of our Order – with a three year indult of exclaustration. His part in the work is blessed by his abbot and by Dom Gabriel. It is tending explicitly to an independent and original form of "Cistercian" monastery. They have received an indult to join the Syro-Malabar rite, their office is in the vernacular of that part of India and it does not include Prime. It is clear from this that it is possible for someone to start out from a Cistercian monastery as his home base and really do something flexible and new. I would be surprised if in reality Dom Gabriel were quite hostile to the whole project in a passive sort of way. I would not think of discussing it with Dom James.

This I think is very important news.

Read the offprint the other night before going on the Night Watch – a cold, bright evening. And thought about it while going around the dark building. No unrest or eagerness. It is clear I am not supposed to start anything now – yet it is clear that if anything is to be done, it will be done simply and cleanly. It is not for me to be concerned or to be hasty. I know less than ever what I am supposed to do, if anything. The one thing that is most clear – I must get out of the doldrums of relative disorientation and get back into the reality of a deep life of prayer here, in these woods which offer themselves so readily.

Today began reading what seems to be a remarkable though poorly written book – *Hermit in the Himalayas* by Brinton – I picked it up by "chance" in the Louisville library last week.

The *Nativity Kerygma*[40] arrived today – very beautifully done. In many ways quite Russian, especially the end sheets – I like the splendor of the colors.

December 27, 1958. F. of St. John

Cold, frosty morning. I try to recuperate outside the wall from the strain of these feasts, sitting quietly under the frosty cedars and looking at the quiet grey sky and breathing the clean air.

Christmas Eve also was quiet and cold and I walked in grey air like this knowing that it would be the sanest moment of these days.

How I need solitude! And yet – I seem to become less and less fit for it the more I need it. And this is getting inexorably more and more terrible.

I honestly begin to wonder whether my being bound by vows to this situation is not in some way a great mistake. Not that I want to be dispensed from my vows; but I can at least hope for some relief, under the vows themselves. Perhaps this hope is also a vain one. The relief has to come from within myself and my impatience perhaps prevents it from coming. One thing is probably sure: that merely putting aside the burden now would be no good at all. The burden is no longer merely juridical, it is something in the very depths of my being. (I know you are not supposed to admit it is a burden. I am weak enough to do so.) Burden: I mean being obligated to stay all the time under Superiors in a Community where, at this point, things seem objectively to cramp and frustrate my real growth. Whether or not this is a delusion . . . Anyway I feel terribly like a prisoner. And the only solution is to do the things they do to keep sane in prisons: to follow faithfully my own routine and salvage what I can of my inner liberty.

The burden of being a prisoner is now upon me for life, whether in or out of a monastery. And if it is a burden it is because my liberty was too weak to carry it bravely and lightly. I have let myself gradually be crushed by it – expecting help from outside, from someone else – and it cannot come from anywhere but within us. I have let myself become gravely alienated. The only honest thing to do is finally to accept the situation with sin-

[40] *Nativity Kerygma* (St. Paul: North Central, 1958, and Trappist, KY: Abbey of Gethsemani, 1958).

cerity and try to salvage some liberty from it. I have ample opportunities, like this one. Writing this is a relief – though it is hardly what I would call making the best of an hour of solitude. I will do what I can.

The end of a year – and the beginning of a very grave year of struggle, Christ, may I not go under!

I understand now Hopkins' last sonnets. Does religious life do this to everyone sensitive?

The *Secular Journal* came the other day. Meaningless to me. I did not like finding my picture in it and did not like the air of sensationalism about the cover. "Now released for publication after 20 years!"

Fr. Tarcisius preached well today about love. But love in a life like this is a terrible problem. It is not something to be undertaken lightly.

I know from experience that all this is somehow good, but it is useless to mouth formulas about it being so. I must suffer all this and sweat blood / out of it will come growth.

December 28, 1958. F. of Holy Innocents

Feeling better because I slept late and got a full 7 hours of sleep for a change!

Yesterday afternoon I spent a long time, as I had been promising myself, over in the lovely field where the Linton houses used to stand. Tremendous view of four horizons, the vast sweep of strange hills, and the great open sky, with grey clouds overhead, and tunnels of light into the West beyond the fire tower.

Really there is no problem, but the act of accepting the solitude I have desired, the solitude of heart – in community. The whole trouble is I do not want it with my whole being. Half of me demands deference and consideration – expects everyone around me, at least in the novitiate, to see and do things my way. How necessary is this? Not as necessary as I seem to assume. I am supposed to form them according to what I think is right for monks. That is true. But . . .

The house is boiling hot. I sit comfortably outside in Summer clothes with only a Winter cowl. In the house the heat is on full blast and is unbearable. I cannot stand ten minutes in choir without sweating. This is utterly ridiculous: a greenhouse for penitents – Monks or geraniums?

With this and a thousand other things I cannot help thinking that life here has become to a great extent meaningless. Not that I am such a terrible ascetic – certainly I am not. But I wonder more and more to what extent a genuine and deep spiritual life is going to be at all possible in such a community. No question of course that the individual can maintain one on his own, but in order to do so he is going to have to cut his own way through the thicket and not just follow the community. At least that is my case.

More and more I am going to quietly have to do the difficult thing that no one else is free to do either for me or with me – and really live my own interior life and seek God according to my own vocation – without fighting or condemning other people and without worrying at the differences between us in outlook, ideals, etc. Everybody knows me now and I think they are quite willing, to a great extent, to mind their business and let me mind mine. Except in the one place where they like to meddle, which is the novitiate. And there I can't expect to have everything there to myself.

If I ever have a chance to lead a really solitary life I must have the sense and the gumption to jump at it. I was not ready for it in 1955 when I agitated for it so wildly. I am not ready for it now. I am not ready to run a community either and have no longer any desire to start one. I hope when the time comes I may really be ready to go off alone. May Christ grant me this great favor.

Dreamt last night that Fr. Tarcisius insisted on the novices going to Communion each one with a cookie suspended around his neck on a string.

December 30, 1958

Today it became to some extent clear why this has been a dark and trying Christmas. We were sitting in chapter in a futile discussion of a point of moral theology – about absolving a dying man who is unconscious and has not expressed a desire for the sacraments. Fr. V. of course taking the strict view. While he was explaining the strict view, Bro. Colman poked his head into the Chapter and made the sign for "Doctor" – Herman Hanekamp had been found dead in his house.

While we argue wisely about administering the sacraments to the dying, someone depending on us for material and spiritual care has died without sacraments. I cannot help regarding it as a significant episode!

Herman, who was once a novice here (in the days before the first world war) is one of the very few members or former members of the community that I have ever had any desire to imitate.

When I first saw him, I was a novice, serving the matutinal mass and I saw this tramp, bearded and tosseled, dark as a Negro, coming up to communion with two Negro kids, when the hosts ran out in the secular church.

A few years later there was a forest fire on All Saints Day and I went out to fight it. It was the first time I ever saw Hanekamp's place, in the valley behind the Vineyard Knob. The fire was all around it and he was protecting his house with backfires, and I remember him coming through the bushes and asking me what happened to his can of coal oil. After the fire I learned a little of his story – how he had been a professed monk, and left when his temporary vows ran out, and they gave him a few acres of woods where he built himself a place to live. He lived out there with a mule and a few goats and chickens. By that time he had been there thirty five or forty years.

I met him again fighting another fire out there in 1951 or 52. After that I used to see a lot of him. I would go out there sometimes and stop by his place. I remember a beautiful Summer evening when we stopped out there looking for Fr. Marion and Isaias who were lost in the woods (a letter from Fr. Isaias who is now married and announced the birth of a daughter!!). Hanekamp was reading an old German book, *The Pilgrim's Journey*, which Fr. Lambert had given him.

Then there was the classic day when we went out to look for the boundary line – Fr. Ephrem came all the way from Georgia – Hanekamp met us up on the ridge and Fr. Ephrem greeted him with contemptuous affection as a vagabond. It was a classic meeting.

Hanekamp said his stomach upset him when he was in the monastery. He was perfectly happy in his lonely valley, and came to mass and communion on Sundays at the monastery. He used to come before daylight, walking through the woods, and when we started to make dams and lakes overnight he walked into one, in the darkness, not having been warned that the brothers were damning the creekbed by which he normally came.

Later, after he had been quite ill out there and we had bought the Linton farms, Rev. Father gave him one of the houses. He came over in the rain with all his possessions in a mule cart. It was a pathetic sight.

He had a radio, and it was over this radio that the news of Pasternak's getting the Nobel Prize came and was relayed to me by Fr. John of the Cross. Fr. John of the Cross was out there all the time. He was out there two days ago and Herman was very sick. He had pneumonia and could hardly breathe. He refused to come to the monastery, and said "Oh, they don't want me over there." Fr. John of the Cross stayed with him a long time and was the last to give him a blessing. Yesterday some of the brothers were over there and say that he was very sick. But someone said "He's faking." Herman had ceased to be picturesque and interesting and could no longer be used for some obscure psychological purpose. If it had been thought that his being over here would have impressed the brother novices somehow, that would have made things different. But he was just old and sick and obviously didn't think too much of the community either.

On the whole, I think he preferred to die alone, and without being a spectacle to anyone.

He is not even being buried in the monastery. A laconic notice announces that he will be buried from the parish church in New Haven, with the pastor officiating.

Later: Fr. Eudes found the body of Hanekamp still warm and gave him absolution and extreme unction.

Significant that on the 28th. in the morning I read *Oedipus at Colonus* and was deeply moved by it.

January 2, 1959

Yesterday began the New Year well with cold, rainy weather, but that is the weather I like – After None I was walking and reading Tauler under the tall pines up behind the Sheep Barn and after Benediction went for a walk and talk with Fr. Tarcisius out around St. Anne's, which was a good thing because I have been too distant with him. And he is such a good, sweet person it would be sad to treat him so indifferently and thus perhaps have a bad effect on him. And he has really outdone himself to be helpful, so that my finding fault with what he did, rather than seeing his good will, was singularly selfish. That was a grace, then, to begin with.

In the morning chapter Rev. Father, because of certain events and circumstances, came out strongly against the reading of fiction and playing classical music on records. He almost seems to be trying to forbid them, under pain of mortal sin. It created quite a sensation because of the question of principle involved and not because very many are either reading novels or playing symphonies. He is definitely down on Fr. John of the Cross for reading and discussing Dostoevsky and Tolstoy. He tolerates my interest in them oddly but without explicit opposition but I gather I am included, though that it does not seem certain. I think what he is aiming at is a group of junior professed laybrothers. It is hard to see how they are going to run a college course in literature here and not read literature. For Rev. Fr., incidentally, all novels are "love-stories," and that is that. It can hardly affect anyone much except as a matter of principle – it takes so much time we haven't got, to read a novel. However I did spend some fruitful hours this Summer sitting in the straw and reading *Dr. Zhivago*. I know Fr. Sebastian is enthusiastic about Sigrid Undset and he looked a bit disgusted. As to what those others are reading, I hardly know.

This morning went to the funeral of Herman Hanekamp in New Haven. Started out in the frost after dawn. The body laid out in the funeral parlor was that of a millionaire, a great executive. I never before saw Herman shaven, in a suit, and, last of all in a collar and tie. He looked like one of the great of the earth. I was a pallbearer along with Andy Boone, Hanekamp's old friend Glenn Price (a great stout man with a lined face like the side of an old building but very humble and gentle). Bros. Clement and Colman were pallbearers and another man with a shoelace necktie.

Rev. Fr. sung the mass, vexed with me because I begged off being deacon when he asked me at the last moment (because at the last moment it became a big affair and if I had known that I would not have gone).

When we came out of the church into the sun, carrying the coffin, the bright air seemed full of great joy and a huge freight train came barreling through the valley with a sound of power like an army. All the pride of the world of industry seemed, somehow, to be something that belonged to Herman. What a curious obsession with the conviction of him as a great, rich man, tremendously respected by the whole world! And we drove back to bury him in the graveyard outside the monastery gate.

The bare woods stood wise and strong in the sun as if they were proud of some great success that had been achieved in secret with their connivance and consent.

And as we carried the coffin through the sunlit yard I listened with exaltation, for it was hailed by the singing of skylarks, on the second day of January.

What has triumphed here is not admired by anyone, but what was despised even by the monks who, they too, could not but help thinking of Herman as a lazy man and an escapist. He had not taken seriously the world of business, so important to us all. And now behold – a captain of industry.

January 11, 1959. Day of Recollection

Spent an hour straightening out our books and now it seems that there is much more room in our bookcase although I only got rid of a few. I am determined not to waste time writing and to enjoy reading. This in itself is a work, and an important one, but hard to get down to sometimes. Some people seem to think that I read an enormous amount but actually I read relatively little – though it is true I do get through quite a few books. Most of my reading is done after dinner walking up and down the road from the woodshed to the mill – and you do not read as much when you are walking.

Does it matter how much you read? What matters is the quality and variety of one's reading. Most monks are enclosed within too narrow limits and read too much of the same things and by losing their perspective lose their capacity to learn from what they read. I am perhaps at the other extreme now, but I really think that in almost everything I read I find new food for the spiritual life, new thoughts, new *discoveries* (for instance the deep spiritual content of Jan Van Eyck's portrait of the Arnolfinis) – a whole new light on my concept of the *hieratic* (in the good sense) in art. Or the Gregg book on non-violence – some LaFontaine "fables" (The *Rêve d'un habitant du Mogra* struck me deeply the last time I was in Louisville and I saw it in Gide's anthology). Three or four pieces on "religion" (decadent) in Edmund Wilson's collection of articles about the '30s (*American Earthquake*) – some things on Mayan civilization – Kierkegaard's *"Works of Love"* – Guardini on Dostoevsky. etc. etc.

There are a hundred things I want to get to.

A very fine interview with Guardini was read in the refectory – a wonderful relief from the complacent windiness of Chesterton *(St. Thomas Aquinas)*. Guardini spoke of power *poisoning* man today. We have such fabulous techniques that their greatness has outstripped our ability to manage them. This is the great problem. Difference between Guardini and Chesterton – Guardini sees an enormous, tragic, crisis and offers no solution. Chesterton evokes problems that stand to become, for him, a matter of words. And he always has a glib solution. With Chesterton everything is "of course" "quite obviously" etc. etc. And everything turns out to be "just plain common sense after all." And people have the stomach to listen and to *like* it! How can we be so mad? Of course, Chesterton is badly dated: his voice comes out of the fog between the last two wars. But to think there are still people – Catholics – who can talk like that and imagine they know the answers.

I should have written long ago what Fr. Lawrence told me of the assassination of Somoza – or maybe I did. It was on a day when he was going to celebrate his murder of some enemies – and because it was a "lucky" day he did not wear his bullet-proof vest. His assailant, a young radical, planning on his having a vest, carefully shot him in four or five places the vest could not protect, and thus it took him longer to die. And while they flew his dying flesh to Costa Rica all his enemies were rounded up and thrown into jail without having any idea what had happened until one of them saw a flag at half mast from his cell window.

The Epiphany was a great day this year.

And Friday, after receiving the relic of St. Bruno from Sister T., I got up at one o'clock by mistake and had a marvelous silent hour in the church before anyone else came down.

January 17, 1959. F. of St. Anthony the Great

A fine, cold day, as it should be.

Hard snow frozen everywhere, and the hills bright with it in the sun. Clouds and sun.

A fine Mass this morning – I had an intention to dispose of and said it for monks everywhere and for vocations. During a recollected thanksgiving fired with desire, heard in the depths of my soul the psalm *"Dominus, illuminatio mea et salus mea, quem timebo – Dominus protector vitae meae, a quo trepidabo?"* ["The Lord my light and my salvation / whom should I fear? / Lord, guardian of my life / from whom should I shrink?"] – a "voice" of great peace and serenity.

And chapter was short because Rev. Father went to Georgia – it was beautiful in the chapel, in the quiet, cold sun.

A letter from S. Spender, about the *Letter to an Innocent Bystander* which I had sent to "Encounter." He passed it on to *Tempo Presente* in Rome and said Silone "ought to read it."[41]

---

[41] Later published in Merton's *The Behaviour of Titans* (New York: New Directions, 1961).

It turns out in the Guardini interview read the other day in the refectory, was a paragraph about me which was left out. It said my books were good but that if I went a few years without writing they would get better. And this is true. I ought to be able to write even less this year than last. (Last year – only the additions to *Art and Worship* and a few articles.)

I like writing in Cyrillics – my Russian exercises, and it seems to improve my handwriting in English, which is a good sign.

Moved by Guardini's wonderful book on Dostoevsky.

The Hammers came over today and we talked about the Desert Fathers' translation, etc.

January 19, 1959

A great problem of the contemplative life. We pride ourselves on renouncing the *highest* natural goods, goods which in themselves are spiritual and easily supernaturalized and tend to lead us to God. For instance, married love in its most spiritual form – or art, music, scholarship, culture, and all the spiritual pleasures which go with them.

The renunciation of these things is not valid unless we are able to go beyond them and to fill the emptiness caused by their loss – to fill that emptiness with God Himself. Only a really spiritual man is capable of doing this – a highly spiritual man with very spiritual gifts.

But such gifts are very often lacking in contemplatives. They would often be more truly contemplative if they accepted, or even *sought* these goods – I mean art, culture. For in "renouncing" them they often create a void which they fill with something lower – preoccupation with business, or worse still, preoccupation with themselves, with their health, their hurt feelings, etc. Worst of all, those who get involved in immature and sentimental "friendships."

January 20, 1959

We are in the Chair of Unity Octave.

In many ways the pamphleteering about church unity annoys me. I find so much of it futile and absurd – largely because of its self-complacently idiotic lack of tact – lack of any sense of what church unity means: union in love.

As long as Church Unity is regarded as primarily a matter of submission to Papal authority, the whole business is going to remain pitifully absurd.

Chair of Unity! Just because something ought to be done, does not mean that those who ought to do it will do it as a result of being shoved around and bullied in to it.

Does anybody stop to say – in some half articulate, human way – that we love the Greco-Russian Christians – or to express a need to be loved by them? Or the Protestants – nearer home?

Each group regards the others with a mixture of pity, tolerance, and contempt. A pamphlet by Père [Martin] Jugie on the Byzantine schismatics is typical. The "Orthodox" Church is treated as absurd because it is "powerless to define" any new dogmas and has not said definitively that one cannot accept what has been defined by Rome since the 8th. century. *Therefore*, there is "no reason" why a Greek or Russian should not make submission to Rome in dogmatic matters. *Therefore* . . . Therefore . . . And out of those therefores comes the comforting assumption that everybody is in bad faith except ourselves.

The Church will never be united by "Therefores."

And people like Père Jugie, who is considered an authority, are those who *do the most to prevent* a mutual understanding between the East and the West. Precisely because he is (was) and knows himself to be (knew himself to be) an "authority" – a *specialist* on the Oriental Church – a specialist on schism. A specialist on what is wrong with other people.

Ought we not take warning from the fact that people like Jugie swarm all over the place in Rome, Paris, Salamanca, and in every seminary and religious community in the Catholic Church? And for that matter, though in a different form, in the Orthodox Church and in all the Protestant sects?

Christianity is full of specialists and authorities on what is wrong with different camps of Christians.

Do you think that when I come I shall find faith, or love, on the earth?

Wouldn't it be a little simpler and more honest to stop and look at what is *right* in different views of Christianity? We don't have to broadcast indifferentism all over the place. We don't have to compromise on anything. We don't have to hedge or pretend. We don't have to deny that the Pope is the head of all Christendom and the successor of St. Peter. But how about some of the things that have been done by Roman authority to antagonize and repel other Christians uselessly, uncharitably?

What an awful weakness it is to *have to insist* that one is *always right in everything*. If we admitted some of our own mistakes, in accidentals, people might be more ready to believe us right in the essentials.

January 21, 1959. St. Agnes
A Haiku

> High winds all night
> Stole the voices of the bells:
> No one knows what they said.

January 25, 1959. Septuagesima Sunday

I was going to write about the wonderful storm of rain that descended upon us on and off for two days – rain coming down on the woodshed in great sheets like a tropical storm in the movies, pouring out over the edges of the roof gutters and spilling on the ground in great pools of foam – the thick rain blew past the shed in tidal waves, hiding everything like the smoke of an enormous forest fire.

Then after that new glasses came and very cold weather. I walked in the cold weather with the new glasses which, being bifocals, and "executive" bifocals at that, made me feel as if I were walking up to my waist in water. A ludicrous experience. I will not bother to wear such glasses out of doors.

Now the Abbot General has written saying he refuses permission for publication of my article on Pasternak, on the grounds that novels are worldly things and the dog should not return to his vomit. I can see the reasonableness of not publishing the article and had thought of that myself, so that is no difficulty. The reasons alleged, and the incomprehension with which they are alleged, pain me a little, but so what. No one seems to suspect that there might be, in Pasternak, something of deep spiritual value and significance. Something perhaps spiritually *more* significant than anything that has yet manifested itself in any of our monasteries.

I do not accept this mania for judging everything according to labels and categories. Contemplative = what is in an enclosed monastery. Spiritual = what happens when you are on your knees. The "Things of God"? = pious exercises according to an approved formula. And the obsessive refusal to allow anything ever to overlap from one category into another. For instance that something outside monastery walls should be a manifestation of God, a thing of spiritual significance, something to do with contemplative life. I am getting to dislike more and more the complacent emphasis of the term "contemplative," and its inherent capacity to encourage phariseeism.

Indignation! Of course we admit there can be "contemplatives" outside monasteries. You do? But you only admit as contemplatives "outside monasteries" people who in every respect behave as if they were inside monasteries, people "in the world" who live, act, and think like monks and therefore might as well be in a monastery. Such distinctions have no significance.

I believe more and more that the rigidity of our spiritual categories and the obtuseness of our monastic minds produces results that are *fatal* to many monks morally, psychologically, and spiritually.

The utterly pitiful letter of ex-Fr. R. from Georgia – apostate after 12 years – The obvious assumption of all that it was his "fault." Does anyone stop to consider the possibility that it was also the "fault" of the monastic community, the Order, the Superiors?

No one of them could have foreseen that. This model religious never really believed in God – as he has at last discovered. And a good thing that he has, for now he has taken the first step towards believing. He entered the monastery on somebody's else's faith and lived there on somebody else's faith and when finally he had to face the fact that what was required was *his own faith* he collapsed. As many others would, or will, collapse when they find out how they stand.

Now it is the alienation implicit in most of our thought, most of our "Doctrine" of the monastic life, most of our rudimentary philosophy, and text-book theology (that fortunately is never really applied to in actual life) which keeps us divorced from our own depths and *alienated from our own true selves and from the Living God.* A certain simple and uncomplicated type can live very well with God in the ordinary pattern of our life. The rest, alas, have to pretend – or sweat blood.

The latter is my vocation. I am absolutely determined to be completely sincere, always, in everything, with myself and with God, in so far as I can, and accept no pre-fabricated answers or spurious solutions.

I will follow my conscience – and my vows – and the Holy Spirit and not expect anybody else in the world to think for me and live my life for me.

The question I ask now may be wild and scandalous. Still, let me ask it. What perplexes me is the fact that this Fr. R. as apostate is still the same Fr. R. who was the exemplary monk. As far as I can see there has been no change, except outward and juridical, in the man. And of course he has ceased to live as a monk.

Those who regard the change as tremendous and obvious must, then, attach all importance to the fact of *being in a monastery* – that above all. That is what makes the difference.

If Fr. R. were only in his monastery with his zeal, industry, capacity for hard work, love of order, kindliness, regularity – he would be a "model religious." He has transplanted all these things outside – that is the end of him. Of course, he has also incidentally given up his faith.

But he himself says he had already given it up in the monastery.

Here is the terrible question and one worthy of Kierkegaard:

Is it not possible that there are *large numbers* of "perfect religious" in their monasteries, regular, lovers of order and hard work, lovers of liturgy, kindly men and women – who have in reality *given up their faith?*

Useless to ask such a question, if all that matters is that they are in the monastery. They are "contemplatives."

To my mind, the danger comes from assuming that all men who are in monasteries and love order and keep our rules and love the liturgy – *have faith*. As if regularity were the sure sign and test of faith, vocation, election.

The honest beginning is to see that *we also* lack faith – that perhaps we, defended by our order, regularity, etc. are enabled to get by with even less faith than people who have to struggle outside.

Fr. R. is the same mixture of a honest business-man and a "social" Christian as almost everyone else I can think of who has the same character and background, whether in the monastery or outside it. Including those who (naturally) are most upset by his case.

January 26, 1959

In the Gospel of Septuagesima Sunday – the workers who worked all day for the agreed wage, complained that those who worked only one hour received the same as they. That is to say: all men have a tendency to make their own work, their own situation, their own condition the basic norm for judging everything and everyone else. If I work eight hours and you work one hour, I assume I ought to have eight times as much pay as you. And this becomes the starting point of all my reasoning. But supposing, by the grace of God, you get eight times as much as was due you? The mercy of God is not my business. If you get eight times your due, then I ought to get sixty-four times your due. Because I am I and you are you. There is a great deal of oriental wisdom in this Gospel and if we look at it as if it were a *Koan* the "logic" of man's every day life soon collapses completely.

We live by abstract ideas that seem to us to be absolute realities – and they are based on our own illusions. The workers who worked all day thought they were defending "justice" and who will deny that justice is real? But who can fail to see that in their case, "justice" was supremely unjust, and they were utterly incapable of realizing it. Their eye had become evil because of the goodness of God and the good they opposed to His goodness was evil. To cure their vision there was no way but to forget about "justice" and to stop thinking in terms of good and evil. But this they could not do, since he who argues against God can only do so in the name of a "good" and a "justice" which he opposes to God (In the name, that is, of evil).

How little we realize the importance of not trying to make ourselves arbiters of good and evil, justice and injustice. We have lost all capacity to judge now that we consider ourselves just judges and insist on judging everything.

God said: "Is it not licit for me to do as I please?"

In monasteries, we agree that it is "more perfect" to keep silent than to speak. So if someone speaks we think him imperfect. And not speaking is regarded as a form of "perfection." So that if someone speaks little, we think he possesses to some degree the reality, the substance of perfection. And if he speaks out of turn he reproaches himself as having let slip a little of his perfection. If we ask to *see* this famous perfection – why, it is a spiritual reality, an object of faith! Manifested by the lack of speaking.

How great is our reverence for nothing.

It is certainly good to keep silent. But only to get free from distracting and delusive words and concepts, and see reality more clearly where it is to be found, not in objects and words, but in ourselves. But if silence itself becomes the *worship of a concept*, then we become the prisoners of what we are seeking to escape. And then we judge like the workers in the vineyard – and make our tyrannical concept the measure of everything that happens under the sun. Thus we get completely out of touch with reality.

Silui a bonis [I have kept silent about the good]. Let me be silent from the worship of monastic concepts.

January 28, 1959

From Berdyaev's "Solitude and Society"

"Man may feel himself infinitely more alone in the midst of his coreligionists than in the midst of men of totally different beliefs . . . his relation to them may be of a purely objective kind. Such a state of affairs is extremely distancing and tragic . . . An increase of spirituality may only aggravate the sense of solitude for it may be accompanied by a total rupture of man's social relationships . . . But there is no way of avoiding such ruptures once man has embarked on a spiritual plane, only in mystic experience, where all things participate in the Ego and the Ego participates in all things. This path is diametrically opposed to objectification, which effects communication only between extrinsic and abstract things."

February 1, 1959. Sexagesima Sunday

A beautiful cold, windy afternoon. So many things to celebrate – (for some reason, though some are painful or foolish, all seem matter for celebration, perhaps because I drank coffee for dinner).

First, the good things. Everything Pope John XXIII does seems to me wise and worthy of celebration and now he has summoned an Ecumenical Council, in which to consider the reunion of the East and West. I am sure everyone is happy about it. And it is an answer to prayer – one which calls forth more prayer that it may lead to a good result.

Then a fine letter from Jaime Andrade in Quito with two color transparencies of the mahogany Virgin and Child he has carved for us. It is superb, strong, simple – very serious, compellingly sacred. Saying more strongly than I had imagined the thing I wanted to have said – with the note of reproach and directness, of accusation, that should be there. He will exhibit her in Quito then she will come by air, which is right. I still do not know if many here will like her or understand. Fr. Lawrence, of course, already does.

After dinner by the gate of the guest's garden thought of finally writing up some of the material on Genesis. This will have to be done, but when?

Speaking to Fr. Lawrence – said that even though I do not go to Ecuador, yet I can be present there in various spiritual ways. But he says no doubt you will go. I replied that it would take a miracle. And he said, "but a miracle is easy, for prayer." I could see at once how right he was. I shall go to Ecuador.

Another complication – this one elaborate and a little sickening. But with many good aspects.

I forget when I got a letter from Fr. Lombardi about his *Mondo Migliore* – Last Spring some time. I wrote him of some of my own aspirations and heard nothing, nothing, nothing. I knew something had happened, but had no idea how much. Finally last Thursday it all came out.

For months he has been struggling with the Abbot General, and Rev. Father, and even Dom Louis got in on it. He wanted to get me over to Rome apparently – to the horror of all my Superiors. What letters, secret consultations have taken place! Finally after the General Chapter Rev. Fr. went to Rome with Dom Louis and saw Fr. Lombardi. Great confabulation. Something or other is agreed upon. Then the Abbot General goes to see Tardini[42] to inquire if Lombardi could get the pope to order me out of here and into his organization. No, says Tardini. Sighs of relief!

Meanwhile what has been agreed – that I should "write for" his movement. Meaning what? I have not been told.

Coupled with his contempt for writers, Rev. Fr. has a kind of assumption that they just sit down and "write" – write anything. Whatever comes into their head.

"It doesn't matter – all he wants is to use your name."

Then Fr. Lombardi was going to come here and see me – at least I would get some information that way. The Abbot General, hearing of this, immediately forbade it and Rev. Fr. had to write in a hurry to cancel the visit, to the obvious annoyance of Fr. L.

Finally, Dom Louis' contribution: I am to write for Fr. L. without having any direct contact with him, even by letter. It is all to go through Rev. Father.

I am – why say it? – sickened by being treated as an article for sale, as a commodity. I feel deeply that all this is a sign of something, radically and terribly wrong – something very much the matter with religious life and our order. I do not say it may not be good and very providential to be thus protected from what might perhaps be a stupid error. Yet the whole thing is so cheap and expresses such a complete spirit of alienation. It is to me a sign of God – how terribly and how inexorably He draws out the falsity of pseudo-Christian tactics. But it makes me sweat to think that the same falsity is in myself and must come out too. Pity the General and Rev. Father! And pity me, if I ever get out into the light of day and my hypocrisy is brought into contact with Christ, say, in the Indians of Ecuador! God have mercy on me. Christ have mercy. Mother of God, intercede for me. There is no truth in my heart, there is no love, there is no cleanness. Have pity! Have pity!

February 7, 1959. Feast of St. Romuald

For the first time read some of the lapidary verse of [Giuseppe] Ungaretti.

His intensity, his earnestness, his discipline, his human feeling.

---

[42] The Vatican's Secretary of State.

As a Trappist, I should write as he does words fit to be carved in stone – with that kind of economy. I mean in verse.

It occurs to me that if Neruda in his last odes is imitating Ungaretti he is doing a very bad job. In Neruda's odes each line is a word, but the whole poem is only a line of uninteresting prose with the words strung out down the page, one on top of the other. In Ungaretti on the other hand each word is a line or even a poem in itself. Was there ever such a sense of words? I think he is quite probably inimitable.

In the refectory they are reading the new translation of the original life of St. Thérèse. I knew it would be different but I had not realized what fine, powerful lines and images had been cut out by the unimaginative Mère Agnes to make everything conform to the ideas of people without originality and without taste.

Flatirons on the feet of the little devils. And she "hated" the size of her mother's coffin. That she was so content with her own sisters and so completely unaware that she had something in her they were incapable of understanding or appreciating. Or maybe too in a very pure and matter of fact way she was aware of it, and it did not matter to her at all.

In any case the thing that overpowers you in everything is the realization of her sanctity. It is always deeply moving – and I am reassured by the fact that I can find it moving.

The foresters were here the other day looking at what we had done to the woods, and on those nice days that begin to feel of Spring I must begin to use the new pruning tools.

A heated discussion today in a Council meeting.

February 8, 1959. Day of Recollection – Quinquagesima Sunday
Reading one of the books sent by Fr. Lombardi to try to find out the precise essence of the movement.

This becomes really clear in the *"Esercizioni"* ["Exercises"] which is simply a combination of a retreat and a study group in which apostolic action is discussed and conclusions are arrived at in common – with the aim of common effort for the good of the Church.

This is all quite simple and obvious and corresponds to what I had been thinking of on my own, but with special reference to intellectuals *outside* the church.

Lombardi's *Mondo Migliore* movement is also highly organized on a diocesan and regional level. The *fraternitas* idea – collaboration of flying squads from diverse orders, is also good. This I had heard of. The efforts in Bologna had become famous.

The chief thing, then – active, coordinated participation in the apostolate for a renewal of the church and of Xstian society from within, not just the reform of individuals. Though the renewal of the Christian life comes down in the last analysis to the renewal of the spiritual life of individuals.

It seems evident to me that from one point of view I *ought* to be involved in something like this – I ought to be collaborating with other people in a constructive work of world-wide scope. The circumstances of my life and my isolation have led to thus being left in the background. I do not collaborate well – or only, shyly and impetuously. The fact that I almost never work in union with anyone else in anything important is probably one of the things most lacking in me.

In the novitiate, in this monastery, such collaborating as I do is a matter of routine – it is not especially constructive. It is merely a matter of the usual discussions that serve to keep life going on in the ordinary way in a sense the discussions whose purposes is to guard against *anything too new* happening.

On the other hand, I have to collaborate with publishers, printers, etc. But here it is all very simple – it is not a question of a common effort to achieve some common Christian end – to build anything new.

My activities are all extremely individual. That is the source of their strength and their weakness.

Strengths = originality, spontaneity, freedom, independence – the added power that comes from obviously personal convictions.

Weakness: subjectivism of the wrong kind, rashness, imprudence, snap judgments, unfairness, prejudice, lack of perspective, lack of depth, lack of discipline.

The greatest weakness may perhaps be that, too sure of myself and too much in love with the sound of my own voice, I may produce quick, superficial effects, gain attention – but without providing any lasting or really vital fruit. The great danger is that nothing is heard but the voice of my own precocity – and not the Holy Ghost.

It is equally obvious that I am not supposed to push ahead madly to try to solve anything. The solution is not up to me. I am not supposed to have any preconceived solutions. I will study what I study, think what I think, write what I write, and leave the disposition of my time and work to my superiors. At the moment, their answer is in effect to protect my individuality and spontaneity and keep me from getting immersed in any movements.

Whether or not this is a wise answer, in itself, is the wise answer for me in practice.

The ideal remains: my ideal as well as the ideal of the movement.
1. To rebuild the world spiritually, from the foundations.
2. The Christian renewal and transformation of society.

But does this mean the imposition, from without, of certain concepts and slogans? The adoption of certain devout practices? Such things alone do not constitute a renewal.

To get everybody back to "going to Church" – that is not yet the answer. The idea is that men should live *first of all as men* – with all their human rights and dignities. Then as *Sons of God*, with their divine and spiritual prerogatives. If Sons of God – Then *Brothers in Christ*.

February 9, 1959
Bad cold. Forty Hours.

Last night I was on night watch. Curious effect of the brothers lined up before the Bl. Sacrament in the sanctuary, chanting their office. Paternosters treated as psalms, each one followed by a *Gloria Patri*, with a profound bow. The Bl. Sacrament surrounded by heavy, gleaming brass. Brass candlesticks, brass tabernacle, a brass roof taken from an old reliquary, forming a canopy.

The fantastic inadequacy of the whole thing suddenly floored me.

What kind of sense could such ceremonies possibly make of the sacramental presence of the Incarnate Word of God? Our curious, matter of fact familiarity with the Sacred Presence – its utter objectification. Painfully struggled with the fact that we do not know what we are doing, saying, thinking, believing – almost as if it would end in a denial of the whole thing – as if the mystery itself were impossible. Could God be really present and allow this presence to be so efficiently and systematically slighted?

This morning I saw it in a different light. It is that our indebtedness to God is so immense that no effort we make to acquit ourselves of it can be anything but foolish. And it is this indebtedness that shocked me. It is infinite. It is this we do not want to see. It is this, also, that we hide from ourselves by our very piety. For our worship is often a way of deluding ourselves that we are paying our debts.

This morning – Solemn Mass outside the sanctuary. I assisted in the transept snorting with my cold behind the credence table, watching the timid maneuvers of my novices, serving as acolytes. Fr. Alberic, eating against his will large quantities of porridge, has become a great shaggy novice, wild eyed and sudden in his movements and still basically gentle. He is fatter than almost anyone, so I suppose that for Lent the porridge had better stop.

Fr. Columban on his back in the infirmary, something wrong with his spine.

February 13, 1959

Kierkegaard's marvelous book on the *Works of Love*.

With pages of careful and passionate thought he returns again and again to the task of making the freedom of Christian love impregnable – how? In the *obligation* laid upon us by God to love our neighbor. A strange paradox and a scandal who think it is a matter of emotional spontaneity. But if that were so Christianity would never transform man or divinize him.

One of the most original pages is the one where he illustrates this by the example of marriage. For a Christian, the wife is first of all a neighbor. For the worldling who attempts for a moment to think in Xstian terms, it might almost seem to be the opposite, as if we had to hope that somehow every neighbor were to be as a wife, which is absurd and impossible.

The wife is a *specially chosen* neighbor, but the important thing is that there is *the choice*, the act of freedom and of conscience, one example of the free choice by which we determine before God to love every man as *our* "neighbor."

When two consciously make this choice, this spiritual choice, with regard to one another, then a great mystery and transformation takes place in the world and God is present in this mystery.

Si Dei praecepta custodiens, filius quis efficitur Dei, *ergo non est natura filius sed arbitrio suo.* [*Any child, obeying God's commands, becomes a child of God not by nature but by his will.*] St. Jerome – *II Lesson of today's Vigils.*

The breathtaking mystery of the freedom of the sons of God: that one becomes a Son of God *by wanting to*. And this is the gift of God – a gift of His spirit – the Spirit of the sonship, the Spirit of adoption. So that if one wishes to be the Son of God he knows that he is the Son of God: provided only his wish is a desire to live and die as a Son of God with all that this implies. Not a mere velleity of seeing in oneself the consolation of Sonship and tasting a feeling of peace.

Two articles much alike. One by Edmund Wilson in a recent book with a section on Israel, the other by Apostolus in *la vie spirituelle* both on the Basilica of the Holy Sepulchre in Jerusalem, that sad, dilapidated symbol of disunity. What a heart-rending thing. What a source of shame. All the abstract talk about sin that is bandied about by all of us who ignore this terrible witness to our sins, in the very place of salvation. And the inscription: Surrexit, *non est hic.* [He is risen. *He is not here.*]

February 14, 1959

ON RETREAT

"Christianity is not indifferent to anything secular – on the contrary it is solely spiritually concerned for everything." *Kierkegaard.*

This very good quote is nonetheless out of context, and the context is interesting for many weightier reasons than the quote. For what I have extracted from K. is nothing new, whereas the context *is* new. (Thought I have already run into that too long ago in Kierkegaard.) It is that "Christianity does not wish a decision in external matters"! That is, it is the worldly attitude to demand distinct outward manifestation of the difference between "Spiritual" and worldly love. For instance – a different kind of object, a different style, a different kind of love altogether. As if one were to love "only God." In actual fact, what matters is the inwardness of Xstian love – the inner spiritual change which in "many cases leaves the external situation unchanged. v.g. the true hiddenness of Xt was His ordinariness.

Of course, this is not absolute. Christianity *does* speak in externals and decisively. But here again her decision is apparently arbitrary, and offends the world. The decision upon certain sacramental signs, which simply and summarily declare the Church's meaning and manifest her inward and spiritual intention which, for the rest, is nobody else's business.

———

With difficulty, but in time, I remember my resolution to keep this book free of resolutions. However I *do* want this retreat to be decisive. And doubtless by writing too much about it I could prevent it from being so.

It is however clear to me that the decisiveness one way or the other does not depend on the conferences which, as far as the material goes, are very miserable. At least so far.

The good father from Los Angeles is without any doubt a pious person, sincere, devout, really humble, limited in his views, earnest, humorless, unimaginative. You do not mind his lack of humor, though, for his humility and earnestness give him a kind of inner lightness – he is not nearly as ponderous as he could be – just conventional. And if he is a saint, which they say, and I hope he is – then he is the kind of saint I am not called to be. The kind it would be sinful for me to try to be.

To think that a community of monks should sit and have the Spiritual Exercises of St. Ignatius preached to them by a secular priest, and not even by a Jesuit. He apologized earnestly, but said we must look at it with the "eyes of faith" and that the Exercises had been heartily approved by the Popes.

The fact remains that the Popes also insisted that religious try to nourish their spiritual life at its source, in the writings, teaching, and example of *their own* founders and fathers. When do we ever hear anything about monastic tradition in one of our retreats, or anywhere else?

Continual rain, and the rain seems to make the red oaks grow redder still.

Contrast with our retreat master the sense, breadth, good humor, and above all the *immersion* in God's Word of Soeur Jeanne d'Arc, in an article on "Chastity and Virginity" which I am going over in view of conferences for the novices!

I let my soul grind away at itself for an hour, without seeking refuge in a book or in writing anything down. What do I do at such a time? What am I attempting? To resolve to be something other than I am, which is futile. Or rather, returning to an old, old question: what shall I be? The question has been settled long ago. There is no point sitting and thinking about such a thing, but to work at the work appropriate for the person that I am.

And here – too careful planning and looking ahead are not much use. Do what you do, read what you read, the rest will follow.

February 15, 1959

The best of the retreat, as far as conferences go, has so far been the really excellent talks on Baptism which, of course, fall quite outside of the proposed scheme of the "Spiritual Exercises." The good Father apologized for digressing. For me no doubt the whole of his message is in this digression. That it is time for me at last to live fully up to the level of what I am, a Son of God. I do not have to be something new, I only have to be what I am. I have known this all along, and I really think I have sought it. If only now I can seek it more completely and more efficaciously.

In the second of these conferences he made some very apt remarks on St. Benedict also, so I can take back what I wrote yesterday.

February 16, 1959

Describing the Last Judgment in the parable of the sheep and the goats the Lord did not say that the ones condemned to separation from Him had done anything especially wrong, that they were thieves or adulterers – He just said that they had *not* done certain good things – And these good things they had omitted to do are all reducible to one – they had omitted to show love for Him in their neighbor – To do good to them in the neighbor. How terrible is salvation and how terrible to miss something so simple – and perhaps those who tend most easily and most tragically to miss it are we who are "consecrated to perfection." We tend to worry about everything but this.

The Gospel of Martha and Mary shows that the one thing necessary is love – not, as usually interpreted, "The Contemplative Life." Love whether in contemplation, or in action: love of Christ in Himself and in our brother, that and that alone is the one thing necessary.

February 17, 1959

The main idea of this retreat for me is one from Kierkegaard: That the man who is constantly seeking an object worthy of love and constantly rejecting every object because he still wants to find one that is *really worthy* is perhaps in the end only pretending to seek and pretending only in order to dissimulate his own complete lack of love. For if one has love in him he will soon find an object worthy of love and will be able to love everyone and everything. That is my trouble – instead of loving I am only "seeking to love" and only developing my own fastidiousness. If only I would put an end to this foolishness. The problem Kierkegaard describes is essentially neurotic, and one feels it was only his own. The description of St. Thérèse's sickness as a child in the new translation shows how neurotic she was – and that a neurotic can nevertheless become a saint if he only learns to love.

Says K.: "The task does not consist in finding the lovable object: it consists in finding the object already given or chosen lovable, and in continuing to find him lovable however changed he is."

February 18, 1959

Tradition. "God has given us a thought of our own and our personal work cannot be done *in the past*. In other words ecclesiastical tradition does not put the voice of the past *in place* of the voice of the present, but gives it full force." *Bulgakov.*

February 24, 1959. Feast of St. Matthias

Morning off. Cold wind but warm sun. I sit in the sun with a torn work-blouse and a worn workjacket and muddy feet and listen to the song sparrows and the bawling heifers.

Last night dreamt I was just about to enter the Library of Congress – a vast, splendid place probably much more grand than the real thing. There was a sidewalk cafe along the outside of the building and thinking to enter the building I got mixed up among the tables of the cafe. I could see the library through the windows. I was moving along seeking the door when a waiter asked me what I desired, as if I were occupying one of the empty tables. I said I would come back later and he was grieved at losing my business. He said, "but that will be too late!" "Will the place be closed?" I said. "No," he replied, "but I will not be here!" And at that moment the alarm went off. How like the whole life of man!

What can I say about the great discovery of my need for the Church, that is for the Holy Spirit dwelling and acting in the Mystical Christ? It is something inexplicable, this greatest of all realities, this reality which is so well hidden by the false front and the externals and the unintended edifice. But I now realize that for a long time I have been slowly, and severely tempted against the Church, and only with the first glimpse of a solution have I realized how deeply I was involved in the problem. And yet it is not really that much of a problem since the Spirit Himself (who helpeth our infirmity) both raises the question and answers it. *Quid petis ab ecclesia?* [What do you seek of the church?]

Fine letter from Czeslaw Milosz in Paris. I had written about *The Captive Mind*. He replied at length about Alpha, Beta, etc. gave information about books, said he had translated some poems of mine into Polish. Sense of dealing, for once, with a real person, with one who has awakened out of sleep. There is no question that the world of the West and I in it, is involved in the deepest and most restless, and most stupid sleep. And how are we going to wake up? (The efforts which Western politicians imagine to be an awakening are only ways of tossing around in order to settle into an even deeper slumber.)

A red-shouldered hawk screams insistently in very blue sky.

February 27, 1959

Yesterday in chapter a theological conference over the fate of unbaptized infants. It is a silly but symbolic question. With all our solemn theology of the mercy of God we still cannot devise a better system than one which involvers the damnation of innocents. Of course they are "damned" etc. They are "happy." But are they? In questions like these I think Wisdom mocks the theologians – the men who so solemnly imagine they are supposed to know and settle everything.

The presuppositions are so childish and embarrassing. How do we approach this question? It has frankly become one of expediency: how to make sure that people will get their infants baptized, and yet how to console those whose infants have died . . .

It is a very good subject on which to say nothing. Except that God has said "ask and you shall receive." It seems to me that anyone who is really interested in the salvation of these infants can at least *ask* for it!

March 1, 1959. Sunday

Yesterday morning, coming out from frustulum, looked up at the Eastern sky over the barns and saw a bouquet of very distant jet planes growing like a silver plant out of a dark blue bank of cloud. The sun, hidden by the clouds, filled the exhaust of the four planes with brilliant light, and they were slowly turning and swinging to the North so that their ropes of silver fire twined in the dawn sky.

And later came to the novitiate chapel after chapter and opened the window and prayed while birds sang in the willow tree.

What they are continuing to do to Fr. John of the Cross is a shame to mention. Tragic and stupid righteousness with which he is being "brought into line" – made to conform. It is true, he has given them reason by being independent. And that is the tragedy. They can feel fully "justified." But in the end it is the old fear of originality, of the person who has "got something," who realizes that mere conformity would be an infidelity to God and to grace – fear of the man who is different from the others and will not (*can* not) sacrifice that difference which makes them fear him because he is so obviously superior. So he is made to suffer for his superior gifts of heart and mind and soul. Made to suffer because those he has helped (whose vocation and spirit he has saved) continue to love him. It makes me sick at the stomach.

March 3, 1959. Tuesday

Yesterday received word from Helen Wolff that Pasternak had disappeared from Peredelkino and had, so the official news said, gone on a "vacation" to the Black Sea "to get away from foreign reporters." I believe this will be the end of him. He has been fearing it, recently, so I hear (he wrote to his London publisher that the end was coming). And now all the ghastly business – the "confession" which he has denied in advance – and his total disappearance. How he needs strength now. Perhaps he is already finished. How strange it is to speak of someone one knows in such terms. (It is strange, at least, to one living in America. Many millions of others are now thoroughly used to it.)

I said my Mass for him this morning. The introit was terribly appropriate:

> "I have cried to thee and Thou O God has heard me:
> O incline Thine ear unto me and hear my words:
> Keep me, O Lord, as the apple of Thine eye.
> Protect me under the shadow of Thy wings.
> Hear, O Lord, my justice – attend to my
> supplication." (Ps. 16)

How like the psalms many of Pasternak's later poems have become. May God protect him and have mercy on this great man.

Father Herrera, a priest of the diocese of Avila in Spain, is here with a seminarian from Nicaragua. Fr. H has stories about the tremendous difficulties of the Spanish priests appointed to teach in the Seminary at Managua – opposition of the native bishops and clergy. The Bishop backs Somoza, to the disgust of the people. I have said nothing of the victory of Fidel Castro in Cuba but it has been a most inspiring event. We are hoping for something of the same in Nicaragua. Fr. Lawrence's cousins and several friends will be involved in it . . . Fr. Herrera – a good poet, wonders whether to become a Cistercian monk some day.

A most significant event. After much thought, prayer, and debate, consulted the *I Ching* as, I think a valid experiment. Not a question of *sortilegium* [divination], but a consultation in the same spirit as that of Jung in the preface. To learn something of my own deeper moral self and to see more clearly, perhaps, into my most hidden motives and problems. Much as one might take a Rorshach test, for instance. That was the spirit of the experiment.

Used not coins but three rather "special" religious medals; one an old bronze one of St. George (yang) on one side and a staff (yin) on the other. One of Our Lady of Cobre, with nothing (yang) on the back. One of Our Lady of Perpetual Help with a hole in it. And, as I say, much prayer. (After all, the Holy Spirit spoke through a drawing of lots when St. Matthias was chosen apostle.)

The answer was a crucial one – struck me very deeply and I think it was astoundingly correct. It was talking "preponderance of the great."

— — "The ridgepole sags to the breaking point.
═══ The fortress to have somewhere to go.
— — Success."

[These broken lines were Merton's attempt to illustrate the hexagrams from the *I Ching*.]

The heavy load – an exceptional time – extraordinary events demanded problems not to be solved by force but by gentle penetration. *Demands superior courage* – to stand firm under the Tree (Sun)

═══
— —

to be joyous as the lake

— —
——
——

even if I must renounce life itself. To stand alone, unconcerned, in the face of death. (I think that in some strange way Pasternak got mixed up in this Hexagram!) What is truest for me – the need to abandon *hubris* and go slow, to drop ambitions, to pull in my horns, love those under me, and stand firm in danger.

March 10, 1959. Tuesday

A happy purposeless afternoon in the woods – most purposeful when I am not doing anything.

Last week I did not have time to write down everything about the Hexagram from the *I Ching*. It does not matter. To a great extent, I think, the necessary change has been made. A deep interior one, rather than an exterior change. On the Feast of St. Thomas Aquinas it was like pulling up the roots of something and I don't quite know how it got done – and perhaps it is not yet done completely. Probably not.

March 15, 1959. Passion Sunday

Same struggle in the depths. All I can do is want what is in one to swing somehow into line with forces I do not know or understand, that are reality.

Wrote a letter on thin paper, with two pages of quotes from the Desert Fathers and sent the lot to Suzuki in Japan. I hope it all reaches him, and that he will write a preface to the little D.F. book.[43] No one else is either so worthy or so capable of doing it.

Regret having given up Russian but that is part of the struggle. If it were only a matter of making a decision according to some general norm outside myself – something on paper – it would be so simple. I feel that to seek such simplicity would be an oversimplification and a betrayal – at least now.

Said Mass for Reiko Hatsumi on St. Gregory's day. From her little book and from Ann Ford's book etc. She is an appealing and important person,

[43] Suzuki's preface, in fact, did not appear in *The Wisdom of the Desert*, but did appear in an appendix to *Zen and the Birds of Appetite* (1968).

and one who suffers, and is loved by God – and many more mysterious things.

John Harris[44] who conveyed to me a message from Pasternak during the worst of the storm in November, is now taking instructions, he tells me, at Buckfast.

Fr. Lawrence has translated Lax's circus poem.

Last night another night of high winds. Listened also to the winds outside while we sat in chapter this morning. The cross is a sign of *liberation*. To this hope I cling blindly. There is no hope of freedom in myself alone, or in simple conformity to what is said and done here. Freedom means battle and faith and darkness, and a new creation out of the darkness.

Darkness battling in the March wind.

The sky before Prime, in the West, livid, "blasted" – fast running dark clouds, pale spur of the firetower against the black West.

Fr. Francis Xavier, the Filipino – a very sterling person – has come early into the thick of the battle that is here. Rebellion against the false and depressing forms of love that pass for charity among us. People try to make a pet of him and he hates it. Then they were kidding him about the Philippines "becoming a state like Hawaii" – with all their stupid innocence, not knowing what American rule means in the Philippines. And they joked about war. He told me he had seen the body of a small boy who had been roasted on a spit by Japanese soldiers.

Love = emotional pressure to make others conform to ourselves so that we may not feel insecure. That is the terrible thing: the fundamental treachery of real and personal values, under the guise of love. In perfectly sincere people. When will we ever become Christians?

Rev. Father does not even trust me enough to hand me a letter from Dom Damasus Winzen with a perfectly routine request for information about an ex-postulant from here who is thinking about entering Mount Saviour. I wonder if it ever should be otherwise, but I suppose it should, one way or the other.

March 18, 1959

The old and the new.

For the "old man" – everything is old – he has seen everything or thinks he has. He has lost hope in anything new. What pleases him in the "old" he

---

[44] An English schoolmaster who served as an intermediary between Pasternak and Merton. Merton's letters to Harris may be found in *The Hidden Ground of Love*

clings to, fearing to lose it, but certainly not happy with it. And so he keeps himself "old" and cannot change; he is not open to any newness. His life is stagnant and futile. And yet there may be much movement – but change that leads to no change. *"Plus ça change, plus c'est la même chose."* ["The more things change, the more they remain the same."]

For the "new man" – everything is new. Even the old is transfigured in the Holy Spirit and is always new. There is nothing to cling to, there is nothing to be hoped for in what is already past – it is nothing.

The new man is he who can find reality where it cannot be seen by the eyes of the flesh – where it is not yet – where it comes into being the moment he sees it. And would not be (at least for him) if he did not see it.

The new man lives in a world that is always being created, and renewed. He lives in this realm of renewal and of creation. He lives in life.

The old man lives without life. He lives in Death, and clings to what has died precisely because he clings to it. And yet he is crazy for change, as if struggling with the bonds of death. His struggle is miserable, and cannot be a substitute for life.

Thought of these things after communion today, where I suddenly realized that I had, and for how long, deeply lost hope of "anything new." How foolish when in fact the newness is there all the time.

It is a year since I first found out about Pasternak in a chance reading of *Encounter* which I picked up in Louisville: the Gerd Ruge (?) interview. (The first thing P. taunted him with was being "so young and yet so decrepit.")

March 19, 1959. St. Joseph

Yesterday afternoon as I was trying to get started on a new version of the Pasternak article a call came from the cellarer, asking me to take some novices over to fight a fire in the woods on the other side of the knobs. It turned out to be almost at the edge of New Haven. Some kids were there and it was practically all out. Most of the novices came home. I stayed to help finish up the fire with a back-pack pump. It was not very hot, so everyone did, with impunity, all the things that would have been disastrous in really dry weather. I went down into a gully full of saplings that had honeysuckle all over them. The fire was climbing up the honeysuckle in sudden bursts but with a little water it went out easily. Then we went over a little rise where fire was smoking and smouldering in the ruins of a house (that had fallen down long before that day). We found more fire rambling

aimlessly through a thicket of sumac. I tried to do the approved thing and
build a backfire but it was a waste of time. The job was soon over.

After the fire – talked to a man with long curly hair and a beard and a
kind of red vest, and another very poor man who, I think, cut some wood
for us. There was also a little boy with a pathetic face and holes in his
pants, whom I had seen some weeks before with an ugly scar on the side of
his head. The big scab was gone and you could see the place of the scar.
His face made you wonder if he ever had anything happen to him in life
worth smiling about, the poor little kid. Later, as we were waiting for a
truck to take us home, two more very little mites came running up the road
from school and one of them with trembling lips asked if anyone had been
hurt in the fire. Old Horgan, with his great barrel of a belly and his face
like the side of an old hill with strange rock formations standing out all
over it, said in a most gentle tone, "It was only a lot of old weeds." And to
the little girl, who came after the little boy, I said, "Your house is all right."
She replied in a sweet, tired little voice, "I know it." Her intonation made
the words sound like a Negro or a crying bird or both.

I came home thinking of nothing but these poor little Christs with holes
in their pants and their sweet, sweet voices. Once again I had seen Proverb
and heard her speak and remained heartbroken with love for her. If only
my love could have some truth in it.

I had a Mass free to apply this morning and offered it for those kids and
for Pasternak and for others as well. But it was no help to my conscience.
The warm chapel and the clean linens and the waxed floor and the drapes
and the lights were an accusation. What is the sense of kidding ourselves?
What can I do?

March 25, 1959

It is not the Feast of the Annunciation but Wednesday of Holy Week.

I have the flu. Fr. Tarcisius has been in the infirmary for three days. I
have been spending part of the time in the novitiate and the rest in Hogan's
alley. Some miserable moments – sick as a dog last night.

Yesterday, obsessed with some dire need, finished revising the old article
on Pasternak, having also finished a shorter and better new one the day before. Forgot to say that when P. vanished from his dacha I wrote to the
General about it and he said because of the new circumstances I could go
ahead and write. Now I discover that P. went to Tiflis of his own free will.
Helen Wolff heard this from Gerd Ruge whom Pasternak telephoned in

Moscow before leaving. He is staying with Tabidges' widow. His own wife has pretty much been like the wife of Job throughout the whole affair.

Brother Labre lies dying in the infirmary with a strange blind yearning stamped on his face by the distortion of suffering. He has spoilt everybody's plans by living on until the moment when it is no longer possible to have a Requiem Mass for four days.

As for the new ritual of Holy Week . . .

In many ways there has been a tendency to substitute light and superficial rites for things that were deeper and more symbolic and more moving. I cannot judge how the hymns at the little hours will be, but St. Ambrose or no St. Ambrose at the moment I am disposed against them. The lapidary simplicity of the former office, with its plain repeated cadences, nothing but Psalm 118, was to me perfect.

April 4, 1959. Saturday in Albis

Ending a beautiful week – Easter Week – as hebdomadary. In spite of the struggle and interior difficulty, this singing of the conventual Mass is an immense grace and a work of love that leaves me happy and more profoundly happy than almost anything else I ever do here. It is the most meaningful and elevating of all our acts, and it seems to include everything, draws everything into focus – so that by the end of the week your whole life is in the right shape. This is, of course, to a great extent because of the sacrifice it involves for me. But so many other things come into it too. The beautiful two hours of reading before dawn when the whole house is silent and everyone else is at private masses. Then having the whole wide sanctuary to move in, and the choir behind you as you offer the Holy Sacrifice. Nor have I any objection to the slightly larger cruets. Then the silence and peace of Thanksgiving afterwards.

Worked several afternoons planting saplings – they came on Holy Thursday. Lovely clear afternoons (except for yesterday when there was a storm of wind and some rain).

Read some Origen on Josue, and Soloviev (Lectures on God Manhood) – some material on Mount Athos – Allport on prejudice. A new book by Jung has come in – *The Undiscovered Self* – which so far appears to be quite good.

The Hammers came over and we had a lively conversation about his leaflet on art which, I realize, I had read too superficially. He demands to be met on completely classical grounds and I am unwilling to meet him there. But the fact is he is a very sane and humble person and his refusal to be carried away by contemporary fashions is in reality a mark of genuine and deep integrity. His visits are always very good and salutary events.

Today I discovered something in talking to Victor Hammer. He was speaking of a young artist who paints falsely, deliberately, in order to make money so as "to be able to paint what he likes" – but V. pointed out that this will not work and that one has to be genuine all the time.

I found myself saying that it is a grave error to imagine oneself too much in control of the situation as to think he knows when he can turn on his genuineness and turn it off again. This, in fact, is a serious form of pride and one has to have the humility to be willing to *struggle hard at every moment* to be genuine and honest, realizing that it is by no means easy to be so. And to fail to realize that is fatal.

Yet it is perhaps what I myself have long failed to realize.

Again, on leaving, Victor spoke of the uselessness of his trying to get publicity and to put himself across; its utter needlessness. How unfortunate for me to realize this as he has. I am not as old as he is, of course. But I am a monk!! So . . .

The Hammers brought Brigg's *Christian Platonists* and Burkitt's *Church and Gnosis* – and Carolyn wanted me to do a broadside. At first, I thought of a "Blast on Peace." But then remembered the "Confessions of Crimes Against the State."

April 10, 1959

"The time is coming when it will be necessary for the man who is to be called 'educated' to know either Arabic, Sanskrit, or Chinese, as it is now for him to read Latin, Greek, or Hebrew." *Coomaraswamy.*

But now an educated man is not even expected to know Latin. In fact many apparently "educated" people in America do not even know English – or one vernacular language. What is the conclusion if the "educated" do not even know their own language well? I would like very much to learn Chinese or Japanese and am seriously considering whether it would not be far better than trying to learn Russian.

April 11, 1959

On the evening of the 6th. (Feast of the Annunciation transferred) I found a letter from Suzuki, very cordial and understanding – ending with a few bold and very remarkable intuitions on Christianity. Typical of his Zen approach yet very close to the Fathers. That we have never really been thrown out of Paradise, that our innocence is preserved even though we are sinners, or even because we are sinners. Etc. Statements that would make theologians fall over into a dead faint, and yet behind them is a sharp intuition of a very great reality – our life in the Risen Christ. The fact is that the Resurrection has restored us to Paradise and that since the Resurrection we are sinners yet innocent *(O felix culpa!)* [O Happy Fault!] All these things that can hardly be said scholastically, still less with a kind of pseudo-empirical scientism, and which still accords with the whole spirit of the N[ew] T[estament]. F. Hilarion is typing a copy of the *Exultet* which I will send to Suzuki. Meanwhile today I wrote him a three page letter.

It seems to me very important, indeed a basic fact of primary importance, that Suzuki and I can speak the same language and indeed that we speak much more of a common language than I can, for instance, share with the average American business man, or indeed with some of the other monks.

Now here is the thing: if in order to conform to the standards and I might say prejudices of the society to which I belong, I were to adopt the formulas and attitudes of the American bourgeoisie, with which, I do not agree and which I do not sympathize with or even comprehend and if, taking this standpoint which is not even my own, I should demand that Suzuki should come over and meet me on this ground that is alien to us both: it would be a terrible infidelity to Truth, to myself and to Christ.

And this is so in spite of the fact that Christian doctrines are embedded in a matrix of these alien social elements in which, exteriorly, I am supposed to be comfortable. Thus if I tried baldly and bluntly to "convert" Suzuki, that is, make him "accept" formulas regarding the faith that are accepted by the average American Catholic, I would, in fact, not "convert" him at all, but simply confuse and (in a cultural sense) degrade him. Not that he does not need the Sacraments, etc. but that is an entirely different question.

On the contrary – if I can meet him on a common ground of spiritual Truth, where we share a real and deep experience of God, and where we know in humility our own deepest selves – and if we can discuss and compare the formulas we use to describe this experience, then I certainly think Christ would be present and glorified in both of us and this would lead to a *conversion of us both* – an elevation, a development, a serious growth in Christ. This conversion "upwards" would be real and fruitful – and a conversion "downwards" (dragging him to a mediocre and exterior acceptance) would be hateful. One will say – No, a conversion downwards would be a sacrifice of pride. Therefore it is good. That is an illusion. It would only be true if it were really a conversion "upwards" – a real growth, an interior development. Actually, to demand a conversion in the sense of mere *conformity* is to demand only the humiliation of the convert, and this is not only false but useless. What is demanded is the humiliation of both, and the mutual elevation of both. That is a true conversion. And who says that Suzuki is not already a saint? This all of course has no bearing on the fact that whatever his case, he would be immeasurably more sincere and more saintly *per se*, if he came to the Sacraments and were a visible member of the Church. But *visibility* (which is all that seems to count for the bourgeois) is not the most important thing. Let us also remember that the visibility of the conversion we demand of others may, perhaps, be demanded not by our charity but by our weakness: as an exterior prop to our own lack of faith.

In any case Suzuki will probably write a preface to the *Desert Fathers* – and I worked on the translation today with great joy.

Our new Fr. Immediate, Dom Columban, came today – very pleasant and turns out to have the same trouble with his stomach that I have. Picked it up in a prison camp. Already, I feel well disposed towards him in every way! But he is really very likable and kind. And quite childlike: charmed with the sight of Boston from the air with the little toy cars on all the roads in so many pretty colors.

April 19, 1959

Visitation closing tomorrow (3rd. Sunday After Easter – modicum). It has been very quiet and orderly. The new Father Immediate has been a good influence. Had several talks with Fr. Paul, the censor, who is here from Conyers – brought here on purpose so that we might see eye to eye, on our various problems.

One thing is certain – it is useless for me to turn out easy essays for extern sisters. For a while I was wondering: there is always a temptation to do what is easy and obvious on the ground that the most obvious is the Will of God. This is too obvious and I am glad. On the other hand it is possible that the things I am interested in (articles on Pasternak, Le Douanier Rousseau, etc.) are not obvious enough. Or not obvious enough to those who get worried about such things.

With Dom Columban – decided that it would be good to have someone I would consult on the larger and more apostolic problems and we hit on Daniélou.[45] I think that is a very sound idea.

The statue came from Andrade, in Ecuador, and is very fine. A very serious and mysterious statue that certainly measures up to the virginal idea and conveys it well.

Tuesday and Wednesday – planting tree seedlings.

Thursday, everyone was out burning brush on St. Bernard's field. I wanted the fires to get away. We started on the windward side and it looked like a battlefield in five minutes – and for the rest of the afternoon. Not everything was thoroughly burned up, however.

Sent the Desert Fathers ms. to J. Laughlin[46] today, though there is more to be done on the introduction – and I want to add more *Verba*. Sent it to Suzuki earlier in the week.

Dom Columban – on what I am doing – collaboration with Suzuki, etc. "do it but don't preach it." This is wise. I might be too aggressive and try to say too much. Really, nothing needs to be said: or nothing much. What matters is to *do* it.

April 23, 1959. F. of St. George

Gorgeous sun. Wrote to Daniélou this evening.

What I need most is time to read. Take it.

Went to Lexington Tuesday to see Fr. Columban in the hospital there. They had him covered with hot packs but still did not know what was the matter with him.

Made a visit to the hospital chapel and looked at the saints in the windows with the eyes of a Protestant (many in Lexington) – was not edified.

But Victor Hammer's place, hidden in the trees behind the public library, and hidden behind an old house (a new low wing behind an old house) was fabulously beautiful. It was like a Carthusian cell, and there was not a shelf, not a cup, not a spoon, not a papercutter, that was not in some way fine and beautiful. It is years since I have seen any such thing and it amazed and delighted me. The little Japanese knife in its sheath; the Japanese scissors with wicker covered handles; VH's own pictures which I now like – with

---

[45] Jean Daniélou, S.J. A French theological and patristics scholar; later named a cardinal by Pope Paul VI.
[46] James Laughlin was Merton's editor at New Directions in New York.

their colors like Angelico. The two Greek vases. His print shop where I sat and read Hesiod's hymn to Demeter while he made some soup. It was a very good hymn to Demeter and very good soup. And the cafe expresso in Turkish cups. Not to mention the brandy (Domecq?). I read to Victor and Carolyn the piece I had brought for her to print as a broadside ("Signed Confessions of Crimes Against the State").[47] Borrowed an excellent book on Mount Athos – and brought it back with Hesiod and a pile of other things from the University Library.

Lexington is not interesting. Frankfort is. Like a Pennsylvania town. With deep valleys and surprises as you come around corners and find the State Capitol over or under you or suddenly at your elbow through a screen of woods.

A bridge, trees, and a group of white Protestant churches.

We came back through Frankfort, Shelbyville, Taylorsville, and rich farmlands where there were only Protestant churches.

But it was nice to get back to the wild knobs with their rocks and their pine trees and the plain sign pointing into the woods with the one word "Trappist."

"Repenting of their sins they fled from the world to the desert of La Trappe."

May 3, 1959. Day of Rec[ollection]

"Le secret de la puissance du message est dans cette liberté de parler de tout et de n'importe quelle manière, mais toujours en fonction de l'Unique, de l'Autre, il faut sortier de tout qui est sociologique, se placer au-dessus, annoncer la justice en fonction de la Sainte Verité ..." ["The secret power of the Message is found in the liberty to speak of everything, regardless of the manner of speaking, but always in the service of the Unique, the Other. One must go beyond the sociological, place oneself beyond it to proclaim justice in the service of Holy Truth."] *Evdokimov* ["Message aux églises"] *in* Dieu vivant, xv.

Which I am just now reading 10 years late. The whole answer is there. Am I wise enough to apply it?

Lax and Reinhardt were down last weekend, Bob Giroux yesterday – and in between I went to Lebanon to get a rotten tooth pulled on a beautiful Spring day (Thursday – April 30). Today – had to give the Conference

---

[47] Later published in *The Carleton Miscellany* i (Fall 1960): 21–23.

Chapter – on the Will of God – Joseph, etc. It is like Summer – or rather, it is Summer though the trees are not fully out yet.

The thing is, when people come to see me, they are not really edified. I have to face this fact – it is disturbing. It is that I am not really a monk and a Christian. It is all very well to cast off invalid exterior forms. But is there anything on the inside? I think perhaps not.

Really need prayer in sorrow of heart.

And more humble thought of how to go about saying and doing what I say and do. I try to act as if I were wise and I do not have the fear of God without which there is no beginning of wisdom. I pray for mercy, but coldly. What will become of me? Mother of Mercy and of Wisdom, take pity on me a sinner.

May 7, 1959. Ascension Day

Yesterday, Vigil of Ascension and F. of St. John at the Lateran Gate, Dom Gregorio Lemercier of Cuernavaca suddenly showed up. A surprising, even devastating visit. He had been promising to come but I had given up expecting him. Now, though he had not planned to come, he did so at the suggestion of Dom Damasus whom he had been seeing at Elmira.

Without wasting time, he came directly to the point – that if I was not fully satisfied here I should leave and start out on my own. That my being here was in reality good neither for me nor for the house. That the cause of the monastic revival at large depended on the generosity of the few clear-sighted ones who could no longer be content with conventional "institutionalism."

His suggestion – that I get an exclaustration, with the help of the bishop of Cuernavaca, move to Cuernavaca, live for a while as a hermit under the auspices of the Monasterio de la Resurrecion until I got oriented.

It was quite a mouthful all at once, but it seemed to me absolutely necessary to take it and do what I could to digest it. He left this morning with the agreement that he would approach his bishop and then let me know and I would write to the Congregation.

The opposition here, of course, will be formidable, and I hate the idea of starting all that again – my heart sinks at the thought of it and the prospect of the battle disturbs me deeply. My feelings are not all on the side of going. On the contrary, it is so wonderful, so quiet in the straw of the woodshed and under these pines by St. Teresa's field – I have to leave all that for the uncertain and the unknown.

Of course, that is just the thing. It is clear.

I realize now how weak and confused I have become – most of the time I have simply played around and daydreamed and am sadly unequipped to take a real uprooting. Hence the need of prayer and thought and discipline and the self purification. All useless baggage overboard!!

This time, it is not of my doing – but God's work entirely!

The one thing that has to be remembered: none of this is of any value if it is simply *forced* on superiors. I have no intention of doing that: a question of loyal cooperation, frankness, and trust in seeking the Truth with them. Obviously taking account of unreasonableness where a half-considered answer is a foregone conclusion. I have no intention of forcing any issue. I have no interest in being a hermit merely to satisfy some desire of my own – and in fact I have ceased to think it terribly important what kind of label I wear.

All I want to find out is, quite seriously, what the Church wants of me.

And if she wants nothing – I am just as well satisfied.

May 8, 1959

Trying to understand the new situation and get into it.

This is going to take some time. I have no intention of trying to force things in myself either. All I want to do is respect the Truth – and see it in every possible light, before coming to a final decision.

1. The fact of Dom G's arriving here is of course providential. But it does not dispense me from thinking and deciding rationally. The mere fact that he comes here by surprise with this proposal does not necessarily mean that it is all decided.

2. Today I have been overpowered by the realization of how much I love *these woods* (and this woodshed). For a moment in chapel (after Chapter) I thought it would be impossible to get away from this. Nor is there any reason for wanting to.

3. Another thing – I have no really strong desire to go away to Mexico. I can see how it would be interesting and valuable – yet it leaves me cold to a great extent. What matters – is it really God's will? What, in the context, does that question mean?

Question – After I have gone to the trouble of moving the world to go to Mexico, will I find there half of what already I possess in the woods here?

It is not enough just to leave here for the sake of a better spiritual life for myself.

Yet I have decided to forget all the ideas of a new kind of foundation.

If it is only a question of my own interior life . . .

Apparently more than that is involved. How am I to find out? Wait. Great sense of the meaning and power of prayer.

May 10, 1959. (Private retreat)

Lax brought down the proofs of [Abraham] Heschel's *God and Man* – which looks very interesting. A Hasid, from Warsaw, teaching in the Jewish Theological Seminary in N.Y.

In the introduction – a remarkable sentence:

As an answer, religion becomes not only false but meaningless and irrelevant as soon as the question by which it is evoked no longer represents a challenge.

A good starting point for a 3 day private retreat.

Yesterday – decided to act and pray as if it were the Will of God for me to leave and go to Mexico – to think in those terms, to pray earnestly for the grace and the guidance I need. Obviously this opportunity cannot be ignored.

If it turns out to have been *not* an opportunity, the fault will not be mine.

I really want to do all I can to get *beyond* the static and meaningless situation in which I now find myself. There is no question that in some way I have to burst out of limitations and find a new level of spiritual existence and that conventional means are not going to be very useful. Whether the answer lies in another country or not is no matter. I really would like to start over again somewhere else – it would feel fresh and clean. No sense in just clinging to what I am accustomed to.

Looked up canonists on exclaustration and learn it is no means as simple as Dom G. made it sound. And yet I am not looking for secularization either![48] However, I am not bothering too much about the practical steps to take just yet. Wait and see what develops. And in any case I want to be frank and non-combative with my superiors. To get out violently is ridiculous and has nothing to do with the Holy Spirit.

May 12, 1959

Third day of retreat. Yesterday, quiet – sunny day – spent all possible time in the woods reading and meditating. Marco Pallis's wonderful book *Peaks and Lamas* was one. And Suzuki. Today a remarkably apt summation of the

---

[48] Exclaustration is the canonical procedure by which a vowed monk leaves his monastery; secularization is the legal revocation of vows and return to the lay state.

situation in the *I Ching*. Came out with *Kuai* (43) "Breakthrough" made up
of ch'ien and Tui.

Generally speaking, a change of conditions, but not one brought about
by *my* efforts still less by activity or force.

> 1. One must resolutely make the matter known
> at the court of the King.
> It must be announced Truthfully. Danger.
> ... It does not further to resort to arms
> It furthers one to undertake something.
>
> 2. When one goes and is not equal to the task
> One makes a mistake.
>
> 3. To be powerful in the cheekbones
> Brings misfortune.
> The superior man is firmly resolved.
> He walks alone and is caught in the rain.
> He is bespattered
> And people murmur against him.
>
> 4. If a man were to let himself be led like a sheep
> Remorse would disappear.

With this and the commentary I have what I already know.

To proceed "with a union of strength and friendliness."

No compromise with evil – yet accept ambiguous situation, remaining
true to my principles, but not attacking those in authority.

Not yielding to temptation to push forward blindly and obstinately at any
cost. Not seeking to enforce my own will. Not using force.

Be on guard in myself against the faults I have branded in the community, etc. Not fighting my own faults directly, but indirectly, by progress in
good.

Moving to *Ka'an* 29 "If you are sincere you have success in your heart
and whatever you do succeeds."

Flowing on like water – Tao.

"Once we have gained inner mastery of a problem it will come about
naturally that the action we take will succeed. In danger all that counts is
really carrying out all that has to be done." Thoroughness – "going forward in order not to perish through tarrying in danger."

I am satisfied that the thing is to wait quietly without any special plans or any special purpose. And not care for how long. The more I am content to wait the sooner the right answer will come, all by itself.

How far I have been from the Truth, every day, wasting my time seeking something in vain. What I seek is simply being – and here it is. Here is the straw, here is the rain, here is the silence.

Oppressed with words, with the falsity and needlessness of most of the things I say to others. What do I expect to find in my words to them? What do I resent not finding? I have nothing to say. How happy I would be to admit it in practice. But I believe that all men, at all times, expect one to say something. What a fool I have made of myself by believing myself wise. And now I dare not be silent, though I have nothing to say.

May 13, 1959

Yesterday all the red roses in the novitiate garden were blooming. Today the rhododendrons by St. Fiacre's shrine came out. It rained again – rained while I was with the novices weeding strawberries. I am finishing the Loch book on Mount Athos I borrowed from Victor Hammer. And am reading the fine study of Borodine on Nicholas Cabasilas. And of course continuing with *Peaks and Lamas* which, in many places, deeply moves me.

May 18, 1959. Whitmonday

Nothing can spoil this morning. The rain has stopped. The birds sing and starlings pursue a crow across the grey sky. Clouds still hang low over the woods. It's cool.

The whiskey barrels by the woodshed stand or lie in wetness, one of them with wet weeds up the navel, others rolling in the soaked chips of wood and bark.

Someone has sawed a keg in half, and it is one of the most beautiful objects on the property at the moment. An example of the *sabi* or *wabi* (simplicity) that Suzuki talks about. With joy, yesterday, I smelled the charred barrel. How beautiful to see it catch rain. (The rain starts again.)

Yesterday I was bitter for a while, growling to myself. "Yes, we have the Holy Ghost all right – in a cage with His wings clipped." But later during the Gospel *"Non turbetur cor vestrum"* ["Let your heart not be disturbed"] came through into my heart directed especially to me and I remembered there was no need to be bitter or to worry, or even to notice what appears to me to be senseless in our life here (the utter stupidity of Pontifical Tierce, for instance – with little brothers standing around like dolls, holding pieces of liturgical lingerie with which to dress the abbot. Why do we have to play at being bishops and canons all the time?).

I do not *have* to react. It is useless. There are much better things to do. And to react is to become implicated – to become prisoner of the same nonsense. I am compelled to condemn. Do not be compelled.

Here comes a small, shining rabbit. A kingbird gurgles and chortles in the cedars. Everything is wet.

If a man were to let himself be led like a sheep.
Qui dederis velut ovem Joseph . . . [Who gave Joseph as a sheep . . .]

From Hesiod
ἀρΧομένου δὲ πίθου καὶ λήγοντος κορέσασθαι, μεσσόθι φείδεσθαι· δειλὴ δ᾽ ἐνὶ πυθμένι φειδώ.

(Take your fill when the cask is first opened and when it is nearly spent, but midways be sparing: it is poor saving when you come to the lees.)

From Suzuki. "When the Way and the Wayfarer are one, what can the outsider do for him?"

And for Feast Day Chapters and other such situations, take this:

"Ordinary people are always one sided – when they see a negation (nonbeing) they fail to see an assertion (being). When they see an assertion they fail to see a negation. But the expert swordsman sees both the affirmation and negation at the same time. He sees that a negation is not just negation but implies an affirmation."

May 20, 1959
Shirley Burden here – we went over the pictures for his book again. It is surprising how hard it is to get an interesting picture in our church (there are some, but they are of people, not of the church) and how immediately dull everything becomes as soon as you get into the mechanized bakery and cheese plant. Completely without meaning or interest.

And yet such fascinating things wherever someone has been human – foolishly human even. Like the little feather duster hanging up in the library and the sign to take care of the books.

He has a very fine spontaneous sense of symbolism.

The book will be very symbolic. I hope my deliberately dry preface will get by. He likes it, anyway.[49]

Rain again. A jeep tries vainly to get out of the creek pulling a trailer that they use for bringing food to the pigs.

May 26, 1959

Tenth anniversary of the ordination.

Offered mass for my own intention – the Cuernavaca situation. That I myself might be mild, patient, determined. That my superiors might be unprejudiced, and do nothing to crush the whole thing by pressure. That the exclaustration might be granted. That I might have the health and strength to carry on from there.

I see more and more the uselessness of making it into a struggle (I have said nothing to anyone yet except Fr. John of the Cross, and Fr. Lawrence knows about it). Indeed I am perhaps inclined too easily to imagine that I am being unreasonably opposed, or rather unfairly.

Up against the complacency of Dom James – who is incapable of seeing any sense in a thing like this. To him it must inevitably appear crazy, willful, absurd. His are the views of the class and society to which he belongs. Does he not read *Time* and the *Wall Street Journal?* Does he not regard all Latin Americans as a sort of inferior breed? And so on. Yet it seems to me I have a real obligation to try to get out from under all that, and to break cleanly with all the conventions tolerated here.

May 27, 1959

Corpus Christi tomorrow. Raining today – novices going out to get flowers.

Yesterday Fr. Chrysogamus played in Chapter a tape recording of a Mass sung in Africa with native drums and music. Some of it was very impressive, especially a rather complex and sophisticated Agnus Dei. The drums were splendid, and the voices were full of power and life, raw, fresh, and wonderful. It was not all first class African music, but very authentic, very moving.

I did not vote in the primaries. It seems to me nonsense to go to New Haven to cast a ballot for someone like Combes or Weatherfield. All the

---

[49] A picture essay on the monastic life at Gethsemani, *God Is My Life*, with photographs by Shirley Burden and preface by Thomas Merton, was published by Reynal in 1960

more so when we are "urged" to vote for "friends of the monastery" or "Good Catholics in need of a job" etc. etc.

This morning I went to see Bro. Clement to find out something about the day's work and came upon him leading a young Holstein bull by the ring in his nose. I stood talking to him by the side of the bull, and stroked the bull's nose a little and looked at his short, brutal looking horns. And I kept thinking two thoughts – all this bull needs to do is to give one good wrench with his neck and sink those horns into me and I'm dead. But the other thought was – thank God here is a living thing and not a machine, something big and warm and alive and unpredictable, with fears and angers and appetites. And I was glad of all this and reassured by it because of the value that is in life itself. So the second thought won out over the first. I am willing to trust life more than machinery.

May 28, 1959. Corpus Christi

A quiet morning reading in the woodshed (for the first time in seventeen years had nothing to do with the decorations). A clear, cool morning – got hot later. Reading Berdyaev's *Destiny of Man* which is, I think, his best book.

In the clear sky two shiny kingfishers chased one another in a wide arc over the mill bottom.

What about Cuernavaca?

Getting impatient to hear something from Dom Gregorio and the bishop. Tempted to think the letter has been stopped, though it is coming marked "conscience matter." And yet – indifferent about it.

How unprepared I am to start a new life. Yet that does not matter.

More prayer is necessary – uncomfortable prayer too, not just sitting under a tree.

How I hesitate to believe it can ever come about. Does that mean I am not really interested?

I am worried about the effects of my leaving.

It will be interpreted as simply giving up and "returning to the world." As a renunciation of my vocation. In a way it is = a renunciation of the monastery because I am no longer satisfied with this kind of life. If that is the case, I must be willing to leave it so interpreted though that is not my intention or my desire. However – am I really so dissatisfied? The question is almost impossible to answer. I am often convinced that I have "nothing in common" with Dom James and with the ideals of the Order at present. To what extent is this an evasion? There is certainly nothing wrong with these afternoons in the woods (but what have they to do with the ideals of the Order?).

The truth is, something inexplicable draws me away from here, something indefinable makes me uneasy here (I do not say unhappy) – always the old story of "something missing." What? Is it something essential?

Won't there always be "something missing"?

Yet always that urge to "go forth," to leave, to take off for a strange land and start another life. Perhaps this is inevitable, just a desire one is supposed to have without fulfilling it.

It was that kind of desire that brought me here.

For the rest, I must be careful not to think about it in terms that – under no sense is a "death of ideals." I really have no ideals. Perhaps what I really want is to get away from ideals and mental image of monasticism and simply live as best I can, just live.

If I had to explain now to Dom James that I wanted to leave to go to Mexico – what on earth would I be able to say? I would be tongue tied.

The things I could never say:

I hate pontifical masses. I hate your idea of the liturgy – It seems to me to be a false, dead, repetition of words and gestures without spontaneity, without sincerity. You like to sing hymns because the melodies delight you. I can think of better ways in which to waste my time. The Africans, with their drums, have got it all over us. There is no routine with them. They are saying what they mean.

I think the monastic life as we live it here warps people. Kills their spirit, reduces them to something less than human. The way people verbalize like parrots in sermons and theological conferences seem to me to indicate a perilous falsification of their spirit. Many of them are no longer quite sane.

I would say this and many other things, all adding up to one: our life here is too much of a lie. If that is really the case, then, since I can't do anything about it, I had better leave. But always the question remains: perhaps it is I who am the liar and perhaps leaving would be the greater lie.

If I get an exclaustration it would be based on the plea that things here have gone beyond reasonable limits, and my spiritual life is being harmed . . . Is that true? Depends how you look at it. In a sense it is true. It is hard, almost impossible, for me to do what, in the depths of my soul, I know I ought to be. What is that? How can I explain it? Do I even think I know?

———

Is not my main reason for wanting to leave an irrational one. The door is half open! Get out while you have the chance you may not ever get another . . .

June 1, 1959

Very illuminating critique of St. Thomas by Berdyaev. The ethics of St. Thomas is, he says, basically hedonistic. Happiness is the end for which man strives. Keep natural law and you will be happy. It is the Grand Inquisitor all over again. Perhaps Berdyaev exaggerates and simplifies but there is a great deal of truth in what he says. At least we tend to interpret Thomism in this sense, though there is also his teaching (artificial and a bit schematized) on the Gifts of the Holy Ghost. In any case, the notion to me is a liberation for, it is true, by seeking happiness I have allowed myself to be enslaved. The profound sense of Newman's "holiness rather than peace." Freedom and creativity. These are the aim. To glorify God.

June 7, 1959

A busy week. J. Laughlin came on Wednesday and on Thursday I got permission to go over with him to Lexington and see Fr. Columban in the hospital again. Same ambiguous situation. They have a psychiatrist working on him now. They think his pain in the back is psychogenic – which it might be.

Of course we had lunch with the Hammers, back in their garden, under the elm trees, in the very small stone paved area behind the print shop. It was very enjoyable – the day was beautiful. Only trouble was that we were late getting to Lexington. We went over driving slowly, through Lebanon and Harrodsburg which is a longer way around. Not only that but we ran into a detour.

Saw Shakertown – the big old dormitories stood among the weeds in desolation. Yet there was still something young about the old buildings, as if their pioneer hopefulness were still in them, as if they could not despair though the Shakers (having refused to have children) were all gone. A strangely touching monument to our ingrained puritanism which is not just silly. It is pathetic and beautiful in its wrongness – J. Green is so sensitive to this in his *Journal* which deals increasingly with Calvinists and Port Royal.

I cannot help seeing Shakertown in a very special light, that of my own vocation. There is a lot of Shakertown in Gethsemani. The two contemporary communities had much in common, were born of the same Spirit. If Shakertown had survived it would probably have evolved much as we have evolved. The prim ladies in their bonnets would have been driving tractors, and the sour gents would have advertised their bread and cheese. And all would have struggled mightily with guilt.

Here we are for the most part no longer puritans – we fall all over ourselves to be non-puritans, yet it is useless, guilt remains. We have become so much puritans in reverse that many of us are frantic. The only solution is to be neither a puritan nor a non-puritan. But that is impossible. This idiotic dilemma is the very heart of Gethsemani. And though it is idiotic, it is not to be despised. It is perhaps very worthy of a certain honor.

The wonderful deep gorge in the Kentucky river – something more splendid than I have seen in years. J. kept comparing it to the rivers in the Dordogne where the caves are and it is like Averyon near Saint Antonin but more brutal. And on the Averyon you find no great towering bridges spanning the whole gorge.

We went to the library of the U of K and Dr. Thompson showed us his study and gave us a mimeographed study of the flagellants.

I think I liked best the country between Lebanon and Harrodsburg.

We had breakfast in Lebanon and supper in Bardstown.

And from J. I heard all the mixed up stories of all the writers in the world. Of Pound, and Rexroth, and R. Queneau (whom I must read) and "The Beats" and a hundred and one others I have forgotten.

The other day the vocation idea took a new turn when I walked into Vespers and "saw" for the first time there might be meaning and wisdom to writing some bishop in New Mexico or Arizona, and making a proposal to live as a hermit near or on an Indian reservation and doing a little work with the Indians. But not as a full missionary life. A kind of hermit mission like that of C. De Foucauld.

The whole thing suddenly made a great deal of sense – a lot more than Cuernavaca, to tell the truth.

New Mexico first appealed to me and still does. Then Arizona – because it is wilder. Now I am suspicious of New Mexico because of the aesthetic

element in it. It does not make sense for me to butt into Franciscan terri-
tory and picturesque missions (though it would be marvelous, for instance,
to live at or near Acoma pueblo, or Toleta or Lajuna or etc.). That is not
for me.

In point of fact, I am writing to Bp. Dwyer of Reno because I am more
sure he is interested – and Nevada is a wild blank with no aestheticism
about it. It is a great *nada* ["nothing"] full of sense to me. Very vast and
empty.

More and more I am convinced I am getting warm and that at last I am
coming to the real thing.

Another idea is the Virgin Islands. (Why not the South Pacific?)

Suddenly realized that if only I can face up to the danger and challenge I
can have my choice of anywhere in the world!!

June 8, 1959

Berdyaev's distinction between ethics of law and ethics of creativeness is a
very good one for me now. So good, perhaps, that it is a temptation. In any
case: the ethics of law says stay at Gethsemani and the ethics of creativeness says go out and do something that has not been done. The ethics of
law says – who is this Berdyaev? What authority has he? He is a heretic.
You are doing your own will. What is "creativeness"? an allusion, which
would lead the whole place into madness if everyone followed the same
principles! It is safer to accept what is established, even if it is not so good.
God works in and though the community. The individual has to conform
to theirs, in order to find God. And so on.

If only it were a simple question! Supposing, for instance, there is really
in me nothing creative . . . But what a question to ask! That is what one
must start by believing and hoping, otherwise Christ died in vain.

Yes, sneers the ethics of law – you have put your nose in Dostoevsky and
Berdyaev and Zen Buddhism and now where are you? On the road to
heresy.

Well, what about St. Paul, and all the saints? What about the gospel?

Certainly, it is a dangerous problem, and I *am* in danger. Thank God for
it. I beg Him to protect me and bring me through the danger. And I still do
not know what to do.

Berdyaev says under the ethic of law the future is determined by a fixed
duty to realize a set purpose – the ethic of law is teleological. The ethic of
creativity leaves the future *immanent to ourselves* and we to its nearness.

"The loftiest purpose projected into the future enslaves us, becomes external to us and makes us anxious."

What my real danger is, is substituting the ethic of my own law for the ethic of a social law – as if my own law were the law of God.

Where there is question of a struggle between a law of my own and the law of the community, a purpose purely my own and the purpose of the community, then the law of the community is to be preferred – and it is a liberation.

Creativeness – presupposes a real *indetermination* of the future. Nothing is *determined* by me until the future becomes present. "Take no thought of the morrow."

Where a community completely determines one to the thought of the morrow, then it is no longer Christian (the purpose of vows – to liberate us from thought of the morrow). But where the morrow is so determined that there is no room for the individual to make a gift of it . . . ?

Meanwhile it is very important to get out of the dilemma. Either Gethsemani or not-Gethsemani. Both. Neither. There has to be a way of rising completely above the division and going above it.

June 9, 1959

Fr. Basil and Alcuin (Hogan) left Sunday.

Frs. Sebastian and Vincent (DeTrinis and Gentry) left this morning. These two were professed.

Fr. Aelred (Walters) leaves tonight.

All very disoriented with the community which they think, and perhaps rightly, is crazy.

All the same their general spirit of rebellion is very disturbing. The almost universal unpopularity of Dom James. His unconscious ambiguities, which he himself cannot see, are far too much for most people. Yes – he is a well meaning man, with all his blind spots, and he is after all a superior. There is not enough supernatural spirit of obedience to superiors and that is why I must be, again, very careful not to simply force my own ideas or my own will on him. May God preserve me from that.

By rights, I really owe it to him to propose, first of all, a request to become a hermit in the woods. I like less and less the term "hermit." I want to live alone – not become a member of a fictitious category. But I owe it to him to ask this permission to live alone here before I ask to leave. And seriously I intended to ask it, but more as a matter of form – "knowing" it would be refused. I did hint at it the other day and he seemed very unwilling and uncomprehending. Yet I must not assume *a priori* that he will be completely unsympathetic.

How tiresome and absurd this argument is, and yet it is necessary. It is my life. I have to make the best of it! More and more convinced that I have to settle this question somehow. Letters from Dom Leclercq and Daniélou. Not about this, especially. But Dom Leclercq is convinced my vocation to solitude is genuine. Daniélou thinks I am on the right track with Suzuki, Pasternak, etc. I mean in my "dialogue" with them.

June 11, 1959

More of this tiresome argument.

Supposing I do get permission to even live in the woods here. It will be a more or less extorted permission. He will make it clear that it is all a concession given unwillingly to humor a difficult and self-willed character.

Yet note that Rev. Father does *not give* concessions in important matters – only in rather unimportant ones. However, no general statement about it is possible. He has no set policy, he does what he can, he gives in as little as he can in matters like this, gives in to some and not to others.

He will give the permission and then compensate for it by laughing about it with the cellarars, etc. and systematically turning the whole thing to ridicule. Yet at the same time he will exploit the situation and make the most of its interesting or edifying side. Benefactors would come out to see the hermit – and would contribute lavishly to the monastery.

Living alone in the woods here might simply complicate life, instead of simplifying it. Complicate the ambiguities of my situation.

The truth is, it is very hard for me to judge the question dispassionately! But the crux of the matter is somewhere here: in a kind of dependence and subjection which is not, I think, merely a matter of religious submission to a representative of Christ, but something much more: subjection to a *whole false idea* created by a man, and a community. What I find intolerable and degrading is having to submit, in practice, to Dom James' idea of himself and Gethsemani and to have to spend my life contributing to the maintenance of this illusion. The illusion of the great, gay, joyous, peppy, optimistic, Jesus-loving, one hundred percent American Trappist monastery.

Is it possible to be here and not be plunged into the midst of this falsity?

Is it possible to abstract from it? And if that is possible, is it healthy – is it anything better than a defeat? Certainly such an admission of defeat is, it seems to me, not allowed. I have seen the effect on one person after another. There is nothing "in the books," in the legislation, to defend against this corruption. (Someone will say – you are awfully prissy about corruption. Is there not far worse corruption *everywhere* else? Yet I think it is surely a moral obligation and a *real* moral obligation as opposed to the fictitious obligations we impose upon ourselves here in such great numbers – precisely in order to maintain the illusion.)

The whole thing is complicated by my illusion – the mirage of contemplative happiness that I am going to have to give up because it cannot lead anywhere. As long as I try to compare the "happiness" possible to me here, (I mean the *actual* joy of sitting around under a tree on feast days) and the "greater happiness" I think I may find somewhere else, I am doomed to frustration and confusion. It has got to be a question of seeing Newman's idea of "Holiness rather than peace"!

The question is not – will I have more time to read and pray in Cuernavaca (and will I live among people for whom I have more respect) but: is this battle to be fought or not? And what for? for an ideal? I am suspicious of ideals, and in fact I have renounced them. Fidelity to "my own inner truth"? Nice phrase – but what does it mean? Freedom from the social conventions and compulsions that exist here.

Is that freedom precious enough to me for me to pay the price of insecurity, hard work, poverty, loss of health, and becoming a displaced person? And all this at the risk of perhaps not attaining the freedom I hope for?

Or shall I be content to be a docile and approved captive, with an easy life, a certain leisure, and the opportunity to engage in verbal rebellion anytime I feel like it?

The answer is obvious. If I have stated the things in its correct terms I am really bound to get out – at least try to – from this community. If I am wrong, I hope I will soon come to see it.

The decision once made, there is the even more difficult task of carrying it out and here I am at my worst. I defeat myself by the very energy with which I fight – the energy is misplaced. Too much of it goes into making excuses, trying to assure everyone I only want to be nice about it, that I do not really want to fight – just want to arrange a million things – and in the end I am where I was before – having done nothing but write a lot of letters and caused a big stir, with no effect.

This time, it must not be so.

June 13, 1959. Feast of St. Antony of Padua

Struck by a Zen *mondo* in Suzuki.

Q: When the lion seizes its prey, whether it be a hare or an elephant, he seizes it with all his power – What is this power?

A: The power of sincerity (lit. the power of non-deceiving).

Whatever may be the depths in this, they are for me. For this is the answer to everything. I find it by intuition, related to Xst's words "When they shall take you before kings and rulers, do not think how to speak or what to say. It will be given you in that hour what to say."

This power of non-deceiving is, for me, the all important thing and I lack it. That is, I have the seeds of it but I do not let them grow. I begin to want to *assure* people of my sincerity, and then I deceive myself. And, of course, I am trying to deceive them – that I am sincere.

Today in direction Fr. Lawrence was talking about the Corn Islands, off the Mosquito Coast of Nicaragua. Two hours by motor launch from Bluefields, the old pirate hide-out, inhabited by a few Negroes who speak a kind of English. Fair climate, apparently. A good place to live in solitude. Though now, Fr. Lawrence, the only one who knows my plans exc. Fr. John of the Cross and Fr. Augustine with whom I have discussed it in confession, wants to come with me!! At that rate I am no longer a hermit before I start. Still, for *one* companion I'd be willing to let him come, but it requires thought.

And now in the woods, I once again revisit the idea of simply staying here, in the woods – with great interior freedom, and applying myself to the main business, which has nothing to do with places, and does not require a beach of pure, white Caribbean sand. Only silence and a curtain of trees.

Yet Corn Islands sound wonderful – in some way, the best of all. Certainly the most legendary. But this thing is not to be done in terms of legend. Already it is becoming little more than an anthology of possible legends.

The power of non-deceiving.

If one were to be led like a sheep! . . .

Kierkegaard's meditation on the tame geese . . .

Today, in any case, I wrote to the Vicar-Apostolic at Bluefields, an American Capuchin, with a German name.

June 14, 1959. IV Sunday After Pentecost

A beautiful, cool clear morning.

I am writing this after my mass. It seems to me that during Mass and thanksgiving one of the big ambiguities has resolved itself out.

The fact is, I do not want purely and simply to "be a hermit" or to lead a life purely and ideally contemplative. At the same time I want to break *with* all the fictions and pretenses, all the facade and latent hypocrisy of the monastic community in which I live.

Yet. I truly seek a very solitary, simple and primitive life with no special labels attached.

However, there must be love in it, and not an abstract love but a real love for real people.

The conclusion then that God is calling me to a kind of missionary solitude – an isolated life in some distant, primitive, place among primitive and simple people, to whose spiritual needs I would attend. *Not* a missionary life pure and simple, nor a solitary life pure and simple, but a combination of both.

No nonsense about asking permission to live as a hermit here – and raising all the futile questions and pretenses this would involve. It would get me into a whole network of lies for the sake of one grain of truth.

No nonsense about presenting the thing as a "desire for pure solitude" or for a more pure fiction than the fiction we already cherish in common. (I mean in this monastery. I am not condemning the monastic life, far from it. Perhaps I shall end up with a quasi-monastic community around me. But no set-forms!)

Later.

A beautiful and deep idea of Abraham Heschel.

"Some people think that religion comes about as a perception of the answer to prayer while in Truth it comes about in our knowing that God shares our prayer."

Came upon this following a half hour of thoughtful reading in Daniélou on Revelation.

God's Truth *'emet'* the rock on which one sets his whole being – not simply a rational light.

The Covenant – God *commits* himself without respect to what we do about it. Our infidelity cannot change the Covenant, which is *unilateral*. Our job, to receive. As Heschel says, to participate. To commune in the mercy of God, collaborate with Him in bringing this knowledge of His mercy to others.

Certitude of faith founded on God's manifestation of his love for us – not on *reasonableness* of that love.

Evidence (intrinsic) functions in the world of things, objects.

In the world of *persons*, it is otherwise. Personality = violence (Scheler) and the silence is not broken save by the free will of the person, manifesting himself – or not, as he pleases. What determines the revelation, and its acceptance? Love. Person makes himself responsible, in terms of love, for the Truth of his revelation. Falsity becomes not *error* but a *lie*.

When God reveals Himself, He is not an object that reason can seize upon.

He is supreme subjectivity – "I am Who am" + "I am Who I am" not "I am being."

Heschel again "It is God who teaches us our ultimate ends."

June 16, 1959. F. of St. Lutgarde

Said Mass this morning for the Nicaraguan revolutionaries. Heard of it starting nearly 2 weeks ago when I read the paper in Lebanon, having breakfast with J. on the way to Lexington.

Saturday, a letter came from Pablo Antonio Cuadra, dated the 8th. (last Monday) and postmarked San Jose, Costa Rica. He had to flee for his life and providentially escaped when Somoza declared martial law and started arresting everybody, closing down *La Prensa*. Pablo Antonio said little about the revolution except that three hundred picked men, all Catholics and good ones, were deposited inside Nicaragua by plane and were fighting. Already, before this letter was written Somoza had announced that the insurrection had been stamped out.

The great problem in this crisis of mine is to keep from going from one fiction to another: from the communal fiction which we cherish as a group, to the private fiction which I cherish as an individual. The more I let myself dwell with desire upon "a solution" the more I become involved in a new fiction of my own. I can tell it immediately by the immense weariness that comes from entertaining falsity.

The Truth is that almost everything I do to "solve" the problem becomes a kind of symbolic act that replaces something else, more real and more concrete, that I do not see how to do.

Hence the ritual of writing letters to bishops and Vicars Apostolic (such letters are already too many).

It is impossible to say what I ought to do. The situation is so vague and everything is uncertain. Is there any hope of obtaining an indult from Rome in the first place? It would be disastrous to stir up a great official fuss and then have nothing come of it.

More and more I realize that what I am really seeking is a spiritual and mystical action – which may need an exterior act, a geographic change, to make it really complete. But there is no hope that a legal act can solve a spiritual problem. It can only clear the way, perhaps –

The more thought, the more silence, the more patience go into this – the better.

June 18, 1959

Growing indifference, yesterday, working in the garden picking beet greens – listening to the roar of the machines on all sides (the place sounds like an airport) and smelling the sweet, sick smell of the soft coal they are burning now in the dairy – I felt very aware of my own inner liberty and lack of concern for such things. Which does not mean that a protest might not be good. But that freedom in no way *depends* on a protest.

More and more I see the folly of simply "protesting."

A "revolt" is of no significance. It is mere reaction. It does nothing for me or for anybody else.

The only thing that matters *is* that perhaps a change to some other place, to a real solitude, or less fictional situation, may really be the will of God.

Strange thing, that expression "the Will of God" – meaning not just "a virtuous act" or "something that would be good to do" – but an act springing from the intimate depths of my own life and my own providential destiny – an act which is new and mysterious and contradicts everything that has so far been planned and arranged. A new departure, in a life that seemingly permits no new departures.

Of this I can say nothing. I can only let myself be led.

Once again, sitting in the woods, I think the woods make sense. But that is not the only point. I debate less and less. It is too absurd to argue or to desire anything well defined. Simply to desire is enough. To desire not to desire – to desire without desiring – it means something very different from what I used to think. Not inertia but a blind gravitation – nowhere!

Maybe I'll end in Japan, even. Who knows?

June 21, 1959

Summer solstice. And this vocation business is making me miserable. Lay awake last night thinking about it. I try to keep off the futile and silly plane in which the advantages and disadvantages of each project go through my mind. In the end the whole thing becomes utterly absurd.

The one project to which I pay least attention is the original one, proposed by Dom Gregorio – to go to Cuernavaca and "then see."

Perhaps what is upsetting me is the fear of uncertainty. If the whole business were really serious, that is if my desire to leave here were serious, the uncertainty would not matter. But the fact is, I must face it – I have no really strong and positive motives for launching out into something completely new. I am just not sufficiently interested in "starting something." And more and more I see the futility, the absurdity, of simply becoming a "parish priest" in some isolated place. (That, of course, is not Dom Gregorio's idea, but the idea that struck me later.)

And I don't especially want to live in Mexico, as a hermit or otherwise.

Wherever I go as a "hermit" I will be at the mercy of everyone who writes, of course, and bothers me. Paradoxically, here I can arrange my time.

The question arises – would it be saner and truer simply to be "bothered" by people with real problems, than to go through a lot of community routines that take up your whole day in a monastery?

If I am asked the question – what do I really want to do? It boils down to what I have done for the best afternoons of last week. The long hours of quiet in the woods, reading a little, meditating a lot, walking up and down in the pine needles in bare feet. If what I am looking for is more of that – why not just ask for "more of that"? It is the easiest solution, the request most likely to be granted and the one that involves no problem for me or my superiors or for the Order – no glory and no fuss either.

On the other hand – is that honest, and is it an interior life?

Or is it simply an escape from the routine of the community – the way a worker escapes from the factory on a weekend and goes swimming at Coney Island?

And by accepting the escape am I conceding it, surrendering to, the routine?

It is a serious question – more serious still is the question whether I have by now been so destroyed by the routine that I can no longer do anything but accept it – with suitable evasions?

June 22, 1959. After Mass. Mass Pro Quacumque Necessitate *[For Any Necessity]*

Best thing is to stick to the idea of Dom Gregorio – unless something else very special turns up. Meanwhile, simply seek to go to Cuernavaca and then from there to Corn Islands off Nicaragua, more or less under the aegis of Dom G. Not, of course, as a "foundation." But open to ideas for formation of a small semi-eremitical community there, very unofficial, with no special canonical status.

First step – to try to get 6 months leave of absence from Dom James to see Corn Islands (and Cuernavaca) and also perhaps, New Mexico – possibility of something among the Indians, there.

Yesterday – worked out a simple plan for a hermitage behind the sheep barn in the woods, but it is too silly. Only if no other way is possible will I take that one.

Better to have something definite – a solitary apostolate among Indians or Latin Americans somewhere with possibility of the foundation of an eremitical group. This is not a blind alley. Everything here is.

The enormous difficulty of getting a leave of absence. Wait. If that does not come through, try for an exclaustration

June 28, 1959

Tired of argument. For the last four days or so have not been thinking about it.

Fr. Raymond – a melodramatic sermon on F. of St. John the Baptist. "BE MEN." The usual. One novice had a kind of crack-up, brought on by this (I had expected it before) and will have to leave.

Strange thing, talking to a disturbed schizoid person – you can tell when the real person comes and goes and when you are talking to the empty, excited mask. And the thing to do is at all costs not to accept the mask as real and to let him know you will deal only with the real person. Try to keep his real self from walking away and ignore the other. The real self needs you to anchor him among the living.

The other night on fire watch I ran into him coming upstairs when everyone else was asleep. He had gone down to "look up something in the Bible" or the Imitation of Christ.

The hot weather has really come at last.

Baffled by the intensity of observation in the G. M. Hopkins notebooks (Thought I would talk to the novices about inscape and poetry to give them a change).

Paul Tillich's secretary sent me a mimeographed copy of his excellent lecture on *Art and Ultimate Reality*, given at the Museum of Modern Art.

I like it and am in basic agreement with it. Expressionism is the style best suited to genuine religious art. He meets problems which I have unconsciously evaded by approaching the question in a way not natural to me – from an "institutional" or social viewpoint. To treat art as an adjunct to worship puts one in an impossible position from the start – unless he confines himself entirely to ikons. I should have given myself more room to manoeuver. It is too late to do anything about it now.

I agree that "There is more of ultimate reality in an apple by Cézanne than in a Jesus by Hoffman."

I was comforted by a good article on "The Liberal Catholic" in *Theological Digest*. I have *got* to live in the fresh air. There is no other way.

On top of it all I am still not convinced I ought to leave, or that I have the right to. No answers to any of my letters.

Opened a new translation of Eckhart, and immediately hit upon this:

"Obedience has no cares, it lacks no blessings. Being obedient, if a man purifies himself, God will come to him in course; for where he has no will of his own, then God will command for what God would command for Himself . . . When I do not choose for myself, God chooses for me."

I am sure now that it has been a temptation, all along, to think that by staying here where I like to pray in the woods I would be cuddling in self-love. Yes, I like it. But the important thing = it is what God has chosen for me. Hence I cannot really start off to go anywhere else unless it is clear that God wants it for me. And so far, no such thing is clear.

"A pure heart is one that is unencumbered, unworried, uncommitted, and which does not want its own way about anything but which rather, is submerged in the loving will of God, having denied self."

I cannot be loyal to that which is deepest and most genuine in my life if I am not first loyal to this principle.

June 30, 1959

Yesterday on the F. of St. Peter and Paul – a letter arrived from Bishop Davis of San Juan, Puerto Rico. He says he has just the thing – offers me the mission of St. William on the Island of Tortola, British Virgin Islands –

where in a population of 4,000 there are 50 Catholics, many others fallen away. The mission is rarely visited. I would live there permanently and he would evidently be glad to have me.

This then is the first reply.

Realizing the danger of being over enthusiastic, I certainly am inclined to think that this is ideal. I wish I could leave immediately!

Unfortunately it is a long way to Tortola, a longer way than can be accounted for in miles.

But in confession with Fr. John of the Cross this morning, it was certainly clear that this was something to accept and that is was much better than Cuernavaca, and that I should plan on an exclaustration to go to Tortola since Bishop Davis is definitely willing to have me.

The thing that strikes me is the *reality* of the whole thing. It is *not* a dream, but sober, practical truth. The kind of truth against which we artificially insulate ourselves in our little world of illusions here. This is something that *really* sounds like the Gospel, and at the same time solitude and *real* "separation from the world."

Some of the points that came up today, and are always coming up.

A The responsibility before God to separate myself from a civilization that is utterly contemptible and false and heading for its own destruction. (Read about the atomic submarines that can fire an ICBM with an atomic warhead *from under water* 1,000 miles from "target." Target being of course an open city with millions of innocent and defenseless people in it. This is utterly beyond bearing.) But here at Geth. I am a kind of spiritual spokesman and figurehead for such a society. Before God I have an obligation to leave the society as best I can. Indians, or the Negroes of Tortola, or etc.

B The artificiality of my position here in the community. My ideals and life all such that the books I write will no longer be able to be read here without disturbing people (already this is true) yet I am following the path by which God leads me. "Solutions" that can be desired here are compromises that are no good either for me or for the community.

C I lead them into the same ambiguities and worse. I draw them here and then they are frustrated and confused and have to leave.

D Letter from Dom Gregorio, cryptic, but asserting firmly that in a case like this the decision is not to be left simply to the abbot.

In any case, I can ask him; and will, in due course for a 6 month leave of absence. Explaining the situation as far as I can. I doubt if he can ever understand that it can be *better* for one to seek this ambiguous and unjuridical kind of solitude. Fr. John of the † like Dom Gregorio, clearly insists on the main point which is to get "elbow room" to go in any direction, and not be *committed* to some special job or course of action or program. This, I agree, is it.

ᴇ Maybe later Fr. J† could also come to Tortola. He wants to. We could have a small, unofficial, eremitical group on the island. *No* new order or foundation. *Nothing – just live for God, with poor and simple people on the island.*

July 2, 1959. F. of the Visitation

I notice that when I have doubts about going elsewhere is sometime during the day, when the day is well gone, for instance in the afternoon, and especially when I am out in the woods or after dinner when I am heading to the woodshed to read.

Yesterday we went out to pick up hay in bales on the Bowling farm, near New Haven. The wide sweeping fields were lovely and so were the hills. The sky was black with rainclouds, etc. We filled wagon after wagon, with long waits in between. And as I sat waiting and thinking with the monks and looking at the dark green woods and the black sky, I was content and thought "This is all you need." But precisely "this" was *not* Gethsemani. We were off the property. The monastery was out of sight. Only the top of the watertower could be seen over the hill.

But when I have been praying and especially after Mass, it comes clear, on the contrary, that the time has come for me to leave.

This morning – second day of a three day prayer over the Tortola business – I said my Mass as fervently as I could, with all my heart. And since it was a cool morning I was clear and awake. It became clear to me that, as far as I can now see, God wants me to throw everything overboard, forget doubts and anxieties and, trusting in Him, go to Tortola. Or at least ask for the exclaustration to go there.

Only if Fr. Daniélou says "no" in his reply to my letter – only if Dom Gregorio has something much better – or if a clearer answer comes, will I reconsider this. As for Gethsemani – unless Rome says otherwise, this is the end.

The decision makes sense. It is not based on any passion I am ashamed of – not resentment certainly. I love the place and the people in it. I have been strongly moved to stay. But it seems to me that my motives for staying are negative.

- you are here and can't get out so don't try.
- what will people think?
- you have a life you can easily live here – it is safe and secure. Why take a risk?
- you are content here – You will always be respected and influential in the community and in the U.S. Is this not God's will?
- it is easy to write books here – you can get all the books you want too . . . etc.
- and you love the novices. They are a kind of family to you, aren't they?

None of these reasons is satisfactory. Every one is superficial and says nothing to the depths of my heart.

Not one of the people who have advised or who might advise me to stay, have anything in common with me. Their advice is something official and stereotyped. But those with whom I feel a bond, or those to whom I can talk with a sense of being understood in my own terms, not only say "go" (somewhere else) but manifest at once by their expression and tone of voice that they think I am right in this.

After Mass, deeply moved, I felt as if I were strongly drawn by the prayers of some very poor, very humble, unknown person among the Negroes on Tortola. As if I were being drawn to the Island that the poor and the humble might have Christ with them.

And I saw my priesthood as something so much greater than myself and than my life, writing, enjoyment, "contemplation," etc. etc. How much more real and meaningful and Christlike, this missionary solitude. I so badly want at last, in this, to be perfectly sincere and to make up for all the other mistakes and sins by this act of love for Christ, in spite of all the appearances and conventions. No use comparing Kentucky and Tortola. Meaningless, simply pray for the grace to accept *all* that will come and do my best at it and *give myself* at last in this way. And let God take care of the results, according to His mercy.

Sr. Pius, the Negro Poor Clare in New Orleans, to whom I felt very close, died on the 15th. of June perhaps without receiving my last letter. But I know she is praying for me.

At Mass, realized clearly my need for more firm and objective faith. I am too concerned with psych. – depth or other – that is all good. But God is greater than all this and once He is present, my own reactions are not the thing to look at! But Him. Then hesitations disappear.

July 5, 1959. Day of Recollection

The only remaining difficulty, in my own mind, is the problem of juridically abandoning the monastic state. (Spiritually there is no problem.) Of course an exclaustration is not precisely that. I would remain a member of the Order. Until when?

However, this would be the main obstacle, in my case, in Rome. At least, so I think.

So perhaps I ought to consider seriously thinking of going to Cuernavaca on a *transitus*, making a novitiate and profession there, and thence going to Tortola. Canonically it would keep everything straight. But perhaps Dom G. is considered too much of an innovator that the Congregation might be difficult on this point also.

The "novitiate" could be an apprenticeship for solitude.

I think this might be the right way to go about it.

In any case I see no further reason for staying in the big, overgrown, commercialized community with all its artificialities and stupidities. I honestly think that the situation here is almost hopeless. The blind leading the blind – if not over a cliff, at least around in circles. Fr. Lawrence will probably have to leave.

Here on one hand you have the ones who believe in mechanical regularity – strict fidelity to the system in force. Certainly that is something – but the systematic regularity that they would like to impose on everyone is empty and futile. A series of gestures and external acts without much inner meaning and hardly able to produce any spiritual fruit excepting the satisfied sense of duty that warms the heart of a conformist – when he has conformed.

For the rest it seems only to produce warped and eccentric personalities.

Not because of the Rule of St. B but because of the hopeless way in which it is interpreted here.

Dom James is not one of those who insist on this regularity. His myth is vaguer and in the long run more harmful: that of the jolly, fervent, family of girl scouts and little boys: the sort of stuff that is his signature and as far as I can tell nauseates *everyone* except the latest additions to the laybrothers' novitiate.

Then there are the men who forget their worries in work (cheese) or books or chant, etc. More vain hopes.

And finally, those who forget their worries in the woods – myself and Fr. John of the Cross.

None of us are really monks. The top sergeants of regularity are only sergeants. Rev. Father is a girl scout. The others are frustrated scholars or business men or housemaids. And I – a frustrated intellectual, pseudo-contemplative, pseudo-hermit.

It is imperative to do something. And I am not yet rightly prepared to act, and hardly know where to begin. The time Dom Gregorio spends here had better be well utilized!! Everything depends on it.

July 12, 1959. 8. Sunday after Pentecost
This week I have been rewriting "What Is Contemplation?" and of course it has come out three times as long and is a completely different book.[50] A lot of water has gone under the bridge since 1948. How poor were all my oversimplified ideas – and how mistaken I was to make contemplation only *part* of a man's life. For a contemplative his whole life is contemplation. The last part of the book is turning into a vocal protest against *vanitas monastica* [monastic pride]. I protest too much. It is a sign of weakness and bad conscience. I will have to revise all that.

The other day I spoke guardedly to Rev. Father about my ideas – in a very general way. He seemed to be expecting something and strangely I got the impression that he was all ready to grant me permission to live as a hermit in the woods here. That was surprising! Yet I don't know if I can say that it makes sense, and so I'll leave it on the shelf. I guardedly spoke of another kind of solitude "among Indians" or "on a small island." Here he was opposed, and took fright and went into the same old argument which he always used, and which in substance is this:

"It is true that you are out of place in this life but it is good for you to be out of place, because this causes suffering and the suffering will sanctify you. Therefore you must not make any attempt to find a better situation, for this is the one willed by God and to seek anything else is self-will and disobedience."

---

[50] Originally published as a pamphlet at St. Mary's College (Notre Dame, Indiana) in 1948. The revised version, called "The Inner Experience," was published as eight essays in *Cistercian Studies Quarterly* (1984–85). Merton had stipulated that it not be published as a book.

It was a friendly talk and I realized afterwards that it is very important simply to *listen*. One has no obligation to argue. If I am to say something that will affect his view of things, it will come out by itself. If I argue I will upset him, and in any case I will be arguing to convince myself.

The point is not "who is right."

Hence what matters is not to produce convincing arguments for this or that viewpoint but what is to be done.

Now it is true that self-will is a danger, and that there is no use doing something – especially so great a "something" – merely because I want to.

I see more and more that I need a genuine *consent* on the part of Superiors, even if they don't quite agree with my views, or I with theirs.

It is not possible for me to see everything as Rev. Father see it. He takes the *status quo* as the will of God that "cannot" be changed. But I think that to submit passively to this false situation is a kind of practical despair – it means really despairing of a truly monastic life.

No, not that either: this is a monastic life of its kind.

It means despairing of a real growth and development.

If our founders had believed this they would have stayed at Molesme and Cîteaux would never have been founded.

The other day, finding out more about Tortola – lost all trace of doubt that it is what I seek. What I desire. No cars, no machinery, not even electric light – extremely primitive. On Friday I was overwhelmed with love of the idea, before my conference (which was on St. Anthony at Pispir). And afterwards I thought I could never again be happy at Gethsemani.

Nevertheless, it *is* more than a matter of likes and dislikes. I am bound to the monastic state – o.k. with an exclaustration I am still a monk. But . . . On this plane I am getting away from the true meaning of my vocation and judging by appearances. And so far as I can, I think I must defy appearances. Yes, it is dangerous.

Is it true that I can be more a man of God, more truly and integrally what I am called to be on Tortola? I believe so. All I ask is permission to investigate the matter and find out.

Borrowed from the Library of Congress Henri Troyat's *La case de l'Oncle Sam*. Journalism but refreshing – it is French journalism, and that is something intelligent. The book is something I need at the moment – to see this country again through French eyes and to realize, with relief, that I am not crazy. The faults of Gethsemani are American – puerility, rationalization, idiot belief in gadgets, fetish-worship of machines, and efficiency, love of a big, showy facade (and nothing behind it) – phony optimism, sentimentality, etc.

In the Library [of] Congress copy of the book someone (a congressman?) has lightly written in pencil the following phrase – thrown in out of politeness and probably not sincere:

"Si j'étais américain je serais fier di mon pays autant pour ses erreurs que pour ses réussites." ["If I were an American I would trust my country as much for its errors as for its successes."]

I like better his remark on a conversation with a couple of models at a party:

"Il y avait en elles autant de profondeur psychologique que dans un savon tout neuf. Comme le savon, elles exprimaient une espèce de réalité sane et propre, une certitude hygiénique, une utilité sans équivoque." ["There was in them as much psychological depth as a new bar of soap. Like soap, they express a kind of sane and proper solidity; a hygienic assurance; and a usefulness beyond cavil."]

For me it is saner, in a monastery, to think this rather than to think, as undoubtedly most do, that such beings are a glamorous, unfathomable temptation. Because, alas, in the monastery we are all struggling to achieve the same thing, only spiritually. A hygiene without offense which will, we hope, mean depth, success and beauty. And all it means is nothing. As much depth as there is in a cake of soap. I am getting sententious.

Animated conversation with the models about the funny sheets.

". . . la recherche du bonheur était devenu un problème d'éducation et presque de gouvernement." ["The search for good humor has become a problem of education and perhaps for the government."]

July 16, 1959. St. Stephen Harding

Yesterday as I was sitting down to get together some notes for the novice's conference, the phone rang and Bro. Simon said Dom Gregorio was here.

Within a few minutes everything was clear.

He will present my case to Rome himself, when he goes in September.

Was a great help in my various doubts and misgivings, showing clearly that it is not "disobedience" or "obstinancy" to present the matter directly to Rome. That I have no obligation at all to go about it in such a way as to give Fr. Abbot every chance to hinder and frustrate desires that are serious and just. That I should not feel myself obliged to use Laws *against* their right purpose which is the spiritual good of souls, not only as primarily the apparent interest of institutions. (I am sure also that in many ways it is better for Gethsemani that I make my position clear and not remain in this hopeless ambiguity where I now find myself.)

What is important is not to succeed but to take all necessary steps.

And I intend to proceed (though I wake up in the night with doubts).

Several things were ironed out in a new way. I have asked Fr. Larraona to decide between Tortola and Cuernavaca – simply asking for an exclaustration. Both bishops have accepted me willingly. Dom. G. brought the document from the Bp. in Cuernavaca.

Then – to go on quietly praying and letting Rev. Father realize I am fully serious.

This all brought real clarity and orientation.

Dom G. came here at great inconvenience to himself simply to help me arrange this. His charity is one of the most striking and comforting things about the whole business because it is obvious that it is beyond all possible engineering of mine and that it is a gift of God. Dom. G. flew Tuesday night, got here Wednesday morning, stayed all day, took a plane from Louisville for Mexico at 1 A.M. He had very little sleep. When have I done half as much as that for anyone, or even for myself! It makes me take stock of myself.

Now too is the time to go into a different regime. I don't need all the library books I have been getting (though Lawrence's *Mornings in Mexico* had two wonderful chapters on Indian towns). More prayer, more sacrifice, more silence – more work. There are still lots of things to think about in the next three months. I have little doubt the indult will be granted.

Still need to get fully oriented. Everything here of course is against this orientation – and must be. Here is a beginning of real solitude – not to be used for self-justification – but for really opening up my being to God.

My view of Gethsemani is suddenly back to normal – deeply moved by Fr. Flavian's first sermon this morning. With a few like him one need have no worries for the monastery. And I *do* love the monastery.

The point is that the roots I have here ought to be taken up and it seems to me that God's will has indicated this. And the tearing up will be painful, and will make me feel lost. I *must* feel that. But it is the only way to make a fresh start and grasp at the immense and special grace which such an opportunity implies. And I am so far from being ready – my own laziness and inertia lie heavily on me.

But God's grace is for such as I – the unworthy. No need to pretend to be worthy, still less to try to make the thing comprehensible to others. (Indeed it will have to be kept hidden, and though I want very much to be understood I will have to resist the temptation.)

Fr. Lawrence (Cardenal) has to leave on account of his health. He saw Dom G. and may go to Cuernavaca.

July 21, 1959. Day of Rec[ollection]

Always I come back to one clear point: Tortola. This is not only the most logical solution but the one that makes the deepest and fullest appeal to me. It is the only one about which I have no doubts.

About Cuernavaca – much hesitation. First the monastery is near the town. If I go there the news will be all over Mexico in four days. The town is a resort. And any position with Dom Gregorio's outfit is ambiguous, not that it matters. But if I went there at all it would be temporarily, to get my bearings – and then on to try something else definitive.

While Tortola would probably be the definitive thing in my case.

Talking to Fr. John † about it today – he agreed

1. Tortola is the best place in itself.

2. It is more isolated and primitive. I could keep everything more quiet there.

3. The apostolic work is slight and one could keep it so.

4. Fr. John of the † wants to move to Tortola and there would be two of us.

I like the situation much better. A pure hermit life at the moment would be an undue strain. Later it would be more likely to work out. Meanwhile it makes sense for me to be helping another to get into the solitude as well as myself.

I recognize the insecurity (largely subjective) of the situation, and it is good. I have to keep struggling against my inertia and passivity and conformism. Here is a thing that is really good, original, worth doing. It is the only thing I can see that, at the moment, represents a real step forward, a real problem. Precisely because of this it makes me insecure, I have to go into something new and unknown.

To stay here is no real sacrifice, no progress, no real virtue, only inertia, acceptance of mediocrity –

The pernicious doctrine, which R. Father preaches with such strength and conviction, that the acceptance of this absurd and mediocre existence is a "crucifixion." We live more and more on the "crucified" plane of the American Middle Class, mentally, spiritually, physically. There is less and less distinction between our life, our spirit / the life and spirit of the mothers of the kids who come here.

The books about Nancy Hamilton, read in refectory – exactly the kind of mentality that prevails here. Everybody loves them. Pretty little girl with no legs. Everyone makes a fetish of her and her sufferings. People fall all over themselves about her trip to Lourdes – she goes in the plane, gets extra big dinner, etc. etc. I am sure she is all right in herself, and hope she is praying for me to get a plane ride of my own and a few dinners. But all the falsity that surrounds her!!

I have *got* to break out of this cockeyed legend.

Was telling Fr. J† I *don't* want to die in this monastery. I can imagine few things more frustrating – all the bro. novices with open mouths gathering around, shuddering deliciously as you draw your last breath.

And if you have played ball with the abbot all your life, his chapter talk on the day of your funeral will intimate that you were a saint. Otherwise, baby . . .

Rewriting *What Is Contemplation?* – making too many cracks about "large monasteries" which are "like factories."

Letter from Bp. Dwyer of Reno – says I can have St. Brendan's parish. Eureka, Nevada. It has been reduced to a mission and the 500 people there are sad. The town has "no future." And no appeal to me either. Get out of U.S.A.

July 25, 1959. St. James

The other day – a letter from Fr. Daniélou whom I had consulted.

He does not have a real grasp of the situation which is complicated enough, I admit.

He insists rightly that I am: 1) a monk 2) a writer and that the two go together.

It is clear that I cannot simply renounce the monastic state, or stop being a writer either. Nor am I called to be a pure hermit.

In the light of this, I have to reconsider my preference for Tortola.

It's true that I might eventually and probably would form a community there. But can I go and simply be a secular priest, even temporarily? Yes –

if Larraona suggests it. But I had better be careful about pushing that decision myself.

Daniélou suggested a *temporary* absence from the monastery. I asked Rev. Father and he said no. So it is exclaustration or nothing.

Which brings me back to Cuernavaca. That is a monastic solution, even though it involves an exclaustration. But again, the choice is up to Larraona.

As things stand I intend to go ahead strictly within the limits suggested by Dom Gregorio and not push my own idea of Tortola – or insist on going off as a secular priest even for the sake of solitude.

Clearly it must be a genuinely monastic vocation – even though juridically it may seem unconventional.

Spoke to Fr. Eudes again – he said that in view of my attitude towards the house here and the impossibility of really making the matter clear to Rev. Father, he agrees the best thing is to go ahead according to this plan (He does not know it completely).

Rev. Father is a good, sweet, and dangerous man because he believes in his own sweetness and does not see the inexorable, self-righteous appetite for domination that underlies it. He is terribly possessive, in a feminine and motherly way, and his reactions to serious opposition are feminine, passive, tearful, moralistic and indomitably stubborn. He cannot and will not see any other view but his own, and this is because of the *fear* that underlies all his outlook and spirituality, without his knowing it. The fear of facing the pitiable falsity of the whole structure to which he has completely committed himself here – It is a great theatrical front with little or nothing behind it – except a lot of pitiable and wasted good will.

And he will not call things by their right names.

He always picks some dramatic, emotional word or phrase to dress up and justify what is essentially stupid and trite.

Hence – life at Gethsemani is a "perpetual martyrdom." "It costs, it costs." "Utter, utter immolation." It is like being "boiled in oil."

In reality the life is utterly comfortable, stupid, harmless: an adolescent evasion of responsibility, justified as abandonment. It is not self renunciation at all, but the crudest kind of self deception. The pain is the pain of a perpetual bad conscience over our pretenses.

And, of course, complicated by guilt at our own personal pretenses and lies, with which we talk to justify our own rebellions. I think it is better simply to face the fact that I am not honestly a monk here and that the customary routines will do nothing to make me one and that in order to be more honest (?) I need to go elsewhere. The problem remains an interior one, of course – and conveniently, we don't define too clearly what we mean by "monks." It is not the word that matters, but the search for truth. Here, as far as I can tell, I am at the end of the line – as far as my own personal search is concerned.

For others, the situation is entirely different.

Medical check-up in St. Joseph's Infirmary last Wednesday. Nothing important.

July 26, 1959. F. of St. Anne

In town, having been at hospital three or four hours longer than I expected, arrived late at the library and hastily picked up three or four books, scarcely knowing what I was getting. One – on yoga and Psychoanalysis – gave the first paraphrase of Patanjali's Sutra that I have been able to understand. Very illuminating. One of those eye opening contacts that makes you look around as if awakening from a long sleep, and wonder what you have been doing for the last 45 years!! So this was a good choice.

Another one, on the Virgin Islands, which I took reluctantly and almost against my will (I disliked the way it was got up) turns out to be one of those stories of someone who went and built a house on a cay off Tortola. Probably more information about Tortola than in anything else in the library. Sea Cow bay – bad. Rats, mosquitoes, wild dogs, pigs, and crazy people. East End, good, etc. etc.

But it all looks different in the merciful perspective of the Yoga book.

Rev. Fr. preached sadly, sadly, on kindness in chapter. In a voice almost extinct. Afterwards, it turned out that on his feast day the Brother novices had sent him an *enormous* (literally) spiritual bouquet – The Choir novices – nothing. That is sad. I suggested they write him personal notes – only two did.

What a mess. He attaches such importance to those silly, false and preposterously expansive expressions of good will (and bad taste).

I believe as expressions of "good" will they are false and do more harm than good. The bad taste is very real. I *can't* promote such foolishness.

Yet they could all have sincerely written him little notes.

I thought it was enough to make him the winning boxer sign, but I suppose it wasn't. Tears, tears, tears!

Says the library book:

"The student of yoga has need to be so intent on the creation of a new self that he has no leisure for grumbling at his environment."

July 28, 1959

Got together and read over the correspondence that took place in 1955, 4 years ago, about my proposal to go to Camaldoli. It is a frightening and disheartening mess (one most important letter, that of Tom V. Moore is missing).

What could have been very simple was turned into a sickeningly complicated and futile jamboree, partly through my own fault and partly though the stubborn and adroit politics of my superiors.

In the end it was settled by Larraona with a NO – and with advice to wait a few years.

I have waited a few years and now am in danger of doing the same thing and making the same mistakes over again. I start out boldly with an attack and make a bold bid for something perfectly legitimate – but when I do I am opposed then I defeat myself by *suggesting* compromise – in order not to displease anyone – and finally end up with nothing.

1. In May 1955 I thought I had applied for a *transitus* [transfer], through the Camaldolese. (copy of this letter missing also.) I suppose the request was presented to the Congregation – but how and with what effect I never learned.

2. After that a letter of Dom Leclercq *discouraged* the idea of Camaldoli and I practically gave it up, making a grab instead for Frascati. Permission to go there was asked and refused.

3. I think my superiors, after the General Chapter of 1955, were ready to let me be a hermit here, but I realized this would never work. The novitiate was the final compromise – something of a change, some silence, and a face saver!!

Today, be *careful*.

Daniélou is coming in where Dom Leclercq came in before. And with him, doubts. OK, I respect his judgment. I have written more to him to clarify.

But the best thing is to *stick simply to Dom Gregorio's plan*, keep my mouth shut, not write a lot of letters, pray and *wait*. And then do what is indicated.

"In silentio et in spe . . ." ["In silence and hope . . ."]

Letter to Bp. Niedhammer of Bluefields, about Corn Island, was perhaps inadvisable. But I did have permission to see him if he came in September, so that alone was sufficient reason. But is there any point in my trying to be *clever* and lead people off the scent? I must not make a game out of this.

Stifling, damp heat this afternoon. Noise of the machines over toward Gannons – pump? power-mower? There has been a lot of rain.

Letter from President Somoza, in answer to my plea not to subject the prisoners of the abortive revolution to torture. Injured innocence! What me? torture prisoners? Denied that such things ever happened in Nicaragua!

It was a revolution of well-behaved, well brought up, Catholic youths. They wanted to make a demonstration – well, they did. All but one was taken alive and only a few shots were fired. It was a demonstration. Somoza can afford to be paternal.

Either a thing is important or it isn't.

If it is not important enough to die for, why bother with it? This is for myself, not for anyone else. I cannot afford to preach to others.

I must admit that the vocation affair is *not* a matter of life and death.

But then why bother with it? Why bother with demonstrations?

July 30, 1959

Fr. Lawrence (Cardenal) left this morning. The last of those in whom I had originally placed hopes for a South American foundation and perhaps the best – a good poet, a good artist and one of the few genuine contemplatives in the place. But the life was giving him headaches and ulcers.

And again I am faced with the problem that this so-called contemplative monastery *ruins* real contemplatives, or makes life unbearable for them. Or can I say it is a "problem" when it has ceased to perplex me? Causes have effects. I am not absolutely sure I can point out the exact causes but in general: the place being a machine, an institution, in which personal values hardly count, in which what matters is the prosperity and reputation of the community and everything else comes after that . . .

Yesterday in Chapter, with what seemed to me to be a feeling that he had definitely scored, Rev. Fr. announced the death of a priest of Our Lady of the H. Ghost who was out of the monastery on an exclaustration and who fell into the Grand Canyon. He was their sculptor and *one of the many* problem children (a few weeks ago he spoke of their 4th. apostasy). Had been out in a diocese in Guatemala and had not done well there. It seemed to me that Rev. Father, piling on all the drama he could muster, was making a very "good thing" out of it. It was almost as if he smacked his lips when he declared that this was "the judgment of God on one who had not kept his vows."

Perhaps I am not charitable but I feel that the self-righteousness of the Order towards these poor people is something terrible.

Here is the question I cannot help asking.

What is the matter with that monastery?

Fr. R. – apostate, in California now, broken by overwork in the monastery.

Fr. T. – apostate in Atlanta, entered Geth. very young, was cute and was spoiled. And Bro. F. with him.

Fr. A. – apostate, on a pseudo-mystical apocalyptic "mission"?

The other pseudo-mystics in the monastery. The plain neurotics. The facade of optimism. The "act" they all put on – the elaborate demonstration of feeling.

The worst problem Rev. Fr. has had, here and there, have been with the people he liked best. Why? Is there something pernicious about his affection? It certainly repels most people. And it is terribly ambiguous. He is one of the most neatly compartmentalized minds I know of. To your face, gushing with affection. In another context, behind your back, laughing at your idiosyncracies with some other officer. In public, demonstrating a great interest in your work. In private, despising it completely. All enthusiasm for the Choir and chant and liturgy and crazy to make records, yet he'll tell you that in choir the thing to do is to "abstract from all that." A most possessive and power-loving abbot, yet once wanted to be a hermit. I wonder if he knows which one of all these men is real? I suppose "he" is really the "Abbot," the real self is the one that confronts guests or new postulants and exudes charm all over the place. That is what he most works at, perhaps, except for the sentimental prima donna that he is in choir, eyes closed, head thrown back, in a luxury of mental suffering.

The thing is that this man is, in a way, very great and yet very small, very astute in some details and yet incompetent in the most essential things – his dealings with the community and with souls. (In this I would be far worse than he – and not so good at the business!)

I can't help hoping that something will clarify the mystery of sorrow and despair that hangs more and more heavily over us without our knowing it. It is heavy, close air, still sunny, that precedes a terrific storm.

August 2, 1959. Monthly Day of Rec[ollection]

Cool again. Blue Sky.

Fr. Gerard's brother is entering (Bob Bryan) – both from the Redemptorists.

Fr. Alberic (Pendergast) does not drink his milk.

Fr. Anselm (Quenon) is invitator and got the wrong section of the Rule in chapter.

A very skinny two week postulant, hugs his chest and his ribs in choir with long bony hands coming around under his armpits and grabbing his shoulder blades.

Yesterday finished what I hope is the final version of the article on the Pasternak affair – it is to be printed in *Thought*.

Sermon in Chapter today by the Chant Master (Fr. Chrysogamus) on the divine Office. Naturally – the Office is the great prayer of the monk, to which nothing is to be preferred, one who does not ardently love the Office is no monk; it is the prayer of Christ; it is in choir above all that we find Xt. etc. etc. All things I have many times said myself. Yet as I listened I thought "there is a big hole in the middle of this somewhere" –

Interesting article by P. Henry in the *Mélanges* for Dom Alexis Presse; quotes a study of earliest monasticism in which certainly the Office has little or no place. The monk, with the consent of the Bishop *receded* from the common life of the Church and from outward liturgical forms.

"Il anticipe à sa manière la vie angélique qui est pure contemplation et pure communion avec Dieu, au-dessus des signes, des symboles, et des images, les sacraments . . . Les célébrations sacramentales et la liturgie en général occupent peu de place dans la vie de moines . . ." etc. ["He anticipates in his own fashion the angelic life which is pure contemplation and pure communion with God beyond songs, symbols, images, sacraments . . . sacramental celebrations and the liturgy in general occupy little place in the lives of the monks . . ."]

In any case – whatever happens in the next three months, they will be crucial. For my own part – the exterior moves have been more or less decided upon. (Remains the question of Fr. Daniélou – and Dom Gregorio will get in touch with him I think.) My business is now the interior preparation for a change, should one occur. And I pray very hard that it will occur.

1. Fidelity to inspirations of Holy Ghost – walking in risk I have no one else to rely on!

2. Prayer and Detachment. A good time to forget about poetry, secular concerns (though I may have to do some fast typing – I'll see, maybe not). Do I have to set aside a pile of mss? Why?

3. I will have to cut off many contacts – break with many American correspondents.

4. Manual labor!! What has been most lacking in my monastic life.

PM AFTER ADORATION

It seems that the best thing would be to make up my mind definitely to *go ahead in spite of all obstacles* to keep working and praying patiently, humbly, perseveringly, to arrive at a new monastic solution according to God's will – and if I fail now, to keep on trying until the day I die. Never to abandon this idea of going on to a more solitary, primitive life, for a more true, less formalized, kind of monasticism.

And to take as my proximate objective – Dom Gregorio's idea – to start with a quasi-eremitical life in Mexico and then when my canonical situation is changed, to start a venture of my own on Corn Island or Tortola or somewhere in the West Indies – or perhaps even Ecuador. But the main thing – if the Congregation says so – is to be a hermit near Cuernavaca: and then see.

August 9, 1959. XII Sun. after Pentecost

The Hammers were over yesterday. Victor had been ill (he had a stroke) but looked very well. He was a little thinner, which is good. I too am a little thinner – since that day with Dr. Mulligan in Louisville, who put me back on meat and off too much starch, one of the banes of our silly diet.

Victor brought the Desert Fathers book which is superbly done – his very best work perhaps. Certainly his best use of uncial.[51]

And several books on Blake from U.K. library (I had asked for them).

When I was in Louisville I picked up, on the wing, "by chance" Blake's poems and realized again how much I love them, how much I am at home with him. Reading the prophetic books with immense enjoyment – feeling

[51] *What Ought I to Do?: Sayings of the Desert Fathers* was printed in a limited edition of fifty copies at the Stamperia del Santuccio (1959) by Victor Hammer.

thoroughly at home in them now, though I don't follow all the cast of characters. It is a life-long study in itself. Just glanced at some of his letters which Victor brought. Blake is *never* merely indifferent. Always if not inspired, at least very alive. Never dead. I love Blake.

Victor doesn't like Blake. As an artist he doesn't like him. And probably not as a poet because he only reads with full understanding only German poetry. And of course his militant classicism. Yet there is in his militancy and classicism a spark of Blake-like inspiration and his devotion to his craft is like Blake's. Dealing with him is to some extent like dealing with Blake though he is no visionary.

I'd like to try an essay on Blake and believe I will, though I have been writing too much.

The second 1/2 of the transformed version of *What Is Contemplation?* (totally transformed) seems satisfactory. The 1st., in which much of the old is left, is poor.

August 15, 1959. Assumption

Rain. sitting in the woodshed listening to the rain and wind.

Rain and sleet fall on the brothers bringing tubs of ice cream over from the deep-freeze for dinner. Five solemn professions, all brothers. I will probably tell F. Alberic (Pendergast) to leave – too much mischief of visiting postulants, starry eyed and confused – an abominable practice.

Was in Louisville Thursday, about the printing of Guerric's Christmas Sermon. Hated the town. It was hot and stupid. Hated all the advertisements, the interminable attempts to sell you something, the unbearable excess of needless articles and commodities. Everywhere the world oppresses me with a sense of infinite clutter and confusion – and this is what is worldly in the monastery also. Too much of everything.

So that the thing that now gives me the greatest joy is my new diet – for breakfast one piece of toast and some fruit!

Terrell Dickey lent me Thurber's book *The Years with Ross*. Interesting, and yet I don't laugh. In a way it is a sad book – saying so definitely that the era and the city I once believed in are both already finished, and belong only to the past. Every name hits me hard – names I had forgotten – Dorothy Parker, Rea Lavin, Scudder Middleton (who was at all those parties Reg would take me to), Reginald Marsh himself, John O'Hara, Scott Fitzgerald. People not of my generation but the ones my generation believed in. And the brave days of Columbia in the Thirties, which Ad Reinhardt still believes in, I learned at his last visit.

Letters from Laughlin, Naomi (happy),[52] Bob Rambusch who has just been at Mount Athos, and Ernesto Cardenal (Fr. Lawrence) now back in Mexico and ready to enter Cuernavaca, but *"triste"* ["sad"].

August 17, 1959
Another letter from Fr. Daniélou.

It is definite and clear, and an intelligent, winning letter. I have not gone over it again yet. These are just first impressions. But deep impressions and I know they are important.

1. He does not completely exclude Cuernavaca. That is for me to decide, but as far as he is concerned he is against any change. I gather he would even be against a change of monastery within the Order. Except, of course, temporary.

2. He is against it for the effect it would have on people. I do have to consider the fact that some people rely on me. So I have to take a genuinely apostolic outlook; I am an apostle of Christ, and not for myself but for Him and for souls. And I cannot honestly risk grave danger to them in order to gratify a desire of my own, be it spiritual.

He tells me then to bear witness to Xt and not to myself. Not to harden myself but to put on Christ. There is no denying the rightness of this. Am I "hardening my heart" simply, by going to Cuernavaca? He does not say that – it remains for me to decide honestly.

3. Strongest point: that at Gethsemani I have really found a genuine and unusual balance between my 2 vocations as monk and as writer. And that whereas I feel myself to be prisoner of an artificial role, I am in reality prisoner of a mission. Yes or no? I am tempted to throw this mission business out of the window. False humility? Does real humility consist in just accepting it?

I trust his judgment as more objective than Dom Gregorio's, deeper, more Catholic, in its way. Yet I still don't know whether Dom G. is not right in a practical intuition that for my own monastic future and for the future of monasticism the thing to do is to leave here. Fr. D. thinks – if I were to make a new foundation, yes. But the time is not ripe for that.

[52] Naomi Burton Stone was Merton's friend and literary agent.

August 18, 1959

What do I need?

Hard question to answer. This morning – I need nothing. Then perhaps what I have now is what I need at other times. Leisure. Time to think. Time to look at the hills, at the horses in the distant pasture and at their beautiful brown color – to call it golden would be to insult it.

I need something beyond my capacity to know. If I call it solitude, I mistake it. Silence, a primitive life.

What I need – as far as I can interpret the desire in my heart, is to make a journey to a primitive place, among primitive people, and there die. It is at the same time a going out and a "return." A going to somewhere where I have never been or thought of going – a going in which I am led by God, a journey in which I go out from everything I now have. And I feel that unless I do this my spiritual life is at an end. Unfortunately, this obscure drive is not recognized by theologians and directors. Certainly it is "nature." But is there no grace in it and with it? I do not know. It is an anxious and imperious thing . . . call it "acting out." I am going to have to act out something like this – it would not be healthy not to. The woods, for the time being, make some such ritual possible here.

But – if you go to Mexico on the strength of that impulse are you free? Are you not subordinating your spiritual freedom to blind irrationality? Maybe that is the trouble. (The book about the *New Yorker* – Thurber's – oppresses me. Civilization oppresses me, or rather all that is new in it does – the most comforting thing in the book is the sketch on the cover – a boat in one of the Manhattan docks. The only good thing about New York is that you can sail from there to France.)

What do I need? If necessary I can get by with plenty of mornings like this. Seriously I need silence, thought, solitude, to enter into myself to see and touch reality, to live the contemplative life.

Ernesto Cardenal sent the *Revista de literatura Mexicana* with his political poems about Somoza. They are very fine, clarity and passion, best political verse of the 20th. century perhaps.

All right – What do I *really* need – ?

1. To be free from the *need* of letters and mail and new books (but to have them in so far as they are necessary or as they come).

2. To be free from my own irresolution and confusions, and distraction: that is, to be free from my subjection to chance and to my own passions.
3. To be free from my need to be admired and approved of, my need to feel fully justified in all I desire, or decide to do.

August 22, 1959. F. Immaculate Heart of Mary
A hot night and a hot morning.

Curious that for the first time in a year or more I have taken a spontaneous interest in a moral conference and participated in it actively – to the extent of getting up and talking three times. And the case? The obligations of an escaped prisoner. Is even a guilty man allowed to escape? Yes. Must he go back? No. I stoutly defended the point that it would rarely if ever be "better" even to "counsel" him to go back. And against all comers, with Fr. Tarcisius, I held that he was not bound to restitution for "damage done to doors and windows" while getting out.

Curious, isn't it?

The last case in which I said anything was one on atomic war, which I could hardly see as moral.

Had a fairly sane and sensible talk with Rev. Fr. yesterday about the business of my problems here and my desire for a more primitive, isolated, and simple life alone and away from the *vanitas monastica* of the community life. Not that we have settled anything, but at least it was a matter of a genuine interchange of thoughts and not just two individuals separately and stubbornly entering their own views and refusing to communicate with one another.

The net result was of course that I had said in various ways that I thought I ought to leave and he had said in various ways that he thought I ought to stay but nothing final was said one way or another.

I felt however that I had sufficiently manifested the state of my mind to him, and that he now knows my desires in a general way. But according to Dom G's advice I said nothing at all definite about Cuernavaca or the indult. On that point, I am still unsettled, and will consult Dom G. when he comes.

Rev. Fr. is going to the General Chapter and probably to Rome and this would be just when Dom G. would present my petition. It would prove very awkward.

But I have still to discuss Fr. Daniélou's letter to Dom Gregorio.

I wrote Fr. D. that I was suspending all decisions until Dom G. came and if he wanted me to go with the project as planned, I would do so. But I can't do anything on my own initiative, as things stand. And furthermore, Fr. D's stand makes it clear that I must sacrifice Tortola as "not monastic" unless we present it as an alternative in Rome and Fr. Larraona picks it for me.

Had a good talk with Fr. Alberic, went for a walk with him on St. Bernard's feast. We came close to sending him home, but he pleaded to stay. And he is a good kid, in his wild way. I wish I knew something of the mystery of his situation. Deep down I am convinced he can make a very good monk – and that I can help him remove the obstacles, if only I can see what they really are.

I hear Gregory Zilboorg is dying of cancer. I must write him a letter sometime those days when letters *are* written.

I continued to be interested and depressed by *The Years with Ross*. It is really a very remarkable book in its way – a historical document. And a very human one. That is the only way one could write the life of an abbot. "The Years With James." It is remarkable the mixture of objective criticism, legitimate impatience, admiration, resentment, and love with which Thurber looks at Ross. Very edifying in its subtle way, and yet also there is something weird about it. Maybe neurotic. Which I guess Ross was and Thurber probably is.

August 23, 1959. Sunday (xiv after Pent.)
As a result of my conversation with Fr. Abbot, he gave us this morning in chapter a little sermon on "seeing the bright side of things" + "not looking at the dark side."

> Two men looked out from prison bars
> One saw mud, the other saw stars.

Item: Things are going well with the Church in America, though not so well in other parts of the world. Look at our school system. Look at the use that is being made of radio and TV for the Faith. Look at the Communions every day, since the new regulations for the Eucharistic fast.

Item: Things aren't so bad in the monastery either. After all, we are *still here*.

Item: Why not tell ourselves with conviction "Day by day in every way things are getting better and better." And *keep* on telling ourselves . . .

Item: Every cloud has a silver lining.

Item: Story of a priest who dreamed he was in hell. Yes. but it was *only a dream!* . . .

One cannot be mad at Rev. Father and does not need to be. He means so well, and there is of course a background of truth, something he is trying to say but cannot. And that is just the problem. Instead of hoping in Christ, we hope in the phrases of the late-lamented and thoroughly forgotten Emile Cone (?). Everyone was smiling and there was a kind of tolerant tongue-in-the-cheek attitude, generally, in the chapter room. Yet that is not good either. It has a *dark side*, and I see it.

August 24, 1959

Yesterday was very hot. I gave a conference on Providence. Today, on Psalm 36. Yesterday finished *The Years with Ross*, and am tempted to write Thurber a note about it. This seems to be a good thing to do. J. Laughlin wants me to write a note to Mina Joy in Aspen, to cheer her up. (He sent me her poems from N. Carolina.) And I will.

Reading Tillich's *Love, Power and Justice* and am excited by it; it is very dense and strong. The substrate of depth psychology makes his thought very substantial. I will certainly write to him about it, especially as he signed the copy for me.

Having been giving deep attention (as deep as possible when one is half awake before Sext) to Butterfield's book on Christianity and History.

Especially the business about the men like Napoleon, Bismarck, and Hitler who wanted to get ahead of history and manage Providence for their own interests. Providence will not be managed. The one great doubt that remains in my own mind – if I go to Cuernavaca, am I getting ahead of my own life and simply evading a limited situation which is fruitful and will continue so in so far as it is providential? (The abbot's view and Daniélou's to some extent) or am I simply resting in inertia and bourgeois comfort and evading the responsibility to embrace a "tragic" and more fruitful so-lution (Dom Gregorio's view, though for him the concept is not tragic. That is from Koestler).

August 30, 1959. 15 Sun. After Pentec[ost]

The postulant visitors who have come for two weeks are still here mostly. Although I don't like the institution, strict rules were applied this year and the thing went better than I expected. At least they did not wander around the monastery talking to everybody.

Two – the most interesting ones – are not really thinking of vocations. One is Paul Pendergast, Fr. Alberic's brother, and it is purely and simply a "visit" but I am glad. He is a very nice kid and Fr. A proudly takes care of him in choir etc. He is shy but relatively sane and would not be as wild as Fr. A.

The other – Rev. Fr. picked up in Atlanta and persuaded to come here. Phil Gage, a high school kid who is getting into the *Atlanta Journal* and writes well. He is intelligent, balanced, sophisticated and altogether unlike what we normally get and I conclude there is no chance of his entering here. Nor will I give him much encouragement in that direction. But I think he will make a good priest some day. The biggest joke of all was the fact that he spent most of last week reviewing a novel for the *Atlanta Journal* – (I gave him work time for this). It was an effort by some English "angry young man" called *The Breaking of Burnabo* and looked a bit silly.

Yesterday, spoke to Anselm's sister Carolyn.

She is a very charming, intelligent, and honest girl who for reasons I cannot easily dismiss has stopped going to church and calls herself an "agnostic."

Actually, it amounts to a kind of final revulsion against superficial and empty Catholicism on the part of one who has all the makings of a tremendously earnest and vital Christian, and who has never seen Christianity as it really is. It is heart-breaking. Yet we talked for an hour understanding one another perfectly, and on a deep spiritual level, because in reality she has very much the same hungers and ideals I have, but has rationalized them out in an utterly different language.

She had been completely unable to understand Fr. A's vocation and had challenged him on it without pulling any punches, and the points she made were *serious*. (This in a letter at Easter.) I had written back suggesting she read Jung's *Undiscovered Self*. She had not replied. She was then working as a nurse in a psychiatric hospital.

When she came and met me I felt sorry for her – she looked a bit haunted and defiant, out on the end of her own limb, no doubt expecting to be pelted with heavy abstract theses in dogma and apologetics. I felt inexpressibly moved by her courage and her loneliness.

So after we talked, sitting on the wall at the end of the front avenue. She said what she had to say about "this place" – living "without normal contacts," "Loving God" being pretense and self-delusion, "praying for others" being no excuse for evading active work outside – "The need to make everything fit a lot of dogmas" etc. etc.

There was no need to argue, but just to explain and to establish clearly that what she meant by these objections was in fact not what she thought she meant and that it was quite possible that behind all her objections were genuine and earnest religious aspirations, but not *conventional* ones.

In other words we ended by comforting one another mightily with our fundamental sense of spiritual agreement, and I am deeply moved at the thought that we share the same ultimate yearning which words and gestures cannot adequately express. I am sad that I did not get to explain that this is the very heart of what is signified by Holy Communion.

I know her problem is deep and severe, and can only reply with an inarticulate prayer that shares her anguish – and a kind of sense that by this sort of sharing we are both saved. The thing that stays with me most clearly is the conviction that this is what we both sensed and felt most deeply, although nothing at all was said about it. And this is the important thing.

Anyone with two grains of sense will probably detect behind all this a sort of sexual attraction. Certainly not explicit or overt, but spiritualized. Well, so what? Does that invalidate anything I have said? We are human and our humanity is part of the mystery of Christ, and there is hardly any spontaneous human affection that does not have some sex in it somewhere.

Certainly, though, I was and am moved by the thought of this child, who is very French first of all (the family is French), very small and delicate, and light as if she would blow away off the wall at any minute – with such light sandals on her feet that I kept thinking that her feet were bare. And her raggedy hairdo, and her very earnest face. And again, the honesty and simplicity of her spirit.

The great relief of coming face to face at least with a *real* problem instead of all the fictions we cherish in the monastery!

Three of the visiting postulants left today – one going tomorrow – but more coming. Here in the woodshed is the 15 year old from Nova Scotia dressed in a work blouse and up until a moment ago, fairly talkative. ("Is there a brook around here?" Like St. Teresa he likes water.)

Serious this afternoon – good long hour in the chapel with the Tabernacle open for exposition. In the end, with my mind empty, thought of seeing what would come spontaneously into it and suprisingly up welled not some subconscious image but Psalm 84, which I said slowly and thoughtfully in the depths.

> *Benedixisti Domine Terram tuam*
> *Avertisti captivitatem Jacob . . .*
> [Lord, you have blessed your land
> You have taken away Jacob's captivity . . .]

Before that – had thought of the seriousness of the hour and of the decisions that are to come. Mine are made. Dom Gregorio comes on the 5th. or 6th. And will fly to France on the 7th. where he will see Père Daniélou. As far as I am concerned there is nothing to do but let things take their course – I see no point in trying to stay here and stagnating indefinitely. Dom G. will go to Rome and present my petition, I believe.

I need a new start and also some direction and support in getting started. For this I have confidence in Dom Gregorio.

A new *monastic* start. I see the ruins of so many mistaken initiatives, so much drifting, so much willfulness in the last years.

I realized today how deceptive and treacherous a person I am, most of all to myself.

It is because I am deceptive that I complicate everything and make gestures to cover any deceit from myself – or to make sure that a legitimate action is not taken as deceptive.

That is the danger now. This going direct to the Congregation seems like a deceit and I am afraid it is so being interpreted. But efforts to make it more honest or more effective will only be a real deception and will not make it either more honest or more effective.

As it stands, it is legitimate and not deceit, though it would be preferable and more open to do it otherwise. It is not purely my idea, but Dom G's so I can feel objective about it and assume responsibility for something more than a personal whim.

The best thing is to be content that it needs no excuse and be patient with the things Rev. Father will say about it, because it will really make him anyway. He leaves Thursday for the General Chapter and will think the whole thing was plotted in his absence. He has a horror of being "outwitted" and taken advantage of. What a skein of insincerities I live in, complicated by my own character. And there is nothing to be done about it here. Put two people like Dom James and myself together and we react on one another with sincerities that cover deceit, each one trying to trick and use the other. And if I say he is worse than I am it is probably in order to justify my own duplicity.

I only hope the whole project is not shot through with duplicity and I have to be careful to see that it is not.

At the moment it seems to me that this anxiety about it is mostly fear of being hated and rejected for what I feel I ought to do. A further deception, perhaps, to calm my own conscience if I draw back – For there is deception both ways. I want to have the glory of a *desire* for freedom and a new start, without facing the required battle.

It seems to me better to face the battle, the rejection, the vilifications and the possible failure. And assume an honest risk of complete loss of face and of reputation and of the pitifully false hope of emotional security I still cling to here, without faith.

And the final deceit that I have perhaps not really been at all fair with Gethsemani – not really humble enough to accept the life with its limitations.

There is truth and falsity in all of this and I cannot any longer hope to disentangle them and come up with a perfectly straight answer.

All I can do is take the steps that seem to be asking to be taken.

Rev. Father is clearly informed anyway, that my life has reached a turning point and that I may turn some unexpected corners.

But let me really turn them and keep going and not come back around the corner to see if he approves and to placate him before going further. So far as I am concerned he is the Mother over whose prostrate body one must step in order to follow one's vocation (N.B. the way *he* paid Fr. S's fare to Buenos Aires after urging him to take solemn vows as a Benedictine there).

September 6, 1959. XVI Sunday after Pentecost

The last week has been busy, active and not especially monastic and today I am really tired – it was almost impossible to participate intelligently in the night office. Yet it was not for lack of sleep. I slept deeply last night and perhaps did not really wake up, just stayed asleep, watching and singing in my sleep.

Yesterday was a fabulous day. Stephen Spender's wife Natasha blew in with a girl from the Coast, Margot Dennis – driving across the continent. They stayed for high mass and spent most of the day here. At first we were very decorous and intelligent walking up and down the front avenue talking about Zen, Freud, music, St. John of the Cross, and the Dark Night of the Soul. Then it went down a notch, became more familiar, and amusing, as we went out to St. Bernard's lake and ate sandwiches and fruit cake and talked about monasteries and abbots, bishops and popes, Corn Island, Mexico, God knows what. This was very charming and maybe I began to look a little less scared. Finally we went to Dom Frederic's lake and went swimming which was the most enjoyable of all. I forgot what we talked about – it didn't matter – but there was something about Mex. Margot, once dipped into the water, became completely transformed into a Naiad-like creature, smiling a primitive smile through hanging wet hair. We sunbathed a bit, then finally they trundled off to Cincinnati with their immense load of baggage.

It is hard to remember when I have ever so completely enjoyed anything – except perhaps the visits to the Hammers at Lexington. And of course it had a devastating effect in the form of distractions, but I don't care. Except of course I had better make a mental note to be very careful in the future when I am going to see more of women with intelligence. I am obviously utterly starved for that kind of conversation, and no woman can resist that hunger I am sure. And in a way it is right that this is so. Everything was really as it ought to be – except that the swimming was an act of disobedience, which may or may not be justified by appeal to a higher rule. I leave that to the mercy of God. Natasha Spender in any case is a charming and dynamic person and one I agree with so immediately and so completely that she is not for me in the realm of "objects" but as much myself as a blood sister would be.

Thursday I took Fr. Alberic and Paul for a walk over to Hanekamp's old place and when we got near there the undergrowth had come up so thick and there was such a hedge of pine saplings and brush that you couldn't get through without danger of getting lost and wasting time. So we came back. I was shocked that this legendary place had now somehow been closed off to me, and with it all the inner life and prayer that were part of the woods for me in 1950–55. This is all finished. Those woods no longer have anything to say and I am a stranger to them. But the pines by St. Teresa's field are full of meaning – part of it a pointing to Mexico or South America.

Wednesday afternoon, cut tobacco. It was already nearly finished.

Reading Jung on religion (not bad) – Some rewriting on *Inner Experience* which is now, I think, a respectable book.

When I got in from the wild party at the lake, Bro. Clement had a tile man there to tile the novices' shower and also put in a new one.

If going to Mexico or Corn Island or Tortola is going to mean meeting very many people and talking a great deal – should I do it? Hard to say yes or no – I *want* solitude and do not want, perversely and though my own fault, to fit into a spurious apostolate. Careful to do only what the Holy Ghost may indicate – and that is going to require *much more* tact, discretion, prayer and interior delicacy than I have now!

September 7, 1959

Happened upon Kierkegaard's analysis on why he "had to" reject Regina Olson. All right, he "had to" – but it was sickness. It shocks me terribly. I wish he had not been so damnably "honest" in his self-examination. If it was less honest to take her, I wish to God he had deceived her and made her happy by his deception – even if it would have been lost in all his writings.

September 9, 1959

On the evening of the 7th. when it was very hot, and all the Louisville priests were coming to begin their retreat, Dom Gregorio arrived. He was here all day yesterday and left last night for Miami, Lisbon, Paris – then to Belgium and then to Rome with my letter to Larroana now rewritten for the third time. And I think in its final form the letter now makes sense. I have great confidence in the judgment of Larraona and that he will see the thing correctly. He may give a cautious answer and prescribe more waiting – but I reminded him that already in 1955 he had told me to "wait" and I was still waiting. Though I don't especially like the political maneuvers that are necessary, still the task of clearly and completely formulating my request has been good for me and there is wisdom in this "red tape" after all. It forces you to think about what you are doing.

Dom Gregorio is more convinced than ever that this is the right thing to do and that Daniélou's letters show he had not understood the situation correctly. He will see D. in Paris.

Pictures of the monastery in Cuernavaca. Interesting new church – but it is clear I am not going there for the monastery or for anything like that, but to have a solitary life – and prepare for a place of my own, perhaps. (Corn Island?)

He spoke of a place the bishop had found recently, ideal for a hermitage, in the mountains near Tepoztlan – can only be reached by horseback.

I am glad of all this, and at peace, see that this is the way to go ahead. But I am not moved by enthusiasm. It is a dry and sober conviction, with a great awareness of risk, which I accept fully. I think there are solid hopes of getting this indult – and that after that the way may be very difficult, but I want to accept all the difficulties. Staying here does not make sense – the life has become too warped and corrupted and the simplicity of the real monastic spirit is gone.

Preached a sermon on Our Lady yesterday. A letter came from Carolyn Quenon. And one from Lax. And a new translation of Pasternak's poems. I have lost interest in literature.

September 15, 1959

The Russians have hit the moon with a rocket – which represents another climax of absurdity and vanity in our technological age. Khrushchev, fortified by this nonsense, lands in America today where he will be secretly loved and respected as a "great-leader" though outwardly and officially the nation will be gruff.

Draghi showed up and talks incessantly of islands. We go to Louisville today about the Guerric booklet which is late already (needed for Christmas).

September 17, 1959

Draghi, with all his well meant and effusive gregariousness is rather tiring. In Louisville – the first part of the day was sensible. Brief business at Terrell Dickey's – Rode downtown in Warren Seekamp's Volkswagen (He is the representative of Fetter who is doing the printing). I picked up a couple of books in the library and then said office in the cathedral.

While I was in the can in the Brown Hotel, heard, over the bootblack's radio, the chatter describing Khrushchev's arrival in Washington. The plane had just been sighted. "There comes ol' Khrushchev," says the bootblack. I said I hoped he would have a good time among us and took off down 4th. street with better things to do than wait for the 21 gun salute and the formal welcome.

When I met Draghi again he was overwrought. First he went to get his car gassed at a garage in the colored section and a crazy man kept looking at him and opening and shutting a clasp-knife. Then he called up a friend – a doctor at G. E. – and discovered he had been shot several months ago. During lunch he told me one horror story after another about rapes and murders that had been taking place everywhere and finally to cap it off he ran over a cat on the road home.

In the evening we stopped by and saw the wife of the Dr. who had been killed – a good courageous little person who has just started teaching High School for a living – and to support her 4 children.

A gay moment in her house, playing Calypsos.

In the end, it was an exhausting day, but that is what it had to be.

The main thing was the movie we went to in the afternoon. He insisted that I wanted to see a movie. Hadn't seen one in 19 years or so and had no desire to see it. Got a good look at the lobby of the place while D. was making phone calls and all the muck that nobody sees, turned my stomach. Couldn't figure out why there was only 1/2 of a naked nymph in the foyer. Other half had been stolen I guess.

The movie – I suppose relatively good – A. Hitchcock's *North by Northwest* struck me as on the whole intolerably stupid – one long tissue of complete absurdities. The movies are a universe of their own in which there is no longer any sense left. Nobody bothered to *act* – well, the villains had to ham it up a bit because they were villains. But Cary Grant – well, he just had to be there. I wonder if he really changed his facial expression *once* in the whole film.

There was simply no explanation for the action. The whole thing seemed to be a game to see how impossible and absurd a situation could become. If they wanted to kill the hero, they couldn't just kill him, they had to try the hardest, most fantastic way, the way least likely to succeed. And of course they never succeeded. The payoff was the part at the end with hero, heroine, and assorted villains chasing each other all over the faces of the colossal Presidents on the cliffside at Mt. Rushmore.

As for the love-making – it was incredibly absurd. First an exchange of supposedly sophisticated innuendoes, uttered through blank, mask like faces, with an occasional fleeting expression of conventionalized lust. Then a bit of manoeuvering around the bunk of the pullman roomette. Finally the cliches in which they made faces at one another, accompanied by inarticulate noises, and a lot of utterly silly passes made chiefly to *look* sensual. I can't imagine that they really were.

Some other time I'll put down more golden thoughts about this fantastic experience.

After 18 years in a monastery I certainly can't believe in movies any more – in fact I had ceased to long before I came here.

September 18, 1959

Have been reading a marvelous book of theology by the Orthodox Father Paul Evdokimov who teaches at Saint Serge in Paris. It is called *La femme et le salut du monde [The Feminine and the Salvation of the World]* but is in reality a whole survey of Sophianic theology. Marvelous and exciting perspectives. Here is a real theologian – one of the few. But one thing helps and encourages me above all. This line:

"Reconnaître le Christ même en ceux qui en apparence luttent contre Lui, mais en réalité se revoltent contre des conceptions et des valeurs faussement Chrétiennes, n'est-ce pas là un acte Chrétien des plus urgents?" ["To recognize Christ Himself in those who by appearance struggle against Him, when in reality they struggle against ideas and values which are falsely called Christian, is that not an urgent Christian task?"]

September 21, 1959. St. Matthew

The evening is bright and cool – nice day for a 1/2 holiday.

Probably this week Dom Gregorio will present my petition to the Congregation in Rome. I wish I were in some sense more "ready." I feel helpless and confused, not knowing at all what will come next, and having been caught up in a whirl of trivial and distracting things for the last week.

The drag of inertia that makes me just want to stay put. The repugnance for the silly and petty battle that will be waged with Rev. Father. His emotionalism, his recriminations. The pressure he will exert. His claims and his reproaches. It could be infinitely unpleasant. I will have to bear it in a Spirit of Truthfulness and calm. Not claiming more than I mean to, not condemning him and the monastery.

If I stay on a superficial level it will be silly and false.

Deeper down – it is a question of the difference between pleasing God and pleasing men. Between sacrifice, difficulty, renouncement, and the easy way, the acceptance of the status quo – passivity.

I believe I have the right and the duty to try to go on to a more pure and simple and primitive form of life. That I have the right to appeal to a higher superior for permission to make this trial. I can ask and wait and see what happens. But the question is, I have to be really sincere about looking for a simpler, poorer, more solitary life, more abandoned to Providence. On the other hand – all the other things that enter in and spoil this: desire of liberty, desire to be out from under a stupid form of authority – desire to travel – to go to a more beautiful and more primitive country. All these things are there, unfortunately, and they are strong. And of course Rev. F. will try to work on *them*, as cleverly as he knows how, in order to hide all the other issues.

From all these things I must be detached. From aestheticism and from love of my own will. That is most important. Otherwise the whole thing will fail.

And be *definite*. Avoid all this futile interior argument and reasoning. The decision has been taken to move forward – the rest remains unknown and it is not for me to decide it beforehand. If I simply try as far as possible to gain interior mastery of this issue, then it will solve itself.

September 22, 1959

F. of St. Maurice and the Martyrs of the Theban Legion – solid nonconformists. I said Mass for my Cuernavaca intention and after that spent a good day of recollection in the woods, which vastly improved my attitude and situation.

The one thing necessary is a true interior and spiritual life, true growth, on my own, in depth, in a new direction. Whatever new direction God opens up for me. My job is to press forward, to grow interiorly, to pray, to break away from attachments and to defy fears, to grow in faith, which has its own solitude, to seek an entirely new perspective and new dimension in my life. To open up new horizons at *any* cost. To desire this and let the Holy Spirit take care of the rest. But really to desire this and *work* for it.

Read a little about Danilo Dolci[53] in Sicily – he puts me entirely to shame and shows up all the futilities of the life I have led here in a new and humbling light.

September 26, 1959

There are no more special difficulties as far as I am concerned interiorly. I have a job to do and I am going ahead with it. The request for the indult has been presented and I have a feeling it will be eventually granted. My job is to do what has to be done in the next two difficult months, to be quiet, accept the pressures and revilings that are inevitable, and not get involved in political tricks – but be prudent in all that is done against me and make sure not to give ground and compromise uselessly. I wrote to Rev. Father about what is taking place, without making known the exact steps.

A copy of two volumes of the *Philokalia* sent by B. Rambusch from Athens, arrived the other day. Magnificent. I had been told it was unobtainable. A new edition – it was begun in 1957. I read it slowly and sedulously – much dictionary work.

September 29, 1959. F. St. Michael

A nice morning but not much cooler, in spite of the brief shower of rain that came down during Vigils soaking the robe I had left out on the line.

Sybille Akers was here yesterday – a very gifted photographer, French, I think, or German, married to a newspaperman in Texas who looks like Pasternak. She brought some impressive things with suggestions for a book – I like the pictures and suggestions but don't know what to do about it now.

My last mss. ("The Inner Experience") lies on the desk untouched. I want to revise it. I want to clean up that room. And get rid of a lot of things and clear the decks for action.

Now they are putting out odious little cigarette lighters with a picture of St. Christopher on one side and the Abbey on the other. I don't look at all the horrors in the Gate House. Fr. Stephen showed me this – he is sending one to his relatives.

[53] A social activist, pacifist, and anti-Mafia worker among the poor.

———

Yesterday, a printed cloth from Mt. Athos came – picture of the Crucifixion and Resurrection sent also by Bob Rambusch. It is an unoriginal and uninspired reproduction of more or less Western models, yet it has considerable character and looks good hanging up over the altar. The Greek lettering is decorative. In the Resurrection Xt is holding Adam by the waist and hoisting him up out of the tomb. Eve is there looking dreamlike, at Bl. Virgin.

Also a splendid little book on [Gregory] Palamas.

I am very happy with these things.

One compromise I would accept – if they would permit the foundation of a hermitage here and three or four of us could live in cottages back where Hanekamp used to be. I would not really want to try it completely alone at first, not here, but even that I would take if nothing else were possible. But the danger is in being too eager to compromise and confusing the real issue.

But it is now clear what the issue is – a more primitive, more solitary life if possible among primitive people, and *out* of the USA.

And there have been so many indications that I belong in Latin America . . . or the Antilles.

October 2, 1959. F. of Guardian Angels

Fine Fall day – trees changing colors. A great screaming of pigs and jabbering of brothers down by the mill: the usual Trappist noise. They chase one batch of pigs away from the trough and lead a new batch down to the trough. Half the pigs sound sick. There is not much life in them after all the screaming.

Rev. Father came back yesterday from the General Chapter looking important and full of cares – with projects for dialogue masses (which in the case of the Choir seems to me absurd when we already have a sung Mass at which everyone wonders what to do. I think Rev. Father wants every private Mass to be a dialogue Mass! God help us!). There is news of this and that, all of it trivial and unimportant. They are rewriting the *Spiritual Directory* and I have not heard if I am supposed to do anything on that job, but everything in me revolts against the mere idea of it. My guess is that Rev. Fr. has discreetly seen that the job will not come my way for fear I might have to go to France and get out of his hands.

Arresting phrases from Evdokimov:

"*Le monachisme, apocalypse vécue, montre la conscience Chrétienne brûlée par l'impatience . . . La prière chante Dieu mais elle a aussi son aboutissement apocalyptique. Elle hâte les événements, dégage l'unique nécessaire, rapproche les temps et rend leur actualité la plus brûlante, aux réponses immortelles, que le Seigneur a donné aux trois tentations du désert . . . Tout destin ne peut avoir d'autre but que de témoigner les choses dernières . . .*" pp. 240–41. ["Monasticism, apocalypse already realized, shows forth the Christian conscience burning with impatience . . . Prayer praises God but is also an apocalyptic manifestation. It hastens events, confronts that which is essential, embraces all times, and makes their actuality more urgent in terms of the immortal answers given by the Lord to the three temptations in the desert . . . Its entire destiny is none other than to bear witness to the Last Things."]

"*. . . les traits propres au mal:* l'imposture, l'existence insensitive, la parodie.

"*toute la vie Chrétienne est vers l'ultime. Dans cette tension il ne s'agit pas de la perfection morale des efforts humaines mais de la participation à l'action transcendent de Dieu . . .*" 247. ["The precise Characteristics of evil: *imposture; unfeeling existence; parody.* All Christian life is oriented toward the ultimate. In this tension one does not move to moral perfection through human deeds but by participation in the transcendent activity of God . . ."]

October 4, 1959. Monthly Day Rec[ollection]. XX Sun. After Pent[ecost]
Had a quiet, uneventful talk with Rev. Father Friday evening. He did not mention my letter and neither did I. Evidently he has heard nothing yet from the Congregation. He is not insistent about the Dialogue Mass, thank God.

I learned from him that Gregory Zilboorg had died about Sept. 17th., of cancer. Rev. Father tried to contact him in N.Y. and found he was dead. I can imagine why R.F. wanted to see him.

A letter from Suzuki came saying he still wanted to write the preface for the Desert Fathers and would do it right away – only that he was "old" and "tired" and could not work during hot and damp weather. But he had been to some meeting of "E[ast] W[est] Philosophers" in Honolulu. I am edified by the simplicity of his letters.

The last month has been too wild. Seeing too many people – but they came. God brought them. Distraction. I am very aware of my lack of inner discipline especially since, in the last week, I have been reading the *Secret of the Golden Flower* [Tung Pin Lu]. A new book by Van Der Post has come in from the library – I wrote to him last week or the week before. Fr. Robert made simple profession today – the only one left of those – 18 or 20 – who entered in 1957. Rev. Fr. is anxious because "Spencer has 40 choir novices."

October 6, 1959. F. of St. Bruno

Today – the best of all days for it – arrived a very encouraging letter from Dom Gregorio in Rome. I had been cleaning up our room and throwing things out and went over to the Abbot's office with some mail – Bro. Simon gave me the letter saying Fr. Prior had just opened it (Rev. Father had a hernia operation in Bardstown today).

Dom G. says he has seen Fr. Larraona twice, up to Oct. 1. when the letter was written (mailed on the 2nd.).

His cryptic message was:

"Larroana m'a aussi dit confidentiellement *qu'il croit que je pourrai recevoir l'aide du moine français* (that's me) *mais que cela dura passer au ses supérieurs – il m'a fait comprendre qu'il prévoit l'opposition mais qu'il ne changera pas d'avis. Je suis très content de cela vous comprenez qu'elle m'aidera beaucoup. Veuillez donc prier le Père céleste pour tout avance bien – je vous averiterai de l'arrivée du moine."* ["Larraona also said *confidentially* that he believes that I will be able to receive the French monk (that's me) but it will have to go through the superiors – he led me to understand that he foresees opposition but it would not change his opinion. I am very happy in that it should be of great help to me. Finally, pray to the Heavenly Father that all goes well – I will advise you of the monk's arrival."]

That is altogether splendid.

The train whistle in the valley reminds me of the first day I came here – the first day we worked, on a grey afternoon like this, in St. Edmund's field. And my gratitude. It is the same gratitude and the same vocation. What has died in my spirit and my vocation here lately has come back to life. I feel at last that I can grow and move forward, and that all life has not been stamped out of my heart.

A remarkable letter, also (same time) from Louis Massignon, about Indian art and its expression of suffering and the sacrifice of the heart which terrified me in *Études Carmélitaines*. There is a great mystery here. I am not going forward to an easy life in Mexico, or to an easy death either. This is precisely what makes me *happy* – the first taste of real happiness in a long time!

Dom G. – in Europe until after Oct. 15 – says he will not be passing through here on his way back. He does not think he would be welcome.

I opened Isaias at the 49th. chapter and read from v. 7 to the end: the marvelous liberation from Babylon and the return.

I have little desire, at the moment, to read anything but the Prophets.

October 12, 1959

After Mass and Communion – I realize that it is utterly shameless and trivial to look at this effort to take a new direction, as merely a development and liberation of my own "autonomous personality." That sounds good and acceptable. It is fashionable, but utterly foolish. What is really important is to see that it is a vocation, a decision of God in my regard, a call to a new work, a new start given by Him and freely accepted by me. But my acceptance must be in the right terms, and above all I must *commit myself* for the unknown and unpredictable work that is to be done and not go about dictating my own conditions and seeking what I think will favor "my development." It is for God to take care of my growth and my happiness.

October 25, 1959. 23rd. Sunday After Pentecost

I have been in St. Anthony's Hospital, Louisville, for the removal of a rectal fistula. Went on the 14th. and got back Friday.

Went in on the 14th. First to see the doctor, not expecting to be kept in town. Also had some business with Fetter. Spent the day riding around in taxis – and with brief moments of respite at the Carmel.

On the Feast of St. Teresa I said Mass at Carmel and gave communion to the nuns. After that went down to the hospital immediately for the operation. Drs. Lucas and Ryan kept me in there a few extra days because of my general condition.

Mostly, it was a very good retreat. I had several quiet days with plenty of time to read and think. (Heschel – *Man Is Not Alone*, Pieper, on *Prudence*,

The Secret of the Golden Flower, and *Villages in the Sun* (Chandon) – to get some ideas about everyday life in Mexico.)

Everyone was very nice in the hospital – I liked the Sisters and the nurses were good kids, all of them with a very good spirit of joy and charity.

Friday, I spent the whole day at Carmel and talked at length with Mother Angela. Somehow it was helpful and comforting and I felt refreshed and appeased after the talk – whereas talking to others wearied and frustrated me, since it did not seem possible to say much that made sense – or came from very deep. With two of the Sisters at St. A's I had talked about problems of religious life and noviceship, etc. – more or less business – with Mother A. is was deeper and from the heart. It is a long time since I have been able to simply open my heart to anyone and fully share confidences, on both sides, like that. I cannot remember how long – It was an unexpected grace. She is all for Mexico and will pray much for the trip.

Mass at Carmel Friday was tremendous – alone in the church with a nun answering hidden behind the grille and the silent presence of the others, unseen. *Animus + Anima* – Adam and Eve. Man divided and seeking unity in the Sacrifice of Christ the Lord. I was deeply stirred by it. Votive Mass of St. John of the Cross (The Proper Carmelite Mass).

Got back in the evening and Suzuki's article had arrived – very fine, with striking intuitions on emptiness, on the Fall, etc.

Fr. Tresmontant says *"C'est au niveau politique que se posent les problèmes moraux les plus graves."* ["The gravest moral problems are found at the political level."] Never was this more true than in our time. Hence the importance of political decisions – and of taking sides in crucial and "prophetic" affairs which are moral touchstones – and in which Xstians are often in large numbers on the side of the unjust and the tyrant.

Problem of atomic bomb. How many Christians have taken a serious and effective stand against atomic warfare? How many theologians have striven to *justify* it?

October 30, 1959

"C'est au niveau politique qu'apparaissent en plein vue les options morales fondamentales de l'homme, et c'est au niveau des principes moraux que se fondent les choix politiques. Si la terme de morale déplaît aujourd'hui, disons qu'une certaine option, en ce qui concerne l'homme – soit amour et respect de l'homme, soit mépris de l'homme – se trouve à la racine des engagements politiques. Le fait qu'une

*morale naturelle soit possible, permet aux hommes, croyants et incroyants, de s'as-
socier pour une oeuvre commune de justice sans référence explicite à la Révélation.
Inversement, l'infidélité à leur doctrine, à la Parole de Dieu, permet à ceux qui
font le mal dans la Loi de s'associer avec ceux qui font le moral sans la Loi. Les
hommes se distinguent essentiellement par cette option fondamentale, radicale,
faite dans le secret de leur coeur, plus que par le titre extérieur arboré.*" ["It is at
the political level that the fundamental moral options appear in plain view
and it is at the level of moral principles that one makes political choices. If
moral language is despised today in speaking of certain human choices – be
it love and respect for men or contempt for them, one finds, at root, political engagements. The fact that a natural morality may be possible, allows
men, believers and unbelievers alike, to join the common work of justice
without reference to Revelation. Conversely, infidelity to doctrine, to the
Word of God, permits those who do evil to associate themselves with those
who do evil without the Law. Men essentially distinguish themselves by
their fundamental choices, radical ones, made in the secrets of their heart
and not merely by some externally flaunted title."] *C. Tresmontant.*

November 2, 1959

A lovely afternoon full of noise. Reading after dinner – snatches from the
Dhammapada – I thought of this clear sky and how it must be like a Mexican sky.

And now, noise everywhere. Hammers all over the roof of the East Wing
– (you could hardly hear the hebdomadary at Sext and None or your own
conscience at the examen) – the buzz saw cutting hickory for the smoke
house. Novices kicking pigs. A huge road-grader sent by the politicians,
roaring up and down significantly on the day before elections. ("Get out
the vote," says Dom J. "Show them that we have power!")

And in the world, the terrible noise over Charlie Van Doren.[54] A sordid
and silly affair which embarrasses everyone and no one with any sense even
wants to read or hear about it. Poor Mark – and all of them.

Nothing has been heard from anyone. Empty mailbox. I know Dom J.
heard something from the General but if it had anything to do with my indult he shows no sign of it.

Sick of writing, sick of letters, sick of self-expression.

[54] The son of Mark Van Doren; he had been implicated in a television quiz show scandal.

Silence and solitude and peace.

Even if everything else is noise, I can be silent within my own house.

Every time I go to Chapter such ties as still bind me to Gethsemani are weakened still more.

Read a little about the Indians who make lacquer at Patzcuaro. The night of All Souls is a great night on the Island of Juntzio (Sybille Akins' photographs of the Indian women sitting with candles on the graves, with food).

Hurray, the buzz saw has broken down.

November 3, 1959

As to voting – at first I was not going to vote at all, then decided to let the decision spring out of "emptiness" – so found myself waiting all alone for the car outside the gatehouse at about 7:45 when the day was at its most beautiful. The ride to New Haven was lovely. There was hardly anyone at the polls in the school gymnasium.

Since the monks had been "instructed" ("only a suggestion") to vote straight Democrat in order to "be on the bandwagon" I decided to vote straight Republican in order not to be on the bandwagon.

Soon after I got back the sky clouded over and the day became chilly and dismal – so at least I went at the best time.

Saw the Christmas folder advertising our cheese and hams, etc. It is revolting – at least the copy is. "Many porkers are called but few are chosen to produce our luscious hams . . ." A few words like that are enough to say all that needs to be said about what has happened to this monastery.

Machines roaring up and down the road, picking up the dirt left by the other machines yesterday. Noise with the compliments of the politicians, glad to have us on their bandwagon, and especially on Election Day.

The day has been completely vile – cold with rain.

Denis de Rougemont: The Western Quest – seeking to resolve the antimony inherent in personal life – an antimony which came into conscious currency after Nicea.

No solution in trying to combine individualism and collectivism in equal parts –

Seeking refuge in one or other extreme = sabotage.

Greek individualism and atomism – or Roman collectivism?

Christian faith and vocation rose above both.

A Crusoe, says DeR, has no real freedom because the tension, the antinomy is lacking. (But Crusoe is a myth.)

Complete absorption in collectivity – also empty of freedom.

Mixture of the two tendencies *does not create personal tension.*

This point is important – and new for me.

"Whoever will not involve himself in the social matter and whoever yields to tyranny are accomplices . . . Those two absconders from the Person, those two fugitives from vocation, are for the same reason saboteurs of the West. They alone, by increasing in number, are capable of getting history stuck in the mud, and putting an end to the Western odyssey of the Spirit." Man's Western Quest, *p. 61.*

"Those antinomies (Liberty and Service) cannot be resolved except thanks to faith in love, and by absolute obedience to a transcendent vocation; failing which the person remains a pure possibility, or the ideal remnant of a tension exposed either to setback or to rupture, whenever one of its poles weakens or suddenly suffers itself to be absorbed by the other."

id. [Man's Western Quest] *p. 40.*

Fr. Alberic left yesterday, in great confusion.

November 4, 1959

"*Les camps de concentration, les massacres, les tortures . . . nous rappelent quelle est l'essence du paganisme: Le mépris de l'homme que l'on sacrifie sans pitié aux mythes et aux intérêts.*" ["Concentration camps, massacres, tortures . . . reveal to us the essence of paganism: contempt for human beings who are sacrificed without pity for the sake of myths and ideologies."]   *Tresmontant. p. 125.*

De Rougemont traces personalism to the Council of Nicea. The *concept* yes. Tresmontant is right in showing how the Old Testament is in reality the first great charter of human rights – in opposition to all the other religious codes for which the individual does not count. But is this exaggerated? What about Confucius? Aman-enope?

November 8, 1959

"*La sainteté est d'abord solitude et déchirement. Il faut quitter une communauté où le mal est installé dans les moeurs, dans les systèmes de 'valeurs' et des juge-*

ments collectifs: c'est 'le monde.'" ["Sanctity is, above all, solitude and a letting go. One is compelled to separate from a community where evil lives in the mores, in the value system, in collective judgments. It is 'The World.'"]

Tresmontant. p. 157.

"La morale authentique consiste précisément à surmonter la 'morale' tribale qui n'est rien d'autre qu'une immoralité collective." ["Authentic morality consists precisely in abandoning tribal 'morality' which is nothing but collective immorality."] *id. [Tresmontant. p. 157].*

Yet of what Laurens Van der Post says about the Bushmen. Tribal morality *degenerated* into collective immorality.

T. says very convincingly that perhaps original sin is not sin which society inherited from one individual, but sin which each individual contracts from society (Adam = man in the collective sense).

Very important idea that one must break with the exterior, "tribal," mechanical and collective society to which one is passively subject, and isolate oneself in order to be actively united in a *spiritual* community which transcends national, social, and especially tribal limitations.

It is clear that fidelity to God for me *cannot* be equated with passive acceptance of the social conventions and prejudices that are part and parcel of life in this community and even go so far as to make up its "spirit." Fidelity demands a break with this kind of conventionalism. It has to be clear and definite.

November 10, 1959

Finished De Rougemont and Tresmontant, two fine books, especially the latter.

I cannot escape the fact that the stagnation of my prayer life here – especially in community exercises like Conventual Mass, is due to deep involvement in the collective sin of American society and American Catholicism – a sin of which we all refuse to be aware. How offer to God prayer as an act of justice when I am living in injustice? An injustice which pervades the whole world and is even greater in the camp of those who can see that we are exploiters. They are worse. The People of God are the poor of the world, in Africa, Asia, Latin America . . .

Rev. Father must by now be fully aware of my application for the indult. Says nothing but smiles very sweetly. And engineers God knows what opposition to it. The other day he tried very hard to get out of giving me a conscience matter letter which had come from Ernesto Cardenal, at Cuernavaca.

I don't expect anything from Rome for at least another three weeks – towards the end of the month. But Sunday, Day of Recollection, saw that it is really getting close now. I am still very busy, too busy, with writing. Typing uselessly perhaps – and compulsively to clean up work that remains to be done. Felt it was necessary to prepare a new edition of *A Balanced Life of Prayer*[55] since the old had run out. Perhaps I should have simply let it die. Yet I am dissatisfied with the edition of 8 years ago.

In town Friday – long wait at Doctor's – the Carmelites were on retreat. Spoke to Fr. Albert, OCD Provincial, who was giving the retreat – about solitude.

Many new books arrive from France. I am too rich in books. Trying to fast a little, at least enough to feel it. Stop getting any more books now.

November 11, 1959

Just read Mark Van Doren's lecture on *Poetry as Knowledge*. He may not be especially fashionable but he is certainly a very good poet and thinks fine. There is even much Zen in it – though not fashionable Zen, and so people can ignore it.

But the true things. All he used to say at Columbia – perhaps that is why I find myself agreeing with everything so completely. Wrote to Charlie to console him for being a scapegoat for the nation's guilt and folly.

Will write to Mark again tomorrow. The wise are not fashionable and that is one sign of their wisdom. So, too, Victor Hammer.

November 15, 1959

Today, Feast of the Dedication of the Church, Father Abbot announced by surprise and without explanation that he is going to Rome tomorrow for an important conference. A complete bombshell – and I have no doubt that one of the main reasons for the trip is my petition to the Congregation. For a while I was secretly angry. It is not going to be easy just sitting here powerless to do anything while he has full power to completely wreck

55 Published by the Abbey of Gethsemani in 1951.

everything by fair means or foul. He is certainly as unscrupulous as any politician can be, and will not stop at anything – as long as it can be made to _appear_ fair. Fr. John of the Cross thinks he is probably going to try to break the Vina election – his candidate did not get the abbotship. What tremendous power to do harm this one man has. Power to wreck people, to make their whole lives miserable and fruitless. To destroy the peace of communities and individuals.

Was going to write another note to Larraona, but perhaps there is no point to it. The embarrassing thing is that there is nothing external I can do that has any point. Just sit still and pray and hope in God. It is one of those occasions when one sees how great a thing is spiritual hope and how much more important than action. I still fully trust that I can get the indult. If I don't get it this time – then later.

Today in the woods I found myself thinking of alternatives. Again, the hermitage here – but it is only a dream. Why am I ready to look for new ways out? More and more the only thing that makes sense is to take the Mexico project not because I like it, but because so far it seems to be most likely to be the Will of God. Not because it seems likely to succeed – but because I think in my heart that I can please God by attempting it. Not dropping it if it seems likely to fail. Staying with it for the love of God and purely for that alone.

For the rest, I am not angry, just tired and disgusted.

I will keep working at my own inconsistencies, my own failings, seek truth, an honest solution – getting out of this immoral and hypocritical mess of a cheese factory – honestly seeking solitude.

November 16, 1959

It is the twenty first anniversary of my baptism celebrated in tribulation. Not the sorrows of Job, just the weariness of struggling with my own resentments and frustration.

Had a bad hour last night, lying in bed awake, wondering how it would ever be possible to fully and interiorly obey if this plan fails. If it is unjustly suppressed because F. Abbot has plenty of dollars and is respected in Rome (And, I thought, no doubt _suadente diabolo_ [by diabolical persuasion], how much his dollars and his prestige are after all indirectly the fruit of my own work. It was a galling thought!).

Confession – since I am weak and selfish and stupid, obedience is for me a very complicated matter, unfortunately. And the question "Can I obey?" is involved in so many ambivalences of which I am not entirely aware. Just know that there is "something wrong" and that my motives are not what they appear to be.

Only if I am *completely sincere* can I do what seems to be the right thing – that is be firm and definite about seeking a solitary life in Mexico and yet accept delays, obstacles, and even apparent failure without impatience.

Yet there is no avoiding the obligation and the honor of obedience. What matters is the purification of my motives and understanding of it. Not to obey as I have obeyed before, simply because it was the thing to do – but in full freedom. Seeing it from *above*. But I am underneath it, pressed down, and smothered by it. Yet so too was Christ in the Garden. But He must not become a pretext for interior evasion of the real issue.

Defeatism is a great temptation. God preserve me.

November 18, 1959

Yesterday it dawned on me with certainty that when Rev. Father said he had been *summoned* to Rome by the General he meant just that. Obviously there is much more to it than I thought Sunday. I can hardly doubt that it has something to do with this exclaustration. But the other day, I understand, Fr. Sylvanus got a communication from Fr. Larraona. Now due to Dom James' invitation in 1952 or whenever Fr. S. came here. S. made his solemn vows as a Benedictine in Argentina *planning to leave* and come here. The vows may have been invalid and Rev. Fr. may have been summoned to Rome to explain. If that is the case, then things are very favorable as far as my own petition is concerned.

On the other hand, it may be something entirely different.

I feel rather sorry for Rev. Father – he is not well and the trip will be hard on him. And he has to go to California in December – the blessing is on the 12th. When I was angry I had some hard thoughts. However, he may still be in a position to block everything.

Wrote to Ernesto Cardenal.

Today Fr. Sylvanus made me a sign that Fr. Larraona is one of eight new cardinals just created by John XXIII. That is very auspicious, I suppose. But auspicious or not, I am glad of it. He is 72 and has worked very hard for all of us. I was very impressed by him when I met him in 1953.

There were 4 articles in the *Louisville Courier* about our retreats and a lot of remarks about Fr. John of the Cross but he refuses to show them to me.

———

Very cold. 18 above this morning. Am tired of my foolish efforts to clean up writing work, yet I go on with them. Not very energetically this week. Yesterday had a good day of recollection in the cold.

Louis Massignon and his Seven Sleepers.[56] Very interesting documents and pictures, with a totally new perspective. How different from the kind of arid Catholicism represented by the new shrine of Our Lady they finally dedicate in Washington this Friday. The blank splendor of what is expensive and big and expressionless. Official architecture, with a face so neutral that it could be Wall Street or Soviet, indifferently. It frightens me a little.

All the Gehl forage boxes lined up in the woodshed – and disks and drills and combines. No more splitting wood, we buy our wood. The novices almost never get to the woods. All cheese and ham in the "Farm Products Building." I suppose all that is more or less inevitable, in the situation here.

The other day, a beautiful, unforgettable, winter wren, running like a mouse all over the pile of logs, and his song as beautiful and pure as Thoreau said it was – as "pure as ice" but not cold either. Winter wrens are much more lovely than the Carolinas of which I am tired = they bicker and cuss all the time and strike me as rather gross, compared with the winter wrens. Beautiful stars at night, the great icy M of Cassiopeia's chain, and down on the horizon the red winking eye of Redebaran.

November 19, 1959

A good letter from Charles Van Doren about his predicament and confusion. He suffers very much – was really very guileless in his "deception" and is now face to face for the first time with deception as *responsibility* after he has already made it, objectively, a reality. Having deceived, he is learning painfully that it is possible for him to deceive. He paid no attention to what he was doing, because the game was so much fun and after all, so real. He was honest in his deception because he knew what people liked in him was really there: and I don't suppose he regarded the rest of it as a deception. Now he is learning. He told me a tremendous story about the Christianis and Lax – and how much they love Lax.

---

[56] A sixth-century Byzantine hagiographical legend about saints who slept through a persecution and awoke, after two hundred years, to find their city of Ephesus a Christian one. Louis Massignon was a French scholar of Islamic and Arabic studies.

I have a koan to work on: "Who is this that wants to go to Mexico?"

I wonder what is going on in Rome?

Get clear about motives – or rather, write them down:

1. I really want to live alone in simplicity and devote myself to thought and prayer.

2. No *typewriter.*

3. Strictly selected books – about 100. Especially hope to work on *Philokalia.*

4. Renounce all *comfort*, the *reputation*, the *security*, the American friendships which bind me here and make me part of the collective falsity and injustice of this society. Renounce this kind of cenobitism.

Hence, to offer to God the hardship and poverty, the obscurity, perhaps unpopularity, the loneliness, the estrangement, the unfamiliarity, the fear and perhaps even the dangers of a new life.

God, I beg you, give me the grace to wholeheartedly embrace all hazards, risks, and insecurities trusting in You, and to do without all false support I have gained here.

To cease to be famous and let myself be forgotten, very gladly.

Deliberately. Concentrate on this. Emphasize it. Remember it every day and act accordingly otherwise I will be back where I started.

Three books to finish correcting and proofreading and that's all – the future, if it wants another, will have to say how six or seven years from now.

A   The Essays – and Xstian Life of Prayer.

B   Existential Communion

C   Inner Experience (?).

Send a few Kerygmas to friends.

Break useless contacts.

November 21, 1959. F. of the Presentation

Yesterday – stupid and distracted, or rather just stupid.

At first wanted to write some more on "The Xstian Life of Prayer" but simply could not write another word.

Preferred finally to stay quiet, and set aside a few books to take where I go.

Today, distracted during the night thinking of the very good pictures Sybille took – and to whom I might send them. Which shows how deeply I am mixed up in nonsense.

But after Mass, suddenly it dawned on me, – the first real ray of the sun – that I will soon actually be going to fulfill a very ancient and very deep desire. It is still difficult to believe. The first stirring before a man awakens from a long sleep – a long, long sleep.

November 23, 1959

After dinner, looked out at the hills and woods and realized with a shock that perhaps within two weeks I will have seen them for the last time in my life.

This thing is like death, but it must be so.

It hardly seems possible – never seeing the woods again. Other woods will not be the same. The strangeness, the exile, the essential. I must be quite determined about that and not let myself be held prisoner emotionally by the soft embrace of this "mother" – this silent, gentle, circle of hills that has comforted me for eighteen years and whose secrets I have come to know perhaps better than anyone here (so many of the monks hardly know there is a forest around the abbey).

That is the one thing that will really hurt. Making up my mind, adjusting my mind to this requires real determination, in the psalms especially. But it is a necessary "death," a detachment from one of the few things I really love deeply and purely.

Realized too how much I have in many ways failed here, failed in love. I have been weak in love and have broken with the community gradually because I did not have the strength to love it with all its faults and with all my faults – all my faults that necessarily come out in this cramped and unnatural situation.

Yet I prefer to die this way before dying in truth.

I would hate to die in this monastery. It would be a complete surrender to mediocrity. But of course it doesn't matter where you die, actually. Yet I do love the community, inarticulately, after all. It is better for them also that I leave here.

Supposing Rev. Father has to resign and there is an election? I don't have to worry about that though for I shall certainly refuse. Fr. John of the Cross thinks I was elected in the early balloting in California (as I was also at Genessee) and Rev. Fr. explained that I would refuse the election.

It is very fortunate that I made that vow.[57]

---

[57] In 1952, Merton made a private vow never to seek or accept election to be abbot.

Today I finished editing and correcting the *The New Man*[58] (Existential Communion) written in five weeks in 1954 (during the Fall vacation) it is certainly one of the works with which I am most satisfied – though it was "unfinished." Providentially. It had gone as far as it needed to go. I can think of few other books of mine that I would have been able to read through from cover to cover after a five year interval.

Tomorrow, to Louisville, to see the Dr. again – and to say Mass for the Feast of St. John of the Cross at Carmel.

November 25, 1959

Yesterday, in town, said the Mass of St. John of the Cross at Carmel, one of the side altars. They had the Blessed Sacrament exposed for 40 Hours.

I was tucked in an alcove like a hermitage.

Downtown, after the doctor let me go (I got out very quickly) I went and made inquiries at the Eastern Airline office and then went to the cathedral. After I had been there for a while, a Mass began (at noon) – and this I regarded as a special grace.

Spent the afternoon at Carmel. Talked too much to Mother Angela.

Drove home in the evening – cold – long blue streaks of clouds over the pale West, behind bare trees.

Outside Carmel about two, a little boy from St. Agnes school was hit by a car. I did not learn of it immediately but went out about ten minutes after the event. He was not badly hurt but lay in the road with a blanket around him, surrounded by people, awaiting the ambulance.

He was in no danger. I gave him a blessing. But a split second after I touched his forehead his whole being lit up and stirred with joy and his eyes shone with faith. It was very beautiful, the response and the stirring of the child, knowing he had been blessed by God. The thought of it stays with me as the most truly beautiful thing of that day.

Otherwise, I talked too much, too much, and not well.

Learning unhappy sidelights on Dom James.

We get back late and I learned he was coming home last night.

Since then I have been depressed.

[58] Published by Farrar, Straus & Cudahy in 1952.

November 28, 1959

It is the Saturday before Advent and since last night there has been snow on the ground.

Thursday I went to talk to Rev. Father, after his return from Rome and learned only that he had seen Larraona and was under instructions from the General not to say anything to anybody about what had taken place.

Though I am no wiser than I was before, the whole atmosphere of the conversation was a relief. Rev. Father, though at first there was some sign of strain and possible resentment whenever my "case" came up, seems generally relaxed and detached and I gather that he is now happy with the unconcern of one who has shifted an unpleasant problem on to the shoulders of higher superiors. This is a great relief to me also because we can now go ahead more objectively, without animosity and resentment. I think my relations with him have never been better and I am very glad of that fact.

It seems evident that the case is close to being settled and I have definite hopes that it will be settled in my favor, I hope soon. The only thing now is *waiting*.

I have no urge to write, little desire for anything except silence and prayer.

Went over last night to interview a postulant, a man in his forties – Tom O'Brien – who turns out to have been the pilot that instructed John Paul[59] in the RAF. We had a talk about him this morning.

December 2, 1959

Adjutor et liberator meus es tu, Domine, ne moveris! [O Lord, you are my helper and liberator. Do not abandon me!]

Though I am impatient at waiting, still I know that I need to wait. Every day that I wait is a better beginning of a preparation. Though there are many things that distract me from one thing that is important.

The preface to the maxims of St. John of the Cross which Fr. Albert wanted for his Carmelites in Wheeling. Today, proofs of the Spiritual Orientation book from the monks of St. John's.[60]

---

[59] Merton's brother who was killed in the war.
[60] *Spiritual Direction and Meditation*, published by Liturgical Press in 1960.

Yesterday, anniversary of the death of Charles de Foucauld – mass partly for his canonization – partly for my Mexican intention – partly for the novices.

Today – visit with the Wassermans and their friends. Could hardly talk. Yet talking too is a preparation – I will have to meet new people, temporarily, before settling down in solitude.

The big reasons for solitude: the true perspectives – leaving the "world" – even the monastic world with its business, vanities, superficiality. More and more I see the necessity of leaving my own ridiculous "career" as a religious journalist. Stop writing for publication – except poems and creative meditations.

Solitude – witness to Christ – emptiness.

Apophthegmata [Sayings of the Desert Fathers] in *P[atrologia] G[raeca]*. [Paolo] Guistiniani again.

Tomorrow, F. of St. Galgan, hermit whom the Cistercians appropriated by putting the habit on him after he was dead!

Knowles on the English mystics. How much I love the 14th. century and how truly it is my own century, the one whose spirit is most mine, in many ways, or so I like to think (Rolle – The Cloud of Unknowing – etc.).

Heard today of the death of F. C. Doherty, Headmaster of Oakham.[61]

December 5, 1959
These have been very dark days.

I thought that the indult would very probably arrive this week and was entertaining hopes of going down on the Feast of the Immaculate Conception or perhaps on the 12th (Our Lady of Guadalupe).

No sign of anything.

Instead of that, Thursday Rev. Father told me blandly that a conscience letter from Ernesto Cardenal had arrived but that he would not give it to me. Instead, he would send it back to Mexico.

It was nice of him to tell me. I assume this is the strategy worked out in Rome together with the General.

I reflect ruefully that after Rev. Fr. went to Rome I was foolishly sorry for him, and at the turmoil he had to take!

[61] Oakham was Merton's boarding school in England.

In effect, I am powerless in trying to get my case past two very astute and ruthless politicians, all the more ruthless because of their complete and unshakable self-righteousness. It is to them *absolutely inconceivable* that I have the slightest right to seek any other form of life.

This is the terrible thing. This whole attitude towards religion – a concept which is completely bound up with an unconscious, ingrained social prejudice – prejudice in favor of all that is firmly established, the entrenched privilege of money, the unchangeable holiness of power.

I am therefore kept from seeking any kind of a personal ideal by a man who is convinced of his own rightness just as he is completely convinced of the rightness of Wall Street and big business, *Time* and *Life*, the Spellman and Sheen type of Catholicism etc. etc. Anything else is to him *inconceivable*, and for one to seek a primitive, non-American, eremitical kind of life is simple folly. (Oh yes, he can conceive *Carthusians* all right. Well established. Firmly entrenched. And I saw a full page ad for *Chartreuse* in colors, from a big French magazine. Big picture of the bottle, coming out of the Grand Chartreuse – little picture of a Carthusian looking into a test-tube.)

At times I feel fear that all the life is going to be inexorably squeezed out of me by this pious system, which, of course, I *must* obey, to which I *must* conform since I have vows. I really am beginning to understand the psalms, about the temptation to despair that beset the poor and the oppressed. To see what is evidently wrong or less good, triumph without difficulty while ideals of truth are crushed. There is no greater pain. Of course, it can always be said: "What is wrong with the setup, after all?" And if you look at it from a certain perspective – that of my abbot – you see no wrong in it at all. Nothing but good. I have rarely met anyone so completely comfortable in his acceptance of his own chosen delusions about life. Outside in the world – "power, pleasure, and popularity." In the monastery – "the cross." They laugh – we suffer. And because we suffer, we are close to Jesus. But they don't laugh. They suffer and have more anguish than we do, even in their pleasures. We – vegetate and dream and sell cheese and get involved in petty projects.

He said – the other day: "Here – no visible results, just chapter of faults," etc. etc. In the cheese building they are all shouting about orders coming in. Chapter of faults? What about Charlie Van Doren?

Wrote to Daniélou.

I still have hopes and sometimes strong ones. One must have courage to hope – dare to rouse hopes that might be dashed. Yet – not rouse them to such a pitch that they have to become delusions. Hope more in God than in a particular fulfillment if that appears to be willed by him.

Hope in Our Lady.

Today at Mass I thought: If I have Her, nothing else matters. But it does matter because this desire for solitude is part of my love for her, her will for me.

December 6, 1959. Sunday – Day of Recollection

Decisions of the General Chapter read publicly today. The solemnity with which we make big decisions about nothing.

One prayer at the Office of the Dead rather than three. One minister at Mass on Feasts of 3 lessons (a good decision). You can mention the president, along with the pope, in the prayer *Pietate*. Dom Deodat de Wilde is Procurator General but without the title of P.G. and in a year they will give him the title of Abbot, of some non-existent abbey, so that he will have "more influence" on the Holy See. Our whole religious life is made up of these fictions, which are symbols and symptoms that no one knows how to read. And yet the general tittering in the Chapter room indicates *something* – if only a refusal to think about it seriously. Which implies at least a germinating realization that there is something to think about.

And then, mind you, the bull is sick and has to have an operation.

The amount of energy we waste in marking time. The monastic treadmill – to imagine we are escaping from something and going somewhere. If only we used this all for some purpose – or even for *no* purpose, instead of an imaginary purpose. The delusion is the terrible thing. *"Divertissement?"*

I am assured that the sales of cheese and hams will run into six figures. Into the hundreds of thousands. Now the brothers have to work overtime, from Prime (early) until supper (late). And all this for a project that is supposed to make us plenty of money so that we will never have to work overtime – so that we will be rich enough for the leisure of contemplation. The leisure of contemplation cannot be bought with money. In the old days when we husked corn overtime through October and November, on those beautiful afternoons, we had leisure *while we worked*. But it didn't make any money. I think that what we want is not leisure, not contemplation, but purely and simply, money. We are monks who want to get rich.

But no, that is not quite it. We do not want to be rich. But we want to be successful, secure, "prosperous." It is not the money we want, but the feeling that we can make plenty of money any time we want to!

We want to be a going concern. To produce for profit.

Before the Bl. Sacrament. I thought first of all of nothing – just the Kyrie of the African Missa Luba. And the people of Africa. The fighting in Rwanda.

Later I thought of my life in the Order and how if I had been a good boy and had played ball with everybody I would by now be an abbot or at least a definitor – and I am very glad that I have been what I have been, namely a non-conformist and a non-participant who clearly prefers being alone in the woods, to anything a monastery has to offer. This much of my life makes sense.

Finally, I asked myself and the Lord if I were really being sincere or if there were some change asked of me: namely to change back to cenobitic ideals (if I ever had any) – and the only thing that came out of it was the word *"qui Spiritu Dei aguntur, ii sunt filii Dei."* ["Those who act with the Spirit of God are the children of God."] – And that I should listen for "follow the Holy Spirit." I cannot conceive that the Holy Spirit is behind this big cheese business, though He is certainly not stopped by it.

In the end, with renewed hope (against hope) I am simply going along on the path that has been pointed out to me though I do not even know if there is a path any more.

Fidelity to the Holy Spirit is the great thing. More trust and peace, less agitation and worry. God can and does do the impossible. I must be without fear and without doubt. And keep on going. Not fighting the abbot (I realized only *après coup* ["after the fact"] that the conscience matter letter to Daniélou was in fact a way of "getting" the abbot for stopping Cardenal's letter. And it did upset him, too).

Read a bit of Voillaume on the poverty of the Little Brothers. Finished Neal Breman's excellent book *The Making of a Moon*.

December 7, 1959

We no longer have Vigil of the Immaculate Conception in the Liturgy. A pity – I miss all the Vigils. Why on earth were they suddenly suppressed?

Said a Votive Mass of Our Lady – for my Mexican intention (recently, quite unusual, I have received a few stipends for my own intentions).

Non erit impossible apud Deum omne verbum. [No word is impossible with God.]

These words in the Gospel struck me today. I should remember them much more. Nothing could be more eloquent for me now than this Advent Liturgy!

Ecce apparebit Dominus et non mentietur: si moram fecerit expecta eum quia veniet et non tardabit, alleluia. [Behold the Lord will come and He does not dissemble. If He tarries wait for Him for He will come and will not delay. Alleluia.]

December 8, 1959. F. of the Immaculate Conception

The Advent liturgy is all speaking apparently of time and of hope for a temporal fulfillment. And yet our hope is not for anything in time, but for the inception of a whole new dimension – extra and supra temporal – into our living eternity. Berdyaev shows that the reign of Antichrist will be, precisely, a total tyranny of mere *duration*, of time in its most external and fictitious sense, in which the present is consistently being devoured by the future – which does not exist. Problem of hope (memory) to establish a right relationship between the past and the future, which give spiritual solidity to the *present*. Dimension of depth, comes from contemplative historical consciousness. This is the key to what has been inviting me to enter for a long time; question of the fact of history in contemplative life.

Grasp of God in the present, as the One who has revealed Himself in the past and holds, in His mystery, the promise of His mercy for the future. When? This we need not ask.

Berdyaev's *Meaning of History* made up of lectures given in Russia right after the Revolution, before he was kicked out, is one of his most important books. The power of his prophetic insight is especially evident here. He really has the best (spiritual) understanding of the mystery of our time. At the same time sees the futility of expecting a real fulfillment in time, and yet affirms most strongly man's creative duty to respond to God in time, even though his response will in the long run be doomed to temporal failure and extinction. But it is *not lost* – it is recovered in eternity.

He demands of man a *"fervent will to miracle and (to) the organic spiritual transfiguration of life."*

Another surprise. Someone arranged the High Mass for my intention today. Fr. Abbot seems well aware what the situation was – I resolutely refused to change it in any way except of course to include all the spiritual needs of everyone in the community, especially those who have trouble with the abbot. I know he would have liked me to throw it wide open to the four winds; so that he could pray "against me" but I didn't give him that satisfaction. I would have thought it an act of servility to do so.

Later, I would have liked to write him a long note – but there are so many things you simply cannot say to him. He is one of those people you have to address only in certain terms he wants from you. They can be flippant, absurd, sentimental, conventionally pious and ascetic even "mystical." But not just straight, honest statements of what you really feel.

What would I have said to him today?

"You have the misfortune to be one of those people for whom I have, in my own way, a deep affection. Deep affection, of course, disturbs me, and I am very exacting and difficult with those who claim my affection. Hence my resolute refusal to accept you except on certain very definite terms, and especially since you too are a very demanding friend, and very masochistic about it, too . . . Thus you see that we are bound to get into difficulties, sensitive, subtly aggressive, you under a cloud of sweetness and I behind a curtain of reserve. Certainly it is difficult for us, between us, to arrive at a clear and frank appraisal of the will of God in anything that concerns us both deeply, in a personal way. Hence though you seem to feel that you are the only person capable of directing me at this juncture, and are very hurt because I barely consult you, I on the other hand have reached the conclusion that you are the last person in the world whose direction I would really trust. Though in most things I can obey you there are very few in which I can agree with you, and this agreement is, to you, all important. You do not easily tolerate any differences of opinion and you absolutely refuse to countenance a disagreement on something as fundamental as the question of vocation – or at least of my vocation. You somehow seem to think that I have been, by making vows, become your personal property.

That the mere thought on my part of seeking God in some other way, under some other superior, and in some other situation, in which I might do better, is utterly inconceivable. I repeat – find it *inconceivable* for me and for all your other monks, to seek God in any other way than here, with *you* as their superior. This is one of the many things about my predicament that I feel obliged to question. All the more so since the matter of personal affection enters in. This is what makes it all the more important for me to go elsewhere . . . etc. etc."

In fewer words, he is absolutely not the director and superior that can help me now – if I am at all capable of judging and perhaps I am not. Perhaps also the question is to a great extent irrelevant.

What I did was write him a short note wishing him a happy birthday and a prosperous trip to California, though I must admit during the Mass I prayed for him to have a little light to see himself as his monks see him. I regret it as usual, but perhaps it was worthwhile. At the same time, if I were a superior, I would not be happy at being disliked by a subject as I sometimes dislike him.

It is, of course, Providence that has thrown the two of us together.

Resolved to be more circumspect with Dom G. if I go to Cuernavaca.

December 10, 1959

I have finally gotten around to reading Pieper's fine little book *Leisure, The Basis of Culture.* It is very sound and no amount of guilt should make us treat his view of contemplation as "pagan" as if that were to exclude "Christian." One thing is sure – we do not in this monastery have any faith in the basic value of *otium sanctum* [sacred leisure]. We believe only in the difficult and the unpleasant. That is why we, in practice, *hate* the contemplative life and destroy it with constant activity.

They have speeded up the machines in the cheese building, and everyone is agog with the orders. "I saw one going out to *Mrs. Irving Berlin!*" said one awestruck novice. We have finally justified our existence.

December 12, 1959. Feast of Our Lady of Guadalupe

Foul, rainy day. It was cold and miserable everywhere, including especially the woodshed – reading Coomaraswamy. Working on Isaias for conferences. Preparing a study on primitive Carmelites since Rev. Father very much wanted me to do it for some Carmelite foundation that asked for something. (They didn't ask for this, but it is what they will get) Mount Carmel and the Carmelite deserts. Anyway it is peaceful work.

In the cheese, everyone is ready to go crazy. Machines at top speed (?). People losing their tempers. Silence broken; mad jokes, rush, confusion. One of the novices flew off the handle after Chapter of Faults and my undermaster – suddenly deciding vocations – tried to get me to throw him out.

The best thing – the only sensible thing – I have done in the past few days was to clean out the drawers of our desk. That was pacifying.

Today – another day on which I had hoped to go to Mexico or receive the indult. Can Dom Gregorio have been mistaken? Still, peace – indifference. There is no use in facing my own desires in prayer. To pray for the glory of God and for His kingdom first of all. Detachment. Interior purity. How much I need this preparation. Whatever happens, this will have been good, this purification, this acceptance of the empty mailbox. The thing is to continue to hope and trust in God without breaking my head in prayers and desires. This has all taken me out of the future and brought me back into the present. Which is as it should be.

A Mexican postulant, Justino Gonzalez, entered last week. today he returned to Mexico.

What else has been done during these three weeks of waiting?

Learned a few new _asanas_ [yogic postures]. Rewrote article on solitude.

Wrote a letter about a mixup on Portuegese translation of some booklets.

Wrote a letter to Lax, very poorly. Double talk flaccid.

Have translated a couple of poems of Jorge Carrera Andrade – he is a charming poet. What he writes about Quito in his early poems makes us recapture the awe and joy and absorption in life that I knew that Summer in Sussex, at Rye, etc. The utter wonder of the sky, the quiet town, the marshes and hills, the bells in the tower, the choirboys. He has a wonderful, clear, deeply mystical poem (yet very simple) about the weathercock on Quito Cathedral, which grows on you more and more. A poem of light, simplicity, space, love. I translated it this afternoon. His Franciscan compassion for small things. His sense of life.

Other things – cut my finger before shaving, trying to assemble the safety razor. Hidden aggression, self-hate! Yah! It was a deep cut, too.

Sent out some copies of the Guerric Sermons. What for? I kept saying "Charity."

I try to list all these things – as if I had been doing something else besides looking in the mailbox.

Talked to Fr. Anselm – not seriously. Talked to this one and that one. No one usefully except perhaps Fr. Placid this morning. Everything here tends to be trivial and foolish. And fictional. Like the plan that is now being cooked up to provide some of the young ones with "two years of college" right here at Gethsemani. What a joke! But this is the kind of thing the abbot likes to do – go through some motions, give the motions a *name* – "College" and that's it.

December 17, 1959

Yesterday, when I was least expecting it, a letter arrived from Rome.

It was a large envelope – had come by surface mail. Too large an envelope. I took it back to the novitiate and read it on my knees before the Bl. Sacrament – and it said "No."

It was a long, personal, detailed letter, in fact a very fine letter, signed by the Cardinal Prefect [Valerio Valeri] and countersigned by Card. Larraona. Two cardinals. What could be more definitive and more official – what could be more final?

They were very sorry. They wanted the right words to pour balm in certain wounds. But my departure would certainly upset too many people in the Order, as well as outside it. And they agreed with my superiors that I did not have an eremitical vocation. That therefore what they asked of me was to stay in the monastery where God had put me, and I would find interior solitude.

It was a serious letter, to be taken seriously.

I felt no anger or resistance. The letter was too obvious. It could only be accepted. And this first reaction was one of relief that at last the problem had been settled.

Had to give a conference to the novices, which turned out to be a bit dizzy.

Afterwards had to call Victor Hammer who is coming over on Saturday and he said he had heard in a roundabout way from Cuernavaca that the indult had been *granted*. But I knew this was impossible.

The letter from Rome was dated Dec. 7th.

The thing that strikes me is that the problem is settled, it is settled in some wider and deeper way than just be negation. It is not just that I must stay here.

Sat alone outside after dinner. Very quiet.

Actually it *is* a solution, and I don't yet know how much of a solution.

A kind of anesthesia. Certainly surprised myself by not getting at all upset and feeling the slightest disappointment. Rather, felt only joy and emptiness and liberty. Funny.

Went out alone, in light rain, to get Christmas trees for the nuns.

Who cares about anything? Here or there.

The letter is obviously an indication of God's Will and I accept it fully. So then what? Nothing. Trees, hills, rain. And prayer much lighter, much freer, more unconcerned. A mountain lifted off my shoulders – a Mexican mountain I myself had chosen.

Actually, what it comes down to is that I shall certainly have solitude but only by miracle and not at all by my own contriving. Where? Here or there makes no difference. Somewhere, nowhere, beyond all "where." Solitude outside geography or in it. No matter.

Coming back, walked around a corner of the woods and the monastery swung in view. I was free from it. I remembered the anguish and resentment with which I saw that same view in March, '47, before my solemn profession.

I will, of course, answer the letter, and may take the opportunity to explain that my idea was not simply to "be a hermit" – but it will make no difference.

I woke up at 12, just when I was about to drink a milkshake in a dream. Could not get back to sleep, so went down at 1 for an hour of prayer, in very silent darkness. Empty, silent, free, opening, into nothing – a little point of nothing that alone is real. What do you ask? Nothing. What do you want? Nothing. Very quiet and dark. The Father. The Father.

Nothing. Nothing. Nothing, Nothing. The place where the tooth was pulled is only just beginning to hurt this morning.

December 18, 1959. Evening – before fire watch

Yesterday afternoon, in the rain, cut some more Christmas trees and took a load of them to Bardstown in a dump truck to the hospital. Fr. Callistus drove – a good, simple, and stable monk. It was pacifying to be there and eat a sandwich and drink some ginger ale talking to Sister Clare and Sister Paul Elizabeth. Came home in the dark, Christmas colored lights strung over the saloon at Smith's Corner, rain falling on the forest. It was a happy afternoon and evening and I felt as if I had never thought for a moment of leaving.

A very great peace and gratitude at knowing that I have really, at last, found my definitive place (found it long since) and that I have no further need to look, to seek, except in my own heart. Of course, it would be exciting to start all over again . . . And it is even more satisfying that the new starts have all ended, and that what I said to Fr. Philotheus when I came down here 19 yrs. ago was true and has been realized. What I have said so much in my own writing – as Card. Valeri reminded me. It is impossible to look through my *Selected Poems*[62] and not see that this is where I belong. That I might have had the capacity to be a hermit in Mexico and many other things too makes very little difference. I am nearly 45 and it is time for one to be content with what I am and finish the work I have begun without seeking a new one.

So at last I can simply abandon myself to God – and it is about time.

Today, cut a few Christmas trees for the house, and a big one for the novitiate. It was not quite raining, but cloudy and cold. Walked home alone by the lake near Bardstown road. The loblolly pines planted during my 1955 crisis are growing well. The whole property is dotted with trees I have planted in hours of anguish. The ones I planted in hours of consolation have not succeeded.

Had a good talk with Rev. Father who is tired after coming in late last night from California – and where else? It doesn't matter. I talked about the cheese question, and people and novices, and toasted nuts, and policies and next year's program, and acted in general like a member of the community.

Lax's circus book came, and a pretty little clock from Mother Schroth.

December 20, 1959. IV Sunday Advent
Lax's Circus book is a tremendous poem, an Isaias-like prophecy which has a quality you just don't find in poetry today, a completely unique simplicity and purity of love that is not afraid to express itself. The circus as symbol

---

[62] *Selected Poems of Thomas Merton*, published by New Directions in 1959.

and sacrament, cosmos and church – the mystery of the primitive world, of paradise, in which men have wonderful and happy skills, which they exercise freely, as at play. But also a sacrament of the *eschaton*, our heavenly Jerusalem. The importance of human love in the circus – for doing things well. It is one of the few poems that has anything whatever to say. And I want to write an article about it.

Victor and Carolyn Hammer came over yesterday. We ate sandwiches in the jeep, in a sunny field, near the shallow lake, drank coffee, ate apples and ginger; I lost a filling from a tooth. He came back to see the chapel – I have hopes that he will make a tabernacle for us and candlesticks. He looked at the chapel without inspiration and said, "This is an awful place." A prophetic utterance, quite unlike the words of Jacob used as introit for the feast of the Dedication. But he offered to lend us one of his painted crucifixes – one of those he did for Kolbsheim.

He gave me one of his little Japanese knives. I cleaned up the room in its honor.

Went out alone to get three trees and a small one in the wasteland along by Andy Boone's. In the evening – two postulants to interview.

A sunny, happy day, yesterday.

December 26, 1959. St. Stephen's Day

I had been fearing that this Christmas would be a terrible one like the last one, but it has been quiet and neutral. Interiorly I have been aloof and resigned in all the community nonsense – and also more united with the brethren on a simple human level *without* nonsense. In other words, it is the pretense that kills me and when I can avoid the official myths and pretenses, everything is relatively sane.

On the 22nd – the only sunny day for a long time, but for the one when Victor came over – I went to Lexington to get his crucifix and came back with two of them.

It was cold in the morning. Took more trees to Flaget hospital, then over the winding road through Protestant country – (conscious sense of liberation there) – to Lexington.

Rush to get books from U of K library, and downtown with Dr. Thompson (after meeting his wife) to a bookstore to buy paperbacks. Lunch at Hammers wonderful as usual.

Coming back suddenly decided to go to Shakertown.

The approach from the West, through the big sycamores in the bottom, past a long stone fence, to the old community house on "Pleasant Hill."

Only the guest house was open and at first I found no one there. The marvelous double winding stair going up to the mysterious clarity of a dome on the roof. The empty third floor rooms with names scribbled all over the walls – the usual desecration – quiet sunlight filtering in – a big Lebanon cedar outside one of the windows. Mr. Renfrew came and we spoke – he lamented the lack of water. No one would come because there was no plumbing. Who cares? I said. He said everybody does.

All the other houses are locked up.

There is Shaker furniture only in the center family house. I tried to get in it and a gloomy old man living in the back told me curtly "it was locked up." He was putting water in a bucket from a pump in the yard. No plumbing, you see!

Mr. R. dug out of an untidy roll top desk a copy of the *Sacred Roll*, the Shaker bible, full of inspirations, which I have only glanced at. But borrowed and brought home.

The empty fields, the big trees – how I would love to explore those houses and listen to that silence. In spite of the general decay and despair there is joy there still and simplicity.

The Shakers fascinate me. Mother Ann Lee thought she was Sophia. The role of the sexes in their mysticism. The pure, entranced, immaculate dancing, shaking the sex out of their hands. And the whirling. God, at least they had the sense to *dance*. I want to study them.

I thought when I got home at night and went to bed I would have prophetic dreams. Dreamt only of a colored boy who had come from very far away to be my friend. Whatever else I dreamed, I have forgotten.

Joe and I ate supper in Springfield, and got home at bed time with the crucifixes, having taken a strange winding road and passed St. Rose in the darkness.

Christmas – the usual mad and silly decorations, and the carols in which I did not become involved at all. Played some austere Ambrosian and Byzantine chants to the novices and went for a walk in the darkening woods alone. Only one carol bowled me over – the first played in the refectory – ancient and pure.

Rejoice, rejoice Emmanuel
Has come to thee o Israel!

It struck the depths of my heart and this morning I suddenly awoke with it loud in my head – at 1:45. I got up and went down as if it were a call and prayed in the very dark, silent church for half an hour, before the bell rang.

December 29, 1959. F. of the Holy Innocents

Fr. Tarcisius preached in chapter and quoted (without identification) from Dostoevsky about God receiving all the sinners who did not think they were worthy. And he said if someone came to the monastery and said there were three million dollars hidden in a hill in the woods next to our property, would not the abbot sign everything away to get that hill? No, said the abbot – after the sermon, the monastery is worth at least ten million dollars.

Two days I have inwardly said no to all the Abbot's preening exhortations after Chapter sermons – not because they are wrong in themselves but because they are all implicitly summations to conform with the party-line which is that this life is a life of great suffering and heroism and therefore most noble and exalted. To prove this he would insistently repeat over and over again things that cause the kind of suffering that is caused by acute boredom. As if to say grimly: You do not agree that this is a life of suffering? At least, I can hold you here and bore you, because I have the power. But you do not have the power to make me think it is not boring – Yes! I have the power to make you resent and resist it: that is all I ask. In this way, he generally gets what he wants in the end: opposition. And that is where I am silly. I still think "no" has a meaning. Actually, this life is made up of situations in which both yes and no are equally nonsense, and all that is lacking is to see (as I now see in the woodshed) that there is nothing lacking.

Beautiful sun on the cedars over there. Pale blue sky, watery clouds, rushing of creeks, there has been continual rain, now ended.

Bro. Antoninus sent his poems. "Gnarled" said Rexroth of them. All clutches, rugged, bitter, really powerful. A puritan, a medieval Englishman, too, Anglo-Saxon words, a poet of heavy substantial texture and full religious feeling. Feeling about sin. Reaction, disgust. Healthy fighting against the sickness of falsity everywhere.

In some poems, like "Gethsemani," he spills it out too long, spins it too thin. The monastery poems, with him as with me, are the poorer ones.

The first conversion poems better. Yet, the last one, a return to Christmas, Phoenix, one of the best. The Magi too, very fine. He is a first class poet, if that means anything. Very glad of his book. He printed it, signed it, sent it to me. I will write to him.

Read some of Peguy's "Mystery of the Holy Innocents" to the novices last evening. And alone in the woodshed on St. Stephen's day some Emily Dickinson, my own flesh and blood, my own kind of quiet rebel, fighting for truth against catchwords and formalities, fighting for independence of the spirit, maybe mistakenly, what the hell, maybe rightly too. Who else, in Amherst in 1859, said anything worth being remembered? Said anything that remains living and natural now.

The great thing Emily D. has done, and very great – she has hidden and refused herself completely to everyone who would not appreciate her and accept her on her own terms. Yet who "knew" and "saw" her. But she gave herself completely to people of other ages and places who never saw her, but who could receive her gift anyway, regardless of space and time. It is like hugging an angel.

December 31, 1959

The last night of the year. Presently, a *Miserere* and a *Te Deum*.

I do not look back on the year. I do not look forward to the next one. I do not bother to step over an imaginary threshold.

Got permission today for a few sessions with Dr. Wygal in Louisville – since I am sure Rev. Father's argument before the Congregation was based on a couple of wild remarks by Zilboorg that I was likely to take off with a woman and leave the church, etc. So it would do no harm to find out if I am just suffering from neurotic instability or what. I do not think I am.

Some books on Shakertown came from U. of K. library today.

Interesting book by Paul Radin on *Philosophy of Primitive Man*. Also Merleau-Ponty and Cornford on the early Greek philosophers.

There is a possibility we might be able to have some special meetings here – two groups of specially invited retreatants, say one of Protestant, one of Orthodox theologians. I mentioned this in passing and Rev. Father seemed willing to permit it. Perhaps it is possible to do here some of things I wanted to do in Mexico.

If perhaps Wygal can prove that there is no danger in my being out on my own, Rome might revise its opinion on the Mexican project. But I don't look forward to anything or pin my hopes on anything special.

For the New Year – renew Cistercian studies – take Cistercian history with the novices.

January 1, 1960

Last evening at Benediction I was over in the transept and Fr. Eudes the weekly reader did not show up so I was roped in as deacon for Benediction. Got the tabernacle key mixed up with the rosary in my pocket and couldn't find it.

The illusion of a New Year . . . will it be better than the last, etc.

Nunc est dies salutis. [Now is the day of salvation.]

In any case I can do here more or less, as far as I can, what I would have wanted to do in Mexico. The attitude of the abbot seems to be that as long as I am in this monastery he doesn't care much what I do. So I can concentrate on solitude, prayer, and meditation, reading and study, such work as I have for souls – primarily the novices and then maybe retreats for special groups. What is lacking in me?

From Merleau-Ponty on Pseudo-scientific Marxism (*Sens et non-sens,* p. 223).

Most intelligent papers I have yet read on Marxism and religion (225–26) – and the most challenging. Religion a symbolic structure, not mere meaningless verbalism, symbolizing relations between men, communion which it "cannot attain" – and which the revolution can attain. This is the thesis that has to be judged and which is judged by history itself.

Existential movement of history – not "scientific" laws or operations but the movement of alienated man "to take possession of himself and of the world."

Quotes Marx as saying – one must above all avoid setting up society again as abstraction "face to face with the individual."

Moving force of history *"l'homme engagé"* – *moteur de la dialectique.* ["The engaged man – engine of the dialectic."]

Big changes in the monastery offices. Fr. de Sales removed from his busy money raising public relations job to the library. Fr. Hilary back from guest house. Fr. Francis of Assisi to guest house, Fr. John of the Cross to doghouse. No – not quite. I was agitating for a vocation director and he is it, more or less.

A quiet day, a quiet afternoon. Woods. Light in the sky, guns banging in the bottoms. Happy New Year. Once more I feel like a member of this community. All the fuss of New Year's Day creates an illusion that we are getting somewhere. Yet it is true – it reminds everyone to take stock of his contributions to, and place in, the community. And I am glad to be still with the novices for what is already a fifth year! Hard to believe it, time has gone so fast.

A beautiful letter from Daniélou yesterday. Very kind and helpful but he did not know the final news, the reply from the Congregation. He said Giorgio LaPira[63] wanted me to come to a Congress of Peace and Culture in Florence in June (Feast of St. John Baptist). No hope – I would not even think of suggesting it to superiors, they would be convinced that I had no love for solitude. And, in fact, it would be a penance to go – but the thought of trying to do something positive and evident for peace is overwhelming. However, It is God's Will that I keep to other ways, the hidden ones.

January 3, 1960. Sunday

The great problem of the confusion and ambiguity by the liberal – say the liberal Catholic individual by his sincerity and good faith – in his occult unconscious association with what is reactionary.

The problem, which I have certainly had to face here – that my own broad and "spiritual" views of monasticism have only served to support a materialistic and narrow monasticism, or rather to confuse and muddle it with evasions and with pseudo-spirituality.

That by and large my work has finally led to the justification and solidification of what I myself have been critiquing, of what appears to be a force of Death.

That what I am fighting against grows strong by virtue of the confusion created by my own fervor in the cause of "good." The appearance of liberty.

If that is the case – then perhaps I ought to stop writing and speaking.

That oversimplification is a defeat.

More liberty – speak out *until you are silenced*. But that too can be a silly, individualistic, illusion.

The solution must be much more subtle, *nuance*.

Actually, by speaking the truth as I see it, I am perhaps preparing the way for others to see it so, for change and development. If my statements have

---

[63] Then mayor of Florence, Italy, and noted Christian activist.

unfortunate consequences, I can guard against them, correct them, react against them, take statements back, if necessary. But go on seeking and thinking and saying what I have to say – if I have anything to say.

But words are easy. The real solution is difficult, it is a matter of my whole life, not merely of my thought and work.

It is clear to me that life, as I have been living it, has been no solution to anything: only an unsolved problem.

January 9, 1960. Saturday

It has been a wild dark week with only short bursts of sun until yesterday.

Bro. Theophane fell down inside a silo onto a pile of alfalfa pellets, so that his fall was broken and he was not killed but he is in the Bardstown hospital with an injured spine.

We said the prayers for the agonizing for Bro. Stanislaus in the Vigil of Epiphany and he died shortly afterwards. Lay in his bier biting his lower lip like a naughty child and like Falstaff, his nose was a pen in a table of green fields. We buried him Thursday morning – the sun came out just for this.

Epiphany, came into the infirm refectory for dinner and Fr. Maurus who has taken another fall in one of his fits was sitting with his forehead gashed open and blood on his cowl and even in his glasses.

Yesterday was in town – talked to Jim Wygal about the whole vocation question and his feeling is that if properly presented the affair could work itself out in the Cistercian Order.

Book on Shaker furniture from the library and Aeschylus.

Fr. Gerald went in to see Dr. Mulligan who kept him late. We ate at Jones's in Bardstown, being too late for supper at the abbey.

Joe Carroll who was driving got a ticket for "improper passing" just after crossing the Salt river in Bullitt County. The state cop was very courteous (but firm) and called him Mister Carroll. Took an awfully long time to make out the ticket, a very young state policeman. Maybe his first catch!

January 10, 1960. Recollection Sunday

The reality of temptation in monastic life – and in my life!

It is clear that I have been severely tempted for a long time and have not avoided sin – the obscure, easily justified sins of self – will, pride, disobedience, infidelity to duty and obligation, lack of faith. Specifically, lack of faith in the protection and providence of God in the ordinary ways of my monastic life. My critical spirit, my judging of the monastery and of the Order, even though I may logically justify myself by a certain "rightness" and still be wrong. And very dangerous for myself and others. In any case, my "rightness" is only a matter of opinion and furthermore it is a cloak for my own weakness and laxity. I am in fact both of these things. And it is not always easy to say where, how, and why. There are exceptions in my life that are fully justified, others partly justified, many are very ambiguous. I have got to begin to face all this more squarely.

January 14, 1960

Floods of rain for St. Hilary's Day.

Yesterday, on the contrary, was bright and warm. J. Laughlin stopped on his way or out of his way to Florida, and Victor and Carolyn Hammer came over. We had a picnic lunch sitting in the warm sun and the dead leaves near St. Bernard's lake, looking up at the pale clouds behind the fire-tower, a joyous and pastoral occasion with even a bottle of red wine.

Victor says he will print the little piece on *The Solitary Life*[64] (an expansion of my "desert" piece done several years ago at La Pire que Vire but banned by American censors of the Order at that time).

Talked a bit of Shakertown and that perhaps the state will buy it and make it a park and monument of it. I must write the new governor about that.

And we talked of monks and cheese and of paper making (Victor wants us to start making handmade rag paper). And of Coomaraswamy (Bob MacGregor of N[ew] D[irections] has been accumulating things on C. – and C's wife wants to read some of C's pieces before republishing them).

Graham Carey has sent a list of small things by Coomaraswamy that he can lend me. And I will certainly do my best to borrow them.

Sent back to L[ibrary] C[ongress] *The Mirror of Justice* but wish I could keep it and study it.

Victor took some measurements in the chapel for tabernacle, etc.

Later, I was tired. I am tired of talking to people about small hermit foundations. The whole thing ends in nausea.

And J talked of poets who had gone crazy more or less like Rexroth now and Delmore Schwartz who shouted across sixth avenue at Bob MacGregor "MacGregor, I'll have you in jail yet!" And who else? Who-

[64] Published by Stamperia del Santuccio in 1960.

ever the man is who wrote *Naked Lunch* which is about every kind of dope and who is a god of the Beats. Also that the climate of Big Sur is not always good. That H. Miller is thoughtful and mild.

J. wants to get busy on *Problems and Paradoxes* and this morning discussed a cover for *Wisdom of the Desert*.

Rain. Sore throat. The weird infection for which I got two potent white shots. Sweats. Weariness.

Trevor Roper's book, which solicits my agreement, and makes one wonder if I am being tempted to treachery. Too much of the instinct to be unfaithful to those whom, after all, my lot has been cast. One has to remain identified to them in and with their faults. This running everywhere in search of rightness and purity ends nowhere. Still, his evaluation of Erasmus, More, the Recusants, and incredibly Newman is moving and right. I wish not to be a propagandist – or is that a decision I have made too late? Silly question. I will try no longer to be one.

January 15, 1960

Out to work this afternoon. Cold. Cutting briars back in the woods where I always go. It felt good to get exercise.

Getting back read the *Ignea Sagitta* [The Fiery Arrow] again – in view of article on Carmelite ideal. It is clear to me that I have simply been fooling myself and looking for consolation and recreation in sensual and secular ways which is all very foolish. This document may be extreme, but it is passionately sincere and always moves me to compunction.

January 17, 1960. II Sun Post Epiphany

Very fine book by J. G. Lawler on *The Catholic Dimension in Higher Education* with splendid quotations from Newman whom I have too long underestimated. A clear and liberating diagnosis of so many ideas that affect us particularly in the monastery – our anti-naturalism, our distrust and hatred of the intellect, of art – our pious pragmatism, the mechanical thinking by which we avoid intellectual commitment and sterilize real thought . . .

"As to Faber, I never read his books." – Newman.

"In small things I went according to my natural inclination – and I still do – instead of considering which was the more perfect course" – St. Teresa.

Compare previous entry Jan 15. Both go together. Teresa [of Avila] would in another context argue with *The Fiery Arrow*. Not a question of being absolute. Principles applied according to circumstances, surely. What is wrong is a confused flight into secular consolations, without discernment. One must *choose* what is healthy and right, for this is willed by God. It need not be pious. It must be sane and productive.

After dinner – read the *Prometheus Bound* of Aeschylus. Shattered by it. I do not know when I have read anything so stupendous and so completely contemporary. I felt like throwing away everything and reading nothing but Aeschylus for six months. Like discovering a mountain full of diamond mines. It is like Zen – like Dostoevsky – like existentialism – like Francis – like the New Testament. It is inconceivably rich. I consider this a great grace on the feast of St. Anthony! A great religious experience. Prometheus, archetypal representation of the suffering Christ. But we must go deep into this. Prometheus startles us by being more fully Christ than the Lord of our own cliches – I mean, he is free from all the falsifications and limitations of our hackneyed vision which has slowly emptied itself of reality.

January 19, 1960. Annual Retreat
Retreat began last night.

As to the preaching – today we were told "The greatest bargains are to be had when doing business with Jesus Christ, the divine trader of Galilee." Certainly this is the right place for such language, but I must be forgiven, I hope, if I remain unmoved by it. Or rather repelled.

However if anyone seriously wants to make a retreat the preaching need not stop him, and I know from experience that something good comes up when you least expect it.

For my own part, I have enough to think about.

And mainly that my great obligation is to obey God, and to seek His will carefully with a pure and empty heart.

Not to try to impose my own order on my life but let Him impose his. Or rather to serve His will and His order by realizing them in my own life. This means certainly *deep consent* to all that is actually and manifestly His will for me.

That having been thought and written – there arrived the missing copies of *La vie spirituelle supplément* – including #50 with Dom Winandy's article on the canonical situation of hermits. It reopened everything. The big wound bleeds. I think certainly I have been unjustly treated. But what can I do?

January 21, 1960. St. Agnes

Snow for St. Agnes. Still dark, but a happy morning.

The retreat talks have mostly been boring and oppressive until one this morning which, though in the same lingo, happened to coincide with what I had been thinking about independently: on simple fidelity to and union with God's will. To me, that is all that matters. But once that is said, the will of God remains a great mystery – except that in present actuality we *possess* it even though we may not see and understand it. In that event understanding is not so important and in any case understanding can flow only from acceptance.

January 24, 1960. III Sun. After Epiphany

I have caught the vile cold that has being going around the community. The stifling heat of the radiators in Church is no help in making it more bearable. Only feel fully normal in the open air, so yesterday afternoon, cutting brush along the creek that divides St. Teresa's field from St. Gertrude's. A nice sunny afternoon. The novices and professed brothers were out there together and it was a joyous occasion – not to mention a rare one. Warmth of sincere charity all through the group – almost all of them kids, crazy, sincere, good kids. It would be wonderful to really *do* something for all of them. But what can anyone do?

As soon as you think of something to be "done" you have to get engaged in the ponderously stupid political machinery of the group life which is geared not to get things done but to prevent anything from being done except the crazy and impossible ideas that please one or two who are in a position to make their preferences felt.

Ups and downs of the retreat. Talks rather uneven. Sometimes blustering, sometimes clowning, sometimes cajoling, never really good. Much amateur psychology in the sense of "observations on the religious character." Some standard, stereotyped pictures of the Mysteries of Christ, especially the passion. An occasional good intuition, a lot of casuistical moral theology à la St. Alphonse, and a lot of ponderous, aggressive humor.

Certainly it is not all lost – but what a retreat for monks!

This is the kind of thing we are up against everywhere.

Read a little of Kierkegaard's *Journal* but the reading was spoiled by the fact that the more intense passages ring in my ears with the urgent and shouting tones of the retreat master!

How " O God" rings in his throat; coming right up out of his belly!

This has happened before in retreats and that is why I prefer to read natural things, when on retreat.

January 29, 1960

On Monday I went to bed more or less for the day and read and thought up there. It was the best day of the retreat. On Tuesday – arrival of some wonderful letters in the mail the best being that of Jorge Carrera Andrade to whom I had written a long time ago about translating some of his poems. Moving and full of thought. I see more and more that there is great meaning in these rare, unexpected, contacts. Went to town – a pleasant sunny day and a rare one. Wednesday – a letter from Laurens Van der Post. And then too arrived a lovely little ikon that Bob Rambusch got for us in Salonika, I believe – He had it cleaned in New York and here it is – not astonishingly beautiful but simple and holy and joyous. It radiates a kind of joy and strength that one would not look for – or see if one looked only superficially. Blessed this ikon today (it had been sold and lost its consecration by the defiling touch of commerce) and prayed aloud before it an Eastern prayer and hymn to the ikon of Our Lady of Kazan (our newcomer is a *Hodogitria*[65] – her coming is a great grace – her presence a great comfort). I have placed the ikon over the altar of Our Lady in the novitiate chapel.

January 31, 1960

I never thought to have had such a thing as a forty fifth birthday. Yet here it is. Why was I always half convinced I would die young? Perhaps a kind of superstition – the fear of admitting a hope of life which, if admitted, might have to be dashed. But now "I have lived" a fair span of life and whether or not the fact be important, nothing can alter it. It is certain, infallible – even though that too is only a kind of dream. If I don't make it to sixty-five, it matters less. I can relax. But life is a gift I am glad of, and I do not curse the

[65] "The One who points the Way"—icons in which the Blessed Mother points to the Christ Child.

day when I was born. On the contrary, if I had never been born I would never have had friends to love and be loved by, never have made mistakes to learn from, never have seen new countries and as for what I may have suffered, it is inconsequential and indeed part of the great good which life has been and will, I hope, continue to be. Because, after all, as I suddenly realize, 45 is still young.

Fr. Barnabas Mary came and gave a good short conference on the Bible as a general background to the Psalms. I liked it and was moved by it. Especially Jeremias 45. Later I discovered from him that the successor to Card. Larraona as secretary to the Congregation of Religious is none other than Fr. Paul Philippe, certainly the best friend I have in Rome! What a birthday present!

February 2, 1960. Purification

At last we have a little sun warm enough to sit in the woods. Which I do.

It is not difficult to be content under this pine tree.

But I have not tried hard enough to be content in community. In fact I have almost refused to let myself be content, as if there were danger in it; something to lose by it. As if by being content I would give in, lose my freedom, be trapped. But actually there is all the difference in the world between contentment and acquiescence. Content is an interior thing and goes with freedom. Freedom depends on it, and he who cannot be content in adversity cannot be free. Contentment has nothing to do either with defeat or compromise, it is the condition for victory. For when I am content I recognize that. *I need no other conditions* and no other situation in order to be free and happy. This is, in one sense, to transcend the whole business!

Freedom, relaxation, and sense of peace from active meditation – merely as *exercise* – in the woods. We live without sufficient use of the intelligence or without right use of it. Forced, compulsive, thought, that is not thought but verbalizing in the interests of conformity.

"I must be about My Father's business." The constant desire of interiority, meditation, the desire of liberation and purity, emptiness, is something I must always be following – not trying to see where it leads. If I follow, it will lead me where I cannot foresee the fulfillment that is waiting. Loyalty to this one call. All the rest is absurd.

Night Watch – Reading Bernanos.

February 3, 1960

One thing is sure: I have got to give up my secret justification of my own indolence and laziness as if these could be as spirituality. My life is very full of silly vanity and I hope I can begin to be honest about it. And some day come to a certain degree of real intellectual and spiritual honesty, instead of a facile pose of honesty which is useless even to convince myself with.

First of all, forget myself, just not pay attention to my own feelings and desires all the time.

Then recognize the superficial thinking, the personal cliches, which enable me to indulge my vanity without having to admit it. One of these is the instinct – a pseudo-prophetic one – to condemn the whole world and preach the coming of the Last Judgment at every turn.

Eschatology is certainly a vitally important part of Xstian revelation but is one that tends to be a pose and a vice if I am not very careful. On the contrary, what I need is the study, patience, effort, and self-effacement that will make what I truly need to be, a genuine Christian humanist – and this is necessary for true contemplation, as opposed to illuminism and quietism. I see it more and more.

I have to begin reading Newman, whom without cause I have neglected as though he were, say, Chesterton. There is all the difference in the world. At the moment I am much more akin to the vanity and absurdity of Chesterton than I am to the solidity and brilliance of Newman. Brilliance is a bad word – for me to desire that is always fatal!

February 6, 1960

Absolute, urgent importance of the following in my life.

1. Not cherishing the idea that my inability to attain my interior goals is due to someone else – the Abbot, the Order. What a ridiculous thought! Yet I waste time on it. True everything here is not ideal, but so what? My life should not depend on anything outside myself and the Grace of God. If I *am* dependent on conditions outside myself. Then by that very fact, whatever those conditions may be, I cannot have true peace.

2. Not complaining and analyzing: but going beyond the surface to have full confidence in the deep action of God's laws and His will, no matter

how superficially confused the situation may be. In other words not waiting to do everything perfect and acceptable, but being content and confident within myself. This is the beginning of true freedom.

February 8, 1960

"Instead of happiness, the able mind will take knowledge as its goal."

J. Burckhardt.

He meant here by knowledge, awareness of tradition in history which gave evidence of the civility of the human spirit. The survival of "one human being." This the object of the contemplation of history.

February 14, 1960

Heavy snow since yesterday.

Cleared up novitiate yesterday at least to the extent of changing the books around and fitting more into the new shelves.

The walls of the chapel are again blackened by the radiators, just as I expected they would be; but we got nowhere asking for a new kind two years ago. Now they will have to put in new guards and we will have to paint the chapel over again.

Monday – visitors from Asbury Seminary and the Bible College in Lexington. Arranged a small retreat for some of the professors in the Summer. And another with Msgr. Horrigan for some of the Bellarmine College faculty.

I thought I would note down the letters received in the past week – Feb 7–13. To see what an "average" week was like and have it on record.

• 2 from Bob MacGregor at New Directions – about *Problems and Paradoxes* and the new difficulty over Suzuki's part of the *Wisdom of the Desert* (killed by censors and Abbot General).

• 1 card from *Thought* saying they received the Carmelite article.

• 1 letter from Jaime Andrade – with pictures of his new work (the mural in Quito) and remarks on Nat. Kerygma.

• 1 note from Cliff. Snow in Louisville thanking me for *Selected Poems*.

• 1 letter from Perry Knowlton at Curtis Brown – re terms for *Problems and Pardons* and paperback edition of *Bread in the Wilderness*.

• 1 letter from St. Procopius Abbey, Illinois, about a postulant who had been rejected here.

• 1 letter from a Sister in Wisconsin who liked *What Are These Wounds?* and wants further material on St. Lutgarde.

- 1 letter from Rosa Maria, in Recife, without her own address – from which I learn that in *my* letter to her of December much cheese and ham advertising was enclosed and she was a bit shocked. No address, so I can't write to apologize.
- 1 letter from Vatican Secretariate of State, with a signed photograph of Holy Father, and blessing for the novitiate thanking us for the Christmas greetings and prayers. This definitely *not* average.

Total: 10 letters.

"It is human for the mature man to give himself wholly, to sacrifice himself to a task *to find the whole in the part that is given to him.*" *Von Balthasar.*

February 19, 1960

This week has not been an average one for letters – a long, handwritten note from Cardinal Larraona, one from F. Cornford's wife (a surprise engineered by Natasha Spender) two or three from J. Laughlin, one from Bob Giroux saying he may come down and even one from Pasternak!

More snow and now, after so many very gloomy days, brilliant winter weather – all the snow freezing and bright sun with a cold wind. Too cold to read outside (Huizinga's *Erasmus*) – hands froze while holding the book.

Dom Phillip the abbot of New Melleray is stopping here for a few days – brought his sub-cantor as Dom Desroquettes is coming back, and will be here from Sexagesima to Easter.

Finishing the *Hidden Face* in the refectory. It has been remarkably revealing and intelligent.

Two wonderful mornings in nov. chapel, all being quiet with snow!

February 27, 1960

End of the month.

Maybe Edith Sitwell's "Jodelling Song" from Facade is the lovliest lyric of the age. It haunts me.

Heard Facade up in Matthew's place (he is now a Family Brother) when Bob Giroux was here the other day. I intend to play parts of it to some of the novices after dinner today.

Yesterday, against all the laws of the Medes and the Persians, I had the novices covering books in the novitiate and played to them some Beethoven and Robert Schumann records – very pleasant. All borrowed from Matthew.

Bob Giroux was here, with a contract, and straightening out lot of snarled threads in the production of *Disputed Questions*[66] and *Art and Worship*. (Captions for the last got lost or something – or never arrived. Maybe never sent. Who can say?)

Graham Carey has sent some of his wonderful Coomaraswamy material.

Got Isaac of Nineveh from Library of Congress. The quaint Wensinich translation. Very impressed with Isaac.

March 3, 1960

It snowed all day Ash Wednesday – yesterday – and there is at least a foot of snow on the ground. Snow is beginning to fall again – more of it.

The cloister was cold under bare feet yesterday but the Church was so overheated that I began to sweat, even in Summer clothes.

Walked in the snow after dinner and read a little about St. Bede. There are so many things to read! Snell on the *Discovery of the Mind* (in Ancient Greece) is enthralling but yet unsatisfactory. Too simplified. We have over-simplified Classical Greece. Only Cornford satisfies me as having approached its true complexity.

Wrote to Suzuki and sent him the poem I wrote the other day, "Messages from the Horizon." Must write to Fromm about the new book *(Zen and Psychoanalysis)* which is on the whole excellent, especially Suzuki's part in it.

Dom Desroquettes suddenly – *à l'improviste* – got rid of the Mass schola and the Mass was very peaceful and monastic for the first time in 10 years – no, not that. But a special quietness and fittingness, because no schola and no director. I wrote him a note and got a nice note in return saying that those most in favor of pushing the chant were at times those who least understood its real meaning. I agree! (This does not refer to Fr. Chrysogamus) I am sure. He is a competent and sensitive musician. (But some of the others!!)

Lent – punctuality – not getting books (already broken but renew resolution!!). More manual labor in P.M. – less writing (but I am stuck with two things already).

There was a wren in my room when I returned from None and the distribution of work.

---

[66] *Disputed Questions* was published in 1960.

March 8, 1960

In the refectory they are reading a long impassioned circular letter from the General, against those who desire to leave the Order and get dispensed from their vows. I am tempted to think he thinks he is dealing with a case like mine, but if that is what he imagines he is certainly wrong – or else we are completely unable to understand one another. What it boils down to is: the Order is always right, the individual is always wrong, whenever there is question whether or not the Order is the proper place for him and whether he could do better, for God and for his own soul, elsewhere. Always a pre-varication! Change out of the question. The situation you are in is always the best for you, and to think of doing anything about it is a crime – the status quo is purely and simply the will of God.

Last night about 8:20 I was suddenly awakened by the fire alarm, looked out and saw the roof of the steel building in flames. Got dressed quickly and went out. Brother monks were rushing about with hoses. Great danger that the five or six propane tanks to the North of the building might ex-plode. Used up a lot of energy running about in the dark, pushing parked trucks, cars, etc. out of the way. Got in the smoke inside with all the others milling around in the dark, putting out the burning pile of wood near the power saws and shooting at the little flowers of flame up inside the ceiling. The fire was out quickly – I expected the whole building to go.

Fire is always disturbing – one always wonders when the main building may get on fire. I found a fire in the night in the guest house a few weeks ago (a smouldering artificial flowerpot, where someone had thrown a ciga-rette).

The Office was delayed an hour. We got up at 3:15. I was exhausted. It took quite a time to get back to sleep after the fire.

Yesterday I got a charming letter from a Shaker Eldress in New Hampshire in answer to an inquiry I wrote her. A touching little leaflet about how the Shakers now quickly face extinction, convinced they had not been a failure. And I am convinced of it too. I think Shakerism is something of a sign – mystery – a strange misguided attempt at utter honesty that wanted to be too pure – but ended up by being nevertheless pure and good, though in many ways absurd. This loyalty, absolute loyalty to a vision leading nowhere. But do such visions really lead nowhere? What they did they did, and it was impressive. It haunts me, at times. I mean the atmosphere and spirit, the image they created, the archetype.

March 16, 1960

There was much more snow, in the last days. It was really deep, the cold weather froze it, and for a long time it did not melt. It was heavy on the roof and leaked through everywhere. I have never seen such deep snow in Kentucky and hear that back in the mountains they have been bringing food to snowbound places by helicopter.

But our snow here gradually got black with the vile coaldust from our chimneys and now rain is washing it away, slowly for it is a warmer day.

Even Khrushchev has the 'flu (though there is not too much of it here for the moment).

It is my week as hebdomadary and I have been inspired by the quiet calm morning Masses and the Office at the Little Hours – singing more slowly, with a feel for the terrible solemnity of our Office and Mass.

Books on Greece, books on Shakers (which I do not get around to reading); Lytton Strachey's _Eminent Victorians_. The life of Manning is a masterpiece. That of Arnold, disappointing. That of Gordon perplexing and disturbing. I believe that his portrait of the religious megalomania of Gordon is distorted and overdone. But I am sure it is essentially true. I feel very sorry for the poor man – and also do not quite understand him. For there are wide gaps in Strachey.

Strachey, Tom Bennett, myself at 18 – and so many other Englishmen laughing at false mystics and holding them off by supercilious objectivity. All Englishmen who are not Thomas [sic] Cromwells or worse, tend to be General Gordons. (Hence Trevor-Roper's fear of monks and his admiration T. Cromwell – of all people to have for a hero!)

March 18, 1960

Cold day with sun. The snow melts slowly.

A jet plane swoops low over the monastery with an interesting roar and then started climbing beautifully into the North, at great speed, with a flight I could not help but love and admire. In a few seconds it was high enough for the exhaust to come out white in a long trail.

Reading [Al] Hallaj in Massignon's translation – about which I wrote him a letter today. Hallaj is right, and our piety is so safe as to be impious.

What a difference between the Greeks and this Moslem. I mean the classical Greeks. But in Aeschylus there's the same kind of fire none the less!

Perhaps I have been struggling with an illusory idea of freedom – as if I were not to a great extent bound by my own history, the history of this community, of the country where I have become a citizen, etc. There are only certain very limited and special avenues of freedom open to me now and it is useless to fight my way along where no issue is possible. This is true not only exteriorly but even interiorly and spiritually. To say that God can open up new ways is perhaps among other things, to admit only that He has provided ways for me, of which I cannot yet be aware since I am too intent upon imaginary and experimental ones.

March 21, 1960

Very important book – *The Humiliated Christ in Russian Thought* – from the Library of Congress. More and more impressed by the seminal and prophetic stuff of Russian nineteenth century. If there were something I intended to study I think it would be that. The *whole* 19th. century grows like a mountain behind us as we move away from it, taking on its true proportions, great, ominous, and pathetic.

Warmer weather – but sickness in the community. Fr. Hilary sweating and pale in chapter today.

March 24, 1960

Went out to work clearing brush near the lake by the Bardstown Road yesterday and got my eye infected. Conjunctivitis, they say. During Night Office and especially during my Mass it was extremely painful today. Now I know what G[erard] M[anley] Hopkins was talking about when, after correcting hundreds of exam papers, he said he felt as if his eyes were full of lemon juice. Get the thing fixed up with ointment and even bandaged, and it was better. Practically no reading all day – spent a lot of time "empty" and it was a happy, salutary day – a gift from God!

Over forty 'flu cases in the community, only the very worst can get in the infirmary.

Vito Casaneli – a postulant from Rome, who was a postulant at St. Scholastica's, Subiaco. He seems to like it here.

March 25, 1960. F. of the Annunciation

Rev. Father lifted the Lenten fast this morning. It is still cold. Many are ill, some dangerously so it seems. My eye is better – to the extent that I can do without a patch – but reading irritates it.

How little I really think – since I write a lot I imagine I think a lot, but that is not true. Perhaps I do try to experience things rather than think them. But not enough.

For example – some pitiable things said (not by me) about the Incarnation. Cerebration – playing with words, as substitutes for real thinking, in contact with realities. A pseudo-docetism, a multiplication of confusing concepts, and each time in order to fit in a new concept to the complex structure, or puzzle, one has to bring in yet another one to justify it, to "make clear" what one is doing – and "keep straight" in one's theology. All this is the sign of a mind that understands no theology, that has never really worked at theology, never given it time or thought – has only imagined that a strong *feeling connected with certain formulas* is an "understanding of theology"!

For my own part I must admit I have not even begun to think deeply on this mystery, and at least I hesitate to talk about it or write about it. The scholastic approach disconcerts me, and I have never really learned any other (or ever really learned that one, either). But those who apparently *have* learned this one, do not impress me; they repel me.

Perhaps if I see less, I may learn to think more, and pray more.

One thing Christ has said: "He who sees me sees the Father also."

In emptying Himself to come into the world, God has not simply kept in reserve, in a safe place, His reality and manifested a kind of shadow or symbol of Himself. He has emptied Himself and is *all* in Christ. *Invisibilis in suis; visibilis in nostris.*[Invisible in his own; visible in ours.] Christ is not simply the tip of the little finger of the Godhead, moving in the world, easily withdrawn, never threatened, never really risking anything. God has acted and given Himself totally, without division, in the Incarnation. He has become not only one of us but even our very selves.

March 29, 1960

Yesterday spent an interesting afternoon talking to Protestant divinity students from Vanderbilt University. A good lively and intelligent group, we got along well together, I think. Perhaps I was going more than half way to meet them through saying that in the lives of most monks there must be something akin to Luther's experience – the discovery of faith and the supreme reality of the divine mercy as opposed to the triviality of formal observance and quasi-magical "works." That from faith in the Divine mercy springs true works, the works of love and gratitude. I felt a very deep and genuine understanding, in the main, had been established by the time the afternoon was over. They were in the novitiate an hour and a half.

One of the Vanderbilt professors [Langdon Gilkey], then a missionary in China, had been in a war-prison camp with our Fr. David (then also a missionary). The Dr. from V was not here this time but I wrote him a letter when I found out about the coincidence.

The 'flu is dying down. Warm sun on Sunday. I had a cold beginning but the sun baked it out of me, though I was not sure it would not attack me again yesterday.

We begin now on project of renewing the dormitory wing – the floors to be torn out and replaced by concrete, on all 3 stories.

March 31, 1960

The breaking up of the Hogan's alley rooms in the old guest house has begun. I have moved into a special cell built over the new stairs by the infirmary. It is practically a windowsill – a wall and a window and this floor is almost on the level of the window, high up on the third floor, looking out over the bottoms towards Rohan's Knob and Holy Cross. It is so far very quiet and I think it ought to make a nice hermitage. Worked putting in the ceiling today: joists and sheet metal on which concrete will eventually be poured.

April 3, 1960. Day of Recollection

Friday the 1st. was a warm sunny day, with a little wind. I went out alone to burn some brush back in my corner of the near woods by St. Teresa's. I took a bucket pump but found too late that it did not work. The fire got away (fortunately at the West was the field's edge) – and started North and East and I could barely control it on the East. Freddy Hicks arrived in the forestry truck, warned by radio from the tower, and got the North end of the fire stopped. I was pretty knocked out. But it was good exercise. All I had to fight the fire with was a small shovel from the flower garden.

Yesterday the Hammers came over in their new little car (a Fiat?) and we ate some sandwiches and drank Chianti under a grey sky out in the pasture, on a stony creek bank from which a squirrel and a woodchuck fled at our approach.

Victor wants to print a dialogue on art between him and myself but I am not sure we would be talking about the same thing.

He brought a fabulous book on wooden synagogues – buildings destroyed by the Nazis in Poland – strange, beautiful old barns with primitive ornaments, full of the inspired atmosphere of the Hasidim. They affect me like Shakertown only more so. What is it, in these places, that moves one so?

And, from the library, the marvelous, enigmatic Heraclitus.

April 9, 1960

Reading Jeremias 32 and 33.

Tremendous lines *(Bible de Jérusalem).*

"Quand elles apprendront tout le bien que Je vais faire, elles seront prises de crainte et de tremblement, à cause de tout le bonheur et de toute la paix que Je vais leur accorder." 33:9. ["Who shall hear of all the good I do for them; they shall fear and tremble because of all the good and all the prosperity I provide."]

April 13, 1960. Wed. in Holy Week

Hot and happy weather. Fasting has helped Holy Week to make sense. For the first time in years I have fasted completely, i.e. with no breakfast at all and it is one of the things I have most badly needed – any idea that I could not fast was an illusion. Based however on experience that the ordinary regime of ten years ago nearly wrecked me. Now that I have a different diet, it is no longer the same story. I am glad and relieved and it has brought me a lot of joy.

Palm Sunday – Lorenzo Barbato, Venetian architect, friend of the Holy Father, brought a stole from the Vatican, blessed by John XXIII – with some medals. Had a good, though hurried, talk with LB in my room – architecture, Japan, wooden synagogues, the dim view I take that the US is the hope of the Xtian world. He argued. Afterwards, I was disturbed at having got mixed up in such horrors and so much talking.

Yesterday, happy in the woods, barefoot.

Last pages of proofs of the *Solitary Life*; from Victor, a secret book, pro manuscripto. Is it good or not? It says something I think needs to be said, but not temperately.

April 14, 1960. Holy Thursday

In a few minutes, the great Mandatum. Clean white summer cowls. We did not wear them this morning for the Mandatum of the poor. Perhaps we do not believe enough that Christ is present in the poor!

One reason why it is easier to fast this Lent: letters from Louis Massignon and his association with non-violent movements of protest, etc. One for the reclamation of perverted youths in Africa. And his association with the Friends of Gandhi.

New sense of the meaning of fasting.

Fr. Lambert dying in the infirmary, after a stroke. I will see him after communion this evening when I go up to watch in his room. Active, joking, extroverted, he has had a hard time here, and in the last year seems to have eaten his heart out with frustration, but was too solid to let it get him down. It must have been hard for him.

Yesterday we finished planting such tree seedlings as we had this year but I have little hope of many growing. The roots got dry or dried out when they were being planted. They came some time ago and there were too many other jobs, and we only watered them sporadically.

Excellent book by Scholem *Major Trends in Jewish Mysticism* and Traherne's *Centuries*, sent by Natasha Spender. Finished Fromm on love. And a little thing by Jungmann, *The Sacrifice of the Church*.

April 24, 1960. Low Sunday

A beautiful Easter – the weather has been warm and bright. Easter night a huge fire roared in the night wind, reaching out at the building and the people at the beginning of the rites of the Vigil. It took half an hour to get from the door to the sanctuary (including the blessing of the fire).

A letter from Jacques Maritain recommended getting together a book with Fromm, Tillich, perhaps Mircea Eliade, to round out my essay and Suzuki's but the Abbot General having spoken to Fr. Paul Philippe about it said "no."

Reading Barzun's *House of Intellect.* Good criticism of the so-called educational "system" which is no system. A sane book about a sick society. I took to heart what was said about useless conferences and committees – Having written to the College of the Bible and Asbury Sem. about their coming "retreats."

Letter from Msgr. Horrigan at Bellarmine Col. yesterday – about seeing one of their graduates who is having a hard time adapting to graduate school in a secular university.

Tuesday – a fine afternoon in the sun, in the woods close by Andy Boone's place where no one ever comes. Then saw Fr. Pastora, Nicaraguan Franciscan who showed up by surprise – did not know that Ernesto Cardenal was in Mexico. Even got a letter from E.C. about my poems coming out in Mexico with Morales' Meditations.

Ed Rice flew to South American this week.

Shirley Burden's book of pictures came and it is a bit disappointing. Flossy gold cover and I think his titles and captions are sentimental. Worse, their sentimentality will be blamed on me!

Rewrote, in a hurry, some completely inadequate notes on Xstian Perfection dating from 1956 – when I took over novitiate. Insufficiency of a concept of perfection that is based on two things only: "obey" and "fulfill your duty of state."

Dom Columban Bissey here for the visitation yesterday – due days ago. Has lost his voice. I had an hour with him yesterday morning. He wanted to know what was this about my trying to leave the Order. Had heard of it from some Belgian missionary, probably a friend of Dom Gregorio. Dom. C. was sympathetic. Got a letter from Fr. Daniélou who has been conferring with Protestants in Sweden.

Last night in chapel I think I felt a slight earthquake tremor.

In refectory they are reading T. Dooley's book about Laos. I envy him his adventures and his chance to do good; am less sanguine about his "Americanism."

Letter from Card. Tardini; saying, if possible, more clearly and strongly than Msgr. Capovilla's confidential notes, that the Holy Father was greatly interested in my "special retreats."

April 29, 1960. Feast of St. Robert

Beautiful days lately – the most perfect days of Spring, day of dogwood and redbud, now ending. Cool, clear days, with all the varied shades of green and red in the thinly budding branches of all the great trees. Later, in the haze of Summer, the soaked green is monotonous jungle. Now it is France and Europe.

Dom C. closed the visitation last night and left today. Was very kind to me, with a genuine disinterested affection, which I accept gladly, touched that one should think of such a thing. Perhaps one of the biggest of my difficulties, and those of so many other monks, is that I do not really believe in the affection of Dom J. though he certainly tries hard and is subjectively sincere by his own lights. But there is something else there, and neither he nor I will ever, probably, be able to say what it is. Of course, *omnis homo mendax* [every man a liar]. Yet certainly Dom J. does practice a great deal of virtue and self-sacrifice in his dealings with his monks. That's just it. That is where the trouble lies. He doesn't completely love them, he sacrifices himself . . . They are merely the occasion for his immolation. How awful that turns out to be for him and for us! This he will never see. Am I any better? God help me!

Yesterday Jack Ford, philosophy prof. at Bellarmine, came out with Tony Benet, grad student at Indiana U. and we had a good afternoon's talk. Part of the "retreat workshop" plan. Each new step leads to more significant regions. But I can still be circumspect (why say that?). Possibility of a skete for retreat, on the hill behind the sheep barn. Have not given it much thought.

A few words with Fr. Anselm, on his way from New Clairvaux to Rome.

Letters from Marina de Berg this morning and a wonderful one from Meg Chatham about the Tillers – two letters from her (she is a Protestant minister's wife) show her to be a remarkable. He too. The work of grace in their hearts is wonderful or so it seems to me.

Conjunctivitis again. In L'ville with dark glasses the other day. Poems of Bert. Brecht – like sackcloth, like brown bread. To what extent is their healthiness illusory? I think it is genuine. But if so, how does he believe what he believes? Or does he? Is this question an illusion also? I like Brecht anyway; he is a good poet. So much better, say, than our esoteric ones. Better than the Beats who try to be rugged but have nothing to say. And Brecht is a most *individual* poet. More individual, perhaps, than those who are so insistent on saving their individuality.

Entranced with the dark Heraclitus.

Do not mind the baroque elements in Eros and Psyche – commended by E. Neumann. It is moving and involves me one degree farther in the world-view of Jung etc. Read the story while riding back in the car the other day.

Monday (May 2) I will try to start putting into effect in novitiate the new ratio studiorum.

May 8, 1960. III Sunday after Easter

Happy Sunday morning in cell – which does all that tradition says it does! How eloquent all these four walls and the landscapes of hills and woods and crazy barns outside my window! I am high up as a stylite, the window goes down to the floor, my head almost touches the low ceiling, birds fly past below me. I sit on the edge of the sky, the sunlight drenches my feet. I have a stool here, an old one, and a desk (my old scriptorium desk) by the bed – three ikons and a small crucifix which Cardenal made. Reading in here is a totally different experience from anywhere else, as if the silence and the four walls enriched everything with great significance. One is alone, not on guard, utterly relaxed and receptive, having four walls and si-lence all around enables you to listen, so to speak, will the pores of your skin and to absorb truth through every part of your being – I doubt if I would be any better off in Mexico!

Making plans for the retreat house up behind the sheep barn – Bro. Clement is friendly to it and working to have it built, and even to pay good money to have it built rather than let the boys from Bellarmine build it.

Yesterday, Derby Day, was raining. I wrote an article on St. Peter Damian having finished the one on Heraklitos earlier in the week.[67]

Answered Milosz's letter written in February. It is deep and sound, and questions my innocent and optimistic friendship with nature, my lack of manichaean poison. Have I right not be poisoned in this way? He sent here five bitter poems of Zbigniew Herbert which he had translated himself.

My answer was inadequate, and I must think of it more. For instance the awareness that nature is *alien* and *heartless* is becoming inevitable, as the awareness of man's own alienation, emptiness and heartliness increases.

It was the swine in the SS who most loved nature, and turned to "her" as a relief from their orgies, to keep human in the midst of degradation they had created.

[67] These essays, variously published, would eventually be part of *Disputed Questions*.

Perhaps this realization (and the awareness of the trite naturalism in art favored by totalitarianism) has made the best minds puritanically devoted to ugliness, to irrelevance, to action painting, and to various studied forms of blasphemy.

It is the turds who have preached happiness and inflicted damnable misery on everyone.

Still reading Barzun. Finished Neumann on Amor and Psyche and returned it to the library. In the cell, here, Vonier's *People of God* and part of *Initiation théologique.*

Fr. Flavian left for Rome last week, bewildered, with Fr. Anselm from New Clairvaux. Rev. Father off to make visitations. It is a relief to have him out of here, with his well meaning, stubborn lack of understanding – almost refused to understand the real needs and aspirations of his monks. Yet he is so kind and tolerant in accidentals – in granting favors by which he hopes to win their support for his own lack of vision.

News from Herbert Mason about Louis Massignon, P. Regamey, etc. with their non-violent demonstration outside the Vincennes prison – Two newspaper clippings which effectively falsify and ridicule the whole thing – the "sane" view of right thinking society. The humane indignation of the police chief who transported them in Black Marias to the tomb of an agent shot by the FLN and gave them a moving speech on their unfairness. It made me think of Dom Gabriel – exactly his kind of "paternal" reaction. Very good politics, good because sincere – utterly sincere. Perfect justification of the status quo, of violence, of torture, of atom bombs, and all that is perpetrated in the name of order and authority. Why so afraid of the "non-violent"? Why so eager to re-educate them?

I shall write to Regamey.

Still have conjunctivitis and have been saying night office privately in novitiate chapel. A totally new balance: about 45 minutes for office and an hour or more for meditation (instead of the 15 minutes of chanting under the neon lights and 1/2 hour of sitting upright in a choirstall for meditation). Meditation in the dark and silence is superb, alert, and alive – none of the torpor, stupidity, alienation, and vanity of meditation in common – (and inevitable strain). Whatever else is true, experience shows that I function well only in solitude.

May 14, 1960. Sat[urday]

After a week without sun, two brilliant May mornings – after chapter I went out and sat on the trunk of one of the pines we felled in the last few days on the site for the Mount Olivet hermitage.[68] Trying to think of the best kind of plan for it. A plan acceptable to Bro. Clement and yet something more than a shack since it is for retreats. A kind of half cloister, facing the hills, catching the view and shade. And a chapel, an airy sanctuary. I think of a small tower in a kind of a cage, so that there can be much air and yet shade and indirect light.

I hate to cut down the fifty and sixty foot pines, slim as grass, waving in the sky.

Maples want to come up, and I have preserved a couple of bastard elm saplings that will grow fast.

Carlo and the Negro with the cigar working on the terrazzo job for the new stairs. Floors almost torn out of brother's dormitory. Novices have to urinate in a pail, since the urinal is gone. Our new one is not yet installed.

Hannah Arendt's *Human Condition* is another cardinal book, a hinge on which one's whole thought can turn. Whole new aspect of action and contemplation, public and private life, it offers a solution to the complex question that has plagued me with its ambiguity so long.

As long as the conflict is between what is *individual* or intimate and what is *social* (this is the modern division) the issue never becomes clear and you can never get to grips with it. The social is simply a continuation of what is *"private"* in the sense of "deprived," restricted, subject to necessity, the satisfaction of material needs.

For the Greeks, the contemplatives and political spheres could be one.

Heraklitos despised the *social*, not the *political* sphere. But because his contemporaries feared excellence, and loved social conformity (behaviour) rather than political action, they thought him a rebel and a misanthrope.

May 16, 1960. Monday

Saturday at noon Victor Hammer came over from Lexington with Geo. Headley who has been to Mount Athos and plans to return there to do some painting. V.H. brought over a finished copy of the *Solitary Life* and I signed the leaves for the others. It is in an edition of 80, in Victor's usual

---

[68] This combination "retreat center" and cottage would eventually become Merton's hermitage.

perfect style. I am very pleased with it. The end sheets are beautiful. The copyright notice and title pages are the first time Victor has used that new Greek seeming type of his. The rest is uncial, very effective. It was a fine clear day not too warm. We ate some sandwiches for lunch sitting in the dry leaves by the old lake, under maple saplings just freshly in leaf. The lake was full, for a change! No mud flats to look at, but cool sparkling water.

Today after dinner Bro. Clement came and got me from the woodshed and we went up to look at the retreat house site on Mt. Olivet. He approved my plans, told some harrowing stories about how the gardens at Mepkin are going to ruin and falling back into jungle.

In ancient Greece the painter was regarded superior to the sculptor. He was admitted to citizenship (Aristotle – Politics) and treatises on painting were written – a painter could be "famous." A sculptor, who had to work harder, was less respected, could not be a citizen, etc. Has this something to do with the fact that the tradition of the Orthodox Church admits painting but not sculpture?

Bro. Clement said the Summit Conference had "ended in three hours" with Khrushchev in a rage about Americans with cameras flying over Russia. One was caught. Duck soup for K. – a nice big spy scare over which to be heartily indignant.

May 18, 1960

Yesterday in Louisville. Bellarmine College, clean and airy with big windows looking out over a wide sweeping view of the trees and hillsides and Our Lady of Peace, for the crazy people (or for people that aren't crazy but need to rest and get organized – like everybody!). (Whole different attitude towards mental illness now that everyone realizes he could have a little of it!)

Spoke to Msgr. Horrigan about plans for the Mt. Olivet hermitage and retreat house and he said he wanted to do a lot of helpful things about it. And I knew he meant what he said – so that it may turn out to be a much nicer and better building than anyone down here has envisaged. He said Fr. Treece would look the plans over and then they would consult Bob Nolan the architect, etc. etc.

So then he took me downstairs and showed me the library and turned me over to the library staff who made me the object of a public cult for a while. I took some books out of the shelves and was the first one to have signed out Wm Carlos Williams' earlier poems.

What had most impressed me was the little book – a pamphlet really – of Robert Penn Warren on Segregation. Powerful and objective, gives a good idea of the problems in its human aspect. A typical American approach, just describing how all these individuals say they feel about the thing. But it adds up to something decent and is not one of these stupid public opinion polls. It is done well and with concern for reality. The reality of the south to which I belong – without ever thinking of it. You can be in a Trappist monastery and never become a Southerner. But I am becoming a Kentuckian and a conscious one. There is no point in trying to evade it. It means of course talking to people and I do that, in Louisville, and Lexington. And I liked the Lexington Presbyterians who came over the other Sunday.

Did not buy a paper to read about Khrushchev's clever trick – but am irritated that such a clown can have the satisfaction of making everyone else jump and dance to his tune.

I was appalled to realize what terrible things are happening in South Africa. I had thought vaguely that *Apartheid* was something like race-prejudice in our own South, like our segregation which is bad enough. But this is much more. A completely degraded, concentration camp existence, not in misery only but in squalor, degradation and suffering. Beating and killing – then the bodies lying on the ground in Sharpeville.

The Afrikaaners are Christian fundamentalists. Bible Christians! What an indictment of Christianity! Yet if they *read* the Bible they would know what they were doing. And we too!!

At least, some of us know that we don't see and that we are secondly, stupid, befogged, helpless. That our vague good will can do nothing. And we are snowed under by useless goods, objects, foods, furnitures, clothes, things, that keep in movement our absurd society of advertising and commerce. We consume and waste and throw away and everyone else in the world starves, and starves miserably. The best that can be said is that we don't *want* it to happen that way. But it does.

I must do all I can at least to learn and understand and try to see things as they are and know what I at least can do about them. It is appalling to be drained and blinded by the mental habits we cultivate here in the name of love and holiness. Yet it is obvious that I am called to pray for the world. Shame makes me doubt the validity of my prayer. It should not.

May 21, 1960

I wonder if the time has come for me *to cease writing for publication.*

Before this, the idea has come to me in passing and I have never really taken it seriously. I have not been able to. Now I think it is getting to be possible and necessary.

Not to stop writing altogether. On the contrary, to write what I really need to write myself, not what the readers of some magazine would like or what "my readers" expect. But to write better, write less, go deeper, further afield. Think more.

Write better – or perhaps not. But to reach further into areas I do not yet know, to write *tentatively* about them in order to begin to understand them better.

To write more poetry perhaps – try something creative – not for inordinate publication, not a sermon.

To stop telling people what I think. They don't need to know what I think and I do not need them to know it.

Not to stop publishing altogether – obviously there are several books waiting to be printed. But do they need to be printed? Or printed *now?*

But eventually to cut down on publication.

To put more feelings into this Journal which is not for publication.

And in which therefore I can speak freely.

(But perhaps what I say for others is more controlled, more responsible, more objective, and therefore better . . .)

This was prompted in part by the fact that I am *still* in trouble with the censors over "Notes on a Philosophy of Solitude" (alias "The Vocation to Solitude").[69] That is the one thing which ought to be published.

But why have so much bother with them for the publication of trivialities like the *Christian Life of Prayer* and the futile appendix to it on Perfection? God knows.

I will talk to Rev. Father today, at least about the censors, and see what is going on.

For the rest the best idea at the moment seems to be to *write less,* to write what I need to say to myself and to God, not for the public. And to *withhold publication except in special cases.* Yet I have to consider to what extent I owe a

---

[69] After some complex revisions, published in *Disputed Questions.*

certain amount of writing to the Church. Hard to say. On the whole I feel like going underground, and thus deeper into the Church. Maybe what I write then will be of more lasting value. Avoid the temptation to seek an immediate result.

Of course there are *letters* to be written and I could write them better and more thoughtfully. My letters are careless, badly written, without thought, hasty and inaccurate, sometimes having value for their spontaneity, not much more.

I still have at least one thing to write, the article on "Liturgy and Spiritual Personalism" for *Worship* which I have put off to next week.[70]

May 23, 1960

Saturday afternoon, I went to see Rev. Father after his return from Visitations in Georgia and South Carolina. The usual business, etc. conversation, the main thing being *nihil obstat*. Finally approvals have come through the Abbot General for all that remained to be passed in *Disputed Questions*.

About the *Primitive Carmelite Ideal* to which Fr. Thomas Aquinas had strenuously objected, there was finally no trouble at all and it was passed without any change.

But the "Notes For a Philosophy of Solitude" – though approved with three changes, merited a very angry letter of about 800 words from the General – a letter which was touched off by remarks I had made about the Order in the Mount Athos article.

He was really furious (the letter was to Rev. Father) and maintained that I was on my way to heresy (not said in so many words) because the censor had exaggerated and misinterpreted a few sentences of mine as if I intended to say that immediate guidance by the Holy Spirit was preferable to, in opposition with, guidance through the Church and religious superiors which I certainly did not say or mean at all.

Of course my language gave way to misapprehensions and to that extent I am responsible. But can one prevent all misinterpretations?

I was disturbed Saturday night feeling that through my own carelessness and in a sense presumptuousness in my use of words I had been unfaithful to God and caused this absurd rumpus. And one which threatens to undo the real work I intended to do.

---

[70] Published in *Worship* (October 1960) and later as part of *Seasons of Celebration* (1965).

In the evening three from the College of the Bible came. Two conferences last night and this morning.

At breakfast, I realized that I did not have to be upset at all, and that everything is in God's hands and He will rectify my mistakes and will keep me humble and that there is honestly in my heart no real problem about obedience at all – just the normal feelings and repugnancies. But I must not and need not speak of them. I must not let myself be deluded into treating them as a problem.

Tauler – *Gemüt* and the *Grund* – turning the whole desire and strength of the soul to the emptiness, the mirror in which God appears – which is the very mirror being of our being!

Who am I? A Son of God.

Richard Pope's difficulty – re the annihilation of the "Self" – no difficulty. My true self is the self that is spoken by God – "Thou art My Son!" Our responsibility (ability and obligation to respond).

Tremendous happiness and clarity (in darkness) is my response: "Abba, Father!"

I *know* you are leading me, and therefore there is *no conflict with anyone.* Nor can there be.

A Glossary of Monastic Terms

abbey. A monastic house whose superior is an abbot.

Abbot General. The elected superior of the entire order of Cistercians of the Strict Observance.

antiphon. A short verse of scripture sung before and after a psalm. The collection of such music was contained in the antiphonary.

ashram. A religious house, usually organized under the direction of an enlightened teacher (*guru*) in Hinduism. Christian monastics have adopted the term for their own use, for example, in India.

breviary. A small book containing the prayers, psalms, and readings of the liturgical office.

Camaldolese. Monastic order that combines following the Rule of Benedict with the eremitical life.

cantor. The monk designated to lead the monastic chant; his assistant is the sub-cantor.

capitulum. A short text of scripture read at the liturgical hours of the day.

Carthusians. Monastic order that emphasizes the eremitical life.

cell. The individual room of a monk.

cellarer. The monk in charge of the temporal needs of a monastery; similar to a business manager.

cenobite. A monk who lives in community as opposed to a hermit.

Chapter, General. The meeting of the abbots of the order to legislate and direct the affairs of the entire order.

Chapter of Faults. The traditional time for self-accusation of lapses in monastic decorum or accusations made by one monk against another.

Chapter Room. Community gathering place in a monastery so named from the tradition of reading a portion of the Rule followed by a commentary by the abbot.

charterhouse. Traditional English name for a monastery of Carthusian monks.

cloister. The monastic enclosure and, by extension, the enclosed quadrangle of a monastery consisting of a covered walkway around an open garden area.

Collation. A small informal meal eaten during the period of fasting (for example, Lent) taken in the evening.

compline. The final liturgical office of the day; the "night prayer" of the monks.

conscience matter letter. Any letter so marked could not be opened by a superior since it contains personal matters of spiritual direction or confessional matters.

contemplatives. Term broadly used to describe those religious who are devoted to prayer with no "active" apostolate like teaching, nursing, and so on.

Conventual Mass. The daily Mass celebrated with the monastic community in attendance.

cowl. A large white hooded garment worn over the habit during liturgical ceremonies.

Day of Recollection. In the monastery, a designated period when a monk was free from normal obligations to engage in more prayer and silence.

definitor. Someone elected or deputed to participate in the government of a religious order, for example, at its General Chapter.

discipline. An instrument of penance, such as a small scourge.

Dom. Abbreviated form of *Dominus;* an honorific term used for a Cistercian abbot, for example, Dom James.

eremitical. Pertaining to the hermit life.

exclaustration. Official permission to leave one's monastery.

family brother. A lay person who lives and works in the monastery but who does not take monastic vows.

Father Immediate. The abbot from a founding monastery who is appointed to oversee daughter houses founded from a particular abbey.

frustulum. A small portion of food.

habit. Monastic dress consisting of a white tunic with a black scapular held by a belt; novices dressed all in white; laybrothers once dressed in brown.

hebdomadary. Priest deputed to celebrate the conventional mass and lead the various offices for a given week.

Indult. A legal document from the Vatican giving a specific permission or granting a specific privilege.

lauds. The official morning prayer of the monastic day.

laybrother. Monk in religious vows who was not destined to full participation in the choir or ordination to the priesthood.

Mandatum. The liturgical rite of foot washing celebrated on Holy Thursday.

matins. The night liturgical office of psalms and readings; also called Vigils.

meridienne. The afternoon rest period permitted, especially, in the summer months.

mixt. A brief "breakfast" in the morning.

nihil obstat. Latin phrase ("nothing stands in the way") indicating that a book has been passed by an ecclesiastical censor.

nocturn. One of the divisions of psalms/readings that make up the night office of Vigils.

none. The midafternoon liturgical office (circa 3:00 P.M.).

novice. An aspirant to the monastic life who lives in community but has not yet been admitted to vows.

office. The ordinary term for the daily round of liturgical prayer that begins with Vigils and ends with Compline.

office, little. Term for a parallel short office in honor of the Blessed Mother which once prefaced the regular office.

Pontifical Mass. Any mass at which a prelate (for example, an abbot or bishop) presides in a solemn fashion.

Pontifical Tierce. The celebration of the third office of the day (circa 9:00 A.M.) presided over by the abbot in a solemn fashion.

postulant. One who stays at the monastery to observe and participate in the life (typically for six months or more) before being admitted as a novice.

préau. The garden area of the enclosed cloister of a monastery.

prime. A short liturgical office celebrated between Lauds and Tierce (now suppressed).

prior. The "second in command" to the abbot or the superior of a monastic foundation (priory) that has not yet reached the independent status of an abbey.

professed. Those monks who are in vows and have the obligation of choir.

ratio studiorum. Curriculum of study for the scholastics.

refectory. The monastic dining room.

schola. A group of monks within the choir who sing as a choir for certain parts of the office.

scholastics. Monks in vows who were in studies leading to priestly ordination.

scriptorium. The common study area where the monks had desks for reading and study.

secular church. That part of the abbey church available for visitors and guests of the monastery.

sext. The midday liturgical office celebrated around the noon hour.

skete. A small monastic settlement with a few monks living under the authority of an Elder; common in the Christian East.

Spiritual Directory. The official book of formation for the Cistercian Order.

tierce. The morning liturgical office celebrated circa 9:00 A.M.

tonsure. The symbolic hair-cutting of a monk; the heads of choir monks were shaved except for a ring of hair; also called the monastic corona or monastic crown.

Trappist. Common name for the Order of Cistercians of the Strict Observance (O.C.S.O.) derived from the reforms initiated at the French abbey of La Trappe in the seventeenth century. The Trappists are to be distinguished from the common observance Cistercians, whose style of life is less rigorous.

vespers. The evening prayer of the monastic community celebrated, typically, circa 5:30 P.M. before the evening meal.

vigils. See matins.

Votive Mass. The liturgy celebrated to petition for a special need or in honor of the Blessed Mother or one of the saints. Such masses could be celebrated on those days that were not otherwise designated in the liturgical calendar.

Index